ENFORCING THE EQUAL PROTECTION CLAUSE

Enforcing the Equal Protection Clause

Congressional Power, Judicial Doctrine, and Constitutional Law

William D. Araiza

NEW YORK UNIVERSITY PRESS
New York and London

NEW YORK UNIVERSITY PRESS
New York and London
www.nyupress.org

References to Internet websites (URLs) were accurate at the time of writing. Neither the author nor New York University Press is responsible for URLs that may have expired or changed since the manuscript was prepared.

ISBN: 978-1-4798-5970-2

For Library of Congress Cataloging-in-Publication data, please contact the Library of Congress.

New York University Press books are printed on acid-free paper, and their binding materials are chosen for strength and durability. We strive to use environmentally responsible suppliers and materials to the greatest extent possible in publishing our books.

Manufactured in the United States of America

10 9 8 7 6 5 4 3 2 1

Also available as an ebook

To Stephen

CONTENTS

PREFACE

Introducing the Enforcement Power

Consider the following scenarios:

- A paraplegic person attempting to access city hall discovers that the building has no elevators.
- A healthy person with a genetic predisposition to a particularly debilitating disease is denied an assignment in a government workplace out of a misplaced fear that exposure to dust in the new work area would exacerbate his predisposition.
- A woman in that same workplace is passed over for a promotion that will require her to work longer, more unpredictable hours because, according to her supervisor, "women always have to drop everything and get home when one of the kids is sick."
- That same workplace promulgates a grooming policy that forbids cornrows.
- A county department of social services tells a gay couple seeking to adopt that it does not consider same-sex couples as "families" for purposes of its adoption requirements.
- A transgendered student in a public high school is required to use the bathroom of the gender she does not identify as.

When we think about the legal claims the people in these examples might bring to challenge the discrimination they suffered, we immediately think about the Constitution. And with good reason: our legacy as Americans includes a Constitution that, while far from perfect, insists, at least on paper, that people enjoy basic rights, including "the equal protection of the laws."

But what does it mean to think about "the Constitution"? One way—the way lawyers understand it—is to think about the Constitution as a legal document, a source of rights that a plaintiff can seek to vindicate in court. This understanding is deeply ingrained: every June, as the Supreme Court nears the end of its term, Americans wait to see how the justices will rule on closely watched constitutional cases.

At the other extreme—the way scholars known as "popular constitutionalists" think about it—one might understand "the Constitution" as a set of principles that furnish the raw material for argumentation far beyond the courtroom: in the political arena, and even in our dealings with each other. This idea of the Constitution also has great resonance. How many times have you heard someone cite "the right to free speech" whenever he is denied a right to speak, even if that speech suppressor is not a government official, and thus technically not subject to the First Amendment?

Between these two extremes—of the Constitution as a lawyer's document and as a set of fundamental principles governing American life—there lies a middle ground. This middle ground understands the Constitution as a foundation for legislation. In particular, the Constitution can be understood as a grant of authority to our representatives in Congress to translate into concrete rules of conduct the principles that "constitute" our rights.

This book examines Congress's power to perform that translation—in the words of the Fourteenth Amendment, to "enforce, by appropriate legislation," the rights that amendment guarantees us. It focuses on the Fourteenth Amendment for a reason: that provision is an absolutely central text if we want to understand what our "constitutional rights" are. One clause of that amendment—the Due Process Clause—is the source of nearly all the substantive constitutional protections we enjoy against deprivations by state governments. Another—the Equal Protection Clause—provides an across-the-board guarantee that state action not unfairly discriminate. The Constitution provides other sources for other rights. But these two are foundational.

Just as important as these rights themselves is Americans' ability to vindicate them. If a state violates a constitutional right, the victim can usually sue. But it is often difficult for a plaintiff to prevail. Sometimes he has a difficult time amassing the proof the Supreme Court has deemed necessary to make out his claim. In some cases this may be because the claim is so enmeshed in a complex bureaucratic or social system that it is difficult for the plaintiff to cut through the haze and identify the single bad actor holding the smoking gun that makes it easier for a court to find a constitutional violation.

Sometimes the problem arises from other barriers courts erect, to ensure that they don't mistakenly find constitutional violations and thus inappropriately limit democratically elected legislatures from enacting the laws they think best. This is often the case if ruling for the plaintiff would involve the court second-guessing a legislature's decision on a technically complex or morally fraught issue. This may sound unfair, but judges have a legitimate point when they cite either their lack of expertise to second-guess complex policy decisions or their lack of authority to second-guess value judgments a legislature might legitimately make.

That's when Congress can step in. The Fourteenth Amendment concludes with the following simple, yet powerful, language: "The Congress shall have the power to enforce, by appropriate legislation, the provisions of this [Amendment]." As noted earlier, such "enforcement legislation" can translate the often-vague language of constitutional rights into concrete rules of conduct that give such rights practical—literally, "enforceable"—effect. As such, the enforcement power is a critical component of the rights we think of when we think of "constitutional rights."

To be sure, Congress has other sources of constitutional authority to legislate to protect rights. Most notably, Article I of the Constitution gives Congress the power to regulate interstate commerce and to spend money "for the general welfare." Over the past half century, Congress has used these powers liberally to enact human rights legislation. During most of that time it has been aided by the Supreme Court, which in the 1930s began deferring broadly to Congress's use of its commerce and spending power for all sorts of purposes. Thus, to return to our earlier examples, Congress could use the commerce power to restrict a state-run business from engaging in discrimination, and it could use its spending power to condition federal education grants to states on their compliance with particular antidiscrimination rules benefiting students. But as the introductory chapter will make clear, over the last twenty years the modern Court has been cutting back on Congress's Article I powers. Thus, the enforcement power may become more important going forward.

And, indeed, the enforcement power *should* be more important. It may be the case that, just as there is more than one route to a destination, there is also more than one constitutional source for federal legislation protecting constitutional rights. Nothing in this book should be taken to question Congress's authority to use its other sources of power to enact human rights legislation that applies to states. But the enforcement power—the power "to enforce . . . the provisions of" the Fourteenth Amendment—is where that power rightly belongs. This is far more than a matter of proper categorization for its own sake—a sort of legal doctrine housekeeping. Rather, it should matter whether Congress bases civil rights legislation on, alternatively, its power to regulate interstate commerce or its power to enforce the Equal Protection Clause. Our political discourse is impoverished if debates about civil rights legislation never have to mention the Fourteenth Amendment or discuss how best to enforce it. Popular constitutionalists have a point when they argue that "taking the Constitution away from the People"[1] makes us appreciate it less and creates a distance between Americans and the document that reflects our most fundamental political and social aspirations.

A more meaningful enforcement power would provide the opportunity for "We the People" to think about and debate the Constitution *more*, through our political process. Along the way, we can enrich our democratic deliberation, strengthen our democratic process, and, most of all, make clear to ourselves that we—not our judges—are the ultimate guardians of our constitutional heritage.

These are reasons enough to consider the questions this book poses.

ACKNOWLEDGMENTS

Lots of things have to come together for a book to be written. Institutions have to give the author the time and support to work out his ideas. Colleagues have to give their time and effort to engaging those ideas, pointing out their weaknesses and suggesting improvements. Curious and diligent students have to pose questions—often questions that seem basic but that, exactly because of that quality, force the author continually to reexamine his own assumptions.

I have been fortunate to enjoy all these advantages. Most of my academic career has been spent at two wonderfully supportive institutions, Loyola Law School–Los Angeles and Brooklyn Law School. Both Loyola and Brooklyn have generously supported my scholarship, through grants, fellowships, and sabbaticals. Colleagues at both schools, and throughout the nation, have given their time to read drafts, listen to presentations, and offer their wisdom. Sonu Bedi, Eric Berger, Aaron Caplan, Ruth Colker, Evan Gerstmann, Joel Goldstein, Joel Gora, Allan Ides, Eric Segall, Steven Siegel, Nelson Tebbe, Alexander Tsesis, Michael Waterstone, and Rebecca Zietlow read either all or parts of drafts of this book; for that I am immensely grateful. I am also grateful to colleagues who have participated in workshops and conferences where I have been able to discuss and work through my thinking on these issues. Students have also helped: their questions and their curiosity have kept me on my toes. Over the past decade of my thinking about the enforcement power, too many students to name have served as wonderful research assistants. You know who you are. Thank you.

Even with all these advantages, this book would not have come to fruition without the faith and assistance of the people at NYU Press, in particular, Clara Platter. My deep thanks go out to her and to her staff.

Finally, my deepest thanks go out to my husband, who not only suffered through delayed dinners and abandoned evenings but made the ultimate sacrifice of reading a draft of this book to provide a nonlawyer's perspective. If academic publishers offered hardship pay, he would qualify.

Introduction

Why the Enforcement Power, and Why Now?

Intellectual puzzles may be intrinsically interesting, but at least in law they hardly warrant the time demanded to read (much less write) a book. Something more should warrant our attention—an urgency, or at least a timeliness, that makes a puzzle worth the pondering.

Congress's power under Section 5 of the Fourteenth Amendment, known as "the Section 5 power" or "the enforcement power," certainly qualifies as an intellectual puzzle. As an authorization to Congress to "enforce" the provisions of the Fourteenth Amendment, the Enforcement Clause is a grant of legislative power amid a catalog of constitutional rights that are for the most part judicially enforceable on their own (i.e., "self-executing") and, indeed, largely aimed at *limiting* legislatures. Indeed, the very idea of constitutional rights presumes judicial, not legislative, enforcement, at least according to the standard understanding of courts as countermajoritarian institutions tasked with defending rights against legislative majorities. As such, the Enforcement Clause's meaning is by no means self-evident.

The search for meaning is further clouded when one discovers the historical truth that the Fourteenth Amendment was originally drafted as a simple grant of power to Congress. The Fourteenth Amendment's ultimate structure, in which Section 1 grants the rights to privileges and immunities, due process, and equal protection, with congressional enforcement power relegated to the end of the entire amendment in Section 5, reflects a change from the original draft offered in Congress. That original draft simply granted Congress power to enforce such rights, without a prior, self-executing grant of those rights. Given that history, how broadly should we read this counterintuitive grant of legislative power to "enforce" constitutional rights? What lessons, if any, should we draw from the format change?

Interesting enough. But the question of the enforcement power's scope also has both a practical importance and a timeliness that warrant its careful consideration today. First, it is nearly impossible to exaggerate the importance of the Fourteenth Amendment. It constitutes the central text of the second framing of the Constitution, in which federal constitutional rights were granted to

Americans not just as against the federal government but also against their own states. Today it is hard to believe that at one time states could infringe individuals' speech rights, conduct unreasonable searches, and inflict cruel and unusual punishment subject only to whatever restrictions state law imposed, but such was the case until the Fourteenth Amendment was ratified in 1868. Thus, the amendment worked a basic change in the federal structure. Indeed, Justice Thurgood Marshall once stated that while the nation survived the Civil War, the (original) Constitution did not.

Second, the enforcement power itself raises fundamental issues of constitutional structure. As noted earlier, the Enforcement Clause is a grant of congressional power to enforce constitutional rights in a document in which rights are thought to be judicially enforceable. Thus, while the Fourteenth Amendment generally raises significant questions of federalism, the Enforcement Clause in particular introduces equally important questions about the separation of powers between Congress and the federal courts. The point can be illustrated by a famous quotation that, in many ways, states the central issue this book addresses. In *Marbury v. Madison*, Chief Justice Marshall, in the course of asserting the power of judicial review, stated that "it is emphatically the province and duty of the judicial department to say what the law is."[1] If that statement is true, then what role does Congress have under its authority to "enforce" the "law" of the Fourteenth Amendment? The most obvious answer, that the Enforcement Clause merely authorizes Congress to prescribe remedies for violations of "the law" as announced by the Court, is both unacceptably trivial and inconsistent with the framers' understanding of Congress's critical role in protecting these rights.[2] But any broader reading of the enforcement power inevitably raises tension with *Marbury*'s statement about courts' power "to say what the law is." This tension is not insoluble. Still, any answer to the puzzle of the Enforcement Clause must resolve, or at least acknowledge, it.

The Urgency of the Issue

A correct understanding of the enforcement power is especially urgent today, given the uniqueness of that power and its moral resonance.

The Uniqueness of the Enforcement Power

As a practical matter, the importance of the enforcement power depends on the extent to which other sources of power allow Congress to achieve the same substantive goals. The Constitution gives Congress various regulatory powers: for example, in addition to the power to enforce the Fourteenth Amendment, Congress also possesses the power to tax and spend "for the . . . general Welfare" and to regulate interstate commerce. If Congress could always accomplish through, say, the commerce power whatever it could conceivably accomplish through the enforcement power, there would be less need to think carefully about the proper scope of that latter power. In recent years, however, the Supreme Court has shown new interest in cutting back on those other powers. Since 1995 it has twice struck down federal statutes as exceeding Congress's power to regulate interstate commerce. The agreement of five justices in 2012 that the Affordable Care Act exceeded Congress's commerce power suggests continued skepticism of that power.

In addition to restricting the commerce power's scope, the Court has also imposed subsidiary restrictions on what Congress can accomplish with that power. It has held that general principles of federalism restrict Congress's ability to "commandeer" state governments—that is, to require them to act according to federal mandates—even when that "commandeering" clearly implicates interstate commerce.[3] Even more important, it has held that, even though a particular statute might be a valid interstate commerce regulation, that source of regulatory authority does not allow Congress to make states liable for money judgments when they violate that law. Thus, for example, the commerce power authorizes Congress to regulate employment, and even authorizes that regulation to apply to states, in their capacity as employers.[4] However, it does not authorize Congress to mandate back pay awards against state government employers.[5] This limitation on remedies is crucial, given how important retrospective relief may be to making would-be plaintiffs whole, and inducing them to sue—and indeed, to helping them find a lawyer willing to take the case.[6] It is important to keep in mind that much—though not all—enforcement legislation can find support in the Commerce Clause as well as the Enforcement Clause. But the availability of a full set of remedies often turns on whether the challenged law is valid as enforcement legislation.

Cutbacks on other congressional powers, most notably the power to attach conditions on state government recipients of federal monetary grants, are also on the current Court's radar screen. In the 2012 decision otherwise affirming the Affordable Care Act's constitutionality, a solid majority of the Court held that the conditions the statute placed on federal funding of a state's Medicaid plan exceeded Congress's powers under Article I's Spending Clause. Early commentary on that decision has identified this cutback on federal power as a potentially significant development, given how much federal policy in areas ranging from education to law enforcement is implemented via conditions Washington imposes on monetary grants to states.[7] Finally, a decision from

2014 called into question, for the first time in a century, the scope of Congress's power to enact legislation carrying into effect our obligations under international treaties.[8] If you wonder what possible relevance Congress's power to enact treaty-implementing legislation has to domestic human rights laws, consider the panoply of human rights conventions the United States has signed since World War II.

Many of these restrictions do not apply to enforcement legislation. First, the enforcement power allows Congress to regulate state action in areas—for example, domestic relations, family law, and criminal justice—that may not come within the Court's new, more restrictive understanding of the interstate commerce power. Second, enforcement legislation may make states liable for retrospective relief, such as damages. As noted earlier, such relief is often a civil rights plaintiff's most important demand. Third, it is also probably the case, although it has not yet been decided, that the "anticommandeering" rule does not apply to federal laws enacted pursuant to Congress's enforcement power. For example, the Voting Rights Act (VRA), enacted pursuant to both the Enforcement Clause and Congress's cognate power to enforce the Fifteenth Amendment,[9] cuts deeply into states' sovereign functions of conducting elections and organizing themselves into governing units. Finally, the Spending Clause's restriction on coercive federal conditions does not, as a matter of logic, apply to enforcement legislation: such legislation, by definition, compels particular state conduct rather than operating as a financial inducement. Clearly, then, the enforcement power has become an attractive, and even indispensable, tool for the attainment of important federal policy objectives.

The Expressive Imperative

Beyond the practical importance of the enforcement power lies its symbolism. Seventy years ago Justices Douglas and Jackson objected to the Court's reliance on congressional possession of the commerce power as the foundation for striking down California's Depression-era "Okie" law, preventing the importation of indigent persons from other states.[10] Those justices took issue with the symbolism of reducing Americans' right to travel from state to state to a matter of commerce, as opposed to a matter of individual rights and national citizenship. In Justice Douglas's memorable words, in his view "the right of persons to move freely from State to State occupies a more protected position in our constitutional system than does the movement of cattle, fruit, steel and coal across state lines."[11]

That same expressive concern animates this book's call to reconsider the Enforcement Clause. Even if, contrary to our earlier analysis, Congress's commerce, spending, and other Article I powers sufficed to achieve everything that could be achieved with enforcement legislation, it would remain important that individual rights legislation be grounded, when appropriate, on the enforcement power. That power directly relates to individual rights: to paraphrase Justice Douglas, it makes clear that the subject matter is constitutional rights, rather than interstate commerce affecting cattle, fruit, steel, coal—or people. Moreover, as enforcement *legislation*, it directly involves the representatives of the American people in giving concrete meaning to the most important constitutional rights we enjoy as Americans. Even a cynic about the legislative process must concede that a congressional debate explicitly focused on a bill's relationship to due process or equal protection sends a different message than one focused on Congress's authority to regulate commerce.

To be sure, individual rights legislation cannot always rest on the Enforcement Clause. For example, because Fourteenth Amendment restrictions apply only to state government, antidiscrimination legislation operating on private employers cannot rest on that ground unless that private discrimination can be meaningfully attributable to the state.[12] (Chapter 8 will discuss this possibility.) However, when federal legislation regulates states in pursuit of liberty and equality rights, the enforcement power should play a prominent role in the analysis, for reasons that are no less important simply because they relate to law's expressive function.

The Muddled State of the Doctrine

If one agrees that the enforcement power is either indispensable, uniquely expressive, or simply a valuable policy tool, then it becomes important to ground it on a stable foundation. Unfortunately, the Court's current enforcement power doctrine is severely muddled. Since the seminal 1997 case *City of Boerne v. Flores*,[13] the Court has required that enforcement legislation be "congruent and proportional" to the underlying right it seeks to protect. As the name implies, the "congruence and proportionality" test requires that enforcement legislation bear some relationship—as will become clear later, more than simply a minimal or plausible relationship—to the unconstitutional conduct against which the statute seeks to enforce.

Justices across the ideological spectrum accepted *Boerne*'s formula. However, in post-*Boerne* cases the Court split badly on its proper application. More important, the Court's application of the congruence and proportionality test is analytically incoherent, impossible to predict, and institutionally illegitimate. We will discuss these problems in chapters 4 and 5. But here's a quick summary.

Analytical Incoherence

In the first several years after *Boerne* a tenuous majority coalesced around the proposition that enforcement legislation had to be congruent and proportional to the underlying right, *as the Court itself applied that underlying right in direct constitutional litigation*. For example, in 2000 the Court accorded skeptical review of enforcement legislation aimed at protecting the equal protection rights of the elderly because underlying equal protection doctrine had identified the elderly as a "nonsuspect class"—legalese for saying that age discrimination does not trigger careful judicial scrutiny.[14] The Court understood that doctrinal decision as a conclusion that age discrimination did not constitute a serious constitutional concern. In turn, that conclusion rendered such enforcement legislation presumptively overbroad, and hence not "congruent and proportional."

The problem with this approach is that sometimes judicial doctrine, and in particular "suspect class" doctrine, does not reflect what this book calls "core" constitutional meaning—that is, the actual constitutional rule—to which enforcement legislation must be congruent and proportional. Instead, such doctrine is better understood as a set of decisional aids that help courts decide cases despite judges' inability to discern that core meaning. The distinction between decisional aids and core constitutional meaning is not an intuitive one: we are accustomed to consider anything the Court says about the constitutionality of a challenged action as an interpretation of the Constitution itself. Later chapters in this book will explain and defend this distinction.

For now, suspend any skepticism, and assume that sometimes the Court decides constitutional cases based on principles that are chosen because judges can competently apply them. When the Court does this, the resulting analysis should not be understood as stating the core constitutional rule that marks the proper reference point for enforcement legislation under the congruence and proportionality standard. To be sure, such analysis may be helpful in demarcating the allowable space for enforcement legislation. But it should not be the final word. Unfortunately, much of the Court's Enforcement Clause jurisprudence in the first decade after *Boerne* ignored the difference between core constitutional meaning and constitutional decision rules when locating the reference point for enforcement legislation.

Unpredictability

The analytical mistake identified here is serious enough, but in recent years the Court has compounded the error by deviating from this template in unpredictable ways. This new phase of Enforcement Clause doctrine began in earnest in a 2012 case reviewing the "self-care" provision of the Family and Medical Leave Act (FMLA).[15] The FMLA was enacted to protect the equal protection right to sex equality—a right the Court has recognized since the 1970s as meriting significant judicial protection.[16] Under the Court's enforcement power template as it existed before the 2012 FMLA self-care case, the Court's own recognition of the serious constitutional issue sex discrimination presents should have led it to give Congress significant latitude to craft enforcement legislation. This may sound paradoxical, but on reflection it is not: if a particular type of discrimination (e.g., sex discrimination) is so problematic that it merits heightened judicial scrutiny, then it makes sense that Congress should enjoy more latitude to legislate against such discrimination. But in 2012 the Court broke with that template and instead reviewed the FMLA's self-care provision skeptically. Based on that review, it found that provision to constitute inappropriate enforcement legislation.

The FMLA case's skeptical judicial review of the self-care provision echoed the Court's reception to another species of enforcement legislation aimed at another type of particularly problematic discrimination. In 2009 the Court considered a claim that crucial provisions of the VRA exceeded Congress's power to enforce the Fifteenth Amendment. (While the Court has never decided whether the Fifteenth Amendment's Enforcement Clause is subject to the same congruence and proportionality standard, prior to *Boerne* it was generally understood that the two enforcement clauses provided Congress with analogous power.)[17] The VRA deals with racial discrimination—the type of discrimination that was clearly of greatest concern to Reconstruction-era members of Congress, and the type that the Court has identified as presenting the most serious constitutional threat.

The Court resolved the 2009 case on a statutory ground. Nevertheless, it expressed doubts about those provisions' constitutionality, suggesting for the first time since *Boerne* itself that Congress exceeded its power when it legislated to enforce a right the Court itself considered constitutionally central. These VRA provisions survived the 2009 case. However, in 2013 the Court returned to this issue. Again it expressed skepticism about Congress's implicit judgments regarding the need for this legislation. But this time it struck down the key foundation for those provisions.[18]

Thus, in recent years the Court shattered its own template according deference to enforcement legislation based on whether that legislation targeted discrimination the Court itself has identified as particularly troubling. As explained earlier, that template was itself problematic. But the Court's recent cases, by abandoning that template, have added unpredictably to that analytical incoherence.

Illegitimacy

This unpredictability has been accompanied by a further loss in judicial legitimacy. The FMLA and VRA opinions were striking in their willingness to second-guess congressional judgments about, respectively, the subtlety and the persistence of discrimination. The FMLA's self-care provision was defended as a means of combating the subtle perceptions employers had about the likelihood that women were more likely than men to lose work time to attend to family-care responsibilities. The VRA's renewal in 2006—the fourth since its original enactment in 1965—reflected Congress's conclusion that racial discrimination in the covered jurisdictions, while certainly mitigated since the worst days of Jim Crow, had not disappeared. Indeed, substantial evidence suggested that such discrimination had declined exactly because of the VRA's deterrent effect and might reappear if the statute were struck down or otherwise allowed to lapse.

Such judgments about discrimination's subtlety and persistence are fundamentally policy decisions. As the book will explain, they require evaluation of large-scale social facts and predictions based on those facts—functions that legislatures, including Congress, have far more competence and political legitimacy than courts to perform. The Court's skeptical review of those judgments in the FMLA and VRA cases reveal a Court that has arrogated to itself the power to second-guess such congressional policy decisions. This type of review is inappropriate for a nonelected court. On top of making judicial review unpredictable, this development has made it illegitimate as well.

The Need for a New Approach

It is time to put Enforcement Clause doctrine on a sound footing. This call to action would be fitting even if the only issues on the table were the fate of the VRA and other legislation benefiting groups that historically have been of central concern to equal protection. But the problem is even more pressing. As our nation becomes ever more pluralistic, new groups will continue asserting demands for equality. Congress will likely play a major role in addressing those demands, given its political accountability and responsiveness to social changes. That responsiveness will take the form, in part, of legislation grounded on Congress's enforcement power.

Such laws will severely strain current Enforcement Clause jurisprudence by forcing the Court to confront arguments that don't easily fit within the Court's current approach to equal protection.[19] First, new groups' equality claims translate imperfectly into the template created by the clause's central concern with racial equality. For example, some classifications, such as those based on sexual orientation, are viewed by some Americans as reflecting matters of the deepest morality; for others, they reflect simple (and constitutionally illegitimate) dislike. Other classifications confound the Court's usual equal protection inquiry into whether the classification is generally relevant to a legitimate government purpose. For example, disability, obesity, and genetic makeup are classification criteria that are undeniably relevant to certain purposes government can legitimately pursue. However, those same characteristics generate feelings of fear and even disgust that, if acted upon by government, mark such discrimination as illegitimate.[20] The complex motivations for these classifications render the blunt tool of suspect class analysis less helpful in determining the latitude Congress should enjoy to enact enforcement legislation. Its unhelpfulness will only grow as new groups continue to demand judicial and congressional protection.

The FMLA and VRA cases discussed earlier reveal an additional reason for constructing a stronger foundation for the enforcement power. As we noted, those statutes responded to, respectively, subtle and persistent discrimination. Such "second-generation" discrimination requires legislation that itself is more nuanced and responsive to the indirect ways in which discrimination manifests itself today. Similarly, the apparent success of older antidiscrimination statutes may mark a permanent uprooting of bias, or simply its temporary suppression. Just as with the enactment of second-generation statutes designed to root out subtler manifestations of discrimination, so too renewals of seemingly successful laws may be appropriate on the theory that the targeted discrimination is merely lying dormant. The public debate in early 2013 about the continued need for voting rights legislation reflected this latter possibility, as VRA advocates argued that, despite real progress, the job of uprooting racial discrimination in voting was not yet complete.[21]

These judgments are difficult. More important, they rest on both awareness of broad social facts and interpretations of those facts that in turn rest heavily on values and ideology. So described, these decisions are fundamentally policy judgments, most appropriately left to legislators. An approach to the Enforcement Clause that allows, or even forces, courts to second-guess such judgments needs reconsideration. This need will grow as Congress continues to renew older enforcement legislation and enact new legislation responding to new patterns of discrimination.

The Book's Thesis

This book argues that Congress, as the legislative voice of the nation, is often better suited than the Court to determine what the Fourteenth Amendment's vague mandate of equal protection requires in particular contexts.[22] It argues that the very nature of the equal protection guarantee makes it largely—though, crucially, not completely—beyond judicial authority and competence to apply in particular situations. At the same time, it recognizes ultimate judicial supremacy in constitutional interpretation, including interpretation of the Equal Protection Clause. This recognition requires a role for meaningful judicial review of enforcement legislation. This argument rests on three insights.

Equal Protection's Core Meaning

First and most fundamentally, leaving aside two special cases noted later, equal protection's core meaning insists simply that government classifications be both rational and free of illegitimate motivations such as simple dislike of the burdened group—what is often called "animus." (These concepts overlap but are distinct: for example, government action may be irrational even though there is no evidence that officials dislike the burdened group.)[23] Of course, judicial doctrine is far more complex than these two seemingly straightforward elements. But much of that doctrine—in particular, the "tiered scrutiny" structure ultimately based on Footnote 4 of the seminal 1938 case *United States v. Carolene Products*[24]—is best understood as a set of judicial decision rules courts use to implement these core equal protection requirements. (Chapter 2 explains the tiered scrutiny structure and its grounding in *Carolene Products*.) For enforcement power purposes, the key implication of this insight is that the congruence and proportionality standard, correctly understood, requires that enforcement legislation be congruent and proportional to the core rationality and anti-animus rules, not the tiered scrutiny structure that judges employ when attempting to apply those rules.

To be sure, equal protection constitutes more than prohibitions on unreasonable and animus-driven classifications. Beyond those rules, the modern Court has also made clear that the clause imposes severe limits on government's discretion to use race in its decision making. The Court's conclusion on this issue is controversial, and its application at the margins unsettled,[25] but at least since 1989 the Court has made clear that the presumptive rule against government use of race stands not as a decisional rule but as a core equal protection principle.[26] In addition, the Court has identified a "fundamental rights strand" of equal protection, which holds that some substantive rights are so important that the Equal Protection Clause presumptively mandates their equal distribution.[27]

These two latter rules constitute core constitutional principles to which enforcement legislation must also be congruent and proportional. As important as they are, each of them applies only to a specific factual context; thus, this book will focus primarily on federal legislation enforcing equal protection's far broader rules about reasonableness and animus. However, chapter 10 will also explain how a reconceptualized enforcement power applies to the race and fundamental rights contexts.

Comparative Competence and Expertise

Second, Congress is better suited than courts to review state laws for the unreasonableness and animus that constitute equal protection's core meaning. Because unreasonableness and animus are different concepts, they require different analyses. Begin with reasonableness. A determination that a state law classifies unreasonably requires an examination into the lines drawn by the legislation—to allow forty-nine-year-old policemen to remain on the force but to require fifty-year-old officers to retire,[28] or to limit the freedom of opticians, but not optometrists or ophthalmologists, to fit corrective lenses.[29] Such decisions are fundamentally legislative, as they involve the drawing of lines that could just as legitimately have been drawn elsewhere, and whose logic and correctness are not susceptible to traditional legal analysis. This lack of judicial competence suggests that the task of reviewing state law line-drawing for reasonableness is better performed by the federal legislature rather than by federal courts. In turn, this greater congressional competence warrants at least some judicial respect for enforcement legislation targeting asserted state violations of the reasonableness requirement.

Review of state laws for animus requires a different analysis. Animus is usually understood as bare dislike or disapproval of the burdened group, enacted into law.[30] The difficulty with this formulation is that government lawyers defending a decision to accord differential treatment can usually offer legitimate purposes supporting that decision. For example, employment discrimination against disabled persons can be justified as a cost-minimization measure, and exclusion of same-sex couples from marriage can be explained as a result of marriage's asserted purpose to promote procreation, even if the real reasons for these measures are, respectively, public discomfort with disabled persons and moral disapproval of gays and lesbians. While it is possible for judges to sift through pretextual and implausible justifications, courts often refrain from such careful scrutiny, in recognition of their inability to legitimately and accurately probe government action for evidence of such illegitimate motivations.

To an even greater degree than with unreasonableness, Congress enjoys more authority than courts to identify animus lurking in state actions. Congress, with its continual electoral renewal and broad national foundation, is the most legitimate voice of Americans' moral sensibilities. As such, it is far better suited than courts to make the fundamentally normative judgment that a given classification is unfair—that is, is based on animus.

Limits on Congressional Power

The third pillar of the book's thesis addresses limits on the enforcement power. The picture sketched so far suggests broad congressional latitude to enact enforcement legislation, based on Congress's superior competence to review legislative classifications for reasonableness and its superior authority to review those classifications for fundamental fairness. But limits must exist on this power, to satisfy both the Court's insistence that the Enforcement Clause stops short of authorizing Congress to interpret the Fourteenth Amendment and the fact that the amendment itself leaves states with significant policy-making discretion.

This book offers an approach to judicial review of enforcement legislation that imposes meaningful limits on congressional power that courts are capable of implementing consistent with their own competence and authority. Chapters 6 and 7 explain the details: for now, the important point is that the Court should both respond to the judgments Congress actually makes when it enacts enforcement legislation, and respect both Congress's and its own competence and authority to make those judgments. As those chapters explain, this review should be deferential, but nevertheless meaningful and legitimate in light of courts' particular role and capability. This is possible, but only if courts conducting that review ask the right questions.

Fundamentally, this thesis does not call for a change in the Court's Fourteenth Amendment doctrine governing either Section 1's grant of particular rights or Section 5's grant of enforcement power to Congress. Rather, it argues for a change in the Court's understanding of that doctrine. That change would enable congressional action that is both justified by Congress's institutional and democratic advantages, and consistent with core equal protection law.

The difference between the Court changing its Enforcement Clause doctrine and changing its *application* of current doctrine may be subtle, but it is real. A fundamental component of that doctrine—the Court's insistence that it enjoys the final word in interpreting the Constitution—reflects a longstanding judicial commitment. It is not likely to abandon that commitment anytime soon, even if some applications of it are subject to legitimate criticism. More specifically, the congruence and proportionality test is nearly twenty years old and was adopted by a large majority of the Court that included liberals and conservatives. But this book aims to clear a path, consistent with those principles, that would allow the Court to escape the current dead end, in which its approach to equal protection has become a hindrance to, rather than a guidepost for, enforcement legislation. Clearing that path requires the Court to rethink the meaning of its approach to equal protection, and what that approach means for Congress's enforcement power. This is not a small change.

A Word about Judicial Supremacy

As the prior paragraph suggested, this book assumes judicial supremacy—that is, the unalterable status of the Supreme Court's statements of constitutional meaning, except via the Court's own overruling or the Article V amendment process. In part this assumption simply reflects a concession to the reality that the modern Court, under both Chief Justice William Rehnquist (1986–2005) and Chief Justice John Roberts (2005–present), has firmly established, at least for our era, the idea of the Supreme Court as the ultimate arbiter of constitutional meaning. That Court is well known (and often criticized) for its willingness to enforce its own understanding of the federal-state balance. It decided *Bush v. Gore*,[31] and with it the election of 2000. That same year it elevated the police warnings suggested in *Miranda v. Arizona*[32] to the status of constitutional requirement, even in the face of Congress's determination that the underlying constitutional requirement of noncoercive police interrogations could be achieved in other ways.[33] In more recent years, the Rehnquist and Roberts Courts have insisted on a role in demarcating the national security power the executive branch can wield in the post–September 11 age. In *Citizens United v. Federal Election Commission*,[34] the Court insisted on its own understanding not just of corporations' legitimate role in the electoral process but indeed of what constitutes a legitimate electoral process in the eyes of the

American people. In starting from an assumption of judicial supremacy, this book concedes the reality of the current age.

To be sure, that current reality has much to commend it. Today, scholars often critique judicial supremacy, calling instead for a "popular constitutionalism" in which "We the People" have the power to determine what the Constitution means. As will become clear, this book is sympathetic to those calls, but it seeks to retain the benefits of a supreme interpretive role for courts. It does so out of respect for the fact that federal courts—including the Supreme Court—have provided at least some countermajoritarian protection for basic constitutional liberties. Certainly, one can overstate the Court's heroic role in American history. After all, in the twentieth century it approved both the segregation of African Americans and the internment of Japanese Americans, and it fell victim to the same national paranoia that led to the repression of left-wing speech. While eventually these mistakes were corrected, the Court waited to do so until either the crisis had passed or, in the case of segregation, until the political branches and the nation as a whole had already taken large steps to repudiate that practice. More generally, some scholars have concluded that, eventually, the Court ends up more or less reflecting the views of the American people.[35]

Still, there is something to the myth. As early as the 1930s the Court was expressing concern with unfair and racist criminal justice systems in the South. Nobody can deny that the Court under Chief Justice Earl Warren (1953–1969) took up the unpopular causes of criminal defendants; when combined with its activism on behalf of racial equality, the offense to political forces was enough to help generate movements to impeach several justices. At least for a period, the Court under the next chief justice, Warren Burger (1969–1986), stood behind judges who ordered unpopular remedies to desegregate schools; it also continued its campaign for sex equality even after political opposition succeeded in defeating the Equal Rights Amendment. The Rehnquist Court struck down flag-burning statutes. Finally, the modern Court has shown at least some backbone in insisting on limits to executive power in the war on terror, even if the ultimate evaluation of its actions in this area remains to be given. Even its controversial decision in *Citizens United* reflects a Court that is willing to vindicate its own conception of civil rights, regardless of public opinion.

Thus, in an era where national security fears, resurgent xenophobia, and deep cultural disagreement threaten constitutional rights, and where government views information control as crucial, advocates of popular constitutionalism risk disabling the power of the one branch that offers at least the hope of providing a broader, calmer perspective more responsive to both rule-of-law and civil liberties–grounded concerns. The fact that historically courts have failed to completely live up to that potential does not justify disarming them by denying their decisions conclusive authority. This book argues that judicial supremacy can be squared, if not perfectly then at least passably, with a proper respect for the ability of "the People," acting through Congress, to give effect to—literally, to "enforce"—the Equal Protection Clause, the constitutional provision that is perhaps most susceptible to popularly determined application.

The Battles Not Joined

Any book focusing on the scope of Section 5's enforcement power must tread a careful path between two hazards. On the one hand, such an inquiry inevitably requires examination of the underlying rights guaranteed by Section 1 of the Fourteenth Amendment—the familiar rights to "privileges" and "immunities," "due process," and, of course, "equal protection." This is not only inevitable but desirable; a book about Section 5 that failed to engage underlying Section 1 doctrine would be hopelessly formalistic. Yet at the same time, introducing underlying Section 1 doctrine into the mix threatens to swamp the focus on congressional enforcement power. Even more fundamentally, today a book addressing any part of the Fourteenth Amendment—or indeed any part of the Constitution—requires either a discussion of interpretive methods or, at the very least, the author's disclosure of any interpretive assumptions he makes. Again, though, deep discussion of interpretive methods, just like deep discussion of the meaning of underlying Section 1 rights, threatens to overwhelm the intended focus on congressional enforcement power. Thus, the need for assumptions, disclosures, and disclaimers.

Begin with the topic. This book assumes that the Fourteenth Amendment constitutes the primary source for the constitutional rights Americans enjoy against state misconduct. Some scholars may argue that that reliance inappropriately denigrates the importance of the Thirteenth Amendment, banning slavery, and its own, nearly identically worded, enforcement clause. Despite its seeming narrowness, scholars have argued that the Thirteenth Amendment's ban on slavery is properly understood as extending beyond prohibiting chattel slavery or its equivalents, to proclaim freedom for all Americans—a concept broad enough to encompass a wide variety of rights. They also note the amendment's potential for broad congressional enforcement, given its applicability to all conduct—not, as with the Fourteenth Amendment, simply the conduct of state governments.

There is much to commend a revitalized understanding of the Thirteenth Amendment. However, a century of legal precedent has identified the Fourteenth Amendment as the primary source for Americans' constitutional rights. That long-standing practice has influenced broader American culture: today, when Americans talk about our "constitutional rights," our gaze turns to the Fourteenth Amendment's "majestic generalities,"[36] especially "due process of law" and "the equal protection of the laws." This is not to say that such rights cannot be found in the Thirteenth Amendment. But refocusing our attention toward the Thirteenth Amendment constitutes another agenda and another book. Those books exist.[37] But this is not one of them. Instead, this book takes as a given both the Court's and American society's location of their fundamental rights in the Fourteenth Amendment.

This book also makes some basic assumptions about rights under Section 1 of the Fourteenth Amendment, and particularly the Equal Protection Clause. Most notably, it assumes that the Equal Protection Clause speaks to more than racial classifications. If the clause is understood only to guarantee some level of racial equality, difficult interpretive and enforcement issues would remain. However, those issues would have been recognizable to the amendment's drafters and enactors in 1866. For example, does the Fourteenth Amendment require racial equality in every sphere of government action, or just with regard to what the framing generation understood as "civil" rights? Does it allow race-conscious government action designed to ensure ultimate equality, or does it require color blindness? Since then, American constitutional law has experienced an extraordinary expansion of contexts and, crucially for our purposes, types of discrimination that equal protection is thought to address.

The assumption that the clause addresses more than race is, I believe, a defensible one, given this book's goals. Ultimately, this is not a book about interpretive method or even about the proper interpretation of Section 1; rather, it is a book about the interplay of equal protection doctrine and institutional roles in the context of congressional enforcement power. It therefore takes as a given the last forty years of equal protection doctrine, and the interpretive theory that produced it. A reader may view this assumption as a case of confusing the familiar with the permanent. Still, it seems doubtful that the Court will abandon wholesale its expansion of equal protection's scope beyond race. Unlike in past situations where the Court has been forced to repudiate long-standing doctrine, the Court's expansion of equal protection beyond race, while certainly not free of analytical problems, has not elicited a fundamental challenge that makes a complete repudiation plausible. Moreover, this assumption is appropriate in order to maintain a careful focus on the Section 5 power. As Justice Scalia has suggested, the expansion of equal protection's scope to areas beyond race has implications for the proper meaning of the enforcement power.[38] Thus, any analysis of that power should hold constant the other variable—that is, the scope of the Equal Protection Clause itself.

This book also assumes that the Court will continue to test enforcement legislation against a standard requiring a reasonably tight connection between the statute and the constitutional violation it targets. This is, in some ways, its most critical assumption. Many scholars have criticized *Boerne*'s congruence and proportionality test as historically unsupported and inappropriately dismissive of Congress's authority to engage in its own constitutional interpretation. Indeed, Justice Scalia, who joined the majority opinion in *Boerne*, later reversed himself, criticizing that test as "flabby" and involving the Court in disrespectful second-guessing of the factual record Congress assembles justifying enforcement legislation.

Nevertheless, *Boerne*'s core insight—that enforcement legislation must exhibit some relationship to Court-stated Fourteenth Amendment law—appears here to stay. A court's scrutiny of that relationship may well be deferential. Indeed, this book will argue for such deference. Similarly, the Court may have to adjust its understanding of what that underlying Fourteenth Amendment law actually says, and thus what constitutes the target for congruence and proportionality review. This book also makes that argument. But it bears repeating that *Boerne* is nearly twenty years old and, when it was announced, commanded agreement across the Court's ideological spectrum. And again, *Boerne* rests on a core assumption about judicial supremacy that both wings of the current Court have embraced—an assumption that, as noted earlier in this introduction, at least sometimes redounds to the benefit of unpopular civil rights claims. A book that hopes to work within the parameters of modern judicial doctrine must make its peace with *Boerne*. The good news, at least for advocates of a broader congressional role in enforcing the Fourteenth Amendment, is that the congruence and proportionality test is flexible enough to accommodate such a role. This book endeavors to make that argument.

A final, more general, caveat is in order. As should be clear by now, this is a book about judicial doctrine. Many wonderful pieces of scholarship have been written discussing discrimination from a theoretical or moral perspective. When appropriate, this book cites and discusses them. But, except as noted later, it does not join that discussion directly.

Still, it bears repeating that the legal doctrine this book discusses concerns congressional power to give concrete form to the vague but morally resonant guarantee of "equal protection." This fact requires courts to apply legal doctrine to phenomena—enforcement legislation—that may reflect the more theoretical or moral understandings of discrimination noted earlier.

Congress is not bound by the strictures of legal analysis. While it is required, of course, to stay within constitutional boundaries, as a politically responsive policy-making institution it also has the power, and, indeed, the obligation, to respond to the nation's evolving moral sensibilities about discrimination: the types Americans find laudable, the types we find acceptable, and the types we find invidious. Those sensibilities reflect, to a greater or lesser degree, theorists' discussions asking, to use one scholar's title, "When is discrimination wrong?"[39] Judicial review of legislation reflecting those sensibilities therefore inevitably requires courts to engage those more theoretical analyses.

Thus, a book about congressional power to enforce equal protection stands at the borderline between theoretical discussions of equality and doctrinal discussions of constitutional law. As such, the book's analysis touches on those more theoretical discussions as it considers how courts have reviewed enforcement legislation grounded on Americans' understandings of what equality requires. In particular, it considers how courts have struggled to translate those understandings into doctrinally coherent terms. This struggle provides yet another reason the enforcement power provides such an intellectually rich question, in addition to one whose proper answer is so important both to the appropriate division of power between Congress and the courts and to the modern relevance of the Fourteenth Amendment's promise.

The Book's Structure

This book is divided into four parts. Part I (chapters 1 through 3) tells, in a highly abbreviated way, the story of equal protection and the enforcement power in American law up to the present day. Of course, the enforcement power is the main subject of this book. But it is impossible to identify and analyze the problems the Enforcement Clause poses without examining, at least briefly, the guaranties that clause authorizes Congress to enforce. Hence, chapters 1 and 2 present a highly condensed version of equal protection's history, explaining how the Court has come to understand both the scope of the Equal Protection Clause and its underlying meaning. Chapter 1 tells the story up to 1937, the year that marks the threshold of the Court's modern era. Chapter 2 explains how over the past seventy-five years the Court has attempted to give effect to that underlying meaning. Chapter 3 tells the analogous story of the enforcement power. It briefly explains the Court's early encounters with that power but focuses primarily on twentieth-century decisions, culminating in the 1997 case *City of Boerne v. Flores*, which established the modern rule governing that power.

Part II (chapters 4 and 5) critiques the Court's current approach to the enforcement power. Chapter 4 explains how that approach misconstrues its own equal protection doctrine and thus tests enforcement legislation against the wrong constitutional baseline. Chapter 5 explains how recent enforcement power decisions have inappropriately second-guessed Congress's judgments on matters that can only be described as questions of policy, rather than law. These chapters also explain how these missteps will likely recur, given the likely path of future enforcement legislation.

Part III (chapters 6 through 8) offers a new approach. Chapter 6 argues that the Court should refocus its congruence and proportionality analysis toward core constitutional rules rather than the decisional aids against which it currently tests enforcement legislation. Chapter 7 offers a series of principles to guide the Court's decisions about when to defer to Congress's judgments and findings supporting enforcement legislation. Chapter 8 considers Congress's Enforcement Clause power to regulate private parties.

Part IV (chapters 9 and 10) applies that new approach. Chapter 9 applies it to what this book considers its primary concerns: enforcement legislation targeting state government action believed to be unconstitutionally unreasonable or infused with animus, and enforcement legislation tackling stubborn or subtle discrimination. Chapter 10 speculates about how this proposed approach might inform Congress's power to enforce other Fourteenth Amendment rights: both the racial equality and fundamental rights strands of equal protection itself, and the substantive rights guaranteed under the Due Process Clause.

This structure requires heavily condensing the story of equal protection in order to prevent it from swamping the book's focus on congressional enforcement. I hope that persons encountering this material for the first time will find this condensed story accessible and sufficiently detailed; I also hope that experienced scholars will excuse the inevitable simplifications and omissions.

This structure also requires a bit of backtracking. Chapters 1 and 2 proceed chronologically, ending with what judges, lawyers, scholars, and citizens face today as our equal protection jurisprudence. Chapter 3 then rewinds the tape, to consider the evolution of the enforcement power. This backtracking is quite artificial: judges live and work in a particular time period, facing and deciding all questions that confront them. Thus, for example, the same Court that initially determined the meaning of the Equal Protection Clause also decided the first cases involving legislation enforcing that clause. Nevertheless, the coherence of the underlying stories—of the meaning of equal protection and the enforcement power—requires unraveling these two stories, interrelated though they may be, and presenting them separately. I hope that the later chapters of the book reconnect these stories in ways that compensate for that initial artificial separation.

Similarly, when part III makes its argument for a new approach, it refers extensively to the cases discussed in part I and the objections to the current doctrine discussed in part II. This organization is also a concession to reality: before part III can work with the cases and the Court's analysis of the issues they present, part I must present them in their chronological context, and part II must critique them in order to point out the need for the new approach part III offers. I hope that the cost imposed on the reader by any repetition is outweighed by the benefits that are gained in presenting some material three times: first as part of a chronological tour, then as the objects of critique, and finally as the subjects to which the new approach is applied.

PART I

How We Got Here

A Brief History of Equal Protection and the Enforcement Power

1

Equal Protection before the Modern Era

As the introduction explained, before we can fully understand Congress's power to enforce the Equal Protection Clause, we need to examine the meaning of the clause itself. Hence, the first two chapters of this book provide a (necessarily) brief and highly compressed history of equal protection.[1] This chapter begins that history by examining equal protection up to the cusp of the modern era. It first considers American legal thinking about equality before the ratification of the Fourteenth Amendment in 1868. This examination of "equality before equal protection" will help illuminate possible meanings of the Equal Protection Clause. It then examines how the Supreme Court construed the Equal Protection Clause up to 1937—a date that marks a turning point in constitutional law, and equal protection law in particular.

Equality before Equal Protection

Speaking very generally, pre–Civil War thinking about equality consisted of two strands. These strands were motivated by very different considerations, but they eventually converged in Republican lawmakers' thinking during Reconstruction. That thinking ultimately found its expression in the Equal Protection Clause itself.

Class Legislation

From the outset, a fundamental concern of American constitutionalism has been to prevent what has been called "the tyranny of the majority." This concern rose to prominence during the period between independence and the Constitutional Convention of 1787. During that period, Americans reconstituted their state governments, newly freed from royal control, to strengthen democratically chosen legislatures and weaken courts and executives. However, those legislatures became forums for what many American leaders saw as irresponsible government that violated property and contract rights. The problem, at least as it appeared to James Madison and other soon-to-be framers, was that the bestowal of unchecked government power in one institution naturally lent itself to abuse, as self-interested political factions used electoral victories to further their group's own interests at the expense of the public good.

It was to prevent this hijacking of government that the Constitution's framers split sovereign power both between the federal and state levels and within the federal level. By splitting power in these ways, it was hoped that no faction could ever gain control of the full apparatus of government at any one time, and thus gain unrestrained power to act in pursuit of its own interests. It is perhaps not as well known that the same concern also motivated Madison's interest in creating a strong national government, completely aside from how power within that national institution would be divided. His thought, most famously expressed in Federalist Number 10, was that the broad geographic scope of the national government would make it impossible for factions—which Madison saw as localized groups, such as particular economic interests or religious sects—to obtain dominant power over the sprawling federal institution.[2]

These innovations—a federalized government of continental scale, consisting of interconnected, mutually checking, institutions at the national level—speak to structure. Yet it is important to understand that the framers saw institutional design not as an end in itself but as a means to ensuring liberty without sacrificing effective governance. Today, we tend to separate our concerns about separation of powers and federalism from our concerns about individual freedom. (Traces of their close relationship periodically surface in protests against an overweening central government or, conversely, calls for federal assistance against despotic local officials.) But the Constitution's advocates saw structure and rights as intimately related. Indeed, so did its opponents, the Anti-Federalists, who, alarmed at the prospect of any overly powerful federal government, insisted on the enactment of a Bill of Rights as a price for supporting ratification.

The relationship between structure and rights matters for how the framers understood the relationship between equality and the concept of faction. To the framers, the threat posed by factions was the prospect of private-regarding legislation—legislation that did not aim at a legitimate public interest but instead sought to promote private goals such as individual power and wealth. This is not to say that the framers or their successors were averse to all regulation. Far from it. As scholars have demonstrated, contrary to the myth of a night-watchman state, antebellum America featured heavy amounts of regulation.[3] But what did concern them was regulation that reflected hijacking of governmental power for purely private goals.[4]

The concern about private-regarding legislation reflects a distant but nevertheless distinct echo of concern for equality. One understanding of purely private-regarding legislation of the type the framers disfavored is that it aims simply at oppressing a particular group—one economic interest seeking an economic advantage over another, one religious sect seeking to impose itself on nonbelievers, or even one region seeking benefits at the expense of the rest of the nation. By the Jacksonian era, these concerns were becoming voiced in a vocabulary that explicitly sounded in equality.[5] At the federal political level, President Andrew Jackson cast his fight against the Bank of the United States as a fight against moneyed interests he accused of seeking unfair advantages through law. In his famous message vetoing the bill rechartering the Bank, Jackson explicitly spoke of such unfair advantages, calling instead for equal government treatment of all.[6] At the state level, concerns about equality led to attacks on corporations, which at the time were chartered not under general incorporation laws but rather through special legislative acts that granted a particular corporation a right to exist and conduct particular business.[7] Corporations, of course, remained a vital feature of American economic activity; however, the agitation against legislatures' practice of granting special corporate charters gradually led states to enact general incorporation statutes of the sort we have today.[8]

Perhaps most important for our purposes, state courts of the era began focusing on the requirement that laws be general rather than specific—that they apply to all rather than imposing burdens or conferring benefits on only a few. Sometimes they grounded this requirement in their state constitutions' "law of the land" provisions.[9] This was a telling development, given the eventual importance of those provisions' successors (including in the Fourteenth Amendment) requiring that life, liberty, and property not be deprived without "due process of law."[10] Other courts grounded this requirement in general, implied principles of republican government.[11]

Running through all these developments was the idea that government's proper role was to remain neutral between individuals as they competed for wealth and power. Such neutrality was understood to be the exact opposite of so-called special legislation, which singled out individuals for benefits or burdens for reasons unrelated to the public good. Of course, such singling out might in fact be necessary for the achievement of some public benefit. For example, a certain industry might be especially noxious or dangerous, and thus merit special restrictions, while other activities might redound to the greater public good, and thus merit encouragement. Indeed, as we will see later in this chapter, the difficulty courts faced in determining when such singling out constituted legitimate public-regarding legislation, and when it did not, became a major problem in implementing this approach.

That task became particularly difficult after the Civil War—both for state courts and for federal courts construing the new Fourteenth Amendment—

because of the rise of industrial capitalism that triggered reformers' calls for regulation of strong economic forces and assistance to weaker groups. That story is also told later in this chapter. For our current purposes, what is important is the idea that, by the Civil War, American legal culture harbored a deep understanding, expressed both politically and jurisprudentially, that singling out for a purely private purpose—what came to be known as "class legislation"—constituted unfair inequality.

There was, however, another strand of equality thought that had moved to the forefront by the Civil War. This was the issue of racial equality: whether it existed, and, if it did, what it meant.[12] By the end of the Civil War it was clear that the war had evolved into a decisive struggle about slavery. With the North's victory and slavery's impending demise, the racial equality question became a central political and constitutional issue. Interestingly, but perhaps unsurprisingly, consideration of that question was heavily influenced by the class legislation concept.

Race, Racial Equality, and Class Legislation

The original Constitution accommodated slavery. Indeed, slavery permeated the document. Its provision counting slaves as three-fifths of a person for purposes of allocating congressional representation, and its reference to congressional representation for purposes of allocating Electoral College votes, made slavery doubly relevant to the selection of national leaders. The Fugitive Slave Clause constituted one of the few constitutional provisions governing the relations between states. Perhaps most remarkably of all, the slave trade constituted one of only two topics on which the Constitution prohibited amendments.[13]

Nevertheless, throughout the first half of the nineteenth century antislavery thought continued to percolate in the North, even as hopes faded that slavery would gradually die out in the South as it had in the northern states. But slavery's opponents varied widely in their assumptions about African Americans, their rights, and their relationship to the nation. For example, many northerners opposed slavery's extension into the nation's territories (a major question at the time given the country's ongoing expansion) for reasons that had little to do with sympathy for slaves or views about the intrinsic equality of persons of different races, and much to do with restricting the competition slavery would pose to free (white) labor.

But antislavery northerners who were less self-interested also expressed ambivalence about the role African Americans would play in a postslavery America. In the 1850s, even abolitionist leaders of the new Republican Party insisted that they did not believe African Americans to be the social or intellectual equal of European Americans.[14] (To be sure, some of that insistence also undoubtedly responded to self-interest—in particular, the political imperative of appealing to antislavery but nonetheless racist voters.) Some northerners did express what we might consider more modern thinking about race, embracing a view that blacks and whites were equal in all respects and calling for the repeal of all laws drawing racial distinctions. But historians have concluded that such views remained a minority, even among those who opposed slavery.[15]

These disagreements were not purely theoretical, even before the Civil War. Free states imposed varying degrees of restrictions on blacks: most prohibited them from voting, and many restricted their ability to contract, own property, or appear in court as a witness, litigant, or juror. But these disagreements became even more consequential during the Civil War, when in the North the war evolved into a struggle not just to preserve the Union but to end slavery. With the anticipated destruction of slavery came the question of what that institution meant, and what was meant by its opposite: universal freedom.

This is not to suggest that the focus on slavery and racial equality completely subsumed the earlier discourse on class legislation. Indeed, perhaps consistent with many northerners' focus on opposing slavery for reasons other than morality, arguments against slavery's expansion were often cast in terms of the attempts by slaveholders to dominate the country. Expressed as early as the opening years of the nineteenth century, and propounded by abolitionists, the concept of "the Slave Power" painted an alarming picture in which a small faction of powerful persons—southern slaveholders—conspired to destroy the civil liberties of all Americans and to gain a stranglehold on federal government power.[16] The idea was not fanciful: throughout the two decades preceding the Civil War, it appeared as though the southern planter elite and their northern sympathizers controlled most of the federal government, including the presidency and a majority of the Supreme Court.

Claims of a slaveholder conspiracy to control government for its own ends and in derogation of others' rights were aided by a series of mob actions in which antislavery speakers were harassed and injured, antislavery journals physically attacked, and free northern African American seamen detained when their ships docked in southern ports.[17] In addition, the gradual polarization of national politics around the slavery issue led to claims that southern political leaders cared only about their sectional interest in promoting slavery, rather than the national interest. Such single-minded concern for slavery's own needs was alleged to extend even into the nation's foreign affairs, with antislavery advocates arguing that southerners provoked the war with Mexico and plotted other adventures in Latin America and the Caribbean, all in order to acquire more slave territory. By the 1850s, opponents of slavery's extension had largely succeeded in portraying slaveholding interests as the most powerful and thus the most dangerous faction in the nation, intent on subverting the common good in a single-minded pursuit of its own narrow interests.

The evolution of the Civil War into a contest over slavery ensured that legal and political thinking about equality during the Reconstruction era would focus on race. The issue arose first as Congress considered the proposed Thirteenth Amendment, banning slavery. The prospect of ending slavery inevitably raised the question about what the status of "slave" entailed—and, conversely, what was entailed by the status of "free." Scholars such as Earl Maltz have argued that, for the congressmen who provided the margin of passage for the amendment and thus whose views presumably weigh heavily, the universal freedom contemplated by the amendment did not imply that the former slaves would necessarily possess all the rights enjoyed by white persons. He concedes that it is probably impossible to determine exactly the views of the congressmen who enacted the amendment and sent it to the states for ratification. But he also observes that the amendment would not have been enacted but for the support of Democrats and conservative Republicans who took a narrow view of the rights implied by the status of free men.[18] Other scholars disagree, arguing that the amendment is best understood as enshrining a broader set of rights, with a correspondingly broader enforcement power.[19]

The ambiguity about the scope of the Thirteenth Amendment—not just among modern scholars but among Reconstruction-era politicians as well—soon had concrete implications when Congress considered another major piece of Reconstruction legislation, the Civil Rights Act of 1866. That bill constituted Congress's response to the so-called Black Codes that the newly reorganized southern state governments had begun enacting. Those laws severely restricted former slaves' basic rights, restricting, for example, their ability to contract, own property, testify in court, and even travel without a white person's consent. In response, the Civil Rights Act provided that all persons, "without regard to any previous condition of slavery . . . shall have the same right . . . to make and enforce contracts; to sue, be parties and give evidence, to inherit, purchase, lease, sell, hold, and convey real and personal property, and to full and equal benefit of all laws and proceedings for the security of person and property, as is enjoyed by white citizens."[20] Proponents argued that the law was authorized by Congress's power to enforce the Thirteenth Amendment. But others, from opponents of broader rights for blacks such as Democratic President Andrew Johnson to proponents of such rights such as

Republican Congressman John Bingham, doubted that the power to enforce the prohibition on slavery extended to supporting the law.

Even though Congress overrode President Johnson's veto and enacted the Civil Rights Act, enough doubts lingered about that law's constitutional foundation to spur work on another constitutional amendment—what became the Fourteenth Amendment. Perhaps surprisingly, much of that amendment has relatively little modern relevance. Section 2, which reduces a state's congressional representation if it disenfranchises otherwise eligible voters, has at times played a role in adjudicating voting rights claims.[21] However, Sections 3 and 4, which deal, respectively, with the political rights of ex-Confederates and the Union and Confederate war debts, are rarely mentioned today.[22]

By contrast, Section 1, which bestows American citizenship on all persons born in the country, and prevents states from abridging "the privileges or immunities of citizens of the United States," depriving any person of "life, liberty, or property, without due process of law," or depriving any person of "the equal protection of the laws," has been an exceptionally fruitful source of law. The meaning of Section 1—in particular, whether it "incorporated" the Bill of Rights to apply against the states, the clause that accomplishes any such incorporation, and the correct understanding of "privileges" and "immunities," "due process," and "equal protection"—has been hotly contested. And, of course, the topic of this book—congressional power to enforce "equal protection"—requires at least some understanding of what Section 1 means by that phrase. For current purposes, however, what matters is that even scholars who otherwise disagree fundamentally on these issues agree that, at a minimum, Section 1 was intended to provide a firm constitutional foundation for the Civil Rights Act.

Did the Equal Protection Clause play a specific, identifiable role in furnishing this foundation? Scholars have been unable to agree on the original meaning of that clause. To consider only two views, John Harrison has argued for a limited reading in which that clause requires government to provide equality in the protection provided by existing laws. This reading allows government, if it chose, to deny a given type of legal protection to everyone.[23] By contrast, Jacobus tenBroek concluded that the clause's fundamental force lay in the "protection" it gives to persons in their natural rights (e.g., the rights to property and contract), with "equal" simply modifying that basic requirement. Thus, for tenBroek, the Equal Protection Clause means that government could not deny such rights, even if its denial applied across the board, to all persons.[24]

Readings that restricted the clause's scope to a certain set of rights competed with a broader understanding, in which the clause requires equality in all government actions, not simply those protecting the rights addressed by the Civil Rights Act of 1866. While this broader reading is perhaps best encapsulated in the Court's epigram in 1886 that "the equal protection of the laws is a pledge of the protection of equal laws,"[25] this view surfaced during the congressional debates on the Fourteenth Amendment. In particular, it finds expression in the view, articulated by key members of the Thirty-Ninth Congress, that the Fourteenth Amendment in general, and the Equal Protection Clause in particular, nationalized the state law rule against class legislation.[26]

These arguments—whether correct or not[27]—introduced the potential for an interpretation that took the amendment far beyond concerns about ensuring the rights protected by the Civil Rights Act of 1866. But that potential took time to realize. As Reconstruction waned, the Supreme Court gave a limited reading to the Fourteenth Amendment and, in particular, denied that the Equal Protection Clause protected anything more than the rights of the newly freed slaves, or perhaps African Americans more generally.[28] Nevertheless, the introduction of class legislation concepts into federal constitutional discourse about equality ensured that this idea remained available for the Court when it turned its eyes away from African Americans and refocused on constitutional limitations on government regulation of the economy.

Equal Protection before *Carolene Products*

When measured in terms of legal doctrine, seventy years is a very long time. The period from the Fourteenth Amendment's ratification in 1868 to the Supreme Court's 1938 decision in *United States v. Carolene Products*[29] witnessed fundamental changes in many areas of constitutional doctrine. Most important for our purposes, the Court's understanding of equal protection—and, indeed, its entire conception of rights—changed significantly. Ironically, though, these changes reinforced core antebellum understandings of equality. Even more important, they find clear echoes in what the next chapter will explain as the modern law of the Equal Protection Clause.

Early Judicial Understandings of Fourteenth Amendment Equality

A basic issue in understanding the Fourteenth Amendment concerns how it allocated meaning to Section 1's three restrictions on state conduct: "abridg[ing] the privileges or immunities of citizens of the United States," "depriv[ing] any person of life, liberty or property without due process of law," and "deny[ing] to any person within its jurisdiction the equal protection of the laws." Ultimately, the Court located most protections for substantive rights in the Due Process Clause, interpreted the Equal Protection Clause as a broad mandate of equality, and denied much significance at all to the Privileges or Immunities Clause.

This resolution is likely a highly imperfect rendering of the drafters' intentions. Today, many scholars believe that any substantive rights the drafters intended the amendment to bestow were granted by the Privileges or Immunities Clause. In addition, as noted earlier, some argue that the equal protection guarantee implied some level of protection for the basic rights addressed by the Civil Rights Act of 1866. Scholars have spent enormous time and energy proposing interpretations of Section 1 that reflect their understanding of what the Thirty-Ninth Congress meant by these vague phrases. This section tells a highly abbreviated and partial version of the Court's early approach to the Fourteenth Amendment, emphasizing the doctrinal evolution that culminated in our modern understanding of the Equal Protection Clause.[30]

The Supreme Court began asserting a role in interpreting the Fourteenth Amendment soon after its ratification. The Court's first encounter with the Fourteenth Amendment, the *Slaughter-House Cases* of 1873,[31] concerned arguments by butchers in New Orleans that Louisiana's grant of a slaughterhouse monopoly to one firm violated the butchers' rights to practice their trade. The butchers concentrated their argument on the Privileges or Immunities Clause, arguing that it granted federal constitutional protection to the right to engage in lawful trades such as butchering. They appeared to have a good argument: Article IV of the original Constitution prohibited states from discriminating against out-of-staters with regard to persons' "Privileges and Immunities," and a leading case from the early nineteenth century had interpreted those rights broadly, to include the right to pursue one's profession.[32] On this theory, the Fourteenth Amendment's obvious focus on limiting state power would suggest that it had nationalized the protection for those "privileges" and "immunities," converting Article IV's pure nondiscrimination rule into a rule of substantive protection. Nevertheless, the Court rejected that argument. Justice Miller's opinion read the Fourteenth Amendment's clause as protecting only what he identified as a limited set of rights appertaining to national citizenship, leaving to state protection the mass of "privileges" and "immunities" that were the subject of Article IV's nondiscrimination rule.

For our purposes, what Justice Miller said about equality was especially important. Despite disclaiming any relevance for the Equal Protection Clause in the case,[33] he nevertheless thought it necessary to observe that the state's regulation of butchers was reasonable and, crucially for our purposes, required the monopoly slaughterhouse to grant equal access to all butchers.[34] He made this observation in the part of his opinion where he stated that this type of law, regulating potentially unhealthful activities such as animal slaughtering, had always been understood as part of states' fundamental power to regulate for the public health and safety—what was known as the "police power" (although that power extends well beyond modern-day policing functions).[35] This identification matters for us because, once the Court began to use the Fourteenth Amendment to justify judicial scrutiny of all types of state regulations, it would take the police power as the baseline for its analysis—that is, it would test alleged violations of Fourteenth Amendment rights by asking whether the challenged action constituted a proper police power regulation. *Slaughter-House* implied the Supreme Court's understanding that valid exercises of that power had to regulate equally all those whose activities (here, animal butchering) triggered the need for regulation.

The dissenters in that case also identified equality of treatment as crucial to the constitutionality of the Louisiana law. They argued—perhaps in simple factual disagreement with Justice Miller's majority—that the Louisiana law granting a monopoly to one slaughterhouse did in fact amount to unequal treatment of the butchers who were not members of the slaughterhouse corporation.[36] In analyzing the effect the Fourteenth Amendment had on state regulatory power, Justice Field in particular[37] argued that that amendment's Privileges or Immunities Clause cloaked state residents with the same protection from their own state governments that Article IV's analogous clause had provided to out-of-state visitors. In other words, he argued that, whereas Article IV's Privileges or Immunities Clause simply required a state to give visitors whatever rights it gave its own citizens, the analogous clause in the Fourteenth Amendment required states to treat its *own* citizens equally as among themselves.[38]

In the years after *Slaughter-House* the Court moved toward the dissenters' position. By 1877, in *Munn v. Illinois*,[39] the Court had unanimously agreed on the principle that state regulation of property (in *Munn*, the rates that could be charged by grain silo operators) had to be imposed in the interest of the public, rather than the interest of a private group. Chief Justice Waite's opinion therefore analyzed the public importance of grain elevators. Finding them to constitute a crucial link in the process of moving crops to market, he concluded that that business was cloaked with "a public interest," thus justifying equal and reasonable regulation of the rates they charged.

Thus, by the 1877 decision in *Munn*, the Court had set in place the building blocks for understanding the role of equality in the Fourteenth Amendment. The Court had recognized—if only implicitly—that the validity of state police power regulations turned in part on whether the challenged law regulated equally all those whose conduct triggered a legitimate need for regulation. Its location of this requirement in the police power meant that, ultimately, this equality requirement would apply broadly—beyond claims made by African Americans, and, indeed, beyond racial discrimination claims of any sort. Finally, as illustrated by *Munn* itself, the Court would sometimes take it upon itself to determine when challenged regulation did in fact aim at achieving a public good and when it aimed merely at enriching or harming a particular class. This template was to guide the Court's thinking about equality—both when considering claims actually brought under the Equal Protection Clause and otherwise—for the next sixty years.

Individual Rights and Governmental Powers

Today, when we think of equal protection, or for that matter any individual right, we think of that right as a trump—something that presumptively outweighs the normal considerations that justify legislation. For example, a restriction on speech—even a relatively less problematic one such as a restriction on the time, place, or manner of speech—requires government to surmount particular constitutional hurdles. This way of thinking has become so ingrained that we determine the existence of a right largely by asking whether its assertion triggers some heightened requirement of justification from government. Thus, for example, it is standard for lawyers today to say that there is no due process liberty of contract, exactly because claims of the deprivation of such a right do not trigger any heightened justification requirement.

But this was not always the way American constitutionalism thought about rights. Understanding how nineteenth-century courts adjudicated rights claims requires that we recognize those courts' very different understanding of how rights (including equality rights) related to government power. This effort takes some creativity on our part. As an analogy, consider the experience of looking at the famous drawing that, depending on how one first perceives it, portrays either an old woman or a young girl. Once we perceive one of those images, it takes an act of conscious refocusing in order for us to perceive the other.

So too with our understanding of how individual rights relate to governmental power. Scholars of late nineteenth-century and early twentieth-century American constitutionalism tell us that the jurisprudence of that period understood "rights" as the residual liberty that remained after government reached the limits of its legitimate power—not as trumps that outweigh what would otherwise be legitimate government action. It was that legitimate power—what lawyers and judges of the time called the "police power"—that furnished the organizing principle of American constitutional law.

Thus, rather than our modern understanding, in which rights by their very nature reduce the scope of government power, with the appropriate scope of that power consisting of whatever is left after we account for such rights, constitutionalists of the period we're examining reversed the picture. In a mirror image of the modern understanding, they started by demarcating the bounds of legitimate state power, with the residual space outside of those bounds taking the form of "rights."[40] A modern scholar described this idea by saying that during this period society consisted of islands of (limited) governmental power, surrounded by a sea of nonspecific rights.[41] Contrast that conception of rights with one from the early years of the modern jurisprudential era: in an important First Amendment case from 1945, Justice Rutledge described the question for the Court as follows: "The case confronts us again with the duty our system places on this Court to say where the individual's freedom ends and the State's power begins."[42] A nineteenth-century jurist would likely have understood such a case as posing the exact opposite question—where the *state's power* ends and the *individual's freedom* begins. Indeed, consider the title of the preeminent constitutional law treatise of that earlier era: *Constitutional Limitations*, not, say, "Constitutional Liberties."[43]

This insight makes comprehensible several aspects of the constitutional law of the era. Most notably, it helps explain the otherwise perplexing failure of courts of that time to consistently identify a particular constitutional rights provision that prohibited the challenged government action. As Owen Fiss recognized when writing a history of this era, Supreme Court constitutional analysis during this period was often not an exercise in parsing the text of a given rights provision.[44] Today, a lawyer confronted with a constitutional rights claim immediately asks, "Which constitutional right is alleged to have been violated?" In the late nineteenth century and early twentieth century, this question was asked less frequently. To repeat, not only was that question asked less frequently, but, in a real way, it would have made less sense to a lawyer of the period.

This understanding of rights applied with particular force to federal constitutional rights claims involving states. Today, a major component of our Fourteenth Amendment rights consists of those provided by the first eight amendments of the Constitution—the individual rights provisions of the Bill of Rights. However, technically speaking those rights do not apply to states; instead, the Court has concluded that the Fourteenth Amendment's Due Process Clause (which *does* apply to the states) included, or "incorporated," them within its meaning. But that process did not begin immediately upon the Fourteenth Amendment's ratification in 1868. Until the turn of the twentieth century, none of the Bill of Rights provisions was incorporated. Even after

1900, the incorporation process proceeded slowly until at least the 1920s, by which time clause-bound interpretations of the more modern sort had begun to find their way into the case law. The main federal constitutional rights that *did* apply against the states in the late nineteenth century—the due process and equal protection rights of the Fourteenth Amendment[45]—were broadly worded and hence less susceptible to careful textual parsing.[46] Perhaps even more important, they were often understood as inherent limits on free governments, and thus more easily absorbed into an analysis that focused primarily on the police power.

This is not to suggest that the police power furnished the sole focal point for constitutional analysis throughout the seventy years between 1868 and 1938. By the end of this period the Court had begun speaking in more modern-sounding, clause-specific terms that accommodated the idea of rights as trumps. Scholars disagree about the timing of that change and its triggers. Victoria Nourse dates the change to the 1930s and attributes it, at least in part, to the rise of repressive regimes abroad, which led American jurists to attempt to construct more explicit barriers to government invasions of civil liberties.[47] Howard Gillman argues that by the 1920s the rise of industrial capitalism convinced progressives of the need to expand the legitimate scope of governmental power, thus necessitating the creation of specific, modern-sounding rights-based trumps on that power.[48] David Bernstein maintains that by or soon after the turn of the twentieth century, courts were beginning to understand rights as more specific guarantees rather than simply as the residual that remained after the police power ran out. He cites the (in)famous 1905 case *Lochner v. New York*,[49] where the Court struck down a law prescribing maximum working hours for bakers, as embracing just such a specific right—the bakers' liberty right to contract for the terms of their own labor. Bernstein argues that *Lochner* served as the template for the Court's embrace of other explicitly recognized liberty rights beginning in the 1920s.[50] Regardless of the timing of this switch and its justification, as we consider how courts viewed equal protection between the end of Reconstruction and *Carolene Products* in 1938, it is important to remember that for much of this period courts embraced what may sound to modern ears like a counterintuitive understanding of American constitutionalism.

The Challenge of Equality

Courts both during and after the police power era struggled with implementing the Fourteenth Amendment's requirement of equal laws. During that era courts' ultimate goal was to distinguish valid police power regulation from invalid "class legislation" reflecting private hijacking of government's regulatory power. But that approach required the Court to pass judgment on the state's regulatory justification and the challenged law's effectiveness in achieving that goal.[51] To be sure, this imperative did not require that such judicial review be intrusive; it was just as consistent with the police power model that the Court would defer to any reasonable police power justification.[52] However, the vague, open-ended nature of the police power inquiry did result in inconsistent judicial applications of that test.

The inconsistencies this approach allowed can be exemplified by two cases decided within two years of each other in the late nineteenth century. In *Gulf, Colorado and Santa Fe Railway v. Ellis*,[53] the Court struck down a Texas law making losing railroad defendants liable for attorneys' fees in small-amount cases. The Court could not imagine a legitimate police power reason for singling out railroads for this burdensome treatment: the statute did not classify on the basis of corporate structure, for-profit basis, common-carrier status, or other criteria that might potentially have revealed to the Court a legitimate public concern. Yet two years later, in *Atchison, Topeka & Santa Fe Railroad v. Matthews*,[54] the Court upheld a Kansas law imposing attorneys' fees on losing railroad defendants in cases arising out of fires caused by railroad operations. *Matthews* relied on the special risk of fire caused by railroad operations as a reasonable justification for the differential burden imposed on railroads. While superficially appealing, *Matthews* begs the questions implicit in *Ellis* about the reasonableness of the legislature's decision to single out railroads for burdensome treatment. Most notably, if there was something unique about fire dangers that mandated a more plaintiff-friendly rule, why were railroad corporations singled out to bear that burden, instead of, say, any corporation whose negligence caused a fire?

This is not to suggest that one or the other of these cases was wrongly decided, or even that they are necessarily inconsistent. Rather, as Richard Kay suggests, the pairing of these cases illustrates the inability of the police power theory to provide determinate, predictable results.[55] Perhaps *Ellis* and *Matthews* can be reconciled. Perhaps not. But it is this very indeterminacy that reveals the inadequacy of this approach to equal protection. That approach could conceivably have provided for more determinate results, had the Court developed a more specific method of answering the police power question. For example, it could have adopted—and consistently applied—a deferential rule that accepted a state's police power argument unless contradicted by clear evidence. Alternatively, the Court could have subjected any law that classified—that is, almost any law at all—to rigid proof standards about why the public good demanded that classification.

To be sure, the police power concept contained within it the potential for such a principled deference standard. Federal and state courts during this period often described the police power as broad, authorizing government to regulate in nearly any manner as long as it was for the community's general good. The breadth of the regulatory power legislatures enjoyed naturally implied a similarly wide discretion as to means: once it was recognized that legislatures could regulate a wide variety of activities to counteract a wide variety of problems, it followed, at least in theory, that legislatures needed broad discretion in choosing the proper regulatory tools. Given that dynamic, it is perhaps unsurprising that language in court opinions of the era spoke of utter unreasonableness, or arbitrariness, as the limit on the police power.[56] Today, that rule finds expression in the core requirement, sometimes described as so fundamental as to be not based on any particular constitutional provision, that government action not be arbitrary—or, in modern parlance, irrational.[57]

Nevertheless, the Court's police power–based approach to Fourteenth Amendment rights (and equal protection rights in particular) did not feature a well-worked-out theoretical foundation for a court's application of a particular amount of deference to a challenged statute. While courts could—and did—note the breadth of state regulatory authority, and from that breadth infer similarly broad legislative discretion to decide when the public good required a particular regulation, the police power approach did not provide guideposts for where courts should look particularly carefully at a challenged action. In turn, without more guidance, "arbitrariness" was in the eye of the beholder—or the judge.

The lack of such mediating deference doctrine left the Court to its own intuitions about a given classification's legitimacy as a police power regulation. Indeed, reading between the lines, we can perhaps see that intuition at work in the railroad cases, *Ellis* and *Matthews*. After all, in the late nineteenth century it was easy to associate fire danger with railroads, and thus easy to intuit that the Kansas law upheld in *Matthews* somehow was reasonable in a way that the Texas law struck down in *Ellis* was not. But intuitions are not legal rules—especially when courts moved beyond potentially easy cases.

As noted at the end of the prior subsection, by the early decades of the twentieth century, the Court was beginning to move toward a more clause-bound approach to constitutional rights adjudication. In particular, the Court's due process jurisprudence was taking clear shape as one requiring identification of a right, and consideration of how much protection that right enjoyed against government infringement. In 1923 the Court decided the first of two cases involving parents' rights to control the education of their children, using a rights-specific analysis that eventually provided the foundation for the modern due process rights we know today, including, for example, the right to abortion.[58] Only two years before the first of these still-influential cases, Chief Justice Taft pushed forward the project of specifying constitutional rights with more particularity when he carefully explained the distinction between due process and equal protection, even while noting their overlap—in particular, the fact that both clauses required at least some level of equal treatment by government.[59] This process of differentiation and elaboration of particular constitutional rights provisions was gradual; nevertheless, by the 1920s it became possible to think about equal protection as becoming both a right in the modern, specific, rights-as-trump sense, and one distinct from due process.

The replacement of the police power approach with the rights-as-trump idea did not take place overnight. References to the police power continued throughout the pre-1937 period; indeed, as noted earlier, scholars disagree on the precise timing of this change. More important for our purposes, the evolution of the doctrine away from a police power focus and toward a more rights-centered focus did not obviate the fact that the Court still lacked a coherent approach to the question of how stringently it should review legislative classifications. Cases like *Ellis* and *Matthews* showed how adrift the Court was when evaluating states' claims that challenged legislative classifications reflected a proper exercise of the police power. The switch in focus from powers to rights did not stabilize its jurisprudence.

Two cases separated by four decades and this fundamental jurisprudential shift illustrate the continuity of this problem. In 1888, in the middle of the police power era, the Court in *Powell v. Pennsylvania*[60] upheld, against a constitutional challenge, a Pennsylvania law prohibiting the sale of oleomargarine. The format of the Court's unanimous opinion was typical for the era: the substance consisted of a long discussion of the police power, followed by exceptionally cursory dismissals of the equal protection and due process arguments. Tellingly, the Court essentially defined equal protection and due process violations as instances of the government exceeding the police power.

A generation later, in 1926, the Court in *Weaver v. Palmer Brothers*[61] struck down a state law (again from Pennsylvania) forbidding the use of used rags (called "shoddy") in bedding materials. The difference in approach is remarkable: while the Court in 1888 focused almost entirely on the scope of the state's police power, the Court in the 1926 case began its discussion by identifying the issue in an explicitly clause-specific fashion: "The question for decision is whether the provision . . . violates the due process clause or the equal protection clause." Indeed, when the *Weaver* Court found a due process violation, it expressly reserved the equal protection question. That action itself reflected an approach that focused primarily on the right, rather than, as in *Powell*, on the power.

While the focus of the two cases was quite different, the methodological conundrum the Court found itself in was similar.[62] In *Powell* the Court considered itself unauthorized to second-guess the state's health-based justifications for the oleomargarine law. In *Weaver*, however, the Court, noting the state's concession that sterilization of the shoddy makes it safe, refused to defer to the remaining potential justifications for the law—justifications Justice Holmes offered in his dissenting opinion.

The point is simple. In both *Powell* and *Weaver* the Court had to decide whether the state's actions were constitutional. While the Courts in these two cases had different jurisprudential focuses—*Powell* focusing on the police power, and *Weaver* on the plaintiff's more specifically identified individual "rights"—the real difference was in the level of deference the Court showed to the state—a difference that was never explained, or even acknowledged. The deference problem survived the jurisprudential transition from one approach to the other. The jurisprudence may have changed, but the same practical problem remained.

The police power–era Court was unable to develop a coherent theory to answer the deference question. In a crucial case decided in 1938, *United States v. Carolene Products Co.*,[63] the Court hinted at such a theory. But it is crucial for our project to remember that that theory was not itself a reinterpretation of the Equal Protection Clause. Rather, it was merely a new way of answering questions the Court had always asked. Even if by 1938 the focus had changed to the scope of the right, rather than the legitimate scope of the government power, the ultimate question—was government acting in pursuit of a legitimate goal?—remained the same.

The Road to Carolene Products

Doctrinal change can occur in different ways. It can be avulsive, if the Court simply decrees old precedent to have been mistaken and self-consciously embarks on a new path. It can also be—in fact, it usually is—more subtle. The Court can reach results ostensibly by applying an old rule, while actually applying a new or modified one; in a later case it can then claim simply to be explicitly ratifying a change that the earlier cases had already implicitly made.[64] It can also reinterpret earlier cases, as reflecting different truths or at least raising different concerns than what they were originally understood to reflect. This section tells the story of how a confluence of these methods allowed the Court to plant the seeds of what would grow into the dominant doctrinal approach to equal protection in the late twentieth century: the tiered scrutiny structure based on Footnote 4 of *United States v. Carolene Products*.[65] Like the Equal Protection Clause itself, *Carolene Products* has an intimate, though troubled relationship with race. For this reason, the story begins with the status of race and equal protection at the dawn of the decade that closed with *Carolene Products*.

The Court and Race in 1930

From today's perspective, the Court's race equality jurisprudence in 1930 can only be described as dismal. "Separate but equal," if not the constitutionally compelled law of the land, was regarded as unquestionably constitutional if a state wished to impose it. In 1883 the Court had upheld a law prohibiting interracial marriages;[66] thirteen years later it upheld the segregation of streetcars—and, with it, presumably all public accommodations—in *Plessy v. Ferguson*.[67] Twelve years after *Plessy* the Court declined to step in to protect the rights of students and teachers who *did* want to associate interracially, when it upheld a Kentucky law restricting integrated education in private schools.[68] The doctrine allowing separate but equal was so unambiguous that in 1927 the Court was able to remark casually that the matter was settled.[69]

As if to compound the insult, it sometimes seemed that the Court did not take seriously the "equal" part of its "separate-but-equal" formula. In 1899 the Court shrugged its shoulders and implicitly pleaded futility when it declined to stop a southern school district from closing its African American high school, even though that decision left African American students without even the facade of "equal" facilities.[70] Indeed, the Court came close to explicitly pleading futility when it found no way to grant relief to the plaintiff in *Giles v. Harris*,[71] even though it was clear Alabama had adopted the challenged state constitutional provisions for the express purpose of restricting African American voting rights, a clear violation of the Fifteenth Amendment. While the post-Reconstruction era witnessed a few victories for African American civil rights plaintiffs,[72] contemporary observers had to conclude that the Court was no friend to their cause.

Nor did the larger social and political picture in 1930 offer any great hope of a change in judicial attitudes. By then Reconstruction was a memory, with the last pockets of real African American enfranchisement and office-holding decades in the past. No realistic hope existed of resurrecting that progress at the national level—indeed, civil rights advocates could not even gain enactment of a federal antilynching bill. By contrast, the Ku Klux Klan was resurgent, with membership numbering in the millions. In 1925, some 40,000 Klansmen marched down Pennsylvania Avenue.

A New Deal for Blacks

By 1940 much—though certainly not all—had changed. The nation was all but committed to an ideologically grounded war against an expressly racist regime.[73] (Among other consequences, this commitment effectively shut down the eugenics movement that had previously thrived alongside forthrightly racist thinking.)[74] At home the Roosevelt administration, after a shaky start, had become committed to civil rights, even if it continued to act tentatively out of concern for disrupting both the impending war effort and the southern component of FDR's New Deal coalition.[75] Public opinion, while certainly not fully committed to racial equality, had progressed to the point where the African American boxer Joe Louis had become a national hero for defeating Max Schmelling in their 1938 rematch; white Americans had been decidedly mixed in their sympathies during their first bout two years earlier.[76]

Constitutional law had progressed as well. Most notably, in 1938 Justice Stone had suggested in a footnote to an otherwise obscure interstate commerce and due process opinion that discrimination against national and racial minorities might merit especially careful equal protection scrutiny.[77] Footnote 4 of his opinion in *United States v. Carolene Products*[78]—what Justice Lewis Powell called "the most celebrated footnote in constitutional law"[79]—became the theoretical foundation for much equal protection law over the course of the rest of the twentieth century. As such, it plays an exceedingly important role in understanding congressional power to enforce equal protection. For that reason, it becomes important to understand how the history just recounted—and indeed the history of equality before the Fourteenth Amendment, discussed earlier in this chapter—led the Court to the threshold of Footnote 4.

Footnote 4

Before telling that story, it may help to have a thumbnail understanding of Footnote 4, so the reader can appreciate the Court's moves in arriving there. *Carolene Products* was a case that considered a food manufacturer's challenge to a federal law prohibiting the interstate shipment of "filled milk"—that is, products that looked like milk (whether liquid or powdered) but contained nonmilk fats (i.e., "fillers"). The manufacturer alleged that the law both exceeded Congress's power to regulate interstate commerce and violated its Fifth Amendment due process right to engage in trade.

The Court had no difficulty holding that the law was a valid regulation of interstate commerce. It then considered the manufacturer's due process argument. The Court concluded that Congress had a rational basis for believing that prohibiting interstate shipment of filled milk furthered the public interest, given the possibility of consumer confusion and consumption of an inferior product that falsely appeared to provide the health benefits of milk. The Court cited evidence Congress had developed in which experts had warned of this health threat. Still, the Court assumed that if a party like the Carolene Products Company was denied the chance to contest that evidence in court, then it would be deprived of its liberty or property without due process. The only question was what showing the plaintiff would have to make.

That's where Footnote 4 came in. Footnote 4 was appended to the part of the opinion's text where the Court stated that it would presume that legislation impairing a due process right was based on facts supporting the legislature's judgment. Thus, the text was answering a question that had bedeviled judicial review since adoption of the Fourteenth Amendment: How much deference should a court accord a statute that appeared to threaten due process or equal protection rights?[80] The opinion's answer: a lot. The opinion put the burden not on the government to prove that its information was correct but on the challenger to prove that it was wrong.

But Footnote 4 provided a caveat to this deference. In three paragraphs, Justice Stone laid out three possible exceptions to the general presumption of constitutionality he had announced in the text. First, he said that that presumption might not apply when a statute appeared on its face to violate a provision of the Bill of Rights—provisions, he suggested, that were more specific than "due process" or "equal protection" and thus potentially more amenable to principled judicial policing.

Second, using language that can only be described as coy,[81] he suggested that legislation restricting participation in the political process might also be subject to more stringent review. Here, he cited then-recent Supreme Court cases dealing with restrictions on voting, the press, speech, and political association. He justified heightened scrutiny of such laws on the ground that they restricted "those political processes which can ordinarily be expected to bring about repeal of undesirable legislation." In other words, courts could not rely on the political process to remedy problems with such laws, since those laws aimed precisely at closing off that process.

Finally, and again coyly,[82] he suggested that a similar lack of deference was warranted for legislation discriminating against "religious, national or racial minorities," and stated that "prejudice against discrete and insular minorities may be a special condition, which tends seriously to curtail the operation of those political processes ordinarily to be relied upon to protect minorities, and which may call for a correspondingly more searching judicial inquiry." As one might guess, it was this final caveat to the text's statement of deference to legislatures that constituted the seed from which modern equal protection doctrine would flower.

At least with the benefit of hindsight, we can see Footnote 4 as a potentially rich source of justification for a new era of judicial concern for equality of the sort we recognize today—nondiscrimination on the basis of race, national origin, and, ultimately, other identity categories that can be analogized with more or less precision to race. The question is, how did the Court get to Footnote 4? The rest of this chapter addresses that question. It does not reveal Justice Stone's motivations, although it does note the very fragmentary evidence about his thinking in 1938. Instead, it sets forth the context in which the Court acted in 1938. It notes first the doctrinal context (the body of case law the Court had to work with) and, second, the social context (the world outside the Court's doors) and how they both might have influenced the Court.

Jim Crow Justice and the Court in the 1930s

Despite the gloomy picture confronting advocates of racial equality in 1930, the Court soon began to take tentative steps that ultimately reconstituted American equal protection law. Over the course of the early and mid-1930s it decided four cases considering criminal procedure issues that ultimately put it on a course where it could reconsider the equal protection status of racial minorities. Three of these cases grew out of Alabama's handling of the young African American males who became known as the Scottsboro Boys.

The Scottsboro cases arose from allegations of what Jim Crow society likely considered the most heinous crime imaginable: the gang rape of a white woman by a group of young African American men. The case involved nine black teenage males who, while riding a freight train, encountered and fought with a group of white male teens. When the white teens reported the fight and police searched the train, officers found two white women who reported being raped by the blacks. After exceptionally fast trials, eight of the nine were convicted and sentenced to death.[83] As the cases reached the Supreme Court, they involved various legal claims, but infusing the Court's opinions in all those cases is a sense of the pervasive inequality of southern states' justice systems at the time.[84]

The first case in the series, *Powell v. Alabama*,[85] dealt with a claim that the defendants were denied the due process right to be represented by counsel, in light of the trial judge's seemingly pro forma appointment of defense counsel. Writing for a seven-justice majority that vindicated that claim, Justice Sutherland made special note of the cases' racial context. He referred to the races of the defendants, the victims, and the young white men with whom the defendants had fought shortly before the alleged rape occurred. He also noted the atmosphere "of great hostility" toward the defendants; the "atmosphere of tense, hostile and excited public sentiment"; and the youth, ignorance, and illiteracy of the defendants. Even more tellingly, he noted that they were charged "with an atrocious crime *regarded with especial horror in the community where they were to be tried*." Again focusing explicitly on the factual context, he concluded that the "defendants were not accorded the right to counsel in any substantial sense," continuing in the next sentence, "To decide otherwise, would simply be to ignore actualities."[86]

The second case, *Norris v. Alabama*,[87] dealt with the equal protection claim of one of the Scottsboro defendants that African Americans were excluded from the juries that tried their cases. *Norris* reveals a Court determined to cut through the fiction of the state's claims that race did not enter into jury selection decisions. First, the Court noted that the facial equality of a statute—here, the race-neutral quality of Alabama's jury selection process—did not end the constitutional inquiry.[88] Second, and even more aggressively,[89] the Court insisted that this inquiry into whether equal protection was denied "in substance and effect"[90] required the Court to make an independent and searching review of the trial record. Indeed, that review included the high drama of the Court's physical examination of the actual jury roll.[91]

The third case, *Patterson v. Alabama*,[92] the companion case to *Norris*, reflected similar aggressiveness by the Court. In *Patterson* the Court brushed aside procedural hurdles to its consideration of a discrimination claim identical to the one made in *Norris*. In an analysis brimming with concerns about fundamental fairness—in particular, the troubling prospect that a procedural default might lead to Haywood Patterson being executed even though Clarence Norris, who made the exact same claim and offer of proof,[93] had won a new trial—the Court insisted that the Alabama Supreme Court reexamine the state law procedural requirement it had relied on to deny Patterson relief.

These three cases rest on a potpourri of legal theories: respectively, due process, equal protection, and the interplay of state procedural law and federal constitutional rights. But, as scholars have observed,[94] they all reflect an underlying awareness of the racial inequality pervading southern justice systems during the Jim Crow era. Justice Sutherland's opinion in *Powell* turned heavily on the facts of the case. While sometimes oblique, his references to the races of the defendants, the victim, and the witnesses suggest its racially charged nature. Even more so, his recognition that the nature of the crime was viewed "with especial horror in the community where they were to be tried" makes clear that the racial identities of the major actors influenced the likely fairness of any trial, and thus the particular importance of counsel.

To an even greater degree than in *Powell*, the features of *Norris* and *Patterson*—respectively, the Court's insistence on reexamining the facts and willingness to disregard state law procedural hurdles—suggest the Court's underlying unease with the state's conduct. In a manner that calls to mind the Warren Court's careful review of state judicial proceedings in the service of racial equality,[95] *Norris* and *Patterson* pierced the veils of formal equality and respect for state court fact-finding and procedural rules in racially charged cases. The fact that the Court breached such ostensibly neutral barriers suggests an underlying discomfort with the conduct of the state in these cases. In light of the other race-inflected cases the Court decided during this period, it is not much of a stretch to suggest that *Patterson* adds to the list of cases that, while ostensibly grounded on other issues, are fundamentally about race.

For its part, *Norris*'s aggressive stance on both the Court's fact-finding role and the doctrinal question whether formal equality satisfies the Fourteenth Amendment reveals a growing awareness of the systemic inequality maintained by southern governments. The Court's growing discomfort with that systemic inequality—in particular with regard to participation in governance, such as juries—provides yet another backdrop for the Court's doctrinal shift in *Carolene Products* toward concern for both the political process and minorities' systemic political underrepresentation.

In the final of these four cases, *Brown v. Mississippi*,[96] the Court confronted Jim Crow's ultimate weapon: physical torture. In *Brown*, sheriffs investigating a murder took custody of an African American they suspected, took him to the crime scene, and proceeded to hang him (nonfatally) and whip him, demanding that he confess and promising to continue the torture until he did. Two other suspects were subjected to severe whipping with a leather strap and also forced to confess. The technical legal issue in *Brown* was whether the coerced confessions violated the defendants' rights under the Due Process Clause. Chief Justice Hughes, writing for a unanimous Court, did not hesitate to condemn the sheriff's conduct, and the state's reliance on the confessions he thereby obtained.

In doing so, Hughes relied not on a particular Bill of Rights provision (indeed, Mississippi correctly noted that at the time the Fifth Amendment's guarantee against self-incrimination had not been incorporated) but rather on the general protections the Due Process Clause provided for fundamental fairness. As venerable as that idea was by 1936, its deployment to prohibit the use of torture surely had new resonance by the mid-1930s, in light of the rise of violently totalitarian regimes abroad.[97] In the key part of his opinion, Hughes stated a set of propositions about what a fair trial demanded—requirements that prohibited the deprivation of counsel and the use of knowingly perjured testimony, mob violence, and, of course, torture. As obvious as these conditions might sound to our ears, and as well supported in case law as they were by 1936, this catalog likely had special resonance to readers who were just starting to hear about the Moscow Show Trials.

But Hughes was not content to stop with sterile, though fundamental, legal conclusions about criminal procedure. Instead, he took up half of his opinion with an extensive quotation of the facts from the opinion of the state supreme court justices who had dissented from the judgment affirming the convictions. In addition to describing in horrific detail the physical torture the sheriff inflicted, that quotation referred extensively to race—indeed, the first sentence of the quotation referred to the defendants as "ignorant negroes," and the second sentence observed that "a number of white men" had gathered at the location where the sheriff inflicted the torture.[98]

Hughes's use of this quotation raises fascinating questions and possibilities. First, in quoting from Mississippi Supreme Court justices, it is quite possible that he was attempting to defuse any criticism of "outsider" judges imposing alien rules on the South.[99] Southern reaction to the Scottsboro cases had been mixed—educated southern opinion was by no means comfortable with the obviously railroaded nature of the Scottsboro trials—but public opinion across the country and around the world had nevertheless latched onto those cases as evidence of the South's incorrigible racism. Perhaps by disclosing the facts of the *Brown* defendants' torture through a quotation from a southern jurist, Hughes may have hoped to mitigate a defensive reaction and ensure the implementation of the Court's insistence on basic procedural fairness. Regardless of the reason, Hughes's quotation from the state court dissent effectively acknowledged the racial nature of the case.

Despite this evidence of the Court's concern about race in all of these cases, it bears noting that the import of these cases for current purposes lies not simply, or even primarily, in the Court's doctrinal analysis. Indeed, Footnote 4 did not cite these cases as examples of racial discrimination. Rather, as with many of the cases Justice Stone *did* cite in Footnote 4, their larger significance lies in the evidence they provided the Court that systematic use of state power against a reviled group constituted a major problem in the United States—a problem that the political process seemed unable to remedy. It is clear that the nation—and indeed, the world—did not understand these cases to concern mainly the racially neutral procedural inadequacies of Alabama's and Mississippi's judicial processes. Rather, those cases were understood to be about race. The Court itself, through its words and the unusual nature of some of its actions, seems to have agreed. By *Carolene Products* in 1938, the example of racial intolerance around the world would prompt Justice Stone to begin expressing that concern explicitly.

Rereading Precedent

But what of the cases that Footnote 4 *did* cite for the proposition that race discrimination merited particular judicial concern? Justice Stone cited two sets of cases for that idea. One set consisted of two cases where Texas attempted to disenfranchise African American voters from voting in the Democratic Party primary—the only election that mattered at the time in Texas. These were relatively straightforward cases of patent racial discrimination, although in the second of the cases the Court split on the question whether the discrimination was attributable to the state or merely to the party itself.

The second set consisted of several cases from the 1920s that dealt with parents' attempts to direct their children's education against state attempts to restrict certain types of instruction. In the most famous of these cases, *Meyer v. Nebraska*,[100] the Court struck down a Nebraska law preventing instruction in German, a vestige of World War I era xenophobia. Other cases of this sort, cited in Footnote 4, dealt with restrictions on ethnic-based private school instruction and military and religious education.

The Court decided these cases not on an equality theory, even though those laws' ethnic, national, or religious bias was obvious. Instead, it decided them on the basis of parents' due process liberty to raise their children as they wish. Given that reasoning, scholars have criticized Stone's citation of those cases in Footnote 4, accusing him of misusing precedent.[101] But this criticism seems a bit unfair. Stone speaks carefully in the footnote. He cites these cases as reflecting examples of *statutes* that discriminate—he says nothing about, and does not rely on, the reasoning of the opinions striking those statutes down.[102] Just like the criminal procedure cases discussed earlier, even though the theories of the opinions may not have sounded in equality, the factual context of the cases reflected inequalities that prompted Stone to cite them as examples of phenomena courts should rightfully worry about.[103]

Internal and External Triggers

Thus, by 1938 Justice Stone had in place a store of precedent he could cite as illustrating the problem of racial and national group oppression. But just as important was the confluence of other factors, both internal to the Court and outside its doors, which allowed Justice Stone to use that precedent to suggest the Court's new concern with race. First, with the Court's retreat from its *Lochner*-era protection of liberty of contract, the way was open for Justice Stone to begin tentatively to seek a new role for the Court, one focused on noneconomic liberties such as fair criminal procedure, freedom of speech and religion, and opposition to racism. Second, the abandonment of the police power approach to constitutional law, in favor of the rights-as-trumps understanding, opened up the possibility of the Court singling out these types of rights for special protection—exactly the type of heightened scrutiny the Court suggested in Footnote 4. Put simply, the embrace of the rights-as-trumps idea opened the door for the Court to exalt certain rights—most notably, rights to racial equality—as trump cards of particularly high value.

As noted earlier, some scholars suggest that this doctrinal change was encouraged by external events.[104] On this theory, the rise of fascism and totalitarianism led the justices to embrace stronger protection for individual rights than would be logically feasible as part of a police power approach.[105] Scholars also note that President Roosevelt's Court-packing plan from the previous year also caused concern about judicial independence in the protection of civil liberties, and hence increased the attractiveness of a model that called for stringent judicial protection of rights.[106]

At the same time, developments in public opinion made a focus on racial equality much more palatable to the American people. As the 1930s progressed, American public opinion grew less tolerant of blatant discrimination. As a general matter, heightened awareness of the struggles of poor and marginalized people triggered by the Great Depression likely increased sympathy and empathy for the black underclass. More particularly, the Scottsboro cases drew national and worldwide attention to racial injustice in the American South. Finally, it is surely the case that the rise of Nazi Germany as an explicitly racist regime led many previously indifferent Americans to embrace at least the idea, if not the practice, of racial equality as a means of differentiating American society from Nazism. Historians have noted that the 1930s witnessed massive changes in American attitudes about race.[107] Those changes surely made it easier for Justice Stone to suggest that racial equality—however it was defined and however it was implemented—had become a central constitutional concern.

This evolution still left major issues unresolved as of 1938. Another sixteen years were needed for the Court to strike down public school segregation, and several more years—over a decade, if one counts antimiscegenation laws—before it dispensed with segregation across the entire range of government action.[108] Indeed, the question of systemic racism and its relationship to equal protection has never been satisfactorily resolved.[109] On this last point, recall that Footnote 4 did *not* cite the Scottsboro cases, just as the landmark criminal procedure cases of the 1960s, which had race lurking just beneath them, were never officially acknowledged as being about race.

Still, by 1938 the Court had staked new ground for its prestige and its role in ensuring the fundamental equality promised by the Equal Protection Clause. This new ground was not based in protecting the existing economic order or even in policing against an amorphous concern with "class legislation." Rather, it was one based in concern about race discrimination. As noted earlier, this concern took decades after 1938 to reach its full implementation—or at least the limits of the Court's willingness to enforce it. But, as noted in the next chapter, by the middle of the century the Court was actively considering the scope of the racial equality requirement. Later, in the final third of the twentieth century, the Court began to experiment with Footnote 4's implications beyond race. The story of that experimentation, and its fate, is central to our story of the enforcement power.

That story is told in the next chapter. But before leaving this early period it is important to note its lasting influence. Even if the police power approach to rights faded out, the era's concern with laws that did not further a legitimate public good remained. So too did the idea that, as a general matter, legislatures enjoyed a great deal of discretion in what the modern Court has described as "adjusting the burdens and benefits of economic life."[110] Today, these insights find expression in the requirement that legislation not be utterly arbitrary, and that it not single out a group simply because the majority dislikes them. These long-standing prohibitions on irrational legislation and legislation based on animus remain today as core requirements imposed by the Constitution, and the Equal Protection Clause in particular.

2

The Rise and Fall of *Carolene Products*

This book's brief tour of equal protection doctrine ends by discussing the impact of *Carolene Products* on constitutional law—in particular, equal protection law—since 1938. That impact cannot be understated, although it is sometimes misunderstood. This chapter begins by tracing the Court's early use of Footnote 4 and its underlying theory, before discussing its relevance for modern equal protection and, hence, for congressional power to enforce the equality guarantee.

The Early Uses of Footnote 4

Footnote 4 provided a potentially broad foundation for judicial scrutiny of legislative actions. Recall from chapter 1 that the footnote cautioned that the Court's presumptive deference to a legislature's decisions might not apply in three distinct situations: when a law seems to violate the textually explicit provisions of the Bill of Rights, when it appears to restrict the open operation of the political process, and, finally, when the law appears to reflect "prejudice against discrete and insular minorities." As mere suggestions that did not apply to the particular facts of the *Carolene Products* case, these vague caveats to the Court's newly announced rule of deference to legislatures opened up expansive possibilities for judicial experimentation.[1] Indeed, the Court's early uses of Footnote 4 were notable for their fluid deployment of the footnote's different paragraphs.

This flexibility is evident in the 1940 case *Gobitis v. Minersville School District*.[2] *Gobitis* was not the only case during the first decade after *Carolene Products* where the Court deployed Footnote 4's insights. But it is illustrative. *Gobitis* considered a claim that a Pennsylvania school board violated the free religious exercise rights of Jehovah's Witnesses schoolchildren by requiring them to salute the American flag and recite the Pledge of Allegiance. The case posed a quandary for the Court, which by 1940 was dominated by Roosevelt appointees who had pledged to avoid second-guessing legislative judgments—here, a school board's judgment that compelled salute of the flag inculcated patriotism and national solidarity. Pulling against such judicial deference was the Court's increasing focus on civil rights and, in particular, the First Amendment rights of speech and religion.

In *Gobitis* the tendency to defer won out, with Justice Felix Frankfurter, the most zealous proponent of such deference, writing an opinion for eight justices upholding the flag salute requirement. For our purposes, the interesting feature of his opinion, and of Justice Stone's solitary dissent, turned on the justices' use of Footnote 4. As expressed in the two opinions, the flag salute controversy implicated all three components of Footnote 4—and, indeed, the principle of judicial deference to legislative judgments to which the footnote expressed possible caveats. First, the right to free religious exercise was explicitly provided in the First Amendment (the religious freedom component of which had been incorporated to apply against the state the same term as *Gobitis*).[3] Second, Justice Frankfurter's majority opinion implied that "all the effective means of inducing political changes" remained open in this situation—that is, the Witnesses and their allies remained able to vote and lobby for a repeal of the law, or at least for an exemption for religious objectors such as the Witnesses.[4] Third, Justice Stone described the Jehovah's Witnesses sect as a small, politically powerless minority, who for that reason should not be left to the vicissitudes of the political process.[5]

For Justice Frankfurter, the presumed openness of the political process (the factor addressed by paragraph two of the *Carolene Products* footnote) justified judicial deference to the balance struck by the state between the religious rights of its citizens and the need to foster national unity—the latter being not a small consideration in the spring of 1940, when *Gobitis* was decided. (Indeed, Court personnel referred to *Gobitis* as "Felix's Fall-of-France opinion.")[6] By contrast, for Justice Stone the specificity of the free exercise right (the factor addressed by paragraph one of the footnote) required "some accommodation" of the powers normally accorded government with the asserted right—in other words, some level of heightened scrutiny. As he suggested later on that same page of his opinion, the stature of the right at issue required what we might call today a "least restrictive means" analysis, an approach he applied when he noted the state's ability to use means other than a compulsory flag salute to inculcate patriotic feelings. As he further suggested, again echoing paragraph one of the *Carolene Products* footnote, the specificity of the Bill of Rights precludes a court from conclusively relying on the state's determination that the action infringing on the right—here, the compulsion of the salute—was more important than the right itself.[7]

Taken together, Stone was suggesting an embryonic form of what we later came to know as strict scrutiny—an examination of the importance of the government interest with a requirement that that interest be pursued in the way that minimized the impact on the right. His heightened scrutiny derived, at least in significant part, from the specificity of the First Amendment rights at issue—a specificity that rendered those rights, in his view, "preferred."[8]

Justice Stone also focused on the discrimination the flag salute requirement visited on the Witnesses (the factor addressed in paragraph three of the footnote). In particular, he took issue with Justice Frankfurter's argument that the existence of political channels for challenging the school board's judgment adequately protected the liberties at issue. Noting that minority groups such as the Witnesses would likely not enjoy "toleration or respect" for their idiosyncratic beliefs, he concluded, citing Footnote 4, that the official compulsion of views conflicting with such beliefs should receive heightened judicial scrutiny. In essence, then, Justice Stone saw Footnote 4's three caveats to judicial deference as independently significant, each one potentially justifying careful scrutiny of a legislature's judgment—and especially so when, as in *Gobitis*, more than one was present.[9]

Gobitis illustrated Footnote 4's potential for explaining and justifying careful judicial scrutiny of legislative decisions. Ultimately, all three paragraphs of Footnote 4 found expression in the Court's constitutional law jurisprudence. Consider the first paragraph. While explicit references to the "preferred position" of either all Bill of Rights provisions or the First Amendment in particular eventually died out,[10] the growth of Bill of Rights jurisprudence, aided by the incorporation of most such rights to apply against the states, ensured that those provisions would continue to attract intense judicial interest. Indeed, vestiges of the First Amendment's particular preferred position remain visible in the Court's insistence on strict, almost absolutist, protection for certain types of speech, even if the analogous protections for free religious exercise and the press have become far more equivocal.

As for paragraph two, protections for speech, expressive associations, and the press found a doctrinal home in the Court's burgeoning First Amendment jurisprudence. The right to vote—a right quite possibly not intended to be covered in the Fourteenth Amendment, and protected in the Fifteenth only from racial discrimination—eventually found a home in the so-called fundamental rights strand of the Equal Protection Clause.[11] And, of course, paragraph three's concern for "prejudice against discrete and insular minorities" became the foundation for much—though, surprisingly, not all—of the Court's antidiscrimination jurisprudence.[12]

Carolene Products and Race Up to the 1960s

While Justice Stone's concern with discrimination against the Witnesses in *Gobitis* found expression in Footnote 4's suggestion of heightened judicial review in cases of "prejudice against discrete and insular minorities," that idea's most obvious application—to cases of racial discrimination—took a surprisingly long time to evolve. Of course, the most (in)famous race case in the fifteen years after *Carolene Products*—the Japanese wartime internment case *Korematsu v. United States*—did famously state that "all legal restrictions which curtail the civil rights of a single racial group are immediately suspect."[13] But just as (in)famously, the *Korematsu* Court did not actually apply heightened scrutiny; instead, it deferred to the judgment of the military even in the face of the dissent's convincing argument that the military itself did not consider the security threat so pressing as to leave no time for individualized loyalty hearings.

Other issues and statements in the opinion also cast doubt on the characterization of *Korematsu* as the first case to apply strict scrutiny to racial classifications as a matter of equal protection law. First, there is the doctrinal problem that the Fourteenth Amendment's Equal Protection Clause—the only such clause in the Constitution—does not apply to federal government action, such as the military's forced relocation of Japanese Americans. Ten years after *Korematsu* the Court "solved" this problem. In *Bolling v. Sharpe*,[14] the District of Columbia schools companion case to *Brown v. Board of Education*,[15] the Court read the Fifth Amendment's Due Process Clause (which *does* apply to the federal government) as containing an equal protection component that eventually became understood as coextensive with the explicit Equal Protection Clause in the Fourteenth Amendment. But in 1944 the Court was not ready to take this step.

Second, and relatedly, note *Korematsu*'s language quoted two paragraphs earlier. It speaks of restrictions on "the civil rights" of a racial group—not burdens on racial groups generally. As fine as that distinction may sound, Professor Michael Klarman persuasively argues that throughout the 1940s the Court continued to operate as if the Equal Protection Clause and the equal protection component of the Fifth Amendment's Due Process Clause both insisted on racial equality only with regard to a certain set of important rights.[16] The Court's focus was faithful to history: as chapter 1 noted, the Civil Rights Act of 1866, whose placement on a solid constitutional footing all agree was a major impetus for the Fourteenth Amendment,[17] bestowed upon all Americans racial equality only with regard to a set of rights the Reconstruction Congress thought important for equal legal status. Given the embryonic nature of Footnote 4's insight into the political process justification for heightened scrutiny of all racial classifications, it is perhaps not surprising that the Court in *Korematsu* and the other race cases of that era continued to focus on the unequal deprivation of particular rights, rather than an across-the-board focus on racial classifications. The Court simply may not have been ready to apply Footnote 4 so aggressively and comprehensively, because the intellectual ground had not been adequately laid and/or because, as explained later, such a move would have been politically risky.

Instead, the Court continued its rights-based approach to equal protection throughout the 1940s, up to and including *Brown* itself in 1954. First-time readers of *Brown* are often surprised by its lack of sweeping language condemning all racial segregation as violating equal protection. Instead, Chief Justice Earl Warren focused on the importance of education to civic equality. This was not necessarily an easy path for the Court. Indeed, Warren had to go out of his way to explain that the increased importance of education to full civic equality in twentieth-century America justified departing from earlier understandings of the constitutionality of segregated education. He had no real choice but to provide that explanation: once he decided to rely on the importance of education, he had to blunt the argument that the drafters of the Fourteenth Amendment could not have intended to require nonsegregated schools, since they themselves established segregated schooling in the District of Columbia.[18] The existence of that hurdle only makes his decision to take that path all the more remarkable.

So why did he do it? The answer is difficult to pin down. But it is surely the case that at least part of the reason had to do with the political ramifications of a broader rule against racial segregation.[19] Most notably, the Court was clearly nervous about such a rule putting the Court on a collision course with the antimiscegenation laws that were still common in the nation—and particularly the South—in 1954. On this view, it might be one thing for the Court to strike down segregation in education but another thing for the Court, in one fell swoop, to invalidate antimiscegenation laws and, indeed, every other aspect of official Jim Crow. In fact, one year after *Brown* the Court used questionable reasoning to dodge the miscegenation issue.[20] In the course of doing so the Court allowed the Virginia Supreme Court to all but defy it, earning it the disapproval of scholars ever since.[21]

Notwithstanding its avoidance of the miscegenation question, after *Brown* the Court very quickly took up the cause of dismantling Jim Crow's other manifestations. In a series of exceptionally short decisions starting the year after *Brown* (known as "the per curiams" because they were all written "by the Court" as a whole rather by than an individual justice), the Court struck down several Jim Crow provisions in public accommodations, ranging from city buses to beaches and municipal golf courses. These opinions are striking because they contain no legal analysis: the first of them merely cited *Brown* without any explanation; the later ones cited *Brown* and the per curiams that came before, again without supporting analysis. As one might expect, scholars have sharply criticized these opinions for relying on *Brown*. After all, *Brown* did not announce a general rule against race classification; instead, it relied on the importance of education and the inherent inequality of segregated public school education, given school segregation's asserted effects on black schoolchildren's self-esteem.

Regardless, the per curiams did their job: by the early 1960s the Court was able to cite them as support for its triumphant conclusion that any type of official race classification is presumptively unconstitutional.[22] (Remarkably, antimiscegenation laws lingered on until 1967.) Strikingly, though, it reached that point not through an explicit application of Footnote 4's political process analysis but through what can only be described as the judicial fiat reflected in the per curiams. This result is doubly ironic. First, it is generally thought that Justice Stone had race, and African Americans in particular, in mind when he wrote the footnote's language about prejudice against discrete and insular minorities.[23] Second, as it turned out, the Court's only real discussion of political process theory in the race context was to come years later, in its consideration of race-based affirmative action policies that were adopted to undo the damage Jim Crow had caused.

Branching Out: Other Applications of Political Process Reasoning

The first real attempts to apply *Carolene Products*' speculation about discrete and insular minorities occurred in contexts other than race discrimination—in particular, discrimination based on sex, legitimacy, and alienage. This is not to say that the Court was insensitive to the precarious political position racial minorities faced in mid-twentieth-century America. Most obviously, *Brown* and the per curiams reflected a concern with the legal status of African Americans, even if that concern was never explicitly expressed in terms of their political power. Moreover, as noted earlier, Warren Court opinions on issues from criminal procedure to the First Amendment reflected underlying concerns with race. Nevertheless, the role of race, let alone any political process–based justification for concern about race discrimination, remained only implicit in these latter areas.

A more explicit focus on Footnote 4's political process rationale arose only in nonracial contexts, and only in the 1970s. At least with the benefit of hindsight, this chronology is not surprising. The Warren Court's primary concern was with race, both expressly and (as noted earlier) implicitly, as well as with speech and political rights and the government's treatment of the poor.[24] This agenda was quite ambitious; thus, looking back, we should not be surprised that it refrained from embarking on expanding equal protection's scope until some of these projects had resolved, one way or another. For this same reason it makes sense, again in retrospect, that when that Court did suggest such an expansion it failed to provide immediately a full-blown theory justifying it.[25]

In particular, any judicial concern with sex equality would surely have seemed quixotic before the advent of the women's rights movement in the mid-1960s. Indeed, in 1961 the Court—by then not shy about moving the law in new directions—had no difficulty upholding a Florida law allowing women to excuse themselves from jury duty. Writing for a unanimous Court, Justice Harlan could not conclude that the exemption was unreasonable, given the presumed reality that "woman is still regarded as the center of home and family life."[26]

By the 1970s, however, things were changing. The women's rights movement was in full swing, and a new Court, which between 1969 and 1972 had seen the replacement of four incumbent justices with Nixon appointees, had turned away from several of the Warren Court's projects.[27] At the same time women, then later other groups, began raising equality claims with increased intensity. These claims presented the Court with a puzzle. By this time questions of sex equality were moving front and center in American society. But, unlike the race equality claims that had dominated the national conversation about equality for decades, women's equality claims could not be understood as clearly justified by the text or the ratifying background of the Fourteenth Amendment, except at the highest level of generality.[28]

Thus, and again with the benefit of hindsight, it makes perfect sense that the Court would turn to *Carolene Products*' political process analysis as a tool explaining why women's (and others')[29] equality claims merited serious judicial consideration. To be sure, the Court's first serious consideration of sex equality did not employ political process reasoning. In the 1971 case *Reed v. Reed*,[30] the Court struck down an Idaho law that favored men over women as administrators of deceased persons' estates. But that case simply purported to apply traditional deferential rational basis scrutiny in finding no justification for the Idaho law.

Two years later, however, in *Frontiero v. Richardson*,[31] the Court confronted head-on the question of whether sex discrimination merited heightened scrutiny. *Frontiero* considered the constitutionality of a military policy that, for purposes of allocating military family benefits, conclusively presumed that male soldiers were their families' primary breadwinners but required female soldiers to prove that status. While it might have been easy (if not completely honest) for the *Reed* Court to find Idaho irrational in concluding in 1971 that men were generally more acquainted than women with business affairs and thus better suited to administer estates, *Frontiero* posed a harder question, given the high likelihood that men in fact were more likely than women to be their families' primary sources of income.[32] Thus, *Frontiero* sharply posed the question whether discrimination against women required more than just a rational basis.

In concluding that such discrimination did require a stronger government justification, Justice Brennan, writing for a plurality of four justices, analogized women to African Americans, essentially the only group to have received heightened judicial protection at that time.[33] Sketching out what eventually became the standard formula for determining a group's suspect class status, Justice Brennan began his analysis by noting the history of discrimination women had suffered and explicitly concluding that the status into which that discrimination placed them was "comparable to that of blacks under the pre–Civil War slave codes."[34] Again analogizing the social and legal position of those two groups, he then observed that both had gained a constitutional right to vote relatively late in our history—indeed, he observed, women did not gain that right nationally until the ratification of the Nineteenth Amendment, a full half century after blacks had gained it in the Fifteenth Amendment. He also noted how such past discrimination contributed to women's continued lack of political power.[35] Eventually, a group's history of discrimination and current political powerlessness became, respectively, the first and third factors of a three-factor test for determining a group's suspect class status.

But more was needed. As criteria for suspect class status, past and current oppression might well identify many groups we intuitively think merit heightened judicial protection, but those criteria are also vastly overinclusive. Rapists, for example, have historically been subject to serious discrimination. As for their lack of political power, one need not stop with felon disenfranchisement laws to reach that conclusion—one can simply point to the lack of any serious organized lobbying on behalf of their interests. Yet few would say that rapists as a class merit heightened judicial protection when legislation adversely affects them.[36]

Justice Brennan's solution became the core of the second suspect class factor: immutability. Again analogizing sex to race, he explained that the fact that the sex characteristic was an "accident of birth" suggested that imposing burdens based on that characteristic "would seem to violate the basic concept of our system that legal burdens should bear some relationship to individual responsibility."[37]

As a legal test, immutability has not fared well. Scholars have criticized it as a practical matter, on the ground that most traits, or at least their outward manifestations, such as skin color and gender traits, can be altered, even if at great physical and emotional cost. But they have also gone further and dismissed the entire idea of immutable traits as hopelessly essentialist, on the theory that concepts such as race and sexual orientation and even sex are largely socially constructed rather than simply existing as an objective fact. If such concepts do not objectively exist, one might ask, how can they be immutable?

But leave these objections aside for the moment. Certainly, Justice Brennan strikes a chord when he expresses concern about discrimination based on characteristics that one can either not change or can change only with great difficulty, and which constitute key components of one's identity. As attractive as this idea might seem, at first blush it seems unrelated to Footnote 4's political process concern. But on reflection a connection appears. Burdening people based on their (immutable) status rather than their conduct—for who there are, rather than what they do—may well suggest a form of "prejudice," as Justice Stone used that term. At least as compared with conduct, basing a punishment or burden on one's (immutable) status inherently seems to reflect a more visceral, elemental dislike.

John Hart Ely attempted to go beyond this intuitive but inchoate idea to explain how immutability might be tied to political process breakdown. He argued that the problem with status-based discrimination was that it was imposed by legislators who, by hypothesis, could never empathize with the burdened group. According to Ely, the legislator's inability to empathize—to put himself in the shoes of the other group—renders him fundamentally unable to be responsive to that group's needs. Such responsiveness need not take the form of legislative victories. But, he concludes, it does entail a willingness to listen and try to understand. Distributing a burden based on a trait that the legislator literally cannot imagine himself sharing makes such openness, if not impossible, then at least systematically less likely.[38]

Thus, it is possible—if one reads between the lines and does so generously—to find a connection between the second suspect class element and Justice Stone's formulation, thus tying all three of *Frontiero*'s criteria to *Carolene Products*' political process rationale. But as the Court soon discovered—indeed, as Justice Brennan discovered immediately upon announcing those criteria in *Frontiero*—application of these criteria raised problems and contradictions that the Court was never fully able to work through.

Leave aside for the moment the first factor, and continue focusing on immutability. As intuitively attractive as one might find the idea that laws should not burden people based on immutable status characteristics, and as possible as it might be to construct a theory tying immutability to political process breakdown, the inevitable fact remains that such characteristics *are* indisputably relevant, at least sometimes. To take an obvious case, a person born blind may not be responsible for his status, but surely government is within its rights to insist that blind persons not be allowed to be pilots. Scholars immediately recognized this problem. So did Justice Brennan, in *Frontiero* itself. Immediately following the passage explaining the justification for disfavoring such status-based classifications, he added the following key language: "And what differentiates sex from such nonsuspect statutes [*sic*] as intelligence or physical disability, and aligns it with the recognized suspect criteria [i.e., race] is that the sex characteristic frequently bears no relation to ability to perform or contribute to society."[39]

Thus, immutability is not enough. Instead, Justice Brennan caveated the immutability criterion by observing that discrimination based on immutable *and irrelevant* characteristics should render the classification suspect. This move gave away a good part of the game, if the ultimate goal was a formula for judicial review that seeks only to correct for political process failures.[40] Now, a characteristic will become suspect, and thus subject to more careful judicial review, *if a court thinks that that characteristic is irrelevant to the government goal at issue*. One can immediately hear the objection: but the existence of a government decision classifying on that ground presumably reflects a legislative conclusion that the defining characteristic *is* relevant.

Thus, rather than remaining substantively neutral and purely process-based, suspect class analysis mutated into an inquiry that turns in part on a court's own substantive conclusion whether the legislature was correct in deeming that characteristic relevant. Consider an example. One of the most prominent and careful appellate opinions of the modern era attempting to apply the Supreme Court's suspect class formula characterized the second factor of that formula in terms that, for all its care, can only be described as vague, arguably circular, and unquestionably value-based (as opposed to process-based). According to that court, the second factor is "difficult to capsulize and may in fact represent a cluster of factors grouped around a central idea—whether the discrimination embodies a gross unfairness that is sufficiently inconsistent with the ideals of equal protection to term it invidious."[41] Reviewing Supreme Court precedent, the appellate court ultimately concluded that this factor required consideration of three subsidiary questions: "(1) whether the disadvantaged class is defined by a trait that frequently bears no relation to ability to perform or contribute to society; (2) whether the class has been saddled with unique disabilities because of prejudice or inaccurate stereotypes; and (3) whether the trait defining the class is immutable."[42] This enumeration is striking: the final question simply repeats the original immutability idea, the first one requires an inquiry into relevance that is explicitly substantive rather than process-based, while the second one similarly requires the court to judge the existence of "prejudice" and "inaccurate stereotypes." So much for process.

But, one might argue, surely the first and third factors of the suspect class formula—a history of discrimination and current political powerlessness—rest solidly on *Carolene Products*' political process theory. But problems arise here, too. The problem with the first factor is an intensely practical—and, in some ways, a deeply American—one. Our history is full of discrimination. African Americans, Native Americans, Irish, Jews, Italians, Latinos, women, gays, the disabled—the list goes on of groups who can make a plausible claim to have suffered a history of discrimination. Of course, our history is also one of overcoming discrimination—not all of it, and not completely. But the arc of American history bends toward justice, even if slowly.

This combination of insights—that many groups have suffered discrimination, but that many have succeeded in reducing or eliminating it—renders the history of discrimination element a far less useful tool than perhaps one might have thought at first blush. It may potentially serve as gatekeeper for some groups claiming suspect class status, but it is hard to envision it playing a decisive role preventing a group from gaining suspect class status when the other criteria would have allowed it.

But maybe it is the third factor that saves the analysis. After all, what could be more probative of a process-based status as a suspect class than the lack of current political power? Unfortunately, this element suffers from both a practical objection and an objection that is grounded in a deeper flaw with process-based analysis. First, as a practical matter, how can one measure political power? Different panels of the Ninth Circuit Court of Appeals debated this issue in the late 1980s when considering the suspect classification status of sexual orientation. One panel—the one that elaborated on the immutability requirement as noted earlier—engaged in a careful investigation of the political status of gays and lesbians in the United States as of the late 1980s. It noted the phenomenon of the closet, which, by allowing the possibility for gays to "pass," hindered their incentive and thus their ability to organize politically. It also noted the government's own argument in that case, dealing with the discharge of an openly gay solider, which defended its discrimination on the ground that the public would hold the military in disrepute if an openly gay person was serving. The court concluded (not unreasonably) that this argument itself demonstrated the political disabilities under which gays labored.[43]

By contrast, a different panel of that court, in a case decided just one year later, took a much different approach. In response to the argument that gays lacked political power, the court simply noted the success gays had recently enjoyed in enacting state and local antidiscrimination laws. The court concluded that this success belied any claim that they suffered from a lack of political power.[44]

The disagreement between these two opinions reflects a broader disagreement courts have had when applying the political powerlessness factor of the suspect class formula. "Political powerlessness" is hardly a self-defining concept. At a practical level, this fact means that courts will find it an unsteady guide to suspect class decisions, as the two appellate panels found when they analyzed the issue so differently and came to opposite conclusions within one year of each other.[45]

But the difficulty with political powerlessness goes deeper. First, in a system where rights are enforced by both legislatures and courts, the political powerlessness factor creates difficulties when a group begins to succeed in making its equality claims heard in legislative halls. To illustrate, consider again Justice Brennan's analysis of sex discrimination in *Frontiero*. When he wrote that opinion in 1973, Congress had already begun to address the problem of sex discrimination. Among other actions, it had included sex in the employment discrimination provisions of the Civil Rights Act of 1964 and approved and sent to the states for ratification the Equal Rights Amendment to the Constitution. One might think that such electoral successes belied any claim of political powerlessness—indeed, writing a quarter century later, Justice Scalia made exactly that point.[46]

Justice Brennan, however, turned these facts around, to use them as evidence that a problem existed—indeed, that the Court should respect Congress's judgment, expressed through legislation, that a problem existed. As counterintuitive as his argument might seem, upon examination there is much to commend it: the fact that other institutions recognize the existence of a certain type of discrimination surely should be probative evidence for a court that a problem does in fact exist. Indeed, this book's thesis, explained in chapter 6, echoes his insight. Nevertheless, it is hard to square the fact of legislative responsiveness with a political process–based argument for heightened judicial scrutiny.

But an even more fundamental problem plagues the political powerlessness element. The brute fact is that, in a well-functioning political process, some groups *should* be largely powerless. Politics is a game of numbers—or, more accurately, power. If a group is simply too weak to gain legislators' attention, then it will lose most of the battles it fights. That fact should not inevitably cast aspersions on the process itself. Indeed, if anything, it marks a healthy, responsive process. Thus, a group's consistent losing record does not necessarily say anything about whether it should be a suspect class.

Scholars have noted this problem and have attempted to resolve it and thus rehabilitate political process analysis. As noted earlier, John Hart Ely argued that the process problem suspect class analysis attempts to correct is the problem not of losing but of not being listened to. Thus, for him the political powerlessness criterion—and, indeed, political process analysis more generally—seeks to determine not whether a group is able to win victories but able simply to participate effectively in the game.

Yet, as attractive as this answer might be to the problem of the "appropriately" politically powerless group, it ultimately fails. As Bruce Ackerman noted in the 1980s, a group may fail to get legislators' attention for good reasons—because nobody agrees with them.[47] Ackerman postulated a group of legal scholars convinced that *Brown v. Board of Education* was wrong, who lobby Congress for a constitutional amendment overruling it. Ackerman speculates—undoubtedly accurately—that that group would receive little of the sincere attention Ely believes to be their constitutional due. Yet that fact surely does not militate in favor of suspect class status, at least without more. Indeed, Ely himself seems to agree with that assessment: in a key caveat to his thesis that "political power" means the ability to get a hearing in legislative councils, he states that political powerlessness inheres in an inability to get such a hearing "for reasons that are in some way discreditable."[48]

The upshot, as suggested by the last phrase of the previous sentence's quotation, is that political process analysis ultimately requires substantive value judgments. The second factor of that analysis includes an explicitly value-based judgment—the requirement that the (immutable) characteristic which is claimed to be suspect be irrelevant for purposes of the challenged statute's goals. And, as just discussed, the political powerlessness factor, as seemingly process-based as it is, ultimately requires such a value judgment as well. All that we are left with is the history of discrimination element. As a matter of logic, that element is certainly probative of suspect class status. But, as we saw earlier, it is inadequate on its own to distinguish between groups that should be suspect classes and those which, while the past victims of discrimination, have succeeded in easing the most serious bias from which they earlier suffered.

The scope and depth of these problems were not immediately clear when Justice Brennan set forth to translate Footnote 4's "prejudice against discrete and insular minorities" formula into constitutional doctrine. Beginning with *Frontiero*, the Court proceeded over the course of the following dozen years to consider a variety of groups' claims for heightened judicial protection. By the time this process had run its course, the contradictions identified here had become clear.

The Path of Suspect Class Analysis

Applying the template Justice Brennan created in *Frontiero*, the Court throughout the 1970s and 1980s decided the suspect class status of a number of groups. Ironically, its ultimate decision to accord sex discrimination a quasi-suspect, "intermediate scrutiny" status (a decision necessitated by Justice Brennan's failure to find a fifth vote for his analysis in *Frontiero* itself) was simply announced in 1976, without any reapplication of suspect class analysis.[49] But the Court's analysis of other groups did rely, either wholly or in part, on application of *Frontiero*'s principles. For example, during this period the Court granted heightened scrutiny to classifications turning on legitimacy, stating that the status of being born out of wedlock "is, like race or national origin, a characteristic determined by causes not within the control of the illegitimate individual, and . . . bears no relation to the individual's ability to participate in and contribute to society."[50] However, at the same time it speculated that, in part because of the relative invisibility of the characteristic, "discrimination against illegitimates has never approached the severity or pervasiveness of the historic legal and political discrimination against women and Negroes." Thus, the Court concluded, that type of discrimination did not "command extraordinary protection from the majoritarian political process."[51] The Court's application of *Frontiero*'s suspect class factors to legitimacy discrimination suggested an ambivalent answer to the suspect class question—an answer that, like its response to sex discrimination, eventually found instantiation in the concept of intermediate scrutiny.[52]

Another early subject of suspect class analysis was alienage. Indeed, even before *Frontiero* the Court had accorded heightened scrutiny to classifications burdening noncitizens. The Court's holding in that early case was supported primarily by old, pre–*Carolene Products* precedent; however, the Court also cited Footnote 4 and asserted that "[a]liens as a class are a prime example of a 'discrete and insular' minority for which . . . heightened judicial solicitude is appropriate."[53]

These decisions did not go unchallenged. Justice Stewart, later joined by Justice Stevens, often agreed with the results striking down the types of discrimination discussed here, but he did so on the ground that the challenged law was simply irrational or, in Justice Stevens's view, not impartial.[54] But the most forceful challenge to the Court's approach came from then-Justice Rehnquist. For example, dissenting in two alienage cases from 1973, he observed that alienage was not an immutable condition, since noncitizens could seek to become citizens and thus remove themselves from the disfavored group. More fundamentally (and more presciently), he noted the diversity of

American society and expressed concern that a judicial search for "discrete and insular minorities" could open the door to a great deal of judicial creativity in expanding the scope of intrusive judicial review. As we will see in the next section, a decade later, in *City of Cleburne v. Cleburne Living Center*,[55] the full Court expressed that same concern.

But Justice Rehnquist had still more to say about this early phase of the Court's use of suspect class analysis. Most notably for our purposes, he dissented from the Court's 1976 decision in according intermediate scrutiny to sex classifications.[56] Much of his objection centered on the fact that the classification at issue in the case—a state law restricting young men, but not young women, from purchasing low-alcohol beer—appeared to treat females, the presumed powerless group, more favorably than males. (As we will again see later in this chapter, in an ironic twist a form of this argument would resurface more than a decade later, when advocates for race-based affirmative action argued that such action should not receive higher scrutiny, since the majority was burdening itself.)

It might appear only a curious detail that the statute in *Craig* ostensibly benefited women. But that detail reveals much about the Court's approach to sex discrimination. In fact, the Court's sex discrimination cases have often taken place in a context where the challenged law arguably benefited women. For example, in the 1981 case *Michael M. v. Superior Court*,[57] the Court upheld a California law treating female actors involved in statutory rape more leniently than their male companions. The following year, in *Mississippi University for Women v. Hogan*,[58] the Court struck down a state university's restriction of its nursing program to women. Justice Powell, joined by Justice Rehnquist, dissented in *Hogan*, arguing that the state law expanded women's educational opportunities and honored the concept of educational diversity. Two decades later, the Court upheld a federal immigration law that favored the foreign-born children of American mothers as compared with the foreign-born children of American fathers.[59]

All these cases required the Court to consider the underlying significance of laws drawing lines based on sex. In *Craig*, *Michael M.*, and *Hogan*, justices inclined to uphold the challenged laws argued that those laws did not burden women—the only group that could make a plausible claim for heightened scrutiny in the context of sex classifications. Justices opposing them argued that those laws, while ostensibly treating women more favorably, communicated a stereotypical message about women that ultimately redounded to their detriment.[60] For example, in *Michael M.*, the statutory rape case, Justice Brennan argued that the state's differential punishment scheme originally rested on a paternalistic concern for protecting girls' chastity. Thus, these cases required the justices to determine the underlying message these laws communicated or reflected—a task that essentially required them to engage in a substantive, rather than a process-based, analysis.

Indeed, this appears to have been the goal of Ruth Bader Ginsburg, the Supreme Court justice who in the 1970s led the ACLU's sex equality project and litigated the most important early sex equality cases before the Court. According to one scholar, her advocacy pushed the Court to go beyond a formal application of a particular scrutiny standard across the board, and instead to consider whether particular sex classifications reflected stereotypes about women's social roles that excluded them from truly equal participation in American life.[61] Fittingly, the most explicit example of this more focused, granular approach to sex discrimination was her own 1996 opinion in *United States v. Virginia*,[62] after she ascended to the Court. *Virginia* will constitute an important part of our discussion of equal protection today. But before we reach the modern era, we must complete the story of suspect class analysis.

Cleburne and the Decline of Suspect Class Analysis

After the 1970s the Court continued to apply precedent that had employed suspect class analysis to denominate a classification as suspect or, like sex and legitimacy, quasi-suspect.[63] But the Court's attempts to apply that analysis to new situations foundered on significant practical and conceptual difficulties. Before long those difficulties led it to begin abandoning that approach to equal protection. The most notable of this period's cases is the Court's 1985 decision in *City of Cleburne v. Cleburne Living Center*.[64] *Cleburne* was a watershed: this section examines its analysis in some detail.

Cleburne considered a city council decision requiring that the operators of a group home for intellectually disabled persons obtain a special permit, which, after a public hearing, the council then denied. The city's decision had the effect of preventing the operators from establishing the home in a particular residential neighborhood. The operators sued, arguing—successfully before the appellate court—that intellectually disabled persons constituted a quasi-suspect class meriting intermediate scrutiny. Applying that scrutiny, the appellate court struck down the city's decision.

The Supreme Court unanimously affirmed the lower court's judgment that the plaintiffs had suffered unconstitutional discrimination However, the justices split sharply in their rationales. Six members of the Court rejected the claim that persons with intellectual disabilities constituted a suspect or quasi-suspect class. Nevertheless, that majority concluded that the city's action lacked a rational basis, and thus failed the Court's most deferential form of equal protection scrutiny. Three members of the Court, while agreeing that the city's action violated the Equal Protection Clause, would have reached that result by applying heightened scrutiny. More strikingly, two members of the majority (Justice Stevens, joined by Chief Justice Burger) expressed doubt about the entire enterprise of deciding equal protection cases based on the application of different levels of scrutiny. Thus, even though these latter two justices joined the majority opinion, the Court's analysis whether intellectually disabled persons constituted a suspect or quasi-suspect class appears to have gained the unconditional assent of only a plurality of the justices.

This ambivalence reflects both the difficulty the Court had applying suspect class analysis to intellectually disabled persons in particular, and the problems with that analysis more generally. The Court, speaking through Justice White, began by immediately cutting to one of the core issues of suspect class analysis. Justice White concluded that the appellate court had erred in according intellectually disabled persons suspect class status because such persons, as suffering from a reduced capacity to function in society, "are . . . different, immutably so, in relevant respects,"[65] both from mainstream society and from persons with different degrees of intellectual disability. For an analysis that purports to abjure second-guessing legislative value judgments, it is striking that the Court began with a bald statement that the affected group was relevantly different.

This initial observation began what proved to be a suspect class analysis that balanced uneasily between traditional political process reasoning and outright substantive conclusions about the appropriateness of special treatment for intellectually disabled persons. Thus, Justice White followed up the preceding substantive argument by stating that legislatures' response to the unique problems those persons faced "demonstrates . . . that the lawmakers have been addressing their difficulties in a manner that belies a continuing antipathy or prejudice and a corresponding need for more intrusive oversight by the judiciary."[66] This argument is obviously process-based; indeed, its use of the term "prejudice" echoes Footnote 4 itself. Yet after detailing examples of legislative assistance to intellectually disabled persons, he then returned to substantive arguments, concluding that those examples "reflect the real and undeniable differences between the retarded and others."[67] He then continued in this explicitly substantive vein, observing that the fact "[t]hat a civilized and decent society expects and approves such legislation indicates that governmental consideration of those differences in the vast majority of situations is not only legitimate but desirable."[68]

At this point, Justice White added to the mix questions of judicial competence and proper institutional roles. First, he expressed unease about whether legislation specially benefiting those persons could withstand the heightened judicial scrutiny that would flow from their status as a suspect class. He then warned that even if courts could perform that function, the very prospect of such heightened review might deter legislatures from acting at all.

Up to this point, then, the Court's analysis combined elements of political process reasoning, substantive evaluation of the relevant similarity/difference claim inherent in the plaintiffs' lawsuit, and a consideration of the appropriate roles for courts and legislatures in situations like this. To all this White added, at the end of his suspect class analysis, a remarkable concession. The final paragraph of this part of his opinion merits a full quotation:

> Fourth, if the large and amorphous class of the mentally retarded were deemed quasi-suspect for the reasons given by the Court of Appeals, it would be difficult to find a principled way to distinguish a variety of other groups who have perhaps immutable disabilities setting them off from others, who cannot themselves mandate the desired legislative responses, and who can claim some degree of prejudice from at least part of the public at large. One need mention in this respect only the aging, the disabled, the mentally ill, and the infirm. We are reluctant to set out on that course, and we decline to do so.[69]

"Immutable disabilities" suffered by groups "who cannot . . . mandate the desired legislative responses," and "who can claim some degree of prejudice"—these are the building blocks of suspect class status. In this concluding paragraph of *Cleburne*'s suspect class analysis, the Court recognized the possibility that other groups in society may possess those characteristics, as might intellectually disabled persons themselves. But because a ruling that these characteristics justified finding intellectually disabled persons to constitute a suspect class might give these other groups a claim to that same status, the Court rejected the plaintiffs' claim to such status. Simply put, the Court was worried about opening up the floodgates to other groups' claims for suspect class status.

There may be good wisdom in the Court's floodgates fear. Similarly, there may be good reason for it to worry that lower courts would be incapable of applying heightened scrutiny accurately, and thus good reason for them to step back and allow legislatures maximum flexibility in designing policies to accommodate intellectually disabled persons. But these institutional competence–based and institutional role–based concerns say very little about the underlying constitutionality of intellectual disability discrimination. They thus say little about Congress's appropriate enforcement power–based role in overseeing how states treat such persons. Indeed, *Cleburne*'s suggestion that courts should generally step aside and give legislatures discretion to make policy concerning intellectually disabled persons leaves open the question whether state legislatures have some particular claim to this discretion, to the exclusion of Congress, when the latter acts pursuant to its enforcement power.

The Court's concession that perhaps intellectually disabled persons (and others) merited heightened scrutiny reveals the status of suspect class analysis as a decisional aid rather than an actual rule of constitutional law. In other words, it reveals that the result of a given suspect class analysis is not itself the meaning of the Constitution but merely a mechanism by which a court can hope to uncover that meaning. If suspect class analysis were itself constitutional law, then presumably *Cleburne*'s "floodgates" concern is an impermissible consideration for a court. Quite literally, if the Constitution were held to mean something (e.g., that intellectual disability discrimination is highly suspect), then a court would be disregarding its duty if it avoided that conclusion by noting that meaning's implications for other groups' analogous claims.

By contrast, if instead suspect class analysis was simply a means of uncovering a deeper constitutional truth, then prudential reasons could legitimately lead a court to dodge the inevitable end point of its analysis, as *Cleburne* did. By justifying his refusal to accord suspect class status to intellectually disabled persons in part by citing this "floodgates" concern (as well as his concern about courts' ability to perform heightened review competently), Justice White revealed that the suspect class decision included at least some measure of prudential judgment. This insight will matter greatly when we consider the degree to which enforcement legislation should be limited by the suspect class status of the group Congress is attempting to benefit.

The decision to deny intellectually disabled persons suspect class status was not, however, the end of the line for the *Cleburne* plaintiffs. Instead, after rejecting heightened scrutiny, the Court then performed rational basis review and found the city council's decision to have failed even that low standard. This is a remarkable holding that merits attention. As generations of law students learn, rational basis review is usually highly deferential. The ease with which government action satisfies that review is suggested by the doctrinal formula, which requires only that the classification bear a *rational* connection to a *legitimate* government interest. The italicized adjectives suggest an easy test: the connection between the discrimination and the government interest need only be "rational"—not "exact," not "tight," not even "the tightest reasonably possible." Moreover, the government interest at stake need not be one of overriding importance: it need only be "legitimate"—not "compelling," and not even "important."

In applying this test, the Court has provided legislatures with even more discretion. To take perhaps the most famous example, the Court has said for more than half a century that, despite the Equal Protection Clause, a legislature may proceed "one step at a time, addressing itself to the phase of the problem which seems most acute to the legislative mind."[70] When combined with the deference by which such legislative prioritizations are reviewed, the weakness of the rational basis standard appears clear.

Yet the test is even more lenient than that. Recall *Carolene Products* itself, which provides the foundation for the modern rational basis test. In that case Justice Stone announced that the Court would presume the existence of facts supporting the legislature's judgment—in the equal protection context, the existence of facts demonstrating a rational connection between the classification and a legitimate government interest. Later courts expanded on this idea, to the point where under rational basis review a court could hypothesize a legitimate justification that might have motivated the challenged law. When the court can hypothesize the justification for the legislature's choice to take "one step" rather than another, and then presume the existence of facts that rationally connect that justification with the challenged classification, one comes to understand how extraordinarily deferential rational basis review is.

Except when it isn't. In *Cleburne* the Court applied an unusually stringent version of rational basis review. For example, at one point the Court concluded that "the record does not reveal any rational basis for believing that the [group] home would pose any special threat to the city's legitimate interests."[71] That conclusion sounds innocuous enough—after all, don't courts always inquire into what the record shows? But in fact it reflects a serious deviation from standard rational basis review. Recall from the previous paragraph that standard rational basis scrutiny allows courts to presume the existence of facts supporting the legislature's judgment—here, that the placement of the group home on this particular site would threaten legitimate government interests. *Cleburne*'s casual observation that the record before the Court did not support the city's judgment signals that it was applying something other than that traditional scrutiny.

Indeed, the Court's review *was* more searching than what normal rational basis review would suggest. To take one example, when the city argued that the home location lay in a floodplain, thus raising the prospect of emergency evacuations that might be more difficult for multiperson residences, the Court wondered aloud why the city allowed *other* multiperson residences, such as nursing homes, in the same area. Again, normally a court would presume the facts that supported the legislative judgment—here, facts that would render the group home a more difficult evacuation challenge than a nursing home. Yet, reflecting its insistence on more proof from the government, the Court simply expressed its own independent disbelief that, for purposes of flood evacuation, intellectually disabled persons were different from the residents of a nursing home.[72]

Why did the Court deviate from its traditional, deferential version of rationality review? The answer may lie in two insights discernible in other parts of the opinion. First, the city offered additional justifications for the permit denial. In particular, it cited neighborhood fears of the intellectually disabled would-be residents. The Court made short work of that justification, noting that such "negative attitudes" did not constitute permissible bases for the city's discrimination. But the very presence of this argument suggests that the city's decision may have been contaminated by simple dislike of those persons.[73]

That dislike—what legal doctrine shorthands as "animus"—constitutes a core prohibition of equal protection. This rule is a subset of what chapter 1 identified as the "public purpose" requirement. Recall that that requirement prohibits government action that is motivated by purely private purposes. On this view, a majority's simple dislike of the burdened group, unconnected to any legitimate purpose government has the right to pursue, constitutes one example of a purely private purpose which renders a law unconstitutional. Chapter 1 demonstrated how fundamental the public purpose requirement is in American constitutional law.[74] In particular, it explained how earlier equal protection doctrine focused on ensuring that states used their "police power" only for the public good rather than to enact "class legislation."

Return now to *Cleburne*. It is reasonable to assume that the presence of such animus led the Court to perform a stricter type of rational basis review—what commentators and courts later called "rational basis plus" or "rational basis with teeth"—to the city's decision. But *Cleburne* perhaps hides a second clue to its unusually stringent application of rationality review. Recall that the Court performed that review only after concluding that intellectually disabled persons did not merit explicitly heightened scrutiny. Recall also that the Court's denial of heightened scrutiny rested in significant part on concerns about courts' institutional competence, both to evaluate legislative decisions treating that group differently and to distinguish between that group and others that could make similar arguments in favor of suspect class status.

These prudential concerns are perfectly understandable for a generalist court unsure of its own competence to make difficult medical and social science decisions. At the same time, as explained earlier, they suggest that suspect class analysis constitutes not so much constitutional law as a decisional aid that helps courts apply the core meaning of equal protection in a judicially manageable way. By extension, when that decisional aid proves itself not to be judicially manageable, as with the *Cleburne* plaintiffs' argument for suspect class status, the Court felt free to disregard the implications of that analysis.

But such analysis still matters. Even if suspect class analysis really is just a decisional aid that does not itself constitute constitutional law, it must at least help illuminate the underlying constitutional rule. If so, then perhaps part of the reason for the stringency of *Cleburne*'s rational basis scrutiny lay in the fact that the plaintiffs made at least a partially convincing argument about their eligibility for suspect class status. Perhaps their partial success convinced the Court, consciously or otherwise, to probe the city's justifications more closely—especially after one of those justifications (the neighborhood's fear of those persons) itself revealed unconstitutional motivations. This explanation might clarify why the Court took the unusual step—sharply criticized in Justice Marshall's partial dissent—of beginning its analysis by considering whether intellectually disabled persons constituted a suspect class, concluding that they did not, and only then holding that the city's action failed the rational basis test. Rather than constituting superfluous dicta, as Justice Marshall argued,[75] perhaps the Court's suspect class analysis set the stage for its application of stricter than normal rationality review.

Cleburne suggests several lessons for suspect class analysis and its relationship to equal protection. First, its analysis of the suspect class question reveals the foundations of that analysis in judicial competence and conceptions of the proper judicial role. The Court's conclusion that intellectually disabled persons are not a suspect class turned at least as much on concerns about judges' ability to accurately distinguish between benign and invidious treatment of that group as it did on a conclusion that such classifications are generally likely to be constitutional. Conceptions of the proper role of courts in our society also played a role—recall the Court's concern that the prospect of heightened scrutiny would deter legislatures from even attempting to craft appropriate responses to such persons. Continuing with that institutional role point, note also the Court's concluding lament that granting that group suspect class status would open the floodgates to similar claims from groups who could claim an analogous social position. That concern—that if the Court granted protected status to that group, it would have no principled way to deny it to "the aging, the disabled, the mentally ill, and the infirm"[76]—says nothing about whether, as a matter of pure constitutional law, intellectually disabled persons merit such status. It does, however, speak volumes about the difficulties courts face in drawing lines.

Second, consider the Court's application of heightened rationality review to strike down the city's permit requirement. The first thing we can say is that that strike-down reveals that the city's action violated a core constitutional principle. Courts do not lightly strike down government actions as unconstitutional. The Court's decision to do so in this case suggests that, unlike the competence-based and institutional role–based nature of its suspect class analysis, the Court's conclusion about the city's unconstitutional animus toward the would-be group home residents reflects core constitutional meaning. That meaning comes through most clearly in the Court's grounding of its decision on its rejection of private biases, and private motivations more generally, as constitutionally adequate justifications for the permit denial. Consider the last substantive sentence of the Court's opinion, which explicitly sums up the rationale for its decision: "The short of it is that requiring the permit in this case appears to us to rest on an irrational prejudice against the mentally retarded, including those who would occupy the Featherston facility. . . ."[77]

This insight—that privately motivated legislation violates the Constitution—does not directly speak to this chapter's investigation of the fate of suspect class analysis. However, it is relevant to this book's examination of the enforcement power, for two reasons. First, as we shall see later in this chapter, the more particularized, direct form of review reflected in the Court's holding has become a main competitor to the more general, but also more institutionally grounded, approach of suspect class analysis. Second, as we shall see in part II of the book, the rise of this more direct, but ad hoc, constitutional review poses serious problems for the Court's understanding of Congress's Fourteenth Amendment enforcement power.

For now, however, these concerns can be put on the back burner. The focus of this chapter so far has been the evolution of the Court's suspect class analysis. After a start in *Frontiero* that promised a largely process-based, Footnote 4–inspired approach to equal protection review, within a dozen years the Court had confronted serious conceptual and practical difficulties with suspect class analysis. Those difficulties made a mark on the Court. After *Cleburne* the Court never again engaged in a serious suspect class analysis, even though within a decade it would be embarking on yet another equality campaign, this time on behalf of gays and lesbians. For many scholars, the earlier phase of that new campaign bore an uncanny resemblance to the early phase of its sex equality crusade. But as similar as those campaigns might have seemed at the time, ultimately they differed dramatically in their use of suspect class analysis.

Suspect Class Analysis after *Cleburne*

After *Cleburne* the Court never again performed a serious suspect class analysis. This was not because the Court had stopped finding equal protection violations, or even because it had stopped seriously looking. Indeed, in the fifteen years after *Cleburne* the Court found equal protection violations in a number of contexts, ranging from traditional categories such as race and sex discrimination to emerging equal protection categories such as sexual orientation, to potentially one-off, idiosyncratic contexts such as land valuation decisions, in addition to approving a new, sui generis type of equal protection claim, the class of one.[78]

Race

Ironically, while one might think that suspect class analysis would be least appropriate in cases involving race or sex, where the Court had already settled on the appropriate standard of equal protection review, those cases provided the context for whatever suspect class analysis could be found after *Cleburne*. Most notably, in the 1989 case *City of Richmond v. J. A. Croson Co.*,[79] the Court considered whether assertedly benign uses of race—colloquially known as affirmative action—merited the same skeptical judicial review as the Jim Crow laws the Court had dispatched during the 1950s and 1960s. Recall from earlier in this chapter that the Jim Crow cases culminated in triumphant statements that race classifications were presumptively unconstitutional.[80] The context for those statements—challenges to racial segregation laws—was arguably quite different from the compensatory, remedial uses of race that states were experimenting with by the 1970s and 1980s. Before *Croson* the Court had provided a confusing and fractured response to equal protection challenges to those modern laws. *Croson*, which involved Richmond, Virginia's, decision to require contractors on city contracts to subcontract out at least 30 percent of the value of those contracts to firms owned by minority businesses, gave the Court another opportunity to clarify its response.

In *Croson* it took advantage of that opportunity. In announcing principles that would guide its future evaluation of affirmative action set-asides, the Court confronted serious arguments that the level of scrutiny should be different for affirmative action laws as compared with prior generations' segregation laws. Four justices had made that argument in the seminal 1978 *Bakke* case:[81] relying in part on political process reasoning, they argued that remedially justified uses of race should only receive what amounted to intermediate scrutiny.[82] Justices continued to make those arguments into the

1980s.[83] Scholars had made similar arguments. Most notably, John Hart Ely, the preeminent academic exponent of process-based constitutional analysis, endorsed such race consciousness on the straightforward theory that such actions reflected the white majority's decision to burden itself, and thus did not reflect majoritarian oppression of a minority.[84]

In *Croson* the Court rejected this argument. *Any* use of race, the Court concluded, required strict judicial scrutiny. According to Justice O'Connor's plurality opinion,[85] strict scrutiny was required in order to "smoke out" illegitimate uses of what she called "a highly suspect tool"—uses that reflected either "notions of racial inferiority or simple racial politics."[86] But what about the political process arguments that were then circulating—arguments that had been made by scholars and by advocates in *Croson* itself, and accepted by four justices in *Bakke*?[87] The Court dismissed them. Using language suggesting that such arguments stood in serious tension with the Court's core understanding that equal protection presumptively required government color blindness,[88] the Court provided only the most halfhearted, formalistic political process analysis. It noted simply that the Richmond, Virginia, city council that had approved the challenged racial set-aside had five African Americans among its nine members. That barren observation, torn from any larger political, historical, or social context of politics and power in the former capital of the Confederacy, was all the political process analysis the *Croson* Court provided. Compared with some of the sophisticated, nuanced political process analysis that was then current in appellate court reasoning,[89] it was an unimpressive performance. Nevertheless, *Croson* heralded a new era of routine applications of strict scrutiny to all race classifications.

Writing about the Court's race jurisprudence shortly after *Croson*, the prominent legal scholar Michael Klarman identified the Court's rejection of political process analysis in favor of "a more openly normative theory of 'relevance,' which banishes certain criteria from governmental decisionmaking on the ground that they should be irrelevant."[90] The Court has continued to adopt this approach to race classifications, even if at times it has wavered in the strictness with which it scrutinizes such classifications.[91] Indeed, in 2013 the Court again explained that race classifications require strict scrutiny for moral and historical reasons reflecting the Court's substantive, rather than process-based, disapproval of such classifications.[92]

Sex

The Court's substantive interpretation of equal protection soon began to extend beyond race. Seven years after *Croson*, in *United States v. Virginia*,[93] the Court provided one of the most detailed statements of its approach to sex classifications since Justice Brennan's analysis a quarter century earlier in *Frontiero*. *Virginia* struck down the Virginia Military Institute's (VMI's) all-male admissions policy. Writing for the Court, Justice Ruth Bader Ginsburg[94] summarized and restated the Court's sex discrimination jurisprudence. That summary noted Justice Brennan's process-based justifications for heightened scrutiny; however, her explanation of the foundations for the Court's jurisprudence went beyond those arguments. (Perhaps ironically, it was Justice Scalia who relied most heavily on political process analysis, when he suggested in his dissent that application of Footnote 4–type analysis justified reducing the Court's scrutiny of sex discrimination to rational basis review.)[95]

Moving beyond a straightforward scrutiny level appropriate for any and all sex classifications, Justice Ginsburg instead acknowledged that different types of sex classifications merited different judicial responses. Recognizing that "[p]hysical differences between men and women are enduring," and that "inherent differences between men and women . . . remain cause for celebration," she went out of her way to approve of certain sex classifications. She allowed states to employ sex classifications "to compensate women for . . . economic disabilities they have suffered," "to promote equal employment opportunity," and "to advance full development of the talent and capacities of our Nation's people." She also recognized "the reality"—particularly relevant to the VMI case itself—that "[s]ingle sex education affords pedagogical benefits to at least some students."[96]

To be sure, even before *Virginia* the Court had imported substantive judgments into its sex discrimination decisions—recall this chapter's earlier discussion of cases from the 1970s and early 1980s, where the Court struggled over whether a given sex classification reflected a stereotype. But *Virginia*'s recognition that some sex classifications may be not only benign but affirmatively helpful to the achievement of full sex equality required an even more granular examination of each instance of sex discrimination, one taking account of the surrounding social context. Readers might detect a resemblance between Justice Ginsburg's recognition of that fact and Justice White's observation a decade earlier in *Cleburne* that some differential treatment of intellectually disabled persons might in fact redound to that group's benefit. Indeed, one can use Justice Ginsburg's language to make the points Justice White made a decade earlier: differential treatment of intellectually disabled persons might recognize that "differences" between such persons and non-disabled persons "are enduring," thus justifying classifications "to promote equal employment opportunity," "to advance full development of the talent and capacities of our Nation's people," and perhaps even "to compensate" intellectually disabled persons for past discrimination. Similarly, one can easily understand "the reality" that special education for such persons "affords pedagogical benefits to at least some students."

One response to the need for such granularity—*Cleburne*'s response—is to abjure heightened review entirely, and to search, as Justice White did, for instances of discrimination that appeared to the Court to violate core constitutional requirements, such as the prohibition on animus-based government action. Another response—*Virginia*'s response—is to insist on careful scrutiny of each and every discriminatory action (here, on the basis of sex), but to approve of those actions that are taken for good reasons, say, to compensate women for past discrimination or, in *Virginia*'s words, "to support diverse educational opportunities" by providing single-sex education in appropriate circumstances. These responses are closely related. Most important for our purposes, they both involve cutting past rigid applications of scrutiny standards, to focus instead on a search for violations of core constitutional rules.

The upshot is that in the post-*Cleburne* era even the Court's continued long-standing skepticism of sex classifications was tempered by its recognition that equal protection review necessitated more than across-the-board application of a single scrutiny standard to a given classification. In *Virginia*, as in *Cleburne*, the Court was distancing itself from suspect class analysis and the resulting tiered scrutiny structure. In its place, it was moving toward a more nuanced application of equal protection's core requirement of noninvidious classification undertaken for the public good. Whereas before *Cleburne* the Court attempted to enforce that goal through application of a particular level of scrutiny to a given type of classification, by the 1990s the Court was growing more comfortable with a more ad hoc, granular approach.

Sexual Orientation

The same term the Court decided *Virginia*, it decided another case that, in retrospect, embarked the Court on a new equality crusade that continues to the present day. In *Romer v. Evans*,[97] the Court struck down, as violating the Equal Protection Clause, an amendment to the Colorado Constitution ("Amendment 2") that prevented state or local government entities from granting protected status on the basis of sexual orientation. (Thus, for example, Amendment 2 wiped off the books Denver's and Aspen's expansions of their public accommodation nondiscrimination ordinances to include sexual orientation.) On a six-to-three vote, the Court struck the amendment down as failing rational basis review. *Romer* made history, as it was the first Supreme

Court constitutional law victory for plaintiffs in a case that was unambiguously about gay rights.

Romer raises several points relevant to our examination of equal protection's evolution. First, the Court failed to consider whether sexual orientation constitutes a suspect class. The issue had been presented to the Court for at least a decade before *Romer*; indeed, in 1985 Justice Brennan protested the Court's denial of review in a case that presented exactly that issue.[98] Still, *Romer*'s failure to address this issue was at least defensible: after all, if a law fails the lowest level of equal protection review, then there is no reason to consider whether a higher level of review is called for. (Indeed, recall that Justice Marshall made just this argument in his partial dissent in *Cleburne*.)[99] Nevertheless, in retrospect *Romer* can be seen as the start of a series of cases where the Court vindicated gay rights claims while steadfastly refusing to decide whether those claims merited heightened judicial review.[100]

Romer was also noteworthy for the character of its rational basis scrutiny. Writing for the Court, Justice Kennedy (who was fated to write all three Court opinions to date vindicating gay rights claims), found Amendment 2 to fail rationality review for two distinct but related reasons. First, he concluded that the law's exclusion of gays and lesbians from the protection of state law constituted a literal violation of equal protection's command that no person or group should be a stranger to the law, or denied its protection. This is an unusual theory, justified, according to Justice Kennedy, by the law's unusually broad scope—denying any protected status at all based on sexual orientation. As such, it does not directly relate to our topic.

However, that broad scope indirectly influenced Justice Kennedy's alternative analysis, which is much more relevant for our purposes. Under this second approach, he concluded that Amendment 2 violated what he called the "conventional and venerable"[101] requirement that legal classifications bear a rational relationship to a legitimate government interest. He concluded that the state's justifications for the law—protecting citizens' rights to decline to associate with people they disapproved of, and conserving state law enforcement resources to combat other types of discrimination—were so unrelated to the law's sweeping coverage that they lacked the rational connection to the law demanded by the rational basis standard. With those (assumed) legitimate justifications unavailable as support for the law, Justice Kennedy concluded that the law could only have been motivated by simple dislike of—what we have called "animus" against—gays and lesbians. As we have already seen, such animus is an impermissible justification for government action.

Romer thus paralleled *Cleburne* in concluding that a government action failed equal protection rational basis review because it was based on animus.[102] To be sure, these two cases arrived at the animus conclusion through different paths. *Cleburne* found direct evidence of animus in the city's defense of its zoning decision as responding to neighborhood fears of the intellectually disabled would-be occupants of the group home. *Romer* did not cite such explicit evidence of antigay animus; rather, the Court reached that conclusion indirectly, as the only possible explanation for the law after it rejected the state's legitimate justifications. But in both cases the Court got to the same place. It applied what we have described as a core meaning of equal protection: that government action must not be based on simple dislike of, or animus against, a group.

If *Romer* had been an outlier case, then it might not be as significant an indicator of the current Court's approach to equal protection. But *Cleburne* and *Romer*, along with *Virginia*, demonstrate that, with the exception of race, the Court has continued to apply a more granular analysis in equal protection cases. This trend is especially noticeable in the Court's thinking about sexual orientation. Seven years after *Romer*, the Court in *Lawrence v. Texas*[103] struck down a Texas law criminalizing homosexual, but not heterosexual, sodomy. The Court, speaking again through Justice Kennedy, relied on the Due Process Clause. But for our purposes the key opinion in *Lawrence* was Justice O'Connor's concurrence. She agreed with the result striking down the law but relied on the Equal Protection Clause.[104] As with *Romer* and *Cleburne*, she found in Texas's decision to criminalize only same-sex sodomy a law that simply expressed moral disapproval of a certain group—again, animus.

The full Court again invoked the rule against animus in its final gay rights case to date: its 2013 decision in *United States v. Windsor*.[105] In *Windsor* the Court struck down Section 3 of the Defense of Marriage Act (DOMA), which defined marriage for federal law purposes as excluding same-sex unions, even when the couple was validly married under state law. Section 3's effect was to deny federal benefits (such as Social Security survivor benefits) to same-sex couples who were legally married in their state of residence.

Again speaking through Justice Kennedy, the five-justice majority in *Windsor* engaged in an analysis that echoed its analysis in *Romer* seventeen years earlier. First, just like in *Romer*, the Court in *Windsor* bypassed suspect class analysis. But in *Windsor* the Court went beyond its particularized analysis in *Romer* to perform an analysis that is perhaps best described as "pointillist," after the painting style.[106] The Court's constitutional pointillism emerges from the fact that, unlike in *Romer*, the Court in *Windsor* did not even test DOMA against standard rational basis review. Instead, it conducted a detailed review of the statute and its legislative history, which led Justice Kennedy to conclude that the Congress that enacted DOMA had acted out of pure dislike and disapproval of same-sex couples.

Justice Kennedy's analysis is remarkable. It is rare that a federal court will explicitly accuse Congress of acting in bad faith or, in this case, out of malicious motivations. Such an accusation is especially aggressive when it results not, as in *Romer*, from a process of elimination that tests the challenged law against possible legitimate justifications and finds them wanting but instead from a direct examination of the legislative materials. In essence, Justice Kennedy called Congress homophobic, not indirectly, but explicitly, based on what congresspersons actually said.[107]

To be fair, Justice Kennedy did set the groundwork for this analysis earlier in his opinion, when he noted that the federal government had historically honored state definitions of marriage when determining marital status for federal law purposes. This observation cast at least some preliminary doubt on Section 3's rationality as an unobjectionable, garden-variety federal decision about who was considered "married" for federal law purposes. It also raised the specter of Section 3 violating a federalism norm, although his opinion disclaimed any specific reliance on federalism.

Despite these explanations and caveats, the fact remains that *Windsor* represents a remarkable deviation from standard equal protection doctrine. It not only bypassed the option of according suspect classification status to sexual orientation but ignored the basic structure of equal protection review, which searches for at least a rational connection between the statutory classification and a legitimate government interest. In its place, Justice Kennedy adopted a far more direct but narrow—that is, "pointillist"—inquiry into the actual motivations of the legislators that enacted the challenged law. Such an inquiry is a far cry from the more indirect, presumption-driven, but generally applicable approach to equal protection represented by suspect class analysis. To continue the art analogy, in *Windsor* Justice Kennedy replaced broad brushstrokes of mixed pigments with pointillist applications of pure constitutional color.

Consider that analogy one further step. The theory of pointillism is that each dot of color attains meaning only when the viewer's eye and mind combine it with every other dot to form an image—a riverbank, a circus horse, or a park on the outskirts of Paris. Constitutional pointillism of the type performed by *Windsor* likewise promises to create a true picture of what the Constitution demands with regard to sexual orientation discrimination, but only when every case is considered together to create the complete image. This approach is worlds away from suspect class analysis—indeed, it is the logically opposite approach. Suspect class analysis *begins* with the outline of an image—for example, race discrimination is presumptively unconstitutional—and then fills in the gaps through application of the appropriate standard of review. By contrast, *Windsor*, like a pointillist painting, begins with a dot of pure color; only after the court (or the painter) applies countless such dots does the outline of the image take shape. Thus, *Windsor* does not just reflect an abandonment of suspect class analysis. It reflects its polar opposite.

Of course, *Windsor* is just one case—and an unusually politically fraught one (even by constitutional law standards), given the complex and unstable politics of same-sex marriage. Nevertheless, Justice Kennedy's decision to abjure even heightened rational basis review in favor of his pointillist approach poses a major challenge to traditional approaches to equal protection. In particular, it heightens the impression, already prevalent before *Windsor*, that the Court no longer considers suspect class analysis a useful approach. At this point in the Court's history, a fair argument can be made that political process analysis of equal protection questions is dead at the Supreme Court, even if lower courts continue to apply it. Part II of this book turns to what that conclusion means for congressional enforcement power.

The Implications

As intricate as some of the case discussions here might have been, their basic point is straightforward: suspect class analysis appears to have dropped out of the Supreme Court's equal protection analysis. Indeed, the gay rights cases suggest that it has disappeared where it matters most—where the Court considers an equality claim made by a group whose suspect class status has not been determined.

This insight has important implications both for equal protection doctrine itself and, as discussed in the rest of this book, for congressional power to enforce equal protection. For equal protection doctrine, the Court's abandonment of the suspect class template means that future decisions ruling on equality claims made by new groups will likely have an ad hoc flavor. In particular, many decisions finding equal protection violations will likely rest on a conclusion that the discrimination reflected animus. As our brief historical tour has shown, animus and irrationality together constitute the core meaning of equal protection, except in the special contexts of race and the so-called fundamental rights strand of equal protection. (We will defer consideration of these special situations until chapter 10.) Aside from those enclaves, however, the history of the Court's equal protection jurisprudence has revealed the centrality of the animus and irrationality rules, whether expressed as prohibitions on "class legislation," legislation motivated by "simple dislike," or action that has no rational relationship to any interest government may legitimately pursue.

The Court's recent decision in *Windsor* may provide a template for such ad hoc decisions. In *Windsor* the Court concluded that the challenged DOMA provision rested on animus—in that case, a simple desire to deprive same-sex married couples of the dignity they enjoyed by having a state officially sanction their union. There was no indication in the opinion that this conclusion flowed from a stricter than usual scrutiny of the statute. For example, the Court never stated that it would abandon its normal presumption in favor of a statute's constitutionality, or the requirement that the plaintiff negate every conceivable rational justification for the statute. Such statements would have at least suggested a heightened level of review. There would have been recent precedent for such statements. In *Lawrence*, Justice O'Connor's equal protection concurrence stated that the appearance of animus triggered heightened scrutiny, even under the rational basis standard. Similarly, our analysis of *Cleburne* suggested that its more stringent rationality review derived from a suspicion that animus lurked behind the city's zoning decision Yet in *Windsor* the Court remained silent on the level of its rationality review, suggesting an unwillingness to be tied down to any particular formula for performing such scrutiny.

The Court's ultimate animus conclusion was similarly ad hoc. Justice Kennedy noted DOMA's wide scope, affecting more than 1,000 rights and responsibilities that flowed from federal recognition of a couple as married. He also used legislative history and even DOMA's title to suggest that its "principal purpose" was to "demean those persons who are in a lawful same-sex marriage." One might see in these arguments echoes of Justice Kennedy's opinion in *Romer*, where he relied in large part on the breadth of the challenged state law to conclude that it reflected unconstitutional animus. But *Windsor* deviates from *Romer* in that it did not even purport to apply the "purpose and fit" analysis that is a staple of traditional equal protection law. Instead, *Windsor* is much more ad hoc.

Indeed, to bring matters full circle, *Windsor* echoes the pre-1937 Court's "class legislation" approach to equal protection. Both of those approaches seek to cut through mediating rules to test the challenged law against equal protection's core meaning. But, as we have seen, both are susceptible to powerful claims that courts lack the competence and legitimacy to perform this review. And they both risk devolving into a standardless, ad hoc judicial second-guessing of the policy underlying the legislative classification.

Postscript

The *Carolene Products* project suffered perhaps its most explicit blow in 2014. In a case upholding the constitutionality of Michigan's decision (enacted by referendum) to abandon race-based preferences in higher education, Justice Scalia, joined by Justice Thomas, explicitly mocked Footnote 4. Justice Scalia has never been a great fan of suspect class analysis. His race opinions are full of eloquent praise for color-blind government action, without any consideration of the relative political positions of the racial groups benefited and harmed by the challenged race-conscious action. In the *Virginia* case, dealing with VMI's males-only admissions policy, he suggested that a principled application of Footnote 4 would result in sex being demoted to a nonsuspect class meriting only rational basis review, rather than what he claimed was the Court's *upward* ratcheting of judicial scrutiny of sex discrimination.

Justice Scalia's dislike of Footnote 4's political process reasoning bubbled up in his concurring opinion in the Michigan case, *Schuette v. Coalition to Defend Affirmative Action*.[108] In response to Justice Sotomayor's dissenting opinion, which relied on Footnote 4 to insist that the Equal Protection Clause prohibited changes in a state's political structure that disfavored minorities, Justice Scalia, in a page and a half of disdainful criticism, attempted to undermine the formal legal status of political process analysis. His attack directly criticized that analysis, describing it as "derived from dictum in a footnote" in an opinion for a four-justice majority.[109] He also criticized the reasoning behind the footnote's "discrete and insular minorities" formula in ways we have touched on earlier. To repeat: Justice Scalia's critique spoke merely for himself and Justice Thomas. But his willingness to explicitly mock Footnote 4 and its underlying analysis speaks volumes about the Court's more general stance toward the footnote and the political process/suspect class analysis it engendered. In a very real way, his willingness to openly criticize that approach simply brings out into the open its more general abandonment by the Court.

* * *

Thus, modern equal protection review finds itself adrift and ad hoc. In the thirty years after the Court handed women their first sex equality victory in *Reed v. Reed*, the Court had found equal protection violations in discrimination suffered by a variety of groups and, indeed, even when the discrimination was not group-based at all. Even though we haven't yet broached the question of Congress's enforcement power, this broadening of equal protection's effective scope would seem, at first blush, to authorize a broader array of enforcement legislation. After all, if equal protection has been held to encompass a broad variety of discrimination, then one would logically expect the enforcement power to authorize federal legislation regulating those same areas.

However, the Court has failed to provide a satisfactory analytical approach explaining this expansion. This chapter has explained how the most promising candidate for such an approach—political process theory based on Footnote 4—has proven incapable of providing courts with an adequate method of approaching equal protection cases. At the very least, the Court's abandonment of that theory, in favor of the more ad hoc approach most recently exemplified in *Windsor*, suggests that the Court itself has lost confidence in that approach, while not embracing any competing alternative.

The result is a wide-ranging equal protection guarantee and thus, presumptively, an enforcement power of equal scope. But that guarantee remains seriously undertheorized. As we will see, the unsettled nature of the Court's approach to equal protection infects the enforcement power. It is against the unsettled backdrop of the Court's equal protection jurisprudence that this book now turns to consider that power.

3

A Historical Introduction to the Enforcement Power

The modern law governing congressional power to enforce the Fourteenth Amendment was stated relatively recently, in the 1997 case *City of Boerne v. Flores*.[1] However, understanding the enforcement power requires that we go back much further than that. Indeed, as with our just-completed short tour of equal protection itself, it requires that we start even before the Fourteenth Amendment was enacted.

The Beginning: Federal Constitutional Limits and the States

Today we are accustomed to thinking that state governments are bound by the Constitution. And, in a technical sense, they always were, in ways that mattered. For example, Article I, after laying out in Section 8 the list of allowable subjects for federal regulation (interstate commerce, naturalization, etc.) and a series of prohibitions to Congress in Section 9, proceeded in Section 10 to enumerate the powers denied to states—for example, the powers to enter into treaties and to coin money. Included in that latter list are what our modern eyes read as rights—to be free of bills of attainder (essentially, laws that expressly single an individual out for punishment), ex post facto laws, and laws impairing contractual obligations—all of which apply to states. Article IV imposed regulations governing states' relations with each other.

But one set of limitations—those contained in the Bill of Rights, enacted shortly after the Constitution itself was ratified—were held not to apply to the states. On reflection this should not be too startling: the amendments that eventually became known as the Bill of Rights were proposed in the first Congress to fulfill a promise the proponents of the new Constitution made to Americans who were suspicious of the new, potentially powerful, central government the Constitution contemplated. The Bill of Rights, it was thought, would ease those fears. Perhaps unsurprisingly, then, Chief Justice Marshall, writing for the Supreme Court in the 1833 case *Barron v. Baltimore*, stated that, while the question of the amendments' application to the states was important, it was not particularly difficult.[2]

Despite the clarity of *Barron*'s holding, the antebellum era continued to feature what Professor Akhil Amar has called "*Barron* contrarians"—lawyers and judges who considered the states bound by the Bill of Rights.[3] As Amar explains, they relied either on textual arguments (which Marshall largely answered in *Barron*) or on claims that the Bill of Rights simply declared the existence of rights that Americans already enjoyed, as a matter either of natural law or, relatedly, the constitutional understandings, both explicit and unwritten, that had developed in England in the centuries after Magna Carta. In our positivist age, we might look askance at an argument that a government was bound to protect a given right when the relevant document, as authoritatively interpreted, failed to impose that obligation. (We're speaking here of the U.S. Constitution; state constitutions protected many—indeed most—of the rights provided in the Bill of Rights.) But courts before the Civil War were much more willing to read such documents as reflecting "the general law" or "principles of natural justice" that limited all republican governments.[4]

Of course, if state constitutions provided rights analogous to those in the Bill of Rights, then the question whether those rights could also be located in the federal constitution might appear somewhat theoretical. Indeed, for the founding generation, which was both highly enamored of local self-government and distrustful of central authority, it would seem appropriate to insist that the new federal government be the entity limited by the Bill of Rights. But by the middle of the nineteenth century, the conflict over slavery had begun to reveal the risks of relying on state law as the only explicit source of such rights.

The crisis over slavery manifested itself in a variety of ways relevant to the protection of fundamental rights. Leave aside the obvious example of the rights deprivations suffered by slaves themselves at the hand of state law; as fundamental a violation of liberty as slavery was, the Constitution accommodated that institution. But even rights the slave system purported to recognize—free persons' rights—came under serious attack in the South as the crisis mounted. Several southern states insisted that northern seamen of color be imprisoned during their time in the state's ports; apparently their very presence threatened the slave system.[5] Indeed, even white persons could not travel to the South and be assured of safety if they attempted to speak out against slavery. When Samuel Hoar, a prominent Massachusetts lawyer, traveled to Charleston, South Carolina, to protest the detention of Massachusetts citizens detained under the black seamen laws, he was compelled to flee under the threat of mob violence. It was a crime in the South to teach slaves to read, even when this education was conducted by ministers in order to allow slaves to read the Bible. Newspapers critical of slavery were banned from the mail in the South. (This particular restriction, by necessarily involving the federal government—which *was* subject to the First Amendment—highlighted the inextricability of the federal government from southern states' repressive policies.)[6] Nor was racism, and its attendant temptations to infringe on rights, limited to the South. For example, in 1859 Oregon sought entry into the Union, under a constitution that denied free persons of color basic civil rights, including the right to hold real estate or invoke the judicial process. Indeed, it even purported to prohibit such persons from settling in the state.

These examples and others like them made it clear to many northerners that states could not necessarily be trusted to protect rights, including those so fundamental as to be included in the Bill of Rights. The question then became the legal basis for federal supervision of states. Congress eventually took the route of imposing new explicit prohibitions on states, via Section 1 of the Fourteenth Amendment, while granting Congress a similarly explicit authority to enforce those prohibitions, via Section 5. However, before examining the drafting of the Fourteenth Amendment and the history of its enforcement provision, it bears taking one last look back at the antebellum era. When we do, we realize that Congress asserted, and the Court validated, an implied congressional power to enforce rights granted elsewhere in the document. In an exceptionally ironic twist, the most prominent example of such enforcement power took the form of federal legislation enforcing slaveholders' rights to recapture their slaves. Throughout the antebellum period the Court upheld and enforced such legislation as within Congress's power, given Article IV's Fugitive Slave Clause. The best known of these cases was the 1842 case *Prigg v. Pennsylvania*.[7] In *Prigg* the Court upheld the Fugitive Slave Act of 1793, including that law's provision of civil penalties against any person who interfered with a slaveholder's right to property in the escaped slave. During Reconstruction Congress relied on *Prigg*'s theory of broad implicit congressional power to enforce constitutional rights to enact enforcement legislation that reflected the Fugitive Slave Act in structure, even while pointing in a diametrically opposite substantive direction.[8]

The Enforcement Power in the Framing Era

Determining the proper understanding of the Fourteenth Amendment presents a challenge that has occupied every generation of legal scholars since 1868. Ultimately, the extent of that amendment's Enforcement Clause necessarily turns on the meaning of the amendment's substantive provisions—one cannot know how far Congress's enforcement power stretches until one knows the scope of the provisions Congress is authorized to enforce. Nevertheless, for now we can bracket the question of the amendment's broader meaning. Eventually, our examination of the enforcement power will have to make assumptions about the amendment's substantive meaning—in particular, the meaning of Section 1, which contains the Privileges or Immunities, Due Process, and Equal Protection Clauses that we immediately think about when we think about the Fourteenth Amendment. The first two chapters of this book told (in a highly abbreviated fashion) the story of equal protection up to the current day. This chapter does the same for the enforcement power. Subsequent chapters reunite these two strands and examine what the enforcement power means today, in light of the Court's current understanding of equal protection.

The Enforcement Power in Congress

The provision that eventually became the Fourteenth Amendment originated when Congressman John Bingham of Ohio proposed an amendment that was reported to Congress by the Joint Committee on Reconstruction in December 1865. That amendment would simply have empowered Congress to enact "all necessary and proper laws to secure to all persons in every State of the Union equal protection in their rights of life, liberty, and property."[9] Bingham's proposal is notable for at least two reasons. First, it includes concepts ("equal protection" and "life, liberty, and property") that eventually appeared in the Equal Protection and Due Process Clauses. Second, it is phrased purely as a grant of power to Congress, rather than as the eventual combination of Section 1's prohibition on state deprivations of rights and Section 5's grant of enforcement power to Congress.

This original draft's focus on congressional enforcement is consistent with Bingham's insistence that states had always been subject to the requirements we now know as due process and equal protection. According to his statements since before the Civil War, the fault of the Constitution lay simply in its failure to grant Congress the power to enforce those restrictions.[10] Bingham was particularly concerned with enacting a constitutional amendment that would support the Civil Rights Act of 1866, an important Reconstruction statute whose aims he supported but which he believed was not authorized by Congress's power to enforce the Thirteenth Amendment's ban on slavery.

Bingham's proposal was amended by the Joint Committee on Reconstruction, which reported out a draft that was quite similar to his original text. But the committee's proposal encountered resistance in Congress and, with Bingham's support, was tabled. However, in the spring of 1866 the Joint Committee again took up the question of an amendment, considering a proposal from another congressman (Robert Dale Owen, the son of the famous English reformer) that took the form of a prohibition on certain state actions coupled with a separate enforcement provision. At the end of that process, in April 1866, Bingham managed to substitute for the Owen version of the proposal the phraseology that we now know as Section 1, which recognized U.S. birthright citizenship and prevented states from abridging citizens' privileges or immunities; depriving persons of life, liberty, or property without due process of law; and denying any person the equal protection of the laws.[11] The package amendment, which also retained versions of Owen's original Sections 2 through 4,[12] now ended with Section 5's current enforcement provision.

As noted earlier, the meanings of "privileges" and "immunities," "due process," and (most relevantly for this book) "the equal protection of the laws" present enormously difficult questions. However, for our current purposes the most important shift is from the original version's character as a pure grant of power to Congress to a self-executing prohibition in Section 1, coupled with an enforcement provision in Section 5. The ultimate reasons for this shift remain open to speculation and scholarly argument, but we can identify some of the concerns motivating members of the Thirty-Ninth Congress. Some objected to the Bingham proposal on the ground that it would authorize Congress to enact a comprehensive legal regime governing liberty and property, with the only limitation being that such laws be equal. This concern flowed from the original proposal's phraseology, which simply authorized Congress to secure persons' equal protection for life, liberty, and property. Some congresspersons suggested that this language was open-ended enough to authorize Congress to intrude on traditional state powers by enacting laws dealing with these rights (e.g., enacting a code of property law), as long as that federal legislation provided those rights equally. This concern would be at least somewhat mitigated by tying congressional power to the "enforcement" of a self-executing and judicially interpreted set of prohibitions on state conduct (e.g., conduct that denied equal protection). In such a case, judicial interpretations of the amendment might cabin the scope of congressional enforcement power.[13]

This new, bifurcated structure provided another, much more concrete benefit in the eyes of its Republican sponsors. Republicans in 1866 worried about the prospect of southern reentry into Congress—indeed, with increased numbers, given the Thirteenth Amendment's obsolescing of the Three-Fifths Clause that had reduced the number of representatives from slave states. This concern provided part of the motivation for Section 2's provision limiting states' representation in Congress to the extent they disenfranchised large groups of persons—the obvious concern being southern disenfranchisement of blacks.

That same concern for the future provided part of the motivation behind splitting Bingham's original proposal into a self-executing guarantee of rights (Section 1) and the enforcement provision (Section 5). Ensuring that the amendment's protections were substantively enshrined in the Constitution, rather than simply authorized if Congress chose to act, helped guarantee against southern attempts to block new protections and repeal old ones when the former Confederate states were readmitted to Congress.

Regardless of the reasons, the shift away from a pure grant of power to Congress and toward a self-executing grant of rights that could be "enforced" by Congress carried serious implications for congressional power. By tethering congressional power to Section 1's prohibition on particular state actions, the amendment's structure at least arguably restricted the enforcement power to directly correcting state misconduct, rather than ensuring the provision of rights.[14] One can make too much of this distinction; indeed, chapter 8 will consider its limits in the context of enforcement legislation that operates not on states but on private parties. Nevertheless, Bingham's original version arguably allowed Congress more enforcement power latitude, by allowing it "to secure" rights by directly providing for their vindication, as opposed to simply enacting remedies when states violate a particular right.

Still, there is great irony in this argument. As noted earlier, a main reason congressional Republicans objected to the simple power grant format of Bingham's original proposal was that it left constitutional rights subject to shifting congressional majorities. Thus, in a real way the new, bifurcated structure was intended to *strengthen* the amendment, by leaving it less susceptible to future Congresses that might be hostile to civil rights.[15] Moreover, to the extent that Reconstruction congresspersons discussed the enforcement power, they generally agreed that it provided Congress the same broad power that it possessed under its Article I power to enact laws "necessary and proper" for executing the powers the rest of Article I provided (such as the power to regulate interstate commerce). The Necessary and Proper Clause had already been construed broadly by 1866, and Reconstruction congresspersons demonstrated their awareness of that broad construction.[16]

Despite these factors militating in favor of a broader understanding of the enforcement power, the Court soon interpreted that power in ways that tethered it closely to Section 1's prohibitions. In particular, it imposed limitations on Congress's ability to enforce those prohibitions—which, to repeat, only applied to states—by regulating private conduct. In the modern era, the Court cabined that power even more, by requiring that even legislation regulating states be "congruent and proportional" to the unconstitutional (state) conduct Congress sought to prevent or deter.

But before turning to these judicial developments, it bears lingering not over the amendment's text and structure but over the first set of enforcement statutes enacted by Congress. Those Reconstruction-era statutes, especially the Civil Rights Act of 1866 (which was reenacted after ratification of the Fourteenth Amendment to place its constitutionality on a firmer footing), the Enforcement Act of 1870, the Ku Klux Klan Act of 1871, and the Civil Rights Act of 1875, are notable for their regulation of private activity.[17] As we shall see when we consider the state action issue in chapter 8, whether the enforcement power allows Congress to regulate private conduct presents a question that is important in its own right. But that question also has a more general importance. If the Enforcement Clause authorizes Congress to do more than simply correct state misconduct,[18] then it might be appropriate to give Section 5 a broader reading more generally—as empowering Congress to go beyond not just Section 1's state action limitation but also courts' interpretations of Section 1's prohibitions.

Reconstruction-Era Judicial Interpretations

Despite the evidence suggesting broad congressional understanding of the enforcement power, as Reconstruction wore on the Supreme Court gave narrow readings both to that power and to legislation enacted under it. As noted in the prior section, much of the Court's retrenchment took the form of an insistence that the enforcement power did not authorize regulation of private parties. For one example, consider the Court's 1875 decision in *United States v. Cruikshank*,[19] where it threw out a federal indictment charging a group of men with violating federal enforcement legislation in connection with a horrific race-based massacre in Louisiana. The Court rejected the indictment's allegation that the defendants had conspired to deprive their victims of the equal protection of the laws. Rebuffing the argument that federal authority extended to ensuring private respect for persons' equal protection rights, the Court wrote, "The only obligation resting upon the United States is to see that the States do not deny the right [to equal protection]. This the amendment guarantees, but no more. The power of the national government is limited to the enforcement of this guaranty."[20]

Eight years later, *The Civil Rights Cases*[21] and *United States v. Harris*[22] applied *Cruikshank*'s statement to strike down legislation that attempted to enforce the Fourteenth Amendment by regulating private conduct. *The Civil Rights Cases* struck down the part of the Civil Rights Act of 1875 that prohibited segregation in public accommodations such as theaters and hotels. *Harris* struck down a law that punished conspiracies to violate others' constitutional rights, without any requirement that the conspirators be state officials. It is possible to read these cases as standing for something less than a rigid ban on Congress using its enforcement power to regulate private conduct—instead, one could read them as turning on the fact that those laws operated even if the state had not abandoned its duty to provide equal protection.[23] Still, the fact remains that those cases have stood as an obstacle to Congress using its enforcement power to regulate private parties.[24] We will return to the state action issue in chapter 8.

These cases reflected the Reconstruction generation's focus on the state action issue.[25] Nevertheless, during this period the Court remained open to aggressive enforcement legislation that targeted obvious state conduct and thus did not implicate that question. Most notably, in cases decided in 1880 it upheld legislation that both allowed removal to federal court of state court cases when a litigant experienced racial discrimination in the state court and fined state officials, including judges, who discriminated based on race when selecting jurors.[26] These decisions are striking, given the degree to which those enforcement statutes intruded into fundamental state prerogatives, such as operating a judicial system. (Indeed, the jury selection case featured federal authorities arresting and holding in custody a state court judge alleged to have engaged in the prohibited discrimination.)[27] It is also notable that these cases explained the enforcement power in terms that hearkened back to the broad "Necessary and Proper" understanding of Congress's enforcement power.[28]

These cases remained as precedents when, nearly a century later, the Court again confronted significant enforcement legislation that did not raise the state action issue. Indeed, they would provide support for the Court's broadest statements about the scope of the enforcement power.

The Enforcement Power in the Twentieth Century

After Reconstruction the enforcement power languished as Congress turned its attention away from civil rights. Congress would not again make aggressive use of its power to enforce any of the Reconstruction Amendments until the "second Reconstruction" of the 1960s.[29] Nevertheless, one case from that era became relevant to modern enforcement power doctrine. *James Everard's Breweries v. Day*[30] considered a federal statute enforcing the Eighteenth Amendment—Prohibition. That amendment was one of several post-Reconstruction amendments to contain an enforcement provision similarly worded to those in the Thirteenth, Fourteenth, and Fifteenth Amendments.[31]

The Court in *James Everard's* gave an expansive construction to Congress's Eighteenth Amendment enforcement power. It concluded that that power granted Congress the wide-ranging discretion it possessed under the Necessary and Proper Clause of Article I, thus adopting the conclusion the Court had earlier reached in construing Congress's cognate powers to enforce the Reconstruction Amendments. Its application of that test was similarly deferential: for example, the Court disclaimed any authority to review the degree to which the law was necessary.[32] Given that deference, the Court had no difficulty upholding the statute's prohibition on manufacturing beer and malt liquors for prescription purposes, given the ease with which such purposes could be used as a subterfuge to manufacture and sell liquor for the beverage purposes the amendment actually prohibited.[33]

The deference exhibited in *James Everard's* is notable for an early twentieth-century Court that, if not as libertarian and suspicious of federal regulation as is sometimes suggested, nevertheless saw its role as carefully constraining governmental power in general and federal power in particular. Still, one can overstate the significance of *James Everard's* for congressional enforcement power more generally. The Eighteenth Amendment addressed a discrete regulatory area. Thus, it did not raise the delicate questions of federalism implicit in the Fourteenth Amendment, which imposed federal restrictions across a wide range of state actions but nevertheless continued to repose significant regulatory power with the states. Moreover, any federalism concerns implicit in Congress's power to enforce the Eighteenth Amendment were mitigated by the fact that its enforcement provision—alone among those cited earlier—gave federal and state governments "concurrent" enforcement power. Nevertheless, the broad dicta in *James Everard's* provided important support when, forty years later, the Court embraced similarly broad congressional power to enforce the Reconstruction Amendments.[34]

By the late 1950s Congress was again ready to take up civil rights. Responding to the rising tide of activism after World War II, Congress enacted a series of civil rights laws, the most important of which were the Civil Rights Act of 1964 and the Voting Rights Act of 1965. While congressional and White House leaders seriously considered basing both of these laws on Congress's power to enforce the Reconstruction Amendments, ultimately, only the VRA was defended primarily as enforcement legislation. (The government continued to argue that the Civil Rights Act was also valid enforcement legislation, but it relied primarily on Congress's power to regulate interstate commerce.) By this time a number of justices on the Warren Court had become amenable to broad congressional power to enforce the Reconstruction Amendments.

The VRA provided the vehicle for the Court to enshrine that willingness into judicial doctrine.

The Voting Rights Act Cases

The Voting Rights Act triggered two landmark enforcement power cases, handed down within several months of each other in 1966. In *South Carolina v. Katzenbach*,[35] the Court considered a challenge to many of the VRA's provisions. In a mostly unanimous opinion, the Court upheld all of the challenged provisions, as appropriate legislation enforcing the Fifteenth Amendment. (The fact that the Court rested its decision on congressional power to enforce the Fifteenth, rather than the Fourteenth, Amendment introduces a note of ambiguity into our analysis; however, for several decades after *South Carolina* it was generally accepted that the same standard applied to federal legislation enforcing both of these amendments.)[36] In particular, the Court, on this issue with one dissenter,[37] upheld the law's most intrusive provisions, requiring that certain jurisdictions get prior federal approval for ("preclear") changes in their voting rules and government structure, to ensure that those changes not diminish minority voting power. The Court recounted the long history of those jurisdictions' restriction of African Americans' voting rights, and their resort to various strategies—from grandfather clauses to "good character" tests to discriminatorily applied literacy tests—to thwart minorities from voting and evade previous court decisions.[38] It noted that challenges to such strategies, even if successful, nevertheless consumed energy and took time, during which elections were held and the denial of voting rights thus successfully perpetrated. The Court reasoned that the preclearance provisions constituted an appropriate response to the possibility that those jurisdictions would continue to implement new evasive strategies, by preventing them from being adopted in the first place.

At first blush, *South Carolina*'s analysis seems straightforward. The Fifteenth Amendment prescribes an unambiguous rule—no racial discrimination in voting—and the challenged VRA provisions aimed to prevent violation of that rule through a set of prophylactic measures. Thus, the Court's upholding of those measures appears simply to reflect its approval of Congress's estimations of the most effective remedies for and deterrents against such violations.

But the Court's approval of Congress's remedial choices carried potentially major implications. The Court expressed that approval by quoting and following the Prohibition enforcement case's statement equating Congress's enforcement power with its broad power under Article I's Necessary and Proper Clause.[39] That formula undoubtedly granted Congress broad powers. Even though the Court had employed that formula for reviewing enforcement legislation for nearly a century, commentators on *South Carolina* nevertheless recognized its importance, in light of Congress's newfound interest in aggressively protecting civil rights. As one prominent scholar observed the year *South Carolina* was decided, "It would be difficult to exaggerate the germinal importance" of the Court's embrace of that broad power.[40]

Nevertheless, in retrospect it appears that the VRA reflected only a relatively modest use of that potentially broad power. To be sure, the preclearance provisions cut deeply into state regulatory prerogatives. But they applied only in jurisdictions where the record of relevant constitutional violations was undisputed; thus, the only real question concerned the appropriateness of the remedies Congress enacted. As we shall see, in the modern era more difficult separation of powers questions would arise when Congress enacted strong remedies for constitutional violations that were less clear-cut.

The other VRA case, *Katzenbach v. Morgan*,[41] centered on a much less central provision of the VRA. But paradoxically, it came to be understood as a much more aggressive statement of congressional enforcement authority. *Morgan* considered Section 4(e) of the VRA, which prohibited states from denying voting rights to persons who had attained a particular grade level of instruction in American-flag schools, even if the school taught in a language other than English. The statutory provision was all but expressly aimed at benefiting Puerto Ricans living in New York City.[42]

Despite its narrow applicability, Section 4(e) raised important conceptual issues about the enforcement power—here, Congress's power to enforce equal protection.[43] The Court had ruled only seven years earlier in a case called *Lassiter v. Northampton County Board of Elections* that English literacy tests for voting did not necessarily violate the Equal Protection Clause.[44] This fact raised the difficult question of how Congress could be "enforcing" that clause by prohibiting a practice that the Court itself had held did not violate it. To be sure, the matter was not quite as stark as that—*Lassiter* had held only that literacy tests *on their face* did not violate the Constitution. Unsurprisingly, then, the parties in *Morgan* dueled over whether New York's literacy law had been motivated by discriminatory purposes, rather than by the purpose of ensuring educated voters that *Lassiter* accepted as a legitimate justification for such restrictions. Indeed, the Court offered as one justification for upholding Section 4(e) the possibility that Congress had determined that the New York law was motivated by "prejudice."[45]

But *Morgan* ventured far beyond that narrow ground and instead offered broader reasons for upholding Section 4(e). First, the Court concluded that the grant of voting rights to Puerto Ricans would assist that community in ensuring equal responsiveness from elected officials—something that the Court reasoned would most effectively flow from being enfranchised. In this sense, then, the constitutional right Section 4(e) enforced was not voting rights per se but rather a distinct right: the right to equal attention and responsiveness from government that flowed from voting power. As we will see, this theory of indirect enforcement of equal protection rights finds a distant echo in recent enforcement power cases. In those later cases, however, the Court was substantially more skeptical of the multistep reasoning supporting the enforcement statute.[46]

Morgan's second rationale was even more expansive. The Court acknowledged that its decision in *Lassiter*, even limited by its facial nature, stood in some tension with Section 4(e). But it stated that Congress had a basis for concluding that literacy tests did in fact violate the Fourteenth Amendment. Even though the Court kept its focus firmly on the particular situation of Spanish language–educated Puerto Ricans in New York, thus avoiding a direct collision with its own earlier acceptance of the facial constitutionality of English literacy tests, this second rationale suggested broad congressional power to engage in independent constitutional interpretation. Justice Brennan tried to cabin that potential by arguing that this congressional power applied only to congressional *expansions* of Court-found rights—an argument that scholars characterized as giving Congress a "one-way ratchet" that authorized Congress to expand Fourteenth Amendment rights but not to contract them.[47] Nevertheless, commentary after *Morgan* recognized its potential for altering the Court-Congress balance.[48]

Justice Harlan, joined by Justice Stewart, dissented. His opinion raises important questions about the power *Morgan* bestowed on Congress and, more generally, about the appropriate roles of Congress and the Court in converting "the majestic generalities"[49] of the Fourteenth Amendment into concrete rules of conduct for states to follow. Justice Harlan insisted that appropriate exercises of the enforcement power could only be triggered by actual violations of the Fourteenth Amendment. In other words, Congress could not "enforce" against an equal protection violation by deciding that a particular practice constituted a violation. Rather, he argued that only courts could identify constitutional violations. He distinguished Section 4(e) from other VRA provisions the Court upheld that same term in *South Carolina* on the ground that those latter provisions remedied racial discrimination in voting—an explicit violation of the Fifteenth Amendment. By contrast, he argued that *Lassiter*'s acceptance of literacy tests rendered New York's test constitutional in the eyes of the Court—a judgment that Congress could not second-guess.

Despite its seeming clarity, Justice Harlan's position raised several difficult questions that would come to plague judicial thinking about the enforcement power. The first, and most fundamental, question is, what exactly constitutes a violation of the Fourteenth Amendment? Justice Harlan's invocation of *South Carolina* presents a clear case: the Fifteenth Amendment prohibits racial discrimination in voting, both Congress and the Court had identified many violations of that prohibition, and thus the Court upheld the VRA's attempts to remedy those violations. Indeed, in his *Morgan* dissent Justice Harlan himself stated the principle that essentially decided that earlier case: "When recognized state violations of federal constitutional standards have occurred, Congress is of course empowered by § 5 to take appropriate remedial measures to redress and prevent the wrongs."[50] But, as chapters 1 and 2 of this book demonstrated, the Fourteenth Amendment—and the Equal Protection Clause in particular—prohibits not a discrete category of conduct that, at least in theory, is easy to identify. Instead, it is a wide-ranging prohibition on arbitrary government classifications of any sort. Justice Harlan recognized this when he identified the relevant question in *Morgan* as "whether a state . . . statute is so arbitrary or irrational as to offend the command of the Equal Protection Clause."[51]

In Justice Harlan's view, that question was answered in the context of Section 4(e) by *Lassiter*'s upholding of the facial validity of literacy tests. Yet that conclusion just raises more questions. For example, what if a particular state's literacy test—or, indeed, a particular official's application of a particular state's literacy test—was motivated not by the legitimate concerns for ensuring educated voters the Court recognized in *Lassiter* but instead by animus against a particular group? Justice Harlan recognized the possibility that the situation Section 4(e) addressed did in fact reflect such invidious discrimination. But his response was that Congress had not amassed an evidentiary record demonstrating that New York's literacy test could be so characterized. Indeed, he recognized the crucial role that facts played in making determinations about equal protection: "Decisions on questions of equal protection and due process are based not on abstract logic, but on empirical foundations. To the extent 'legislative facts' are relevant to a judicial determination, Congress is well equipped to investigate them, and such determinations are of course entitled to due respect."[52] But he found no such record supporting Section 4(e).

Thus, Justice Harlan's disagreement with the majority ends up being relatively narrow. Taking him at his word, if Congress had developed a sufficient factual record detailing a prejudice-based motivation for New York's law, then he might have voted to uphold Section 4(e). But consider how fundamental the stakes are for Justice Harlan. For him, *Morgan* implicated the fundamental division of power between Congress and the Court, with the latter entrusted with sole authority to declare constitutional meaning. Yet his analysis suggests that the case comes down, at least in large part, to a question of congressional fact-finding.[53] Indeed, the majority appeared to agree: Justice Brennan's majority opinion explained its decision to defer to Congress's constitutional judgment based in part on empirical facts, such as the availability of Spanish-language news sources in New York that made Spanish-speaking New Yorkers just as educated about public issues as their English-speaking neighbors.[54]

Let's think about the implications of that last conclusion. If the requirement that Congress develop an adequate factual record is all that stands between it and the ability to second-guess the Court's interpretation of the Constitution, then fundamental separation of powers lines between the two institutions appear far less substantial than might appear at first glance. This is especially true when such interpretations turn, in Justice Harlan's words, "not on abstract logic, but on empirical foundations." On the one hand, as he explained, congressional competence in fact-finding may tilt the power balance in favor of congressional power, given the role facts play in uncovering constitutional meaning. By analogous logic, it should follow that special conditions of judicial *incompetence* to apply its own constitutional rules also suggest increased congressional power. As we will see in the next chapter, this insight will have major implications for the modern enforcement power.

The Enforcement Power between the VRA Cases and *Boerne*

In the three decades between *Morgan* and the 1997 decision in *Boerne* announcing the congruence and proportionality test that courts apply today, the Court decided several other enforcement power cases that merit mention for their impact on modern law. Two years after *Morgan*, the Court in *Jones v. Alfred A. Mayer Co.*[55] upheld a key provision the Civil Rights Act of 1866, granting "all citizens of the United States . . . the same right . . . to inherit, purchase, lease, sell, hold, and convey real and personal property,"[56] as legislation enforcing the Thirteenth Amendment ban on slavery. Readers may notice the irony in that holding: it was in part because of concerns about the Thirteenth Amendment's foundation for that statute that the Thirty-Ninth Congress began work on what became the Fourteenth Amendment. Nevertheless, *Jones* accorded a broad meaning to congressional power to enforce the Thirteenth Amendment, even though it expressed at least some doubt about the scope of the amendment itself.[57] It stated that, whatever Section 1's self-executing ban on slavery might mean, Section 2's Enforcement Clause gave Congress "the power to pass all laws necessary and proper for abolishing all badges and incidents of slavery."[58] *Jones* concluded that such "badges and incidents" included private refusals to engage in contractual relations with others on the basis of race, which the Civil Rights Act was read to prohibit.[59]

The Court's analysis has struck commentators as potentially allowing Congress to interpret the Thirteenth Amendment. On this theory, the Court allowed Congress to define "slavery" to include its "badges and incidents," which in turn Congress had broad power to combat.[60] In that case, *Jones* could be read as reaffirming *Morgan*'s suggestion from two years earlier that Congress's power to enforce the Reconstruction Amendments included the power to legislate its own understanding of those amendments' meaning. Alternatively, *Jones* could be read as simply granting Congress broad remedial power to implement a command that the Court may believe exists in Section 1, but which may be too difficult for the Court to vindicate on its own. Under this reading, the Court itself has done the interpretive work of equating "slavery" with its "badges and incidents," leaving Congress only with the power to implement that Court-stated meaning.

This distinction may seem highly metaphysical. But, as we've already seen, it means a lot whether Congress has the authority to interpret the Constitution or merely to enforce the Court's interpretation. That distinction is especially important when it comes to equal protection. The exceptional breadth and vagueness of the Equal Protection Clause means that a congressional power to interpret that guarantee would give Congress significantly more power than a power merely to enforce judicially stated rules. *Jones*, while certainly not clear on this point, at least suggests that, in the closely related Thirteenth Amendment context, the Court was open to that broader congressional power.

Two years after *Jones* the Court issued a rare (for this era) decision striking down an enforcement statute. *Oregon v. Mitchell*[61] involved the 1970 amendments to the Voting Rights Act. Most notably for our purposes, it considered provisions that ensured eighteen-year-olds' right to vote in both state and national elections. The Court gave a deeply fractured answer to the question whether those provisions were constitutional. In a five-justice majority expressed through two separate opinions the Court held that Congress could extend the vote to eighteen-year-olds in elections for *federal* office. However, a different five-justice majority rejected Congress's attempt to extend the franchise to eighteen-year-olds in elections for *state* office. In rejecting the Enforcement Clause argument, the three opinions making up this latter majority (solo opinions by Justices Black and Harlan, and an opinion by Justice Stewart for three justices) agreed that the Fourteenth Amendment did not speak to the type of voting discrimination targeted by the statute. Of those three opinions, Justice Harlan's provided the most detailed analysis. He carefully reviewed the history of the Fourteenth Amendment and concluded that the Reconstruction generation simply could not have understood Section 1 as covering voting rights.[62] Justices Black and Stewart came to similar, though not identical, conclusions.[63]

One way to express this conclusion is that the Fourteenth Amendment's scope, or "jurisdiction," did not sweep sufficiently broadly to make the federal law "appropriate" enforcement legislation.[64] As we shall see, this "jurisdictional" approach to the enforcement power would not be available when the modern Court considered challenges to legislation enforcing equal protection—ironically, due to the Court's own expansive understanding of the Equal Protection Clause's "jurisdiction."

Six years after *Oregon*, in *Fitzpatrick v. Bitzer*,[65] the Court held that the enforcement power authorized Congress to provide for retrospective relief, such as back pay and damages awards against states. *Fitzpatrick* thus upheld such remedies provided in amendments to the Civil Rights Act of 1964 that extended the 1964 law to cover state government employers. The *Fitzpatrick* Court proceeded on the assumption that those amendments constituted valid enforcement legislation,[66] and focused instead on whether the enforcement power authorized the retrospective remedies the plaintiffs sought.

Fitzpatrick's implicit approval of the challenged statute's enforcement power foundation became relevant in the *Boerne* litigation because of how the statute *Fitzpatrick* interpreted related to the Fourteenth Amendment. In addition to authorizing retrospective relief such as back pay awards, the 1964 act also dispensed with the requirement that plaintiffs prove that the employer acted with discriminatory intent when it discriminated on the forbidden ground (e.g., race or sex).[67] This fact was significant because, only three weeks before deciding *Fitzpatrick*, the Court had held that such intent *was* required when a plaintiff sued directly under the Equal Protection Clause itself.[68] Thus, it appeared that the enforcement legislation sustained in *Fitzpatrick* had dispensed with the constitutional requirement that a state government employee claiming job discrimination prove discriminatory intent—a requirement the Court had just held constituted part of the law of the Fourteenth Amendment. In other words, in *Fitzpatrick* the Court upheld Fourteenth Amendment enforcement legislation that imposed a broader liability rule than that required by the Fourteenth Amendment itself. As we will see, this aspect of *Fitzpatrick* became an important issue in *Boerne*.

The relationship between Congress's enforcement power and the Reconstruction Amendments' discriminatory intent requirements, only implicit in *Fitzpatrick*, took center stage four years later, in *City of Rome v. United States.*[69] *Rome* concerned the scope of Congress's power to enforce the Fifteenth Amendment—a power that, as noted earlier in this chapter, is expressed through an identically worded enforcement provision in that amendment that has been interpreted identically to its Fourteenth Amendment analogue. It considered the constitutionality of Voting Rights Act provisions that required federal "preclearance," or prior approval, of state actions that only had discriminatory *effects* on minority voting rights, rather than being motivated by discriminatory *purposes*. The case dealt with, among other things, plans by the City of Rome, Georgia, to annex surrounding areas that were populated predominantly by whites. The lower court found that those annexations, while not undertaken for the purpose of diluting black voting strength, would nevertheless have that effect; on that ground, it held that they were subject to the preclearance requirement. Before the Supreme Court, the city argued that the Fifteenth Amendment's Enforcement Clause did not authorize Congress to regulate state actions that only had such discriminatory effects.

The Court's consideration of this issue was sharpened considerably by the fact that, the very same day the Court decided *Rome*, it also decided a case holding that the Fifteenth Amendment itself only prohibited actions undertaken with a discriminatory purpose.[70] Thus the question implicit in *Fitzpatrick* was sharply presented in *Rome*: If, as the Court had held that very day, a constitutional antidiscrimination provision itself prohibits only actions taken with discriminatory motives, may Congress nevertheless enact an enforcement statute that prohibits actions where such motivations need not be proven, but instead which "merely" create discriminatory effects?

The Court's answer was a clear "yes." Citing *Morgan* and *South Carolina*, the Court concluded that, in jurisdictions with a history of racial discrimination in voting (the only jurisdictions subject to the VRA provisions challenged in *Rome*), it was proper for Congress to prohibit government actions that had discriminatory effects on minority voting rights. In the Court's view, such legislation was justified because the prohibited actions, when taken by governments that historically had violated the Fifteenth Amendment, raise the risk of purposeful discrimination.[71] One way to understand this analysis is that the Court viewed the enforcement legislation as a rule of evidence—that is, an evidentiary presumption that bad intent lurked behind many facially neutral government actions that exhibited "only" discriminatory effects.[72] Another way of conceptualizing this idea is that Congress, like fishermen, can cast a wider net than strictly necessary in order to catch the fish it is going after.

While an environmentalist might be concerned about real fishermen casting such wider nets and thereby harming the broader ecosystem, Congress, within limits, can enact enforcement legislation that catches "innocent fish" in its search for its real target. (Again, though, it is possible that many seemingly "innocent fish" are actually just hiding their guilt.)[73]

However one conceptualizes such legislation, the important fact is that both *Fitzpatrick* and *Rome* allowed Congress to use its enforcement power to prohibit constitutionally innocent actions—that is, actions lacking the provable bad motive the Court had identified as a prerequisite to finding a constitutional violation. These cases thus continued to expand the allowable space for enforcement legislation that prescribed rules that went beyond Court-stated constitutional meaning. The cases can be explained in different ways: as resting on Congress's power to reach its own constitutional interpretations, its fact-finding power, or, as in *Rome*, its power to prescribe conclusive evidentiary presumptions. Regardless of the analytical lens through which one viewed such legislation, the important fact is that during this period, as long as Congress was protecting a right that the Court had recognized was within the scope (or "jurisdiction") of the relevant amendment, the Court was willing to grant Congress significant latitude to prohibit more conduct than the Constitution itself did. However, as we shall see, in *Boerne* the Court, concerned about Congress's aggressive use of the enforcement power, cabined that latitude.

The Road to *Boerne*

The Court decided other enforcement power cases between *South Carolina* in 1966 and *Boerne*, the case establishing the modern rule for the enforcement power, in 1997, but the cases discussed here provide the template for that power as the Court approached that latter watershed case. *South Carolina* accorded significant deference to Congress in the course of upholding aggressive enforcement legislation designed to remedy states' acknowledged constitutional violations. *Morgan*—controversially—upheld Congress's power to decide for itself when state conduct violates equal protection. *Jones* arguably gave a similarly broad reading to congressional power to enforce the Thirteenth Amendment. By contrast, in *Oregon* the Court split badly on the foundational question whether the Fourteenth Amendment spoke to the type of discrimination the enforcement legislation targeted.

Fitzpatrick, while not explicitly deciding the issue, has come to be understood as upholding enforcement legislation that dispensed with the constitutional requirement that a state government employee claiming unconstitutional discrimination prove discriminatory intent. *Rome* reinforced this conception of the enforcement power, in the context of legislation enforcing the Fifteenth Amendment. As such, these two cases reflect the distinct yet overlapping justifications for enforcement legislation the Court validated in the 1966 VRA cases. In one sense, their approval of Congress's abrogation of the discriminatory intent requirement reflects the statutes' character as remedial—essentially, making it easier for plaintiffs to obtain judicial relief for unconstitutional state action. In this sense, they reflected the Court's analysis in *South Carolina*. But that same abrogation can also be understood as altering the underlying constitutional rule, which, after all, prohibits only *intentional* discrimination. The muddiness of the distinction between remedial and substantive legislation would continue to dog enforcement power doctrine—indeed, it would become the main issue in enforcement power cases after *Boerne*.

Together, these cases formed the backdrop for the Court's enforcement power doctrine as *Boerne* loomed. *Boerne* considered the enforcement power foundation for the Religious Freedom Restoration Act (RFRA), enacted in 1993 by a huge bipartisan majority in response to the Court's 1990 decision in *Employment Division v. Smith*.[74] In *Smith* the Court, all but reversing decades of precedent, held that most generally applicable restrictions on conduct did not violate the clause of the First Amendment guaranteeing free religious exercise. For example, using the facts of *Smith* itself, a law restricting drug use could not be challenged as infringing the religious freedom of members of Native American churches whose ceremonies included ritual ingestion of banned substances, as long as that law did not single out religiously motivated uses of drugs.

For several decades before *Smith*, the Court had often insisted that even such generally applicable laws must satisfy heightened judicial scrutiny if their effect was to impair religious exercise.[75] Writing for six justices in *Smith*, Justice Scalia criticized that approach as allowing every person to become "a law unto himself," authorized to violate otherwise valid laws as long as that violation was motivated by religious belief. While Justice Scalia did not overrule the scattering of earlier cases that found such general laws to violate the Free Exercise Clause, he distinguished them (unconvincingly, in the eyes of many) by arguing that in each such case the plaintiff had joined his Free Exercise Clause claim to another constitutional rights claim.

Smith was politically unpopular, on both the left and the right. Responding to that broad-based political outcry, Congress enacted RFRA, which prohibited any government action[76] that "substantially burdened" a person's religious exercise unless that action was proven to be "the least restrictive means" for attaining "a compelling government interest."[77] Congress did not make these terms up. Instead, these latter two concepts—least restrictive means and compelling government interest—effectively make up the stringent doctrinal test called "strict scrutiny," which is used to review government action that either infringes on a fundamental right or discriminates on the basis of a suspect classification.[78]

RFRA's mandate that courts apply "the most demanding test known to constitutional law"[79] reveals the stakes that statute posed for the enforcement power. Its use of such judicial tools as the statute's liability standard, and its insistence that courts use those tools in particular circumstances, suggested that Congress was seeking to wrest away from the Court the power to interpret the Constitution. That suspicion was heightened by the findings Congress included in RFRA, which the *Boerne* Court was careful to quote. Those findings spoke to the framers' recognition of religious freedom as "an unalienable right," concluded that neutral laws might burden religion as much as laws targeting religion directly, accused *Smith* of "virtually eliminat[ing]" the requirement that government justify neutral laws that impose such burdens, and concluded that the pre-*Smith* doctrine was a "workable" means of accommodating religious liberty and governmental needs.[80] Congress then announced its purpose in RFRA as, among other things, to "restore" the doctrinal test used before *Smith* and to ensure its use "in all cases where free exercise of religion is substantially burdened"—not only in situations featuring the joining together of two rights claims Justice Scalia described in his *Smith* opinion. These findings and statements of purpose suggest that Congress disagreed with *Smith* as a matter of constitutional law, and insisted on its own prerogative to "restore" the constitutional test it thought was "workable" and consistent with the framers' intentions. So understood, RFRA posed a stark challenge to the Court's supremacy in declaring constitutional meaning.

But it was not obvious that such a challenge was doomed. Most obviously, *Morgan* suggested that Congress enjoyed at least some latitude to reach its own independent conclusions about what the Constitution required. Other enforcement power cases also supported RFRA's constitutionality. Recall *Fitzpatrick* and *Rome*. Both of those cases upheld enforcement legislation that dispensed with constitutional requirements that discrimination plaintiffs prove discriminatory intent. Those precedents provided powerful support for RFRA. After all, by requiring that any government action substantially burdening religion meet a particular test, all RFRA did was dispense with the same intent requirement that those earlier statutes did.[81]

Indeed, three years after *Smith*—and, tantalizingly, only a few months before RFRA's enactment—the Court inadvertently buttressed the argument for

RFRA by, on its own accord, applying strict scrutiny to a statute that the Court concluded targeted religious rituals. The case—*Church of the Lukumi v. City of Hialeah*[82]—was unusual: a Florida city enacted an ordinance restricting the killing of animals, but the ordinance contained so many exceptions and carve-outs that it was hard to deny that it aimed solely at prohibiting the animal sacrifice rituals of a small Caribbean religion whose adherents had settled in that area. When confronted with a statute that clearly targeted religious practice (unlike Oregon's generally applicable, nondiscriminatory drug law at issue in *Smith*), a unanimous Court had no qualms concluding that strict scrutiny was the appropriate test—which, unsurprisingly, the ordinance failed.

Lukumi tightened the analogy between RFRA and the laws upheld in *Fitzpatrick* and *Rome*. In all three cases, all the enforcement statute did was wipe away the intent requirement. Indeed, *Lukumi* seemed to place RFRA on even a stronger footing, since RFRA's abrogation of the intent requirement was followed by its command that courts apply strict scrutiny—the standard the Court itself (in *Lukumi*) held was appropriate in cases where that requirement was satisfied.

Still, even if "all" those statutes accomplished was to wipe away the intent requirement, that's still a lot—such legislation constitutes a strong antidiscrimination remedy. But previous enforcement cases also featured aggressive remedies. Most notably, the VRA preclearance provisions upheld in *South Carolina* cut deeply into state sovereign prerogatives. That ruling provided an answer to RFRA's critics who argued that RFRA's severe restrictions on government action rendered it an unconstitutional intrusion into those same prerogatives.

But if the argument for RFRA's constitutionality was strong, so was the argument against it. As noted earlier, the law's findings and stated purpose made it clear that Congress intended the law as a rebuff to the Court's decision in *Smith*. Indeed, RFRA constituted a stronger rebuff to *Smith* than Section 4(e) of the VRA (which *Morgan* upheld) constituted to *Lassiter*. In upholding Section 4(e) (the Spanish language voter provision), *Morgan* speculated simply that Congress found the New York voter literacy law unconstitutional. That suggestion presented less than a full-on challenge to the Court's equal protection doctrine, which in *Lassiter* had found such literacy tests *facially* valid, thus leaving room for a conclusion that, *as applied*, any given state's test might still be unconstitutional. By contrast, RFRA applied generally to every instance of government action imposing a substantial burden on religion. As such, its insistence that courts apply strict scrutiny to such action squarely collided with *Smith*'s decision rejecting use of that test every time government substantially burdened religious exercise.

In addition to that separation of powers–based concern, RFRA also raised serious federalism issues. Its applicability to any state government action that had the effect of substantially burdening religion meant that it would apply across a limitless variety of government actions, from restrictions on alcohol and drug consumption, such as the drug law in *Smith*, to everyday zoning restrictions. *Boerne* itself concerned a zoning dispute, in which a Catholic parish wished to demolish part of its church located in a historic district but ran afoul of historic preservation rules.[83] In *Oregon v. Mitchell*,[84] the Court held that federalism concerns prevented Congress from requiring by statute that eighteen-year-olds be allowed to vote in state elections. While zoning prerogatives perhaps do not rise to the level of centrality to a state government's identity as its voting rules, such ordinary, local, regulatory decisions constitute the bread and butter of state and local regulatory authority. RFRA's breadth, applying to all such decisions, was therefore potentially troubling. This was particularly true given that the statute required that such government action satisfy strict scrutiny's demanding requirements.

One last point requires consideration before moving to the Court's decision in *Boerne*. That case did not arise in a vacuum. By the mid-1990s the Rehnquist Court was in the middle of implementing its federalism revolution—a series of cases that redefined the federal-state balance, and the Court's role in policing that balance. Before the 1990s it had been settled law for half a century that Congress's regulatory power was effectively unlimited. Congress had utilized its Article I power to regulate interstate commerce to regulate activities as disparate (and, at least superficially, as local) as small-scale loan-sharking, racial discrimination in small, rural restaurants, and even how much wheat a farmer could grow for his own personal consumption.

Along with this wide berth for federal regulation, by the late 1980s the Court had settled on a rule that left to Congress itself the decision when it was appropriate to regulate not just local activities but state governments themselves. There were limits: even the Court's most generous statements of congressional power under the Commerce Clause recognized some role for judicial review, even if it was only at the margins. And, as discussed earlier in this chapter, the Court did reject a component of an enforcement statute in *Oregon v. Mitchell*. But those limits seemed to count for little as a practical matter, especially when compared with the broad swaths of regulatory areas the Court had opened up to federal supervision.

This all started to change in the 1990s. The replacement of Thurgood Marshall by Clarence Thomas completed a thin but durable majority coalition that sought to rein in federal power and reassert the Court's role as an umpire between Congress and the states. Starting in 1992 the Court decided a series of cases that recast the federal-state balance. Over the course of the subsequent five years, the Court reduced federal power to regulate states themselves, increased the force of states' sovereign immunity, and cut back on federal regulatory power over private parties on matters traditionally regulated by states. By 1997 the Court had decided cases on all of these issues. Thus, it was primed to consider pruning one of the few remaining sources of significant federal power that had remained untouched up to that point: the enforcement power.

The Decision in *Boerne*

The federalism cases discussed in the previous paragraph had for the most part been sharply split five-to-four decisions.[85] But the Court's decision in *Boerne,* striking down RFRA, was six to three, with at least one and potentially two of the nonjoining justices expressing agreement with the Court's enforcement power analysis, and the third expressing no opinion. The Court's relative consensus in *Boerne* suggests that that case implicated something more than federalism. That something more was the separation of powers concerns that RFRA raised.

Justice Kennedy's opinion for the Court focused heavily on the separation of powers. Indeed, as he canvassed the enactment history of the Fourteenth Amendment, he emphasized the separation of powers aspect even when, as he conceded, the amendment's federalism implications overshadowed those concerns in the minds of the members of the Thirty-Ninth Congress.[86] Of course, Justice Kennedy had to deal with *Morgan*'s suggestion that Congress enjoyed power to interpret the Constitution. He finessed that suggestion, stating that even this more aggressive rationale for upholding Section 4(e) "rested on unconstitutional discrimination by New York,"[87] while ignoring the key question of who (Congress or the Court) had made that determination. He was on somewhat stronger ground when he noted that *Morgan*'s result rested on two rationales, only the broader of which implied an independent congressional power to interpret the Constitution. The existence of these two rationales allowed him to affirm that precedent as validly resting on the narrower one.

With *Morgan*'s broader rationale brushed out of the way, Justice Kennedy then turned to whether RFRA validly enforced the Due Process Clause (the Fourteenth Amendment provision through which the Free Exercise Clause was "incorporated" to apply to the states).[88] So incorporated, the Free Exercise Clause unquestionably applied to the states and just as unquestionably guaranteed religious freedom. Thus, he could not argue, as Justice Harlan had in *Oregon,* that the challenged enforcement statute regulated an area the Fourteenth

Amendment simply did not address. Instead, Justice Kennedy had to decide whether RFRA was appropriately tailored in enforcing an obligation—to respect free religious exercise—that undeniably applied against the states.

At this point, he encountered the argument we noted earlier, that RFRA simply erased the discriminatory intent requirement imposed by *Smith* with regard to religious freedom, just as earlier enforcement statutes had abrogated the analogous requirement with regard to racial discrimination. This was in many ways the key point of the opinion. This was where Justice Kennedy confronted *Rome*'s and (implicitly) *Fitzpatrick*'s approval of other enforcement legislation that, at least in theory, did no less than what RFRA did.

It was at this point that Justice Kennedy made his crucial move. He insisted that remedial measures must be "congruent and proportional" to the targeted harms.[89] He then applied this requirement by comparing RFRA unfavorably to the VRA with regard to the record of unconstitutional discrimination Congress had uncovered. He concluded that while the Congress enacting RFRA had uncovered instances of generally applicable laws burdening religion (e.g., autopsies performed in violation of religious beliefs), that record lacked examples of laws enacted out of religious bigotry—the only type of law that violated the Free Exercise Clause, at least as Justice Kennedy read *Smith*.[90] Thus, his primary response to the *Fitzpatrick*/*Rome* analogy was to fault the lack of a factual record made by Congress about the existence of underlying constitutional violations. Just as Justice Harlan had done in his *Morgan* dissent, Justice Kennedy demarcated the line between congressional enforcement of the Constitution and congressional interpretation of the Constitution by reference to the state of the factual record Congress amassed.

Justice Kennedy also concluded that RFRA's scope was simply too broad. Quoting *Rome*, he acknowledged that "[p]reventive measures prohibiting certain types of laws may be appropriate when there is reason to believe that many of the laws affected by the congressional enactment have a significant likelihood of being unconstitutional."[91] *Rome* allowed him to make that argument: recall that the VRA provisions at issue in that case applied only to jurisdictions that had a history of unconstitutional conduct. But RFRA, he said, was not confined to situations where such a risk appeared. Unlike the VRA's most stringent remedies, RFRA applied across the nation and across the board to every species of everyday government action, such as the zoning decision at issue in *Boerne* itself. In two other unfavorable comparisons to the VRA's preclearance provisions, he noted that those provisions both contained a "bailout" provision allowing a covered jurisdiction to escape the law's requirements if it demonstrated respect for minority voting rights, and, as originally enacted, had to be renewed after seven years.

Justice Kennedy then supplemented his complaint about RFRA's breadth with one about its depth—that is, the strictness of its liability rule. He noted that RFRA's least restrictive means/compelling government interest requirement was the strictest test known to constitutional law. Hearkening back to Justice Scalia's opinion in *Smith,* he suggested that application of that test would "open the prospect of [legally] required religious exemptions from civic obligations of almost every conceivable kind."[92] Returning again to the lack of a congressional record demonstrating the existence of unconstitutional discrimination, he concluded that this type of burden "far exceed[ed] any pattern or practice of unconstitutional conduct under the Free Exercise Clause as interpreted in *Smith.*"[93]

In sum, RFRA failed Enforcement Clause scrutiny because, while enforcing a right that was recognized by the Fourteenth Amendment, it was out of proportion to either that right (as the Court defined it) or the violations of it that Congress had identified. *Boerne* thus established a new template for Enforcement Clause scrutiny. Before *Boerne,* the only enforcement legislation to have failed judicial review in the modern era was the state voting rights law in *Oregon.* But that law, as understood by the Court, regulated an area that was simply beyond the scope—beyond what we have called "the jurisdiction"—of the Fourteenth Amendment. By contrast, RFRA *did* seek to enforce a recognized Fourteenth Amendment right. Indeed, it did so in a way (by removing *Smith*'s discriminatory intent requirement) that reflected earlier enforcement legislation the Court had upheld.

The conceptual challenge posed by RFRA's protection of a judicially recognized Fourteenth Amendment right required the Court to probe the statute more deeply, to determine whether Congress's protection of that right crossed a metaphysical line from congressional enforcement of the Constitution to congressional interpretation. As noted earlier, the Court located RFRA on the wrong side of that line, based on Congress's inadequate record of government actions taken because of hostility to religion.

To be sure, *Boerne*'s scrutiny of Congress's legislative record and its application of proportionality review were not completely novel, if one looks hard enough at the precedent cases. At least on one reading, *South Carolina*'s upholding of the VRA's core provisions rested on the record of Fifteenth Amendment violations racked up by southern governments. Similarly, *Rome* upheld the VRA's "effects" test because of the risk that government actions creating discriminatory voting effects reflected hidden discriminatory motivations.

But, at least in retrospect, those cases were easy. The covered jurisdictions' record of Fifteenth Amendment violations in *South Carolina* was so plain that the Court hardly needed to refer to Congress's record: indeed, as it noted, all it had to do was look through its own opinions. Similarly, the VRA provisions challenged in *Rome* again applied only to states that had a demonstrated record of voting rights violations: in such jurisdictions, it was easy to suspect that changes with bad effects on minority voting power likely featured discriminatory intent. Thus, these cases arguably featured legislation that rested, respectively, on a record of solid facts demonstrating its need or a self-evident connection between the statute's liability rule and the underlying constitutional violation.

Boerne is notable because the Court scrutinized the record and that asserted connection more carefully. This more careful scrutiny may have been driven by several factors. The Court may have simply had an intuition that, unlike the jurisdictions covered by the VRA, the fifty states as a group were not guilty of widespread animus toward religion. The Court's unfavorable comparison of RFRA's broad reach with the VRA's more narrow geographic and temporal scope may suggest that it thought RFRA was too broadly (and perhaps sloppily) drafted. Or the Court may have simply been offended at Congress's direct criticism of the *Smith* decision, and anxious to cement its own interpretive superiority when it and Congress expressed diametrically opposed views on constitutional law.

Was *Boerne* Correct?

As one might expect of a case that carried such heavy implications for federalism, separation of powers, and individual rights, *Boerne* has been controversial among scholars. Much of that scholarship has been careful and nuanced, for example, arguing that the Court reached the correct result but for the wrong reasons.[94] A similarly careful evaluation of *Boerne*'s correctness here would consume many pages—pages that this book project has elected to spend explaining how best to live with *Boerne* rather than critiquing it.

Still, a few words are appropriate about the correctness of this watershed decision. First, as a historical matter it is hard to see how the congruence and proportionality standard easily jibes with the Thirty-Ninth Congress's understanding that the Enforcement Clause gave Congress the same wide-ranging power granted by Article I's Necessary and Proper Clause. To be sure, that latter power—and, by extension, Congress's Enforcement Clause power—may have always been understood as somewhat narrower than is sometimes thought. That proposition is highly controversial and itself requires much analysis. But even if both of those powers are more limited than commonly understood, it still seems jarring for the Court to put Congress to the test of its facts, to the extent *Boerne* did when it questioned RFRA's fact-finding record.

On the other hand, one can understand the Court's problem. Fourteenth Amendment rights have flowered enormously since 1868. In particular, equal protection has blossomed into a wide-ranging guarantee of equal government treatment. Indeed, as chapter 2 demonstrated, the Court has expanded equal protection's "jurisdiction" far beyond concern for racial equality on matters of fundamental juridical rights such as contract and property rights and equal access to the judicial process. Today, the Equal Protection Clause mandates equality for all groups (and, indeed, individuals without any particular group affiliation), across the entire range of government action. If Congress enjoys the near-limitless power under the Enforcement Clause that some readings of the Necessary and Proper Clause give it, to ensure that states act equally anytime they classify—that is, almost anytime they act—then the enforcement power has become broad indeed.

Of course, *Boerne* did not involve an equal protection right. Still, if the question is the proper scope of the enforcement power as a general matter, the wide-ranging character of *any* judge-found Fourteenth Amendment right might be enough to signal caution when considering the scope of that power. When one adds to the mix the possibility of Congress all but defying the Court on the meaning of core constitutional terms, and seeking, as Congress seems to have done in *Morgan,* to vindicate its own interpretation by use of its fact-finding power, one can perhaps understand why both conservatives and liberals signed on to *Boerne*'s pushback.

Regardless of the reasons, the Court's analysis in *Boerne* suggested that it would not obligingly defer to Congress when considering enforcement legislation enforcing a constitutional right that was not self-evidently being broadly violated. Instead, Congress would have to demonstrate both the existence of such violations and the proportionality between such violations and the challenged enforcement statute. The outlines of these requirements were visible in *Boerne.* But they became even clearer over the next decade.

PART II

Where We Are Now

The Enforcement Power in Today's Court

4

The Modern Enforcement Power

Principles and Paradoxes

Regardless of what one thinks of its merits, the Court's opinion in *Boerne* gave every indication that it reflected the Supreme Court's consensus view about the scope of Congress's enforcement power. Six justices from across the Court's ideological spectrum, from Justices Stevens and Ginsburg on the left to Justices Scalia and Thomas on the right, joined the opinion.[1] Of the remaining three justices, one and possibly two were sympathetic to the majority's analysis of Congress's enforcement power: Justice O'Connor expressed explicit support for it, and Justice Breyer suggested his partial agreement. Justice Souter refrained from expressing an opinion.

In retrospect, this unusually broad consensus was probably doomed, given the Court's sharp divisions (then and now) about the scope of congressional power. Recall from the last chapter's discussion of the lead-up to *Boerne* that the 1990s witnessed a campaign by the Court's five more conservative justices to rein in federal regulatory power. Those justices' concern for policing the federal-state balance focused particularly on federal regulation of the states themselves. The four more liberal justices on the Court consistently resisted such cutbacks on federal power.[2] *Boerne* may have gained the support of both liberals and conservatives because of RFRA's direct challenge not to the federal-state balance but to the Court's own role in interpreting the Constitution. But in later cases applying the *Boerne* standard, the federalism dynamic appears to have resurfaced, and with it the Court's preexisting divisions on that issue.

After *Boerne* I: The Centrality of Judicial Doctrine

Soon after *Boerne* the Court's familiar liberal-conservative divide reappeared, now on the question of how to properly apply the congruence and proportionality standard to equality-enforcing legislation.[3] An early fault line concerned the role of judicial doctrine in identifying the constitutional wrong Congress had authority to target with enforcement legislation. In 2000 the Court decided *Kimel v. Board of Regents*,[4] which considered the constitutionality of the Age Discrimination in Employment Act (ADEA) as legislation enforcing the equal protection right to be free of state government employment discrimination based on age. As with many cases that would come after it, *Kimel* involved a statute whose application to states was unquestionably valid under the Commerce Clause. However, because in those cases the plaintiffs sought damages, back pay, or other types of retrospective relief, their claims required the Court to consider the statute's enforcement power foundation, since the Commerce Clause had been held not to authorize Congress to provide for such relief.

In *Kimel*, the five-justice majority that throughout the 1990s had pushed for tighter limits on federal regulatory power held that the ADEA exceeded Congress's enforcement power. Importantly, the majority's analysis relied heavily on the Court's own equal protection doctrine when determining the scope of the constitutional violation the ADEA purported to target. In particular, the Court observed that its suspect class jurisprudence had identified age discrimination as a nonsuspect classification, meriting judicial review under the deferential "rational basis" standard we encountered in chapter 2.

The constitutionally innocuous status of age discrimination provided what Justice O'Connor, the author of *Kimel*, called "the backdrop" for her scrutiny of the ADEA. She concluded that because the Court generally treated age discrimination as constitutionally benign, Congress faced a high hurdle in demonstrating that the ADEA was a congruent and proportional response to the problem of *un*constitutional age discrimination in employment. Her conclusion meant that Congress had to demonstrate not just a pattern of age discrimination by states but a pattern of discrimination that was either so irrational or so infused with animus as to fail the Court's rational basis standard. Examining the ADEA's legislative record, she found no such pattern. In turn, that conclusion meant that the ADEA could only be constitutional if it was so narrowly drawn as to be proportional to this seemingly trivial constitutional problem. Given the ADEA's breadth and the relative severity of its requirements, the five-justice majority held that the statute failed that requirement.[5]

The Court again made its own judicial doctrine central to its understanding of Congress's enforcement power in the next Enforcement Clause case, *Board of Trustees v. Garrett*,[6] decided one year after *Kimel*. *Garrett* considered the enforcement power foundation for the employment provisions of the Americans with Disabilities Act (ADA). On its face, the ADA's employment provisions seemed to present the same situation as the ADEA. Just as the Court had identified age discrimination as a nonsuspect classification, it had also held that disability discrimination merited similar treatment. And, indeed, the same five-justice majority that decided *Kimel* followed that earlier case. Just as *Kimel* had concluded that Congress had failed to present an adequate record of unconstitutional state age discrimination, so too the same justices in *Garrett* concluded that Congress had similarly failed to present an adequate record of unconstitutional state discrimination on the basis of disability. Thus, the majority held that the enforcement power did not support the ADA's employment provisions.

However, *Garrett* presented two difficulties that posed a larger challenge for the Court. First, in enacting the ADA, Congress amassed a far more extensive record of discrimination than it did in the ADEA—including examples of employment discrimination perpetrated by state governments. Second, the Court's disability discrimination jurisprudence was more ambivalent than its analogous case law dealing with age discrimination. In particular, sixteen years before *Garrett*, in *City of Cleburne v. Cleburne Living Center*,[7] the Court had sent conflicting signals about the constitutional status of disability discrimination. We've encountered *Cleburne* earlier, in chapter 2. Recall that it dealt with a city council's decision to prohibit the establishment of a group home for intellectually disabled persons in a residential neighborhood. As chapter 2 set forth in some detail, *Cleburne* began its analysis by reviewing the lower court's decision that intellectual disability constituted a quasi-suspect classification that merited heightened judicial scrutiny. The Court rejected the lower court's conclusion, holding instead that intellectual disability discrimination merited only rational basis review, the lowest level of judicial review under the Equal Protection Clause.

But that seemingly straightforward conclusion—a conclusion that would appear to put disability and age discrimination at the same constitutional level, with the same implications for congressional enforcement power—was in fact substantially more nuanced. First, *Cleburne*'s answer to the suspect class question appeared to turn heavily on two factors that spoke more to judicial competence than to underlying constitutional law. As chapter 2's discussion of *Cleburne* noted, the Court in that case expressed serious concern about the practical difficulties lower courts would face if they had to inspect closely every instance in which government treated intellectually disabled persons differently from mainstream society. In addition, the Court concluded its suspect class analysis with a frank admission that it was not inclined to grant suspect class status to intellectually disabled persons, out of fear that such a holding would open the floodgates to similar claims from other groups who could claim analogous social status. These worries, as reasonable as they are, speak primarily to practical concerns about courts being able, respectively, to apply heightened scrutiny competently and to draw principled distinctions between intellectually disabled persons and the several other groups the Court suggested would have analogous claims to any protected status the Court bestowed on the intellectually disabled.

But *Cleburne* contained even more ambiguity, which further blurred the seemingly easy analogy between age and disability discrimination. After deciding that disability discrimination received only rational basis scrutiny, the *Cleburne* Court went on to apply that scrutiny. However, as we saw in chapter 2, the *Cleburne* majority applied an unusually stringent version of rational basis review. Contrary to that standard's normal rule imposing on the *challenger* the burden of *disproving* every conceivable rational justification for the discrimination, the *Cleburne* Court remarked upon the *government*'s failure to provide evidence *supporting* its discrimination. Indeed, the Court brushed past several seemingly rational justifications for the city's decision, focusing instead on evidence that the city had acted in response to constituents' dislike and fear of intellectually disabled persons. Accordingly, as chapter 2 noted, the Court struck down the city's decision, concluding that it failed even rational basis review—at least rational basis review as ratcheted up in that case.

Thus, the underlying constitutional jurisprudence of disability discrimination was far more ambivalent than the Court's corresponding age discrimination jurisprudence. When combined with the more extensive record of actual discrimination Congress had compiled in enacting the ADA, the seemingly easy path from *Kimel* to *Garrett* should have been acknowledged as considerably more challenging.

The *Garrett* Court's response to this complexity was simply to deny it. It described *Cleburne* as a case applying standard rational basis scrutiny, ignoring the unusually strict character of the Court's review in that case and blithely describing the outcome as reflecting the rare situation where an instance of discrimination against a nonsuspect class was so irrational as to warrant striking down. Having thus tamed the Court's disability discrimination jurisprudence, the *Garrett* Court then turned to the ADA's compilation of a record of discriminatory acts by state government employers, to determine whether that record demonstrated the existence of a significant constitutional problem that warranted the ADA's response. In testing that record against its newly announced understanding that disability discrimination posed no particular constitutional problem, the Court imposed a harsh and exacting review. It insisted not just on instances of employment discrimination by states, and not even instances that an impartial observer would characterize as irrational or based on animus. Instead, it insisted on examples that were so irrational or infused with animus that they would have failed the Court's rational basis standard of review, despite all the pro-government presumptions that standard incorporates.

The Court's insistence that these examples fail its rational basis test is significant. Recall from chapter 2 that the rational basis test is intended as a paradigm of judicial restraint. As such it might well be admirable. But here the Court was not deploying that test to *defer* to legislative action but as a tool for *not* deferring to (federal) legislative action.

Consider just one example of that lack of deference. In *Garrett* the Court dismissed, as irrelevant, examples where subunits of states (such as counties) engaged in discriminatory conduct. It is true, as the Court explained in justifying this move, that those subunits are not protected by the state sovereign immunity enacted by the Eleventh Amendment. But there is no logical reason a subunit's lack of Eleventh Amendment sovereign immunity should matter to the question whether states are violating the Fourteenth Amendment. After all, states, counties, police departments, and cities are all subject to the Fourteenth Amendment.

Such details need not detain us, for the pattern is clear. In *Garrett* the Court pushed past all obstacles that threatened to make the ADA's enforcement power bona fides a closer question than the ADEA's validity in *Kimel*. After denying—against the facts—any difference between the Court's previous treatment of disability and age discrimination, it then sliced and diced the ADA's legislative record to make it as thin as the ADEA's. After the Court's plastic surgery, the two cases looked alike. Unsurprisingly, the statutes in those cases suffered the same fate.

Two years after *Garrett* the Court confirmed the centrality of its own underlying equal protection doctrine to the fate of enforcement legislation, even while upholding enforcement legislation for the first time in the *Boerne* era. In *Nevada Department of Human Resources v. Hibbs*,[8] the Court upheld, as legislation enforcing the equal protection right to sex equality, the family-care provision of the Family and Medical Leave Act. That provision provided employees (including, most important for our purposes, state government employees) with uncompensated leave time to care for an ill family member. The FMLA suffered from some of the same weaknesses as the statutes found to lack an enforcement power foundation in earlier cases: a somewhat spotty record of actual constitutional violations by states, and findings that were made either by a Congress previous to the enacting one or by private entities whose conclusions were never translated into formal legislative findings.

Nevertheless, a six-justice majority that included two members of the *Kimel* and *Garrett* majorities upheld the legislation. Analogously to *Kimel* and *Garrett* (though with the opposite effect), *Hibbs* relied heavily on the suspect status of the discrimination the legislation sought to deter. Writing for those six justices, Chief Justice Rehnquist explained that the quasi-suspect status of sex discrimination made it "easier for Congress to show a pattern of state constitutional violations."[9] The chief justice was as good as his word: his review of the FMLA's supporting evidence was markedly more lenient than the review he himself had accorded the ADA two years earlier in his opinion for the Court in *Garrett*. To take one notable example, he accorded importance to a federal study of family-care leave policies in private business—a stark contrast to his insistence in *Garrett* that the only evidence relevant to the ADA's Enforcement Clause foundation was evidence of discrimination by state governments themselves (and, indeed, not even subunits of states).[10]

The Court's willingness to infer from this evidence the existence of sex discrimination by states can only be attributed to its recognition that sex discrimination posed a more serious and widespread constitutional problem than disability discrimination—a recognition that found expression in the Court's grant of heightened scrutiny to sex discrimination. Indeed, *Hibbs* explicitly acknowledged not just the constitutional seriousness of sex discrimination but its stubbornness. It recounted the story of sex equality legislation and noted that successive legislative efforts, starting with the Civil Rights Act of 1964 and continuing to the FMLA three decades later, recognized the persistence of sex discrimination in employment and attacked it with ever more nuanced remedies.[11] At the more personal level, Chief Justice Rehnquist himself may have learned that lesson when, in the 1990s, he was forced to leave his chambers to assist his daughter in child-care duties when his daughter (a lawyer) found her work demands to be incompatible with her parenting responsibilities.[12]

The Court's reliance on its own underlying constitutional doctrine when evaluating enforcement legislation reappeared yet again the next year, in a case that, in retrospect, marked the close of the first stage of the Court's post-*Boerne* enforcement power jurisprudence. In *Tennessee v. Lane*,[13] the Court considered Title II of the ADA, which regulated disabled persons' access to "services, programs, or activities of a public entity."[14] While some of the government activities Title II regulated might be regulable under the Commerce Clause, many others might not be. And to repeat a point we made earlier, even if the Commerce Clause did authorize regulation of those state government activities, it would not further authorize Congress to provide for retrospective remedies when states violated those requirements.

Lane involved two plaintiffs, George Lane and Beverly Jones, paraplegic persons who were unable, respectively, to appear in court as a criminal defendant and to pursue her occupation as a court reporter because a Tennessee state courthouse lacked the disability access the ADA required. Both plaintiffs sought, among other things, damages for the state's statutory violation. Perhaps the Commerce Clause might have reached Jones's access claim, given its basis in economic activity (employment). The Commerce Clause would have been harder for Lane, given the Court's restrictions on that power. But regardless of whether the Commerce Clause authorized Congress to regulate either plaintiff's access to courthouses, the viability of their claims for damages inevitably raised a question under the enforcement power.

In *Lane* the Supreme Court upheld the challenged provisions as valid enforcement legislation. *Lane* is somewhat tangential to this book's topic, because the Court concluded that those provisions constituted valid legislation enforcing Americans' Fourteenth Amendment rights under the *Due Process* Clause, rather than the Equal Protection Clause. Nevertheless, *Lane* remains relevant for us. First, this book's thesis about congressional power to enforce the Equal Protection Clause applies, at least generally, to Congress's power to enforce the Due Process Clause: after all, the Enforcement Clause applies to the entire Fourteenth Amendment, which includes both of these rights. Indeed, chapter 10 discusses how this book's suggested approach might apply to due process rights.

Second, and of much more immediate relevance, the Court's analysis in *Lane* followed logically from the *Kimel-Garrett-Hibbs* trilogy of equal protection enforcement cases. Writing for the five-justice majority in *Lane*, Justice Stevens explained that the ADA's public services provisions were properly analyzed, in this particular case, as enforcing Americans' due process right to access the judicial process. On the one hand, that more narrowly focused approach meant that as precedent, *Lane* was limited. But it also made it easier for the majority to uphold the statute: by considering only one particular application of the statute (i.e., to courthouse access), Justice Stevens effectively altered the denominator of the fraction that makes up part of the congruence and proportionality formula. Indeed, the dissent registered exactly that complaint.[15]

We can leave the dissent's objections to the side. For our purposes, the important point is that Justice Stevens's approach focused the Court's attention on the due process right to access courts. In turn, that focus allowed the Court to judge the congruence and proportionality of that particular application of the ADA against the standard of the Court's own underlying Fourteenth Amendment doctrine governing that judicial access right. There was a reasonably well-developed jurisprudence governing that right, developed in cases where, for example, states required litigants to pay filing fees in order to commence a civil suit. In *Lane* Justice Stevens noted that the Court evaluated such obstacles against the principle that "'within the limits of practicability, a State must afford to all individuals a meaningful opportunity to be heard' in its courts."[16] He concluded that the ADA's requirement that operators of public services make "reasonable modifications" to allow disabled access to structures (including, in this case, courthouses) closely tracked the Court's constitutional requirement about access to courts more generally.

Thus, by *Boerne*'s seventh anniversary the Court had firmly established a methodology for evaluating challenges to enforcement legislation. That methodology turned heavily on the Court's estimation of the relationship between the scope of the challenged statute and its own underlying constitutional law doctrine addressing the right Congress was seeking to enforce. In the equal protection context, this methodology tied the fate of enforcement legislation to the Court's suspect class analysis. As explained earlier, if, as in *Hibbs*, that analysis gave special judicial protection to a group, then enforcement legislation benefiting that group would receive deferential judicial scrutiny. But if suspect class analysis resulted in that group not receiving such special protection, then, as in *Kimel* and *Garrett*, enforcement legislation would receive a more skeptical judicial reception.

This approach raises troubling conceptual and logical problems. As part I of the book explained, the modern Court has largely abandoned suspect class analysis when deciding equal protection cases. That abandonment has created an anomaly: today, the fate of enforcement legislation turns on the result of an analysis the Court has otherwise abandoned. As troubling as this situation is as a purely logical matter, it also creates the significant practical problem that enforcement legislation benefiting emerging groups—that is, groups who have not had their suspect class determined—lacks the reference point by which that legislation can be tested. This is not a theoretical concern: enforcement legislation benefiting gays and lesbians, transgendered persons, and persons with particular genetic makeups either is on the legislative agenda or, in the case of genetics, already exists. Solving this problem is one of this book's aims.

The Constitutional Status of Suspect Class Analysis

This problem requires that we consider the constitutional status of the Supreme Court's underlying equal protection doctrine—in particular, its determinations of particular types of discrimination as either suspect, quasi-suspect, or nonsuspect. At first blush this might appear to be an odd question: If those determinations—for example, that sex is a quasi-suspect classification, or disability a nonsuspect classification—are the result of Supreme Court constitutional decision making, then aren't they necessarily "constitutional law"? But closer examination reveals this is not always the case. Importantly for our purposes, it is often not the case with regard to the Court's suspect class decisions.

The idea that certain types of discrimination are particularly suspect ultimately traces back to the Court's 1938 opinion in *Carolene Products*, discussed in chapters 1 and 2. As those chapters discussed, in *Carolene Products* the Court announced that henceforth it would generally presume the existence of facts supporting the constitutionality of a legislature's action—for example, facts showing that a regulated item (like the "filled milk" in *Carolene Products* itself) injured the public's health and thus merited regulation. However, it appended a footnote to that statement—the famous "Footnote 4"—suggesting that in certain situations that presumption might not be appropriate. Among those situations are those marked by "prejudice against discrete and insular minorities." The Court described that phenomenon as "a special condition, which tends seriously to curtail the operation of those political processes ordinarily to be relied upon to protect minorities, and which may call for a correspondingly more searching judicial inquiry." As chapter 2 explained, the "prejudice against discrete and insular minorities formula" eventually evolved into suspect class analysis.

Pause, however, before moving on to the concept of suspect classes. Both Footnote 4[17] and the text to which it is appended speak in terms of presumptions. Read carefully, the text does not say that most normal commercial regulation is constitutional because in most cases the legislature *has* a constitutionally sufficient reason for imposing the regulation; rather, it says that the Court will *presume* the existence of facts supporting such justifications. Similarly, the problem with legislation discriminating against discrete and insular minorities is *not* that there is something inherently unconstitutional about such laws; rather, according to Footnote 4, the problem is that those groups are unable to engage in political activity against legislation that harms them. In turn, that lack of political access justifies withholding the presumption that the legislature must have had good reasons for what it did.

The presumption-heavy nature of these statements is no accident. Scholars understand *Carolene Products* as the Court's reaction to its earlier insistence on scrutinizing economic regulation to ensure that it was truly supported by a legitimate public purpose. Contrary to some overly simplistic accounts of that period, such review was not unremittingly hostile to regulation. During that earlier era, sometimes called the "*Lochner* era" after a famous 1905 case striking down a law establishing maximum working hours for bakers,[18] the Court upheld much regulation, including innovative regulation responding to the new needs of an industrial society.[19] Nevertheless, as chapter 2 explained, the underlying assumption of that era—that the Court had a significant role to play in ensuring that economic regulation truly aimed at promoting the public good rather than at hijacking government power for purely private ends—had proven problematic by 1937.

The response, first intimated in *Carolene Products* and then fleshed out in succeeding decades, was to ground judicial review on a set of presumptions about the likely public purpose underlying a particular piece of legislation. According to the text of the *Carolene Products* opinion, in most cases the Court would presume that challenged legislation enjoyed adequate factual support to justify courts upholding it as aimed at a public purpose. However, the footnote to which that statement was appended—Footnote 4—cautioned that that presumption might not apply in three situations: when legislation seemed to facially violate a Bill of Rights provision, when a law infringed on the political process (as with a voting restriction), or when it seemed to be the result of a flawed political process—when, for example, a law harmed a disliked minority that is presumed to have less access to that process. As chapter 2 discussed, the suspect class analysis that grew from the seed of Footnote 4's third scenario turned heavily on judicial determinations about when it was appropriate for courts to presume that a particular classification tool was likely constitutional.

Return now to the modern era of enforcement legislation. As we saw earlier in this chapter, in cases such as *Garrett*, *Kimel*, and *Hibbs* the Court tied the fate of enforcement legislation closely to its own determinations about whether the benefited group constituted a suspect class. But if we understand those suspect class decisions as reflecting only process-based presumptions rather than statements of core constitutional rules, then those decisions do not conclusively state constitutional law. Such presumptions may help courts uncover violations of such core rules, by identifying situations where courts should investigate more closely. But they are not constitutional rules in and of themselves.

This is a subtle distinction, but a crucial one. Recall *Garrett*, the ADA case we discussed earlier in this chapter. In that case the Court relied heavily on the nonsuspect status of disability discrimination as support for its skeptical review of the enforcement power foundation for the ADA's employment provisions. Yet, as we discussed earlier, the Court's disability discrimination jurisprudence turns heavily on the Court's unease about the practical implications *for courts* if disability was deemed a suspect classification. Recall that in its flagship disability discrimination case, *Cleburne*, the Court expressed concern about courts' ability to do a competent job of scrutinizing government decisions to treat the intellectually disabled differently from nondisabled persons. It also conceded that perhaps the intellectually disabled satisfied the criteria for suspect class status, but it expressed yet another concern about judicial competence—this time, the ability of courts to handle the suspect class claims that other groups might make on the heels of a decision denominating the intellectually disabled as suspect. It is appropriate for the Court to worry about such matters: after all, it has to consider the workability of any rule it might lay down. But those worries reveal that the suspect class status of the disabled was not based unequivocally and simply on the Court's confidence that most such classifications were in fact constitutional.

Once the Court explained that its decision denying the group suspect class status was based on concerns about the *judicial* workability of such a rule, it should have been much more open to the possibility that *Congress* is not subject to those same concerns, and thus merits broader latitude to enact enforcement legislation benefiting that group. Such openness to enforcement legislation still requires some hard thinking about the limits of congressional power and the appropriate way for courts to enforce those limits. Chapter 6 considers the case for congressional power, and how courts can best police it. For our purposes here, however, the key point is simply that such limits should not turn exclusively on the suspect class status of the group benefited by the legislation. Logic suggests that that status is certainly relevant. But it should not play the determinative role that it did in the Court's post-*Boerne* cases.

5

Constitutional Law and Legislative Policy

Chapter 4 explained how the first decade of the Court's post-*Boerne* jurisprudence created difficulties arising from the Court's (mis)understanding of the constitutional status of its suspect class jurisprudence. In recent years, the congruence and proportionality test has raised a distinct, though related, problem. This second problem is every bit as serious as, and indeed potentially even more challenging than, the suspect class problem chapter 4 described. This second problem arises when the Court considers two phenomena that, paradoxically, seem to have little in common with each other: when discrimination persists, and, conversely, when it appears to have been eradicated.

The Problem of Persistence: *Coleman* and the Self-Care Provision of the FMLA

The first variant of this problem arises when discrimination is stubbornly persistent. From its earliest applications of the congruence and proportionality standard, the Court has recognized that stubborn or persistent discrimination may justify unusually strong enforcement legislation remedies.[1] Nevertheless, after *Boerne* the Court's perception of the persistence of a particular type of discrimination did not appear to play a direct role in its evaluation of enforcement legislation until 2012. Until that year, legislation enforcing equal protection rights faced a predictable constitutional fate: if the group benefited by the law was a suspect or quasi-suspect class, it received deferential review, while if the benefited group did not enjoy that status, legislation protecting its equality rights received skeptical review.

In 2012, however, that template cracked. In that year the Supreme Court struck down a statute enforcing the equal protection right to sex equality—a right that, as chapter 2 explained, the Court has embraced through its denomination of sex as a "quasi-suspect" classification. The next year, it struck down a provision of the Voting Rights Act. Even though that statute was based mainly on the Fifteenth, not the Fourteenth, Amendment, its analysis of Congress's power to enforce racial equality with regard to voting bears important similarities to its analysis of Fourteenth Amendment enforcement issues.

The first of these cases, *Coleman v. Maryland Court of Appeals*,[2] struck down part of the Family and Medical Leave Act. Recall that in the 2003 *Hibbs* case the Court upheld as valid enforcement legislation FMLA provisions that granted to state government employees leave time to care for sick family members. Even though it applied equally to men and women, the Court reasoned that the family-care leave benefit helped women in particular, by mitigating employers' perceptions that family-care duties were mainly women's duties, which made women less reliable and therefore less desirable as employees. The Court explained that because the FMLA targeted sex discrimination—a quasi-suspect classification—it was easier for Congress to amass a record of constitutional violations justifying the provisions as enforcement legislation.

Coleman was a different story. *Coleman* considered the FMLA's *self*-care provision, which extended to state government employees time off not to care for sick family members but to care for the employee him- or herself. Defenders of the self-care provision argued primarily that it protected women's employment opportunities by ensuring that employers did not discriminate against women when they took time off for pregnancy-related illnesses or to recover after childbirth.

They also argued that the self-care provision was a necessary adjunct to the statute's family-care provision (the one upheld in *Hibbs*), to ensure that the family-care provision did not have the perverse effect of worsening sex discrimination in the workplace. On this last point, they argued that, despite the family-care provision's sex neutrality, employers would still tend to perceive that provision as redounding primarily to women's benefit, on the theory that women would be more likely to be their families' primary caregivers, and thus the employees most likely to take advantage of FMLA-granted family-care leave. Thus, those advocates expressed concern that, standing alone, the family-care provision would be seen by employers as a women's benefit, making women even less reliable as employees. They suggested that providing self-care leave, which would likely be taken on a sex-equal basis, would mitigate that perception. Given that the sex-neutral family-care benefit was itself a prophylactic device, this particular argument defended the self-care provision as a type of double prophylactic.[3]

The Court rejected both arguments.[4] Justice Kennedy, writing for four of the five justices in the majority, began by denying that there existed a pattern of sex discrimination in the administration of disability leave benefits (which he suggested would include leave for pregnancy-related disabilities). Justice Ginsburg, dissenting for four justices, dismissed that observation as beside the point. For her, the issue was not discrimination with regard to sex per se in the administration of those benefits but, rather, discrimination with regard to *pregnancy*-related leave, which she noted was specifically included in the self-care provision. For Justice Ginsburg, pregnancy discrimination *was* sex discrimination; thus, by ensuring that women had adequate leave time to attend to pregnancy-related health issues, the FMLA's self-care provision ensured sex equality in the workplace.

So understood, this first argument in support of the self-care provision implicates what we have called the "jurisdictional" issue in Enforcement Clause analysis. The Court, in a 1974 case called *Geduldig v. Aiello*,[5] held that pregnancy discrimination did not constitute sex discrimination. One might well disagree with this conclusion—indeed, many observers have.[6] But if one begins with the Court's assumption—that is, if one begins with the assumption that the Fourteenth Amendment's concern with sex discrimination, that is, the "jurisdiction" of that concern, does not extend to concerns about pregnancy discrimination—then the plurality's analysis of the self-care provision follows, more or less naturally.[7]

As important as it is to the underlying question of what constitutes sex discrimination, the pregnancy discrimination/sex discrimination argument does not illustrate the full extent of *Coleman*'s general importance for congressional enforcement of equal protection. The real importance flows from the second argument for the self-care provision, even though the plurality described it as an "alternative justification,"[8] and even though it constituted a fallback for Justice Ginsburg.[9] Recall that that second argument maintained that family-care leave by itself would harm women, as the FMLA would come to be seen as nothing but a women's employment benefit, given employers' perceptions that family-care duties generally fell to women. Thus, the argument went, attaching a sex-neutral *self*-care leave provision to the *family*-care leave provision would help mitigate employers' perceptions that the FMLA made women even less reliable than men, and thus less desirable.

Justice Kennedy simply didn't buy it. He cited evidence predicting that men and women would both likely take only five days of self-care leave per year, an amount that he concluded was simply too small to counteract any gender imbalance in employees' availing themselves of family-care leave. He condemned the double prophylaxis argument described above as "overly complicated" and "unconvincing," and thus rejected this ground for upholding that provision as valid enforcement legislation.

This part of *Coleman* paints a picture of a Court demanding to know that enforcement legislation will be effective—at least minimally—in combating the asserted discrimination. Understood more broadly, the Court's rejection of this argument points to a larger problem that will likely confront the Court with increasing frequency. As the first wave of antidiscrimination legislation enacted beginning in the 1960s matures, scholars have argued that discrimination, far from being eradicated, has simply evolved into more subtle forms.[10] Blatant refusals to hire or promote people based on forbidden grounds such as race or sex have given way to so-called second-generation discrimination, where neutral-seeming policies and practices are developed that continue to frustrate the goal of equal opportunity. Thus, for example, outright racial discrimination may evolve into neutral policies about grooming that impact blacks more than whites, or outright sex discrimination into analogous policies (indeed, about issues such as the availability of emergency leave) that impact women more than men. Such discrimination may not even reflect the invidious motives with which we sometimes associate the concept of "discrimination." As one scholar put it, describing Justice Ginsburg's analysis of the self-care provision in *Coleman*, "workplace discrimination against women includes actions that well-meaning and rational employers adopt to avoid [for example,] the real costs of pregnancy and child rearing."[11] For example, an employer concerned about office efficiency could impose stringent limits on flexible scheduling of the type parents—in our society, especially mothers—often need.

In response to such second-generation discrimination, policy advocates have called for second-generation remedies. The FMLA's family-care provision is a prime example of such a remedy. As explained earlier, that statute's self-care provision is an even subtler example. For our purposes, the most important characteristic of such a provision is its subtlety and indirectness in combating discrimination. However, it is exactly those characteristics that led the *Coleman* Court to question the statute's effectiveness, and thus its validity as enforcement legislation.

As historically disfavored discrimination, in particular based on race or sex, takes on these more indirect forms, Congress is likely to enact more of such second-generation weapons to target it. Leave aside the "jurisdictional" question of whether certain types of conduct (e.g., pregnancy discrimination) even constitute sex discrimination. Beyond that issue, *Coleman* also suggests that such subtle weapons will encounter a Court that hesitates to defer to what it believes, in its own words, to be "overly complicated" arguments about the need for or effectiveness of such a provision.

The Problem of Legislative Success: The VRA

At the other extreme, at least ostensibly, from the problem of persistent discrimination lies the "problem" of discrimination that has been successfully eradicated. A year after *Coleman*, in *Shelby County v. Holder*,[12] the Court struck down the formula determining which jurisdictions would be subject to the preclearance provisions of the Voting Rights Act. As we discussed in chapter 3's examination of the *South Carolina* case, those provisions require covered jurisdictions to get prior federal approval for (i.e., "preclear") changes in the jurisdiction's voting or governance structure, to ensure that such changes do not impair minority voting rights. As such, they cut deeply into state sovereign prerogatives.

The coverage formula was originally enacted in 1965 and renewed in 1970, based on minority voting statistics in then-recent elections. Since then the entire VRA, including the preclearance provisions and their coverage formula, has been periodically renewed, most recently in 2006, although the coverage formula has not been updated since the 1975 renewal. Thus, that formula is old. However, the statute features an updating mechanism. It provides that a jurisdiction can be either "bailed out" of the preclearance requirement (i.e., released from regulation if it convinces federal officials that it has a record of nondiscrimination with regard to minority voting rights and thus deserves to be released from regulation) or "bailed in" (i.e., brought under the preclearance requirement if it is adjudged to have engaged in such discrimination).

Despite the bail-out and bail-in provisions, the Court in *Shelby County* expressed serious concern about the alleged obsolescence of the coverage formula, and whether that obsolescence rendered that part of the VRA invalid enforcement legislation. To repeat a point we made in chapter 3, the preclearance provisions were originally upheld as legislation enforcing the Fifteenth Amendment. Under current law, Fifteenth Amendment enforcement legislation is subject to the more deferential standard enunciated in the 1966 *South Carolina* case. However, *Shelby County* was vague about both the amendment under which the VRA was justified and the standard of review it was applying.[13] Thus, we should consider *Shelby County*'s analysis when thinking about the current state of Congress's Fourteenth Amendment enforcement power. For our purposes, the key component of that analysis is its conclusion that the preclearance provisions had so succeeded in eradicating discrimination in the covered jurisdictions that they were no longer necessary and, hence, were invalid enforcement legislation. That conclusion raises the question of when enforcement legislation ceases to be appropriate because of its very success.

At first blush an enforcement statute's success in eradicating the targeted discrimination does not pose any particular paradox. After all, legislation is designed to accomplish a goal, and if an antidiscrimination statute accomplishes its goal of eradicating discrimination, we should be pleased. The problem arises, however, in determining whether in fact a statute has succeeded.

Determining the success of an antidiscrimination statute requires more than simply examining the frequency of the particular instances of discrimination that motivated the statute's enactment. Instead, it requires a determination that the discrimination has been eradicated rather than merely temporarily suppressed.

In the VRA context, for example, defenders of the statute acknowledged improvements in the covered jurisdictions' records of minority voter registration and turnout. However, they argued that that success was largely due to the preclearance provisions' deterrent effect, an effect they argued would disappear were the Court to strike down either those provisions or their coverage formula. Moreover, and in a way that recalls the arguments in *Coleman* over the FMLA's self-care provision, defenders of the preclearance provisions' coverage formula also argued that covered jurisdictions had sometimes resorted to more subtle, second-generation mechanisms of diluting minority voting rights.

Judging these arguments requires difficult evaluations of evidence. For example, Justice Ginsburg's defense of the coverage formula's constitutionality in *Shelby County* noted the trend line of Department of Justice objections to preclearance requests. She argued that the increase in Department of Justice objections over the twenty-five years since the VRA's previous renewal in 1982 suggested that the preclearance requirement was in fact deterring violations that would otherwise occur. She also found support for the law in her comparison of the covered jurisdictions' relatively worse win-loss percentage in litigation under Section 2 of the VRA (which applies nationwide and directly prohibits racial discrimination in voting). Justice Ginsburg reasoned that differences between these two rates indicated that the covered jurisdictions were still disproportionately responsible for voting discrimination in the United States.

Constitutional Law/Constitutional Policy

The determinations the Court had to review in *Coleman* and *Shelby County* consist of more than mechanical analyses of data. They are instead better described as policy judgments, based in part on data but also on experience with and intuitions about how government officials and politicians operate in different parts of the nation. Describing such judgments as predictions captures some, but not all, of their flavor: after all, a scientist can make a very accurate and objective prediction about what will happen when two particular chemicals are combined. In order to fully capture the character of the types of determinations with which we're concerned, we need to recognize that such predictions are partly based on experience and intuition. They are thus an art, as much as a science. They are policy judgments.

Such policy judgments will likely become more prominent in future enforcement legislation. As the first generation of antidiscrimination laws, such as the Civil Rights Act of 1964, have become well established, the blatantly exclusionary discrimination that motivated their passage has become less prevalent and visible. (Of course, even originally these laws were concerned with subtle, as well as obvious, discrimination. But with the decline of the most obvious manifestations of discrimination, its more subtle variants have risen to prominence.) Just as *Coleman* struggled with the self-care provision's double-prophylaxis response to this evolution, *Shelby County* struggled with what now comes into focus as an analogous issue: whether that early legislation has in fact served its purpose and is no longer needed. As Justice Ginsburg's defense of the VRA illustrates, that issue requires consideration of two related questions: (1) Has the problem been solved, and (2) has the problem evolved into a more subtle variant?

Chapter 9 will offer some conclusions about the VRA debate; for now, the point is simply to flag the issues that debate raises. These issues are thorny and are likely to remain so. Antidiscrimination law, like any policy, evolves as the relevant social landscape evolves. In the case of antidiscrimination law, that social landscape has changed quite a lot since the first wave of significant federal antidiscrimination legislation in the 1960s. First, discrimination itself has changed. The outright—indeed, explicit—refusals to hire minorities or women that marked the backdrop of the Civil Rights Act of 1964 have mostly disappeared, due largely to evolving social views about the appropriateness of such blatant discrimination.

The decline of overt, "first-generation" discrimination did not, however, eradicate the underlying problem. Just ask Ann Hopkins.[14] Hopkins was an executive at Price Waterhouse, a major accounting and consulting firm. By all measures she was quite effective: she generated business and did exemplary work. Nevertheless, she was passed over when she applied for partnership. Because of her sex? Strictly speaking, no. Price Waterhouse had female partners; it was never suggested that the firm had decided that, because she was a woman, Hopkins could never become partner. Instead, her application for partnership encountered objections that her demeanor didn't jibe with the firm's leaders' expectations about how women should act. She was described as "macho," advised to "take courses at a charm school" and "walk more femininely, talk more femininely, dress more femininely, wear make-up, have her hair styled, and wear jewelry."

Intuitively, that sounds like sex discrimination. But if the firm responded to that intuition by explaining that a woman who *did* appear more stereotypically feminine would have made partner, then we are led to recognize that sex discrimination means more than a "Help Wanted: Men Only" sign hung on a window. Indeed, we are led to recognize that discrimination of any sort can mean more than explicit exclusion. It can mean, for example, a workplace ban on hairstyles that are perceived to be culturally favored by a particular ethnic group. Or a firm culture where important decisions are made at a men's-only club.

It could also mean a firm culture that worried about whether a prospective executive would likely be missing at important times because of family emergencies, and thus a culture that disfavored women because they were perceived to be more "unreliable" since they were families' "go-to" person for such emergencies. The core of the FMLA was its assurance that employees could take (uncompensated) leave time to care for a sick relative. On its face such leave is a sex-neutral benefit, available equally to men and women. Yet advocates for the law successfully argued that it was necessary in order to overcome not explicit, first-generation discrimination but the subtle, second-generation discrimination that arose from employer perceptions about traditional sex roles—in this case, perceptions about which family member was more likely to leave work to care for a sick relative.

The FMLA's family-care leave provision did not combat that stereotype in a direct way, for example, by outlawing sex discrimination based on perceptions of family-care responsibilities. Instead, it took a more subtle approach. By providing a sex-neutral family-care leave benefit, it sought to change employer perceptions more organically, by encouraging all workers—including men—to take time off to care for ill relatives. The hope was that, over time, employers would be weaned away from considering women employees less reliable than men, as men and women began to be perceived as equally likely to take time off to care for ill relatives. The perceptions the FMLA sought to change were not explicitly exclusionary; instead, they were based on assumptions about how men and women lived. The FMLA attempted to change those perceptions by changing the reality on which they were based.

Of course, the problem did not end there. As our earlier of discussion of *Coleman* explained, women's rights advocates feared that the provision of family-care leave by itself would have the perverse effect of making women seem even *more* undesirable as employees, since now they would have a federal law right to take time off for family-care responsibilities. Thus, those advocates insisted on tying family-care leave to personal-care leave, on the theory (at least in part) that provision of a benefit that was perceived as sex-neutral would mitigate employers' perceptions about the differential costs such leave exacted, depending on the sex of the employee.

As we noted earlier, the *Coleman* plurality simply did not accept this argument, calling it "overly complicated" and "unconvincing."[15] Justice Kennedy's choice of words is telling. The argument *is* complicated—or at least it is nuanced, in the sense that it requires several steps of reasoning and, importantly, an understanding of social reality. Perhaps just as important, the argument sketched out here is one that, quite literally, only a legislature has the capability to recognize and instantiate into law.

To see this last point, consider the following thought experiment: a female state government employee sues her employer, alleging unconstitutional sex discrimination because the employer offers family-care leave but not self-care leave. (In this hypothetical, nobody, male or female, enjoys self-care leave.) The plaintiff could make the argument that women's rights advocates successfully made to Congress—that this *equal* treatment (no self-care leave for anyone) redounded to women's detriment, since the combination of provision of family-care leave but denial of self-care leave inevitably created a situation where women were thought to be more likely than men to miss work.

Think about how a court would have to respond to this argument if it was made in a lawsuit. It would require the court to consider the equality implications of an entire structure of leave policies, none of which might be motivated by an intent to burden women, and none of which would explicitly harm women, but which combined to create a perception that unquestionably harmed women. That task would be challenging enough for a court. But assume it found that this interlocking structure constituted a constitutional violation. What possible remedy could the court impose? Could it require that employers insist that men take the same number of family-care leave days as women? Could it mandate self-care leave to balance out this dynamic?

The difficulty a court would have in both identifying a constitutional violation and fashioning relief in this hypothetical lawsuit reflects the policy-heavy nature of decisions such as those underlying the FMLA. Those decisions are firmly grounded in constitutional concerns about sex equality. But the liability and remedy decisions a court would have to make in this hypothetical lawsuit—the same decisions made by Congress in the FMLA—reflect more than pure constitutional analysis. Instead, they reflect what one might call "constitutional policy making." This phrase is not a lawyer's term of art: it simply refers to the translation, the implementation, and (literally) the enforcement of constitutional principles into concrete policy. As one might expect from the two parts of that compound term, such implementation requires both an understanding of constitutional principle and a capability to engage in policy making.

Legislative and Judicial Capacities to Make Policy

Such compound decision making will only become more common in the future, as obvious constitutional violations (the "Men Only" caveats to state government "Help Wanted" ads) recede into history, and more nuanced burdens emerge as the primary barriers to full equality. Staying with the example of sex discrimination, feminist legal scholars have long argued that true sex equality requires more than simply the eradication of explicit lines classifying on the basis of sex. Instead, it requires the dismantling of structures that systematically operate to the detriment of women—for example, workplace structures that penalize employees' decisions to take time off for child care in a context where women are presumed to be the primary family caregiver. Indeed, some scholars has gone further and proposed that workplace equality law shift its focus away from uncovering discrete instances of alleged discrimination, and toward restructuring the workplace more generally, by imposing a duty on employers to establish procedures designed to lessen the risk of such discrimination.[16]

As suggested by the thought experiment a few paragraphs earlier, courts would have a difficult time evaluating whether discriminatory workplace structures violated the Constitution, particularly given the rule requiring equal protection plaintiffs to prove that the government intended to discriminate. But even if courts could surmount the liability hurdle, the sort of restructuring necessary to remedy such a violation would severely tax judges' capabilities. It would be even more difficult for courts to go further and insist on the *creation* of *new* structures and procedures that aimed at the opposite result—real equal opportunity. Both dismantling discriminatory structures and mandating equality-generating structures in their place would require the type of constitutionally inflected policy making that legislatures do far better than courts.

Sometimes, of course, courts must engage in such policy making. Congress does not always step in with enforcement legislation. When it doesn't, it is up to the courts to do their best to implement the Constitution's commands, as they attempted, with only partial success, when overseeing the desegregation of the public schools over the last sixty years. But when Congress does step in, as it did with the FMLA, the Court must decide how much policy-making latitude to accord Congress.

The VRA reflects a different, but related, constitutional policy-making dynamic. When the VRA was first seriously challenged in 2009, one of the main arguments made against it was that it had succeeded in its goal of eradicating discrimination, with the result that it was no longer necessary, and hence, "inappropriate" enforcement legislation. (Recall that the enforcement clauses of both the Fourteenth and the Fifteenth Amendments authorize Congress to enact "appropriate" enforcement legislation.) The VRA's defenders responded, in part, that the law remained necessary and thus "appropriate" because without it the jurisdictions covered by the preclearance requirement would revert to their old discriminatory ways. Of course, a law's deterrent effect is often hard to measure, since the very basis of that effect requires measurement of an alternative universe in which the law does not exist. Measurement of that sort is sometimes possible: for example, experts can study a criminal law's deterrent effect by comparing two jurisdictions that are alike except that one has a particular law on the books while the other does not. But such comparisons are difficult. And as hard as they are as a general matter, they are doubly challenging when considering the VRA's preclearance provisions, since, by design, those provisions applied only to jurisdictions that presented unique histories of racial discrimination in voting. Quite literally, there was no noncovered jurisdiction that was otherwise identical to the covered ones, and thus no valid comparator.

Thus, the VRA's deterrent effect was difficult to evaluate. But this did not stop the justices from expressing skepticism when its defenders invoked that argument. During the oral argument in the 2009 precursor case to *Shelby County*, Chief Justice Roberts replied to the government lawyer's deterrence argument by recalling the story of the man who claimed that he had a special whistle that repelled (i.e., deterred) elephants. When asked for proof that the whistle actually did repel elephants, he simply blew the whistle and then observed to the onlookers that, indeed, there were no elephants around.[17] Four years later, that skepticism found expression in the *Shelby County* decision striking down the formula determining the preclearance provisions' geographic reach.

The Court's skepticism about the continued need for the VRA's preclearance provisions shares important similarities with its skepticism about the usefulness of the FMLA's self-care provision. Both of these judicial judgments reflect what can only be described as an unwillingness to defer to Congress's policy judgments about what is needed to ensure the equality the Court itself recognizes as constitutionally central. It should be clear that Congress's decisions to include the self-care provision in the FMLA and to renew the VRA with the same coverage formula reflect policy making—what we called earlier "constitutional policy making." Those decisions resulted from a process in which facts about the world were filtered through legislators' own ideologies and values and preferred substantive outcomes, with the resulting preferences presented, debated, and compromised, resulting in the final legislative product.[18]

In the FMLA, for example, women's rights advocates pressed on Congress the argument that the family-care leave provision, as beneficial as it might be in breaking down stereotypes about women's primary role in family caregiving, carried risks. In particular, it might create the perverse effect of making women even less attractive as employees, since it bestowed a benefit that, at least currently, was perceived as primarily assisting women.[19] The question for Congress was a difficult one: Would the provision of family-care leave in fact lead employers to further skew their preferences toward men? If so, by how much? What would be the best way to counteract that effect? Would those countermeasures impose too much of a burden on employers?[20] Seen through this lens, the *Coleman* Court's breezy skepticism about the sex equality benefits provided by the self-care leave provision appears to reflect nothing more than simple disagreement with Congress's analysis of the problem.

The same could be said for *Shelby County*'s dismissal of the deterrent effect of the VRA's preclearance provisions. The Court's response to that argument, in toto, is provided in this quotation: "Under [the deterrence] theory, however, [the preclearance provisions] would be effectively immune from scrutiny; no matter how 'clean' the record of covered jurisdictions, the argument could always be made that it was deterrence that accounted for the good behavior."[21] One can hear in this response the echoes of Chief Justice Roberts's elephant whistle question, four years earlier. Yet, as Justice Ginsburg argued in the dissent, a variety of data was available which the Court could have considered to assess the reality and size of that deterrent effect.

Still, one can sympathize with a judge's frustration at being asked to assess the continued need for a statute based on a counterfactual argument about deterrence. Such judgments—just like judgments about the *initial* need for a statute (such as the FMLA's self-care leave provision)—require more than evaluation of objectively available evidence. Those judgments also require, literally, the exercise of *judgment*—that is, application of one's own experiences and values and intuitions to the cold hard facts. Indeed, as two scholars have stated, policy making quite literally consists of "the process by which officials exercise power on the basis of their judgment that their actions will produce socially desirable results."[22] In our system, we elect representatives—those who share our experiences and values and intuitions—to make those judgments. Thus, even if one sympathizes with Chief Justice Roberts's exasperation at having to decide whether a statute, like his elephant whistle, really deters unwanted conduct, one should also consider whether a better path lay open than simply rejecting the deterrence argument outright.

Policy and Predictive Judgments in Enforcement Legislation

The FMLA and VRA examples reflect the increasing burdens the Court's Enforcement Clause doctrine imposes on judicial review. As reflected in *Coleman* and *Shelby County*, the Court's approach entails it engaging in quintessential policy-type judgments, about either the effectiveness of the challenged legislation (as in *Coleman*) or the continued need for the law (as in *Shelby County*). But such judgments are exceptionally difficult for courts to make with any degree of credibility. They constitute textbook examples of courts inappropriately second-guessing legislatures' policy-making discretion. It is common to find in the Court's opinions on all subjects an insistence that it has no business disagreeing with a legislature's judgment about the policy wisdom reflected in a particular statute. Judgments about whether a statute has completely eradicated the constitutional evil or merely forced it into dormancy reflect simply another type of policy decision. In both cases, the underlying decision reflects a judgment about the effectiveness of a particular legal rule in changing human conduct, and the continued need for that rule in order to safeguard that change. In neither case is the decision easily susceptible to an answer based on conventional legal or doctrinal analysis.

Despite its poor fit with courts' competence and appropriate institutional role, this type of review seems to be exactly what the congruence and proportionality test calls upon judges to perform. So understood, it becomes less surprising to read Justice Scalia's critique of the congruence and proportionality test. While originally signing onto that test in *Boerne*, seven years later in the *Lane* case he abandoned it. In separate opinions in *Lane* and *Coleman*, he explained that his decision to reject that test flowed from his concern that it ensnares courts in a policy-reviewing role for which they are unsuited, and requires them to "grad[e]" Congress's "homework"—that is, to review the legislative record to ensure that Congress found an adequate evidentiary basis for the legislation. He also expressed concern that the congruence and proportionality test is one that "cannot objectively be shown to have been met or failed."[23] Indeed, in *Coleman* he trenchantly observed that both the plurality's and the dissent's application of the test seemed plausible to him.

The underlying insight of Justice Scalia's critique is clear. As enforcement legislation becomes more policy-inflected—that is, as such legislation evolves away from straightforward restrictions on blatant discrimination that demonstrably exists, and instead employs more nuanced means to ferret out subtler discrimination or discrimination that appears eradicated but may simply be lying dormant—it will become harder and harder for courts to review the constitutionality of such legislation without intruding into Congress's policy-making domain.

But despite Justice Scalia's protests, the congruence and proportionality test appears here to stay. At the very least, it appears inconceivable that the current Court (or, indeed, any reasonably imaginable future Court) would abandon the general concept of judicial supremacy in constitutional interpretation. Judicial imperialism knows no ideology: both liberals and conservatives on the Court appear willing to enforce what they believe to be basic constitutional principles against contrary congressional judgments. Nevertheless, all (again except Justice Scalia) agree that the Enforcement Clause gives Congress at least some authority to "enforce" the Fourteenth Amendment by enacting prophylactic rules of conduct that exceed what the Constitution directly requires.[24] Review of such prophylactic rules for anything more than the barest rationality inevitably entails comparing the scope of that rule with the scope of the constitutional violation it targets—in other words, review for congruence and proportionality, or its functional equivalent.

* * *

Chapters 4 and 5 have identified two distinct problems raised by the Court's attempt to apply its modern, more aggressive approach to reviewing enforcement legislation. The next two chapters offer solutions to those problems. Chapter 6 deals with the suspect class problem chapter 4 identified. It argues for a "refocused" enforcement power, one that judges the congruence and proportionality of enforcement legislation against the correct standard—namely, the core constitutional rule rather than any judge-crafted decisional heuristic. Chapter 7 deals with problems posed by judicial review of the policy choices implicit in legislative policy. Chapter 5 has explained this problem in the context of the FMLA and VRA; it has also argued that this problem, just like the suspect class problem raised in chapter 4, will likely recur. We have identified this policy-review problem as fundamentally raising a question of judicial deference to legislative judgments. Chapter 7 addresses "the deference question." Chapter 8 then considers the distinct question of Congress's ability to enact enforcement legislation aimed at private parties.

Chapters 9 and 10 then apply the book's approach. Chapter 9 applies it to concrete examples of federal legislation enforcing the fundamental equal protection principles we've discussed up to now. Chapter 10 expands the scope and considers how this book's approach applies to federal legislation enforcing other Fourteenth Amendment rights (including particular equal protection principles not addressed in chapter 9). The book then concludes by offering some thoughts about the proper role for enforcement legislation in a constitutional democracy such as ours.

PART III

What to Do about It

Constructing a Modern Enforcement Power

6

Refocusing Congruence and Proportionality

Chapters 4 and 5 identified two basic problems with the Court's current approach to the enforcement power. First, since *Boerne* the Court has tied its review of equal protection enforcement legislation to the suspect class status of the group that legislation seeks to benefit. As chapter 4 explained, this approach establishes a false baseline for measuring congruence and proportionality, given the status of suspect class doctrine as merely a doctrinal heuristic rather core equal protection law.

In practical terms, this flaw has two implications. First, it leads the Court to apply mistakenly strict review to enforcement legislation benefiting non-suspect classes. Second, it makes it difficult for the Court to review enforcement legislation for congruence and proportionality when the Court has not yet determined the suspect class status of a group. This latter problem is only magnified when we realize that the Court appears to have sworn off creating new suspect classes. Thus, when the Court begins reviewing enforcement legislation benefiting emerging groups, it will find itself doctrinally adrift.

Chapter 5 addressed a second problem. As antidiscrimination law matures, courts will encounter both legislation that imposes more nuanced and subtle remedies and legislation that appears to have succeeded in eradicating the targeted discrimination. These two phenomena pose related challenges in the Enforcement Clause context. As exemplified by the *Coleman* case, legislation attacking subtler, more nuanced forms of discrimination will encounter the objection that its remedies are too indirect and attenuated to constitute an effective response to discrimination. Similarly, *Shelby County* illustrated the phenomenon of the Court finding an enforcement statute unnecessary, and thus beyond Congress's power to enact, when it has so succeeded that the Court is unconvinced that it remains necessary as a deterrent to backsliding.

The first of these problems requires a basic rethinking—what this chapter calls a refocusing—of the Court's approach to the congruence and proportionality standard. This chapter provides a template for such a refocusing. The second of these problems requires us to examine how much deference a court should accord congressional judgments underlying legislation that is challenged as either too indirect or no longer necessary. Chapter 7 considers this question—what we have called "the deference question."

The Need for a Refocused Approach to Enforcement Legislation

The Court's post-*Boerne* approach to congruence and proportionality—as exemplified most starkly in the *Garrett* case that rejected the enforcement power foundation for the Americans with Disabilities Act's employment provisions—makes it impossible for the Court to accord appropriate latitude to Congress to enforce the Equal Protection Clause. As chapter 4 explained, the Court's insistence that enforcement legislation be congruent and proportional to the Court's own equal protection doctrine mistakes that doctrine for underlying constitutional meaning. Contrary to *Garrett* and cases like it, it is that underlying meaning that should serve as the reference point for the congruence and proportionality analysis. Sometimes judicial doctrine equates with that underlying meaning. But sometimes, as with the Court's institutional competence–based refusal to grant suspect class status to disability discrimination, it does not.

This chapter therefore proposes that the Court refocus its congruence and proportionality analysis. It does not call for replacing that standard. Any Enforcement Clause doctrine that allows Congress to vindicate its own interpretation of the Fourteenth Amendment would both raise theoretical concerns about the separation of powers and create serious practical difficulties of checking otherwise unbounded congressional power. The congruence and proportionality test, by requiring enforcement legislation to respond to both the type of constitutional violation it targets (congruence) and the magnitude of that violation (proportionality), strikes as sensible a balance as doctrinal language can between giving Congress appropriate latitude and tethering enforcement legislation to constitutional meaning.

Nevertheless, an intellectually honest understanding of the Enforcement Clause requires that congressional power not be hamstrung by limitations that attend judicial review. Such limitations grow out of courts' inability to discern equal protection's true meaning or their understanding of their limited institutional role. It is laudable when courts limit their constitutional scrutiny of state conduct in response to such realities. But those realities do not apply to Congress. Thus, they should not limit congressional enforcement power under Section 5 in the same way that they limit courts' power to decide direct constitutional challenges under Section 1.

A Refocused Enforcement Power

An appropriately refocused enforcement power rests on the proposition that Congress possesses the power to enforce the *real* Equal Protection

Clause—that is, the core constitutional rule that clause enacts. This thesis implies that such a concept exists—that is, that there exists an identifiable set of principles or rules we can describe as the core law of the Equal Protection Clause. Before we can consider that thesis, we need to be clear about what we mean by "core" law.

The distinction between core equal protection law and penumbral principles rests on a conception of what courts do when they decide cases. If everything courts say about the Constitution counts as such core law, then no such distinction exists. But as we know from chapter 4's analysis of the *Cleburne* case, sometimes courts will decide constitutional cases based on principles that primarily reflect their own institutional capabilities—in particular, their understanding of the limits of those capabilities. In *Cleburne*, the Court grounded its refusal to accord heightened scrutiny to intellectual disability classifications largely on concerns about courts' ability to distinguish both between invidious and benign singling out of that group, and between that group and others that might claim a similar social status as the intellectually disabled and thus demand similar judicial protection. These reasons have nothing to do with the constitutionality of intellectual disability discrimination but have everything to do with courts' ability to apply the constitutional rule—what this book calls "core" constitutional law.

This distinction between core constitutional law and institutionally limited judicial statements of that law is not a new one. Lawrence Sager's 1978 article on underenforced constitutional norms (mentioned in chapter 3) distinguished between what he called "analytical" and "institutional" reasons for reaching a result in a particular constitutional case.[1] (Not coincidentally, Professor Sager identified the enforcement power as one of the main areas of constitutional doctrine that distinction implicated.) Professor Sager's typology tracks our distinction between "core" constitutional law and institutionally limited judicial constitutional principles: to quote him, "[T]he important difference between a true constitutional conception and the judicially formulated construct is that the judicial construct may be truncated for reasons which are based not upon analysis of the constitutional concept but upon various concerns of the Court about its institutional role."[2]

At times justices have explicitly acknowledged this distinction. Most recently, in his dissent in the 2013 *Windsor* case striking down part of the Defense of Marriage Act, Justice Alito stated that "[t]he modern tiers of [equal protection] scrutiny . . . are a heuristic to help judges determine when classifications have that fair and substantial relation to the object of the legislation" which equal protection requires.[3] Yet they often ignore it, as chapter 4 explains they did in the *Garrett* case, when the Court refused to recognize the institutional competence grounding of its earlier decision in *Cleburne*. It is perhaps unsurprising that the modern Court often ignores this distinction: after all, if it acknowledges that its decisions may not exhaust the Constitution's meaning, then it inevitably implies that other institutions, particularly Congress, may have a legitimate claim to authority to fill in the resulting gaps. For a Court that likes to see itself as, literally, the supreme arbiter of constitutional meaning, such a concession is not attractive.

But regardless of whether the Court likes it, the fact remains that parts of the Constitution, including the Equal Protection Clause, enact broad rules that courts may be incapable of applying to their full limits. As discussed in chapters 1 and 2, that clause reflects a broad equality rule, applicable to all groups (indeed, to all persons regardless of their status as a group member)[4] and all government action. To be sure, it does not require perfect equality—even as a theoretical matter separate from its judicial enforceability, equal protection does not require states to classify with complete precision. Such a rule would subject state governments to judicial and/or congressional correction even for minor classification mistakes. Respect for state legislative processes, and for state autonomy more generally, and the unlikelihood that the Thirty-Ninth Congress intended such a radical revision of American federalism, render such a rule undesirable as a matter of policy and implausible as a matter of original meaning or intent. But even if the *depth* of the equal protection requirement may not be unlimited, its *breadth* is: the Court has made it clear that equal protection requires at least reasonable treatment of all groups (and, indeed, all individuals), in every instance of government decision making.

Such a broad rule implies a similarly broad scope for the enforcement power. In contrast to the analysis in *Garrett*, a congruence and proportionality test that looked to this broader rule as its reference point would not review enforcement legislation skeptically simply because the Court considered itself unable, for institutional reasons, to accord heightened scrutiny to the group that legislation benefits. Such level of scrutiny decisions would be relevant, to be sure. But they would not dictate the fate of such legislation, as they did in *Garrett* and cases like it. Instead, analysis under a refocused congruence and proportionality test would shift the inquiry away from such institutionally bounded conclusions. In their place it would focus on whatever core equal protection rules could be derived from the Court's equal protection jurisprudence.

This approach requires that we parse Supreme Court decisions carefully to determine the content of those core constitutional rules. The need for this task flows from the fact that courts, including the Supreme Court, may do several things when they decide constitutional cases. In ascending order of fundamentality, they may decide the case in front of them (i.e., decide who wins and who loses), announce and apply doctrinal rules that help them decide the case (e.g., by deciding that sex classifications merit intermediate scrutiny and applying that scrutiny to the case at hand), and announce core rules of constitutional law. Courts need not perform all three tasks in any given case. For example, a court may rule for an equal protection plaintiff without deciding whether the challenged classification merits heightened judicial scrutiny.[5] Nor is there any necessary relationship between these three tasks—in other words, performing a "higher-level" task does not require that tasks down the ladder also be performed. For example, the Court may decide that a constitutional claim merits a particular level of judicial scrutiny, and then remand the case to the lower courts with directions to apply that scrutiny. For our purposes the important point is that this approach to the enforcement power requires us to read Supreme Court opinions carefully to determine exactly what those opinions say.

As an illustration, recall *Garrett*, the ADA case discussed in chapter 4. *Garrett's* skeptical review of the ADA's enforcement power bona fides rested heavily on the Court's conclusion that disability discrimination was not a matter of great constitutional concern. The sole support for that conclusion was the Court's earlier decision in *Cleburne* to accord only rational basis scrutiny to disability discrimination. However, as we saw in chapter 2, that aspect of *Cleburne* is best understood as resting heavily on subconstitutional doctrine, given its foundation in the Court's (admirable) concern for its ability to competently apply heightened scrutiny to intellectual disability classifications. Thus, a careful reading of *Cleburne*—the type of reading this book argues we must do in order to perform congruence and proportionality analysis properly—reveals much less about constitutional law (and hence about the scope of Congress's Enforcement Clause power to enact the ADA) than *Garrett* so breezily suggested.[6]

Does this analysis mean that *Cleburne* says nothing of relevance to the enforcement power? Hardly. First, the fact that the Court struck down the government action in that case means that some underlying equal protection rule was transgressed. Courts do not lightly strike down government action—at least so they say. Taking them at their word, the decision in *Cleburne* means that the Cleburne City Council crossed an actual constitutional line when it prevented the intellectually disabled persons from establishing their group home. The content of that line—the aspect of the case that convinced the Court to strike down the government's action—reflects a constitutional rule. The task—an important one—consists of uncovering the content of that rule.

We've already noted (again in chapter 2) that *Cleburne* is unusual for applying relatively stringent review under the guise of the rational basis standard. Recall that under that standard, when the government offers a legitimate reason for the challenged action, the court does not insist on a tight connection between that justification and the government's action—a "rational relationship" will do. Nor will a court examine that proffered justification carefully, to ensure that it was the actual motivation for the government's action.

Yet in *Cleburne* the city offered a legitimate reason for its action: the concern about safe evacuation of a multiperson residence located within a floodplain. The Court's rejection of the city's explanation suggests that some other aspect of the case superseded the normal deference courts accord under the rational basis standard. In *Cleburne* the Court was likely not convinced by the flood evacuation argument because the trial court had found that city residents' fear of intellectually disabled persons constituted part of the city's motivation.[7] This direct evidence of an illegitimate government motive likely convinced the Supreme Court to disregard the possibility that the city's action was motivated by benign concerns. Indeed, the Court stated as much.[8]

Thus, the Court's analysis in *Cleburne* both recognizes the force of equal protection's anti-animus rule and demonstrates that such animus toward intellectually disabled persons exists in modern America. Of course not every decision harming that group will be infected with animus. Even when an action is thus infected, such illegitimate goals may not always be perceived; perhaps other municipalities will be more discreet about appearing openly receptive to plainly illegitimate citizen biases. But the Court's detection of such motivations in *Cleburne* is surely a data point relevant to a congressional determination of the extent to which disability discrimination is driven by animus.

As important as it is to realize that the Equal Protection Clause prohibits discrimination grounded in animus, and that such animus continues to exist in some contexts today, this insight does not add much to our understanding of what the clause prohibits. Thus, this aspect of *Cleburne* does not state much new constitutional law. However, a careful reading of the case provides additional important evidence about constitutional meaning. In particular, while its conclusion on the suspect class question may not itself constitute constitutional law, its analysis of that issue is surely relevant to what that law means in a given context.

Let's consider that analysis. In the course of denying intellectually disabled persons suspect class status, the Court nevertheless acknowledged that they have suffered a history of discrimination. Even if it was not enough to convince the Court that they ultimately satisfied the Court's criteria for suspect class status, this sort of intermediate conclusion would surely be relevant to a congressional determination that such discrimination ran a high risk of being irrational or reflecting animus. The "history of discrimination" element is part of the suspect class inquiry for good reason: it provides at least circumstantial evidence that current disfavored treatment reflects old, invidious attitudes. More precisely, it reveals the historical occurrence of exactly the sort of systematic disadvantaging that equal protection disfavors.

Even if satisfaction of that element does not prove the case for suspect class status, it can surely play a legitimate role in a congressional determination about animus. This is especially true when, as in *Cleburne*, the Court denies suspect class status largely due to concerns about courts' institutional role—concerns that do not apply to Congress. As we noted in chapter 2, the Court candidly admitted that one reason for that denial was that the Court could not distinguish suspect class arguments made by other groups that suffered similar histories of discrimination, prejudice, and relative political powerlessness.[9] This admission seems tailor-made for understanding *Cleburne* as a case where the record revealed good reasons to be concerned about this type of discrimination, but where the Court felt itself unable to take the normal doctrinal step of identifying the group as a suspect or quasi-suspect class. These insights reveal a great deal about what equal protection requires, courts' inability to enforce such requirements, and the content of the gap between those two concepts.[10]

Note something interesting about this analysis. Of the three levels of content we can find in court decisions (results, doctrine, and law), only the last one explicitly states core constitutional meaning. Nevertheless, both *Cleburne*'s result and its doctrinal analysis help us understand that core meaning. It is this careful reading of judicial precedent that is required when courts undertake the refocused congruence and proportionality review this book calls for.

The Difficulties of This Approach

Looked at one way, the approach suggested here does nothing more than tweak the Court's current view of Congress's enforcement power: it retains the congruence and proportionality test but merely substitutes the correct focal point for that inquiry. But that substitution makes all the difference. The correct focal point for the congruence and proportionality test—the actual meaning of the Equal Protection Clause—is both vague and heavily value-laden. As such, it becomes a much more difficult matter for a court to determine whether a given piece of legislation is congruent and proportional to the target that should count—the clause's actual meaning.

Consider what we know about equal protection law—the true law at the core of the Equal Protection Clause. We know, at the very least, that it prohibits irrational discrimination. We also know that it prohibits discrimination that is motivated by animus—or, to state the requirement affirmatively, it requires government to act only in pursuit of legitimate, public-regarding goals.[11] And we know that these rules apply across the range of government action, from crucially important decisions about racial segregation in key government institutions such as schools and prisons to seemingly minor questions concerning a local bureaucrat's decision about the terms under which a homeowner will be hooked up to a municipal water supply.[12]

We may know more equal protection law than this, but for now consider only this description. These statements provide us with only the haziest outlines of what equal protection requires in a given case. Does it require that opticians enjoy the same rights as optometrists to fit corrective lenses? Does it require that a fifty-year-old policeman in excellent physical shape be allowed to remain on the force, or does it allow the government to force him to retire? Does it allow government to prohibit someone prone to epileptic seizures from being a pilot? How about someone who is asymptomatic but genetically predisposed to epilepsy? Does it prohibit single-sex public education?

To answer these questions, we need to apply the rationality and public-purpose requirements noted earlier. But applying those requirements may require significant knowledge of the empirical world—for example, the risks of having lesser-trained opticians fit corrective lenses, or the likelihood that a genetic predisposition to epilepsy may manifest itself without warning. It may also require a sensitive understanding of society's values—for example, is disability discrimination understood to be fundamentally unfair, and thus appropriate only in very limited circumstances, or a morally neutral feature of government's everyday need to decide who is qualified to do what?

When posed as challenges to enforcement legislation, these questions would be much simpler for courts to answer if they stuck with the approach exemplified by *Garrett*. Under that approach, a court would reason that since opticians, the aged, and the disabled are not suspect classes, discrimination on those grounds presents no serious constitutional problem. Thus, enforcement legislation targeting that discrimination would receive a skeptical judicial reception. (The suspect class status of genetics discrimination has not been decided and poses interesting questions.)[13] *Garrett*'s approach would accord much more latitude to legislation targeting sex classifications, given the Court's well-established rule subjecting sex classifications to heightened scrutiny. And indeed, as chapter 4 noted in its review of post-*Boerne* case law, these contrasting treatments of enforcement legislation track the Court's actual results, at least until the more recent *Coleman* and *Shelby County* cases. More to the point, the built-in thumbs on the scale (against legislation benefiting nonsuspect classes and in favor of legislation benefiting suspect classes) made the Court's task much easier—even if that ease was purchased at the cost of analytical coherence.

By contrast, if the congruence and proportionality inquiry asks instead whether age or disability or sex discrimination violates the core constitutional rule against irrational or animus-based discrimination, then the inquiry becomes much less straightforward. Consider disability. While the *Garrett* Court had no difficulty concluding that states may "hardheadedly—and perhaps hardheartedly"[14] decide that disability status is relevant to an employment decision, the Court refused to consider the larger scope of the rationality/public purpose question. In particular, it failed to consider whether disability discrimination in employment often reflected not harsh-but-efficient sorting but the operation of stereotypes that lacked a strong grounding in fact. Indeed, in deciding that disability discrimination was in fact rational (or at least not irrational), the Court explicitly focused on the content of its own, judicially crafted "rational basis" test.

What's wrong with the use of that test? Doesn't it, after all, ask whether a particular act of discrimination was irrational? Not exactly. Recall from our earlier discussion of *Carolene Products* that the judge-made rational basis test, with its presumptions in favor of the government and its placement of proof burdens on the plaintiff, stacks the rationality inquiry in favor of the former. There may be good reason for that deck-stacking, *when it is the Court that is reviewing the government action*. In that case, it is appropriate for the Court to give every benefit of the doubt to the legislature, in deference to the latter's authority to make policy decisions. Such deference is especially appropriate when (as is usually the case when the Court performs rationality review) the Court is confident that the plaintiff class is free to engage the political process to protect its interests.

But this deference to the legislature plays much less of a role when the Court, rather than deciding an equal protection claim brought to it in the first instance, instead reviews enforcement legislation. In that case, the deference-to-the-legislature justification cuts *in favor* of enforcement legislation, rather than justifying a skeptical reception grounded on the benefited group's lack of suspect class status. At the very least, judicial review of enforcement legislation should feature an inquiry into the irrationality of the targeted state conduct that is unskewed by the presumptions and proof burdens that mark the standard rational basis test.

What would such an unskewed, "pure" rationality inquiry look like? Supreme Court case law gives us some clues. The most famous examples of stricter-than-normal rationality review involve discrimination against groups that have some claim to be a discrete and insular minority and to thus merit explicitly heightened review—most notably, the *Cleburne* case discussed earlier and *Romer v. Evans*,[15] the 1996 case involving sexual orientation discrimination, both of which we discussed in chapter 2. In those cases the Court, while ostensibly performing mere rational basis review, nevertheless appeared to insist on a tighter-than-usual fit between the government interest and the classification. In *Cleburne* the Court refused to credit the government's flood evacuation justification for denying the group home permit, noting that other multiresident communities were allowed to locate in areas presenting the same flood risk as the area where the *Cleburne* plaintiffs wanted to live. Similarly, in *Romer* the Court refused to credit the state's justifications for the challenged law, concluding that the law imposed a much broader burden on gays and lesbians than was necessary to advance the proffered interests—so much broader that the law could not be explained as attempting to further those interests.

Less discussed, but perhaps more instructive, is an obscure 1980 case, *Railroad Retirement Board v. Fritz*.[16] In *Fritz* the Court applied its standard deferential version of rational basis review to reject an equal protection challenge to a federal law that classified among railroad employees for purposes of pension eligibility. (The fact that the case involved a federal rather than a state law does not change the underlying analysis for our purposes.)[17] Justice Brennan dissented, and applied a more stringent version of rationality review. His opinion is instructive because it applied a purer version of heightened rationality review than the majorities in *Cleburne* and *Romer*, cases where commentators and other justices strongly suspected that the Court was in fact performing heightened scrutiny without saying so.[18] By contrast, in *Fritz* there is no indication that Justice Brennan was applying such *sub silentio* heightened scrutiny—indeed, he agreed with the majority's conclusion that, as garden variety economic regulation, the challenged law merely had to satisfy rational basis scrutiny. Justice Brennan simply argued that such scrutiny had to be meaningful.

Justice Brennan's rationality review in *Fritz* differs from standard rational basis review in two fundamental ways. First, he insisted on discovering the government's actual purpose in enacting the challenged law and testing the law's reasonableness by reference to that purpose. This differs radically from the Court's normal rational basis practice of accepting a statutory purpose that *hypothetically* might have motivated the legislature. Second, Justice

Brennan insisted on a meaningful, rather than merely a remotely plausible, fit between the statute and that actual purpose. Applying this tighter fit requirement in *Fritz*, he essentially reweighed Congress's policy conclusions—the so-called equitable considerations determining which groups of workers would have their pensions cut—that the majority identified as a plausible congressional motivation for its allocation decisions.[19]

Justice Brennan's brand of rationality review imposes real burdens on courts. Consider first his insistence that the Court not hypothesize the legislature's purpose, but instead that it uncover its actual purpose. As Justice Stevens noted in his otherwise sympathetic concurring opinion, this approach would involve the Court in a difficult search for a unitary legislative purpose when, in fact, complex legislation enacted by a diverse legislative coalition likely features multiple, sometimes conflicting, purposes. It would also create the anomaly that one state's statute might be struck down if the Court analyzed it based on that legislature's purpose, while the identical statute in another state might survive if the legislature identified a more palatable purpose.[20] Other forms of government action would pose even more daunting challenges to a rigorous purpose inquiry. For example, think about voter referenda: How would a court determine the purpose of a provision that was enacted through a popular vote of several million citizens?[21]

Second, consider Justice Brennan's review of Congress's estimation of the fairness of the classifications it drew—the so-called equitable considerations we mentioned earlier. As explained more fully later, it is exceptionally difficult for a court to second-guess those sorts of judgments with any legitimacy, exactly because they largely partake of moral reasoning rather than logic or empirics. One can perceive this problem in *Fritz*, where Justice Brennan was forced to reargue the "equitable considerations" that the majority held justified Congress's actions—essentially disagreeing with what the majority assumed to be Congress's reasoning about the fairness of the lines it drew between different classes of pensioners. As much as one might sympathize with the losers in Congress's classification scheme, Justice Brennan's out-and-out policy disagreement with Congress over that scheme's fairness raises serious questions about the Court's proper role in second-guessing the results of the democratic process.

None of this is to say that courts are incapable of, or should never perform, a stronger version of rationality review. That stronger version is on display every time the Court engages in intermediate or strict scrutiny, and even when it engages in heightened rational basis review of the type on display in *Cleburne* and *Romer*. In many cases such stronger review is appropriate. But for courts to engage in such review every time a statute implicates equal protection—that is, every time a statute classifies—would entail a major arrogation of power to the federal courts at the expense of state legislatures (and, as reflected in *Fritz*, at the expense of Congress as well).

Scrutinizing legislative action poses even more difficulties for courts when a plaintiff challenges a law on the ground that it reflects animus. Many classification decisions inevitably take the form of decisions about fundamental fairness—that is, an intuitive sense that two groups are or are not relevantly similar. Return to the disability example. As we noted earlier, *Garrett* remarked that state government employers could "hardheadedly—and perhaps hardheartedly" decide that accommodating a disabled employee would cost the state more than it was worth.[22] Yet, such a decision could also reflect more than cold, rational (and thus constitutionally permissible) classification. First, as noted earlier, it could also reflect stereotyping about disabled people that would perhaps lead an employer to irrationally underestimate a disabled person's ability to perform her job well. Second, and more important for our current purposes, it could also reflect deeper phenomena: a discomfort about being around disabled people, even a dislike, and perhaps even a sense that they are morally compromised. Such tragic feelings have deep roots; one need not go as far back as Victor Hugo's story about Quasimodo[23] to find evidence of popular disgust toward the disabled.[24] Congress made such findings in its record supporting the ADA.[25] Moreover, recall that the city council in *Cleburne* relied on residents' fear of intellectually disabled persons to justify their exclusion from a neighborhood.

Judicial review of a claim that such discrimination reflects animus requires a court to second-guess the legitimacy of the public's feelings about the targeted group—to second-guess, in Justice Scalia's memorable terminology, whether the challenged law reflected an (illegitimate) "fit of spite" rather than a (legitimate) "*Kulturkampf*."[26] As suggested by our earlier critique of Justice Brennan's analogous second-guessing in *Fritz*, this task fits awkwardly with courts' roles as unelected arbiters of law. Natural law scholars may be more comfortable with judges playing that role. But such approaches to judicial review are controversial, given our commitment to democratic decision making, and our political culture's rhetorical insistence (unrealistic as it may be) that judges not import their personal values into their deliberations.

Constitutional provisions such as equal protection may place some moral decisions beyond the power of democratic majorities to make. For example, public embrace of a racist theology or morality would presumably not justify a return to slavery or apartheid-type legislation, as long as, respectively, the Thirteenth and Fourteenth Amendments remained on the books.[27] But a court that identifies those off-limits areas by reference to its own moral sense risks serious criticism and allegations of illegitimacy. As Learned Hand, a prominent federal judge in the middle of the twentieth century, once put it, referring to the Supreme Court: "For myself it would be most irksome to be ruled by a bevy of Platonic Guardians, even if I knew how to choose them."[28]

Congress's Expertise and Authority

The last section concluded by suggesting that courts may find it difficult to engage in a pure, presumption-free method of scrutiny, even if only to ensure that legislatures not classify irrationally or based on animus. That difficulty suggests that perhaps judges are doing the right thing when they limit their ordinary equal protection review to a very deferential version of rational basis scrutiny. But is Congress any better at reviewing and, if necessary, countermanding state action? We must ask this question because deciding whether the Enforcement Clause justifies a given statute requires that we determine how much latitude Congress should enjoy to enact legislation enforcing the same vague and morally inflected equal protection guarantee the Court has such difficulty with. The fact that courts are not institutionally designed to scrutinize much discriminatory state action does not prove the case for broader congressional power if Congress is equally poorly suited to that task. However, it turns out that, at least theoretically, Congress possesses the qualities that warrant significant, though not complete, confidence in its ability to make these determinations.

Whether this theoretical argument can be converted into a practical one responsive to legislative realities is considered in the next chapter. But for now, consider the theory. First, consider Congress's capacity to review the rationality of state legislative classifications. As noted in the previous section, a great part of the Court's hesitancy to second-guess the rationality of state legislation rests on a recognition that the entire enterprise of legislating consists of drawing lines—allowing optometrists, but not opticians, unfettered freedom to fit corrective lenses, or allowing police officers to stay on the force when they turn forty-nine but not when they turn fifty. Courts are generally thought to lack the capability to competently decide, say, the fitness for duty of the average forty-nine-year-old policeman or the public health risks of opticians fitting glasses without the patient first visiting an optometrist. Even more fundamentally, the very task of making those decisions—the task of balancing the benefits and burdens of social life and assigning those benefits and burdens by drawing a line separating winners and losers—is inherently a political one, best performed by political bodies rather than courts.[29]

To drive the point home, consider an example—one of many—where the Supreme Court did in fact draw such a line. In *County of Riverside v. McLaughlin*,[30] the Court decided how promptly states had to provide a probable cause hearing to persons arrested without an arrest warrant. In a previous case, the Court held that the Fourth Amendment required that states provide such hearings "promptly." As it explained in *McLaughlin*, such a vague standard caused a spate of challenges to government policies on this issue, putting lower courts in the position of making what the Court itself called "legislative judgments."[31] Nevertheless, the Court felt it had to provide a standard (at least in the absence of enforcement legislation, which was not forthcoming).

In *McLaughlin* it did. It announced a forty-eight-hour rule: delays less than forty-eight hours were presumptively constitutional unless the delay was for an illegitimate reason, while delays of longer than forty-eight hours were presumptively unconstitutional unless the state could prove the existence of unusual circumstances justifying the longer wait. The Court did not base its selection of forty-eight hours on any legal text or common-law rule; in announcing that rule, it simply said that a forty-eight-hour limit "tak[es] into account the competing interests articulated in" the earlier case announcing the "promptness" requirement.[32]

In essence, then, the Court, faced with the prospect of lower courts making "legislative judgments" about the constitutionality of delays of particular durations, made a legislative judgment of its own. There is nothing inherently wrong with that. The Constitution, as understood by the Court in the earlier case, required, albeit vaguely, that probable cause hearings be "prompt," and it was reasonable for the Court to worry about lower courts reaching inconsistent answers to the question of what "prompt" meant. Nevertheless, one cannot describe the Court's line as any less "legislative" (the Court's own word) than those drawn by the lower courts. Nothing in standard legal sources pointed to forty-eight hours as the appropriate line, as opposed, say, to twenty-four, thirty-six, or seventy-two. Instead, the Court balanced interests and drew a line (even if the line marked only the presumptive, rather than the absolute, constitutional line). Such line-drawing may be necessary. But we should recognize courts' limited capacity and legitimacy to engage in such conduct.

Congress, however, is not similarly limited. First, as a legislature it has the same institutional capacity as state governments to make the classification decisions courts may properly decline to second-guess for reasons of institutional competence. Of course, our federal system limits Congress's ability to override state choices without a specific grant of authority. But that qualifier goes to the source of power, not to whether Congress as an institution possesses the same raw competence as a state legislature to make policy judgments.

Second, Congress enjoys similar politically grounded legitimacy that state legislatures enjoy to make such judgments. Federal courts properly refrain from second-guessing state legislatures' judgments in part out of respect for legislatures' electorally based authority to make policy, and thus for the legitimacy of that policy. But Congress possesses analogous electorally based authority. Indeed, Congress enjoys even more such authority, given the combination of its national scope with Section 5's explicit conferral of power on Congress to enforce the Fourteenth Amendment's nationwide restriction on states. The relevance of Congress's national scope is discussed more later. For current purposes, it is enough to observe that, if policy making is most legitimately done by elected legislators as opposed to appointed judges, then Congress does not suffer the same legitimacy deficit as courts when it comes to reviewing states' legislative work product.

So far, this argument has tentatively suggested that Congress enjoys superior competence and authority, relative to courts, to review the *rationality* of legislative classifications. What about congressional review of *moral judgments* state legislatures make when they classify? Here, the argument for Congress is even stronger. Recall the reason courts do not enjoy great legitimacy to second-guess such decisions: as moral judgments, they are not susceptible to dispassionate legal or even policy analysis. Instead, they are fundamentally matters of belief and perspective. As such, decisions based on them must be made by democratic deliberation, unless the Court has decided that a constitutional provision speaks to that matter and removes it from democratic debate.

Congress's views regarding moral judgments are especially authoritative. The Equal Protection Clause, as a mandate for equality across all groups and all government contexts, enacts a nationwide rule that, at the very least, prohibits discrimination grounded on a verdict that the burdened group is morally inferior. The national scope of that rule appropriately bestows significant authority on Congress, as the one governmental institution that is both continually electorally renewed and of explicitly national scope, to discern and instantiate the nation's moral judgments. Even as compared with the presidency, Congress is superior, given its more frequent renewal (two years instead of four), the local-district basis of the House, and the Senate's explicit broad geographic basis. On that last point, consider the fact that in 2012 someone could have amassed the electoral votes to become president by winning only eleven states.[33] Those states would account for fewer than half of the Senate votes needed to enact a statute.

The upshot is that Congress has a stronger warrant than courts to perform more intrusive review of state legislation for compliance with equal protection's core requirements of rationality and public purpose. Still, the argument is by no means complete. First, as a matter of separation of powers, courts retain a role in ensuring that Congress not exceed the admittedly vague prohibitions the Court has found in the Equal Protection Clause. Without a judicial check, broad congressional power to *enforce* the vague equal protection guarantee could effectively become an unlimited power to *interpret* that guarantee. Second, as a matter of federalism, the analysis so far does not change the fact that the Equal Protection Clause leaves some regulatory leeway to states. The limited nature of equal protection's restrictions on states requires that congressional enforcement of that guarantee respect those limits.

In sum, this theory justifies broad congressional power to enforce the Equal Protection Clause. That power is often broader than that courts enjoy when they decide equal protection cases themselves. But separation of powers and federalism imperatives mean that this power has limits. The Court has insisted on a role in policing those limits, despite the fact that it possesses less competence and authority than Congress to translate equal protection's vague promise into concrete rules. The challenge is to envision a method for the Court to exercise that policing function credibly.

A Brief Word on Other Equal Protection Law

Before turning to the judicial check promised at the end of the last section, we must consider whether equal protection law exists beyond the requirement that classifications not be irrational or based on animus. If such additional law exists, then congressional enforcement legislation implicating those rules must also be congruent and proportional to it.

Such law does exist. First, the Court has identified a set of interests that it considers so important that government must presumptively distribute them equally. This so-called fundamental rights strand of equal protection is more analogous to the Due Process Clause, in that it is based on the identification of particular rights rather than the act of classification in itself. Chapter 10 of this book speculates about applying our analysis to other Fourteenth Amendment rights, including due process rights. That speculation applies as well to how Congress can legitimately enforce the mandate for the equal allocation of the rights the Court has identified under this strand of equal protection law.

A second important strand of equal protection law—not judicial doctrine but actual law—concerns race. For at least the last quarter century the Court's race jurisprudence has eschewed reliance on *Carolene Products*–type political process analysis and instead insisted that racial classifications are presumptively unconstitutional because of their underlying incompatibility with the Equal Protection Clause. Recall from chapter 2 that in the 1989 case *Richmond v. J. A. Croson Co.* the Court came close to explicitly denying the relevance of political process analysis in the race context, before providing only the flimsiest political process reasoning to support its decision to apply strict scrutiny to the challenged race-based contracting set-aside.[34] In the years since *Croson* the Court has continued to reject a political process–based approach to race. In 2007, a plurality rejected the argument that the consensus-driven process by which a school district adopted a race-conscious student assignment plan justified a reduction in the stringency of judicial scrutiny.[35] In 2013 the Court reversed a lower court decision for failing to apply sufficiently strict scrutiny to a university's race-conscious admissions policy; in that case the Court remarked upon the need for such scrutiny without breathing a word of political process analysis.[36]

There is great irony in the Court's refusal to engage in serious political process analysis in race cases. After all, it is generally thought that Justice Stone was thinking about race, and about African Americans in particular, when he speculated in Footnote 4 that "prejudice against discrete and insular minorities" might constitute a "special condition" that prevented the normal workings of the political process and justified heightened judicial review.[37] More recently, scholars in the 1970s engaged in a serious conversation about the appropriateness of political process analysis of racial classifications' constitutionality.[38] With *Croson* and its progeny that discussion appears to have been settled, at least in courtrooms, against employing this mediating doctrinal principle when evaluating the constitutionality of government uses of race. Instead, as a prominent scholar noted soon after *Croson*, the Court has opted for what he described as a more "normative" theory explaining the presumption against race-conscious action.[39] Indeed, other scholars have identified a normative strand—sometimes as the dominant strand—in the Court's thinking about race long before *Croson*.[40]

This choice has major implications for Congress's enforcement power. Whatever one thinks of the Court's decision to subject assertedly benign racial classifications to strict scrutiny, its rejection of a political process methodology and embrace of a more "normative" analysis of the question confirm that that decision constitutes true equal protection law. This description is borne out when one considers individual justices' opinions in race cases since *Croson*, which are replete with references to such normative concerns.[41] As a normative interpretation of the Equal Protection Clause, unmediated by political process analysis, the presumption of color blindness adopted by the Court constitutes part of the small group of core legal principles that together make up the law of equal protection, and to which enforcement legislation must be congruent and proportional. As with the fundamental rights strand, this book defers until chapter 10 consideration of Congress's enforcement power with regard to racial equality.

The fundamental rights strand of equal protection and presumption against the use of race combine with the rationality and anti-animus/public purpose rules discussed earlier to constitute the sum and substance of equal protection law. While perhaps initially surprising, the relative paucity of that law becomes more understandable once we realize the broad applicability of both the rationality and public purpose requirements and the *Carolene Products*–based tiered scrutiny structure, which together account for much of the Court's equal protection jurisprudence. Significantly, with the important exception of the *Carolene Products*–based tiered scrutiny structure, all of these principles constitute core equal protection law, to which enforcement legislation must be congruent and proportional. Thus, real limits exist on the enforcement power, at least as a theoretical matter. This realization returns us, then, to the practical question of how courts should police those limits.

The Judicial Check on the Enforcement Power: A Preliminary Sketch

Even though the existence of core equal protection law implies limits on congressional enforcement power, as a practical matter the breadth of the rationality and anti-animus requirements appears to provide Congress significant latitude to enact enforcement legislation. This impression is strengthened when one considers the arguments for both Congress's superiority over courts in judging the reasonableness of lines drawn by state laws and its analogous superiority to instantiate into concrete rules the nation's moral understanding of equality. The developing picture is one in which superior congressional competence and authority combine with the vagueness and breadth of the underlying constitutional command to bestow on Congress near-limitless enforcement power, unchecked by courts.

But courts can exercise both meaningful and legitimate review of enforcement legislation. The challenge for them is to perform congruence and proportionality review with an eye to both the actual decisions Congress makes when it enacts enforcement legislation and courts' appropriate institutional role in reviewing those decisions. When courts ask the right questions, and confine their analysis to the functions they can perform well, they will find themselves able to exert meaningful limits on Congress, consistent with their role in our system.

The Rationality Requirement

First, consider what Congress in effect decides when enforcement legislation second-guesses state laws' determinations about the reasonableness of a given classification. Given that the constitutional rule is reasonableness, an enforcement statute would be congruent and proportional only if a constitutional violation inhered in the unreasonableness of that classification. In other words, in the absence of any credible concern about animus (or any issue about race classification or fundamental rights), enforcement legislation can satisfy the congruence and proportionality standard only if there is a serious risk that the state law classifications at issue are unreasonable—not just inaccurate, but unreasonably so.

In most cases this would be a difficult standard for Congress to meet. It would likely not be met by much legislation for which Congress relies on its enforcement power purely as an expedient for evading the limits the Court has imposed on its interstate commerce power. Much interstate commerce regulation reflects pragmatic concerns about economic and social life: how safe consumer products should be, what types of disclosures securities issuers should make, and analogous matters. Such fine-tuning of our economic and social relations is not triggered by, or even relevant to, the type of systematically inaccurate classification required to warrant a congressional conclusion that the regulated state conduct was unconstitutionally irrational.

To be sure, some federal legislation may be justifiable on both interstate commerce and Fourteenth Amendment enforcement grounds. For example, state government employment discrimination clearly affects interstate commerce (and thus can be regulated under Congress's power to regulate such commerce) while also potentially raising concerns about systematic unreasonableness rising to the level of unconstitutionality. Thus, some legislation may be supportable on both grounds. Indeed, in the *Kimel* case, the Court acknowledged that the Age Discrimination in Employment Act it found invalid as enforcement legislation had previously been upheld as valid regulation under the Commerce Clause.[42] (But don't forget that the Commerce Clause allows plaintiffs to recover only limited remedies from states, thus making the enforcement power a necessary tool—or at least not a redundant one—in Congress's regulatory arsenal. Indeed, the issue in *Kimel* concerned the availability of more expansive remedies than the Commerce Clause authorized.)[43]

In deciding whether Congress's power to enforce the anti-irrationality rule justifies a given type of regulation, courts can draw on the wisdom of their own equal protection doctrine, even when, as explained earlier, that doctrine does not state core constitutional meaning. In particular, courts can employ their nonconstitutional doctrinal rule expressing confidence that most interest groups in American society are able to protect themselves in the nation's legislative halls. This presumption casts doubt on a claim that garden-variety commerce regulation—regulation, for example, of consumer products manufacturers and issuers of securities—is in fact regulation responding to systematically irrational mistreatment of a particular group and thus is also valid under the Enforcement Clause.

The preceding explanation suggests a role for the Court's own doctrine—even its subconstitutional doctrine—when evaluating laws justified as enforcement legislation. Still, it bears repeating that the type of unreasonableness Congress has the power to enforce against is susceptible to proof by broader means than that which the Court has employed in its rational basis jurisprudence. The constitutional unreasonableness that Congress has the authority to correct goes beyond the unreasonableness of the court-focused rational basis standard, with its presumptions and evidentiary burdens on the plaintiff. That judicial standard, it will be recalled, reflects the competence and legitimacy deficits inherent when courts evaluate legislative line-drawing. Such deficiencies do not exist in Congress; as a legislature, Congress should be presumed to possess all the technical competence and political legitimacy of any state legislature. Thus, the type of unreasonableness that serves as the proper benchmark for enforcement legislation is broader—what earlier in this chapter we called "pure" irrationality, that is, irrationality judged from an unbiased, presumption-free baseline.

This type of unreasonableness—the type to which enforcement legislation may properly respond—is more susceptible to broad, indirect proof. Consider again *Garrett*. The Court in that case, considering Congress's record of disability-based employment discrimination justifying the ADA's employment provisions, applied the court-focused rational basis standard when deciding whether such discrimination was likely unconstitutional. This led it to impose strikingly high hurdles on Congress's evidentiary task. Most notably for our current purposes, the Court excluded, as irrelevant, evidence of society's stereotypic assumptions about disabled workers, even though it makes perfect sense to think that such attitudes, if they in fact exist, infect state officials as much as other Americans.[44]

Under the approach this book calls for, the Court would review Congress's judgment about the reasonableness of state employment disability discrimination without such artifacts of judicial self-restraint. With apologies for using a key word twice but in different contexts, the important question would be whether Congress reasonably found that this type of discrimination was unreasonable. In asking that question, the Court would consider Congress's specific talents and abilities, rather than its own. Those abilities would include Congress's capacity to draw inferences about broad social facts—here, for example, that employers of all types, public and private, typically undervalue the contributions disabled persons can make and overestimate the costs of most workplace accommodations, even when those mistakes do not derive from animus.[45]

The relevant question this inquiry targets—did Congress reasonably find that the targeted state conduct reflected serious, systematic unreasonableness?—would impose real restrictions on the enforcement power. It would not allow Congress to target a nonexistent problem, or one that was unlikely to appear in any significant amount. But at the same time, by freeing the rationality inquiry from the limitations inherent in direct judicial review of state action, this approach gives proper latitude to Congress's competence and political legitimacy to examine state conduct and craft appropriate responses.

The Anti-animus Rule

Consider now enforcement legislation motivated by a concern about state action infected by animus. How would a court evaluate the adequacy of Congress's rationale for such an enforcement statute? One approach would be for the Court simply to examine that same state conduct and reach its own conclusions about states' likely motivation. The Court took this approach in the context of a direct constitutional challenge to the *federal* law excluding from federal marriage benefits same-sex couples validly married under state law.[46]

But that approach is not optimal. If animus is fundamentally a moral conclusion—that is, a conclusion that a certain type of discrimination is inherently unfair—then courts are ill-equipped to make that judgment. Sometimes they have no choice: in the absence of enforcement legislation, a court confronted with a plaintiff's equal protection claim must decide whether the complained-of discrimination is based on animus.[47] But is there a better way for courts to evaluate a claim that a particular enforcement statute targets animus?

There is. Again, begin with the implicit judgment that Congress is making, and the foundation for Congress's authority to make it. Here, the judgment is that some nontrivial amount of state conduct is motivated by animus—

that is, it violates our sense of basic fairness. Because that conclusion flows from moral insight, the question for the Court would be Congress's accuracy in perceiving a national moral consensus condemning the particular state practice as unfair. In other words, the Court would not inquire whether a particular pattern of state conduct violates equal protection's rule against animus. Instead, it would ask whether Congress, in its capacity as the representative of the nation's moral sense, reasonably concluded that "We the People" had made that judgment.

In performing that inquiry, courts should broadly review society's attitudes toward the targeted discrimination. Courts should inquire how major civil society groups, such as corporations, unions, universities, and professional and social affinity organizations, view the discrimination. They should examine even the positions taken by courts—it would be relevant whether judicial decisions had found some instances of discrimination against that group to have been grounded in animus, or even that the group satisfied all or some of the criteria for suspect class status. Indeed, it would be appropriate to consider even the views of state actors themselves—for example, if a number of states or state subdivisions had enacted policies forbidding that discrimination, that would surely be evidence of a general social consensus condemning it.

Gay rights legislation provides one timely example of this dynamic. In the past, antigay prejudice has had a distinctly moral edge to it. Gay men and lesbians were thought at various times to be evil, unnatural, or not fully developed as humans, and deeply morally compromised. Later, these views evolved into a consensus that they were "merely" mentally ill. Of course, over time these views have changed, and are still in the process of changing. Hypothesize now that Congress enacts the Employment Non-Discrimination Act (ENDA), banning sexual orientation discrimination in employment, and justifies application of the law to states as legislation enforcing the Equal Protection Clause. Under the approach suggested by this book, Congress could justify the law by arguing that such discrimination was irrational and/or, more relevantly for current purposes, that it reflected animus.

In considering the anti-animus argument, a court would examine whether a national consensus existed condemning such discrimination as inherently unfair. That argument would have been hard to make in 1920, or 1950, or even in 1980. Back then there was simply no such consensus about the unfairness of sexual orientation discrimination—indeed, most Americans would likely have viewed exclusions of gays and lesbians as sound regulation for the health and good morals of the community. Corporations did not protect gays from dismissal, schools and professional associations attempted to screen them out, and legislative and judicial protection was unknown.

But today the picture is different. Corporations' antidiscrimination policies include sexual orientation as a protected category, universities and bar and medical associations go on record as opposing such discrimination rather than engage in it, and a growing percentage of state and local governments provide protection as well. Indeed, even courts have joined in the trend, not necessarily by vindicating all claims of sexual orientation discrimination, but at least by recognizing their plausibility—for example, by recognizing that gays satisfy at least some of the criteria for suspect class status or for protection under analogous state equality provisions.

One can render the analysis even more precise. Ten or fifteen years ago it was probably the case that Americans were coalescing around a consensus that it was unfair to fire a person from a job because she was lesbian. But such a consensus did not exist about the unfairness of depriving that same person of the right to marry her partner. The conduct reflecting an asserted consensus on the marriage issue—state laws providing for same-sex marriage, private entities' provision to same-sex couples of rights normally given to married couples, and statements of support for marriage rights—was simply not as pervasive a decade ago to warrant a judicial conclusion that Congress was reasonable in finding such a consensus. The point of this distinction between employment and marriage is that judicial review of the reasonableness of Congress's conclusions supporting a given piece of enforcement legislation can focus fairly precisely not just on the particular basis of the discrimination (here, sexual orientation) but on the particular social context the legislation addresses (here, employment or marriage).

The more general point is also straightforward. A court evaluating ENDA, a federal marriage-rights law, or any other enforcement legislation justified as combating antigay animus would face the task of determining whether American society views sexual orientation discrimination in a particular context as presumptively unfair, or at least troubling enough to warrant serious concern. If a consensus exists that it is, then there is every reason for a court to allow Congress to enact legislation targeting state action inconsistent with that consensus.

As with congressional determinations of state laws' reasonableness, judicial review of congressional determinations of state law animus should aim merely at checking Congress's answer to the question, rather than providing courts' own answer. Of course, at some point the two inquiries overlap—but it is important to keep in mind that the Court's inquiry would aim merely at reviewing Congress's perception of the nation's views, not directly evaluating those views itself. Even less does this approach involve the Court imposing its own moral views on a given matter.

Thus, even though the review described in the prior paragraphs might be difficult, it remains more straightforward, and more legitimate for courts to perform, than if it sought to make the animus determination directly. Unlike the Court's current congruence and proportionality analysis, the review called for here would not involve the court in reaching *its own* questionably legitimate conclusion about what Americans *should* believe about the morality of a particular type of discrimination. Instead, it would involve the court determining whether *Congress* reasonably perceived what Americans *do* in fact believe. Among other benefits, this approach would ease at least some of the sting gay rights opponents might feel from a federal determination that a particular type of state discrimination is fundamentally unfair, since that determination would emanate from an open and politically legitimate congressional process rather than simply being announced as the conclusion of an unelected court.[48]

Finally, note that this consensus-based approach to animus-combating enforcement legislation contains a self-limiting mechanism. Because Congress is presumed to be politically responsive, there is no reason to think that interest groups that have failed to make their moral case to the American people in other forums would succeed in securing federal enforcement legislation. The history of social movements in America is usually not one where those movements begin with Congress. As William Eskridge has argued, they may begin with a struggle for the most basic protections in courts, where claims are made for at least minimal tolerance and protection from persecution. They may then proceed to other venues, public or private, state or federal.[49]

As a matter of political dynamics, it would be a rare situation where an interest group achieves little success in its broader dialogue with American society but nevertheless succeeds in obtaining federal enforcement legislation. This is especially true today, given the polarized national political climate. As we all know, today it is quite hard to get the bipartisan, supermajority agreement that has become the prerequisite for significant federal legislation. The resulting inaction may make Congress unpopular, but, paradoxically, it means that legislation (including enforcement legislation) that does manage to get enacted likely enjoys broad support. The political check built in to this approach to the enforcement power should replace at least some of the reassurance against congressional overreaching that the Court obtains from the suspect class–based approach it has employed up to now. And it provides that reassurance in the course of offering a much more legitimate role for judicial review.

Let's conclude this argument with a broad observation. Scholars sometimes argue that, in most cases, the Supreme Court's decisions ultimately reflect Americans' views.[50] The process may be bumpy: for a time the Court may appear out of step with Americans' evolving views, either far out in front or far behind. The adjustment process may be slow, sometimes requiring decades. And to be sure, this observation does not always hold: at times the Court holds fast to what it perceives to be core constitutional values despite public pressure to change. But according to these scholars, in most cases the Court eventually settles at about where American society stands on a given issue.

Apply this final insight to our proposal. At base, our proposal calls for the Court to defer to any reasonable congressional determination—that is, any rational judgment supported by the empirical facts—that the American people condemn a particular type of discrimination as fundamentally unfair. Accepting Congress's answer when that answer is reasonable, and reviewing that answer only to the extent the Court has the tools to do so competently and credibly, leads to a result that is fundamentally consistent with what scholars argue the Court does generally when it decides constitutional cases. Ultimately, then, this approach is consistent with what the Court is thought to do as a general matter.

The Special (?) Case of Sex Discrimination

Sex equality presents an important, but difficult, case for this approach to the enforcement power. Sex discrimination presents a thorny issue for process-based constitutional theorists. The prime academic proponent of process-based theory expressed his difficulties with the topic when, applying Footnote 4's own terminology, he observed that women were neither insular nor a minority, nor the victims of the mean-spirited treatment we normally think of when we think of "prejudice."[51] The Court itself has focused its sex discrimination jurisprudence on the concept of stereotyping, striking down government action that perpetuates traditional sex roles that diminish women's (and, ultimately, men's) opportunities.[52]

But identifying stereotypes involves making difficult judgments about social reality. In *Virginia*, for example, the Court struck down Virginia Military Institute's all-male admissions policy, even while it quoted, seemingly approvingly, from a brief for women's colleges stating that all-women's colleges help "'dissipate, rather than perpetuate, traditional gender classifications.'"[53] The Court's simultaneous disapproval of VMI's single-sex admissions policy and seeming approval of other institutions' analogous policies suggests that what differentiates them is the social meaning conveyed by the given policy—whether it sends a message breaking down traditional sex roles or, as in the case of VMI's policy, reinforcing them. Distinguishing between those two opposite messages requires a nuanced understanding of society, one that reflects not simply the actions of state governments but conduct across all American institutions, public and private.

At one level it is tough to argue that sex discrimination or sex stereotyping is based on animus, at least if one defines that term to include some idea of subjective fear or dislike. Instead, stereotyping—the reinforcement of traditional conceptions of women's and men's social roles—may be better understood as a form of systemic irrationality. This may not be immediately obvious: one might think that such stereotyping is simply different from the classic type of arbitrary classification one thinks of when one thinks about irrational discrimination. But the comparison holds. For example, Justice O'Connor has criticized the "reflexive" and "unthinking" use of sex classifications as a hallmark of unconstitutional government action, suggesting that such thoughtless use of sex as a classification tool reflects irrational decision making.[54] Just as employers may systematically undervalue the contributions disabled persons can make, so too employers, schools, and other institutions can systematically resort to familiar understandings about men's and women's social roles. To take one ironic example, when a widower-father challenged the denial of Social Security "mother's benefits" after his breadwinner wife died, the government's lawyer—and, indeed, several justices—expressed incredulity at the very idea that an educated male would choose to be a stay-at-home parent.[55] In that case, *Weinberger v. Wiesenfeld*,[56] the attitudes of that lawyer and those judges illustrated the exact unreflective stereotyping the plaintiff (successfully) challenged.

As with other examples of irrational government action, sex stereotyping is best identified by institutions that are capable of drawing inferences from broad social facts. As with those other examples, the relevant facts about sex stereotyping are also best found by an institution like Congress, with its broad awareness of and responsiveness to American society. To see this, consider again the VMI case. When one recognizes, as the Court did in *Virginia*, that same-sex education may either impair or promote equal opportunity for all Americans, the task becomes one of reading the social message communicated by VMI's policy. That task was eased in *Virginia* by the Court's rejection of the sincerity of the state's pro–equal opportunity motive for VMI's exclusionary policy. But in other cases, where the state's asserted motive is not as easy to impugn, the task will require a more subtle reading of that social message. Such messages are much better detected by Congress than by courts.

But the matter is not as simple as this. Despite our first-blush intuition that it is not based on animus, the ambiguous character of sex discrimination, and, more specifically, sex stereotyping, places that phenomenon in an uneasy middle ground between the concepts of irrationality and animus that constitute two of equal protection's core commitments. In particular, to the extent that sex stereotyping reflects not just traditional conceptions of gender roles but, rather, conceptions that reflect unflattering assumptions about women's capabilities and moral worth, it may be plausible to characterize such stereotyping as based on animus. On this view, sex stereotyping is not morally neutral role segregation. Instead it is a hierarchy-enforcing system that takes as its starting point assumptions about women's inherent incapacity to play roles that society values: government leaders, participants in the economy, warriors.

If this is true, then we can draw two lessons. First, and more narrowly, in such a case it may be appropriate for courts to recognize sex equality enforcement legislation as grounded, at least in part, on Congress's estimations of society's *moral* views about which sex classifications impair or promote women's equal worth. That recognition opens the door for broader deference to Congress, given its unique capability to discern Americans' moral views and instantiate those views into legislation.

Second, and more conceptually, understanding sex discrimination as implicating both irrationality and animus helps us see the relationship between these two concepts. That relationship goes beyond sex discrimination. For example, disability discrimination may also reflect a combination of a misunderstanding of disabled persons' potential to contribute to society with deeper, more morally inflected if usually only implied, views of those persons' lesser moral worth. Understanding such connections may help us appreciate the complexity of Congress's judgments in enacting enforcement legislation. In turn, an appreciation of that complexity may assist the Court in determining the proper intensity and focus of its review of that legislation.

The Next Task

Even if the preceding analysis has convinced you about the general correctness of this approach to enforcement legislation, very difficult questions remain. In particular, the directive to courts to "review" enforcement statutes' determinations about irrationality or animus leaves open the question of how strict or deferential that review should be. This question—what the next chapter calls "the deference question"—in turn raises follow-on issues about congressional competence and authority, not just to make the ultimate conclusions about irrationality or animus but also to find the facts that support those conclusions.

The next chapter addresses this issue by considering the amount of deference that is appropriately due to congressional determinations supporting enforcement legislation. It also reengages the issues chapter 5 raised about judicial review of enforcement legislation that tackles stubborn discrimination or discrimination that seems to have disappeared but is suspected of merely lying dormant. These issues also require courts to make difficult judgments about when to defer to congressional determinations. The next chapter provides a way forward on all of these questions.

7

The Deference Question

Chapter 6 set out an approach to the enforcement power that accounts for both judicial supremacy in interpreting the Constitution and Congress's particular competence and authority to determine what types of discrimination fail equal protection's core commands. Nevertheless, that approach opens up the prospect of very broad congressional power. To the extent that breadth threatens to convert congressional *enforcement* power into *interpretive* power, it risks subverting the division of power between Congress and the Court that underlies the Court's understanding of Congress's enforcement authority. However, that chapter argued that the proper division of power can be maintained if the Court develops an appropriate methodology for scrutinizing the determinations that support congressional conclusions about animus and irrationality.

Chapter 5 examined a different type of challenge to the enforcement power, one that has arisen because of the maturation of much antidiscrimination enforcement legislation. As that chapter explained, the persistence of discrimination in the face of direct attempts to eradicate it has led Congress to enact more nuanced remedies. Such laws have been challenged as exceeding Congress's enforcement power because, according to their critics, they have only a tenuous connection to the constitutional violations they ostensibly target. At the same time, the progress achieved by other antidiscrimination laws has triggered claims that such legislation has effectively obsolesced itself, and therefore constitutes unnecessary and hence unconstitutional intrusions on state prerogatives. In response, defenders of such legislation have argued that the progress is either more apparent than real, or is fragile and dependent on the continued deterrent effect the enforcement legislation exerts. Together, these latter challenges to enforcement legislation require the Court to judge either the effectiveness of, or the continued need for, particular types of enforcement legislation.

Thus, both of the previous chapters require us to consider the latitude, or deference, that Congress merits when it enacts enforcement legislation. This chapter considers "the deference question." A proper answer to that question is crucial if the book's suggested approach to the enforcement power is to be convincing.

The Court's Deference Problem

As one might intuitively expect, the amount of deference a court accords legislative determinations supporting a statute (such as fact-findings or policy conclusions) often determines the outcome of a challenge to that law. For example, if a court exhibits a great degree of deference to a statute's factual foundations or to the legislature's asserted need for the law to achieve an important social goal, then it will likely uphold that law. By contrast, if a court refuses to credit those legislative determinations, the statute may well be in trouble.

This issue is related to, but distinct from, the standard of review a court uses to review a law's constitutionality.[1] For example, under the strict scrutiny standard the Court uses to judge certain types of laws (e.g., race classifications, intrusions on fundamental rights, and content-based speech restrictions), a court will insist that the statute be narrowly tailored to further a compelling government interest. However, the findings supporting that law may be reviewed deferentially, skeptically, or through some intermediate standard. For example, in a 1994 case considering a First Amendment challenge to a federal law regulating cable television operators, the Court reviewed the law under a heightened level of scrutiny but nevertheless stated that courts must defer to the predictive judgments Congress made in crafting a factual foundation for the law, given the technical and economic complexity of the industry Congress was regulating.[2]

The distinction between the Court's general level of review and its review of a challenged law's factual foundations is intuitively sensible. To use the cable TV example, a court might be justly skeptical of government-imposed restrictions on cable operators' speech but at the same time recognize that the challenged legislation regulates a highly complex or technical area, where courts would feel uneasy second-guessing the foundations for the legislature's judgment. Of course, the intuitive nature of this distinction doesn't erase the difficulty it causes: at base, there remains a serious tension between, say, judicial suspicion of government speech restrictions and deferential review of Congress's regulation of a technically and economically complex industry such as cable television. To put the point more generally, the question of judicial deference to congressional fact-finding stands in a tense relationship with legal doctrine, especially when that doctrine calls for suspicion of the law, but that law reflects complex policy making of the sort to which courts normally defer. Later in this chapter we will addresses this tension more explicitly.

Regardless of what we eventually conclude about its relationship to underlying constitutional doctrine, the deference question constitutes a critical component of judicial review of legislative action and is not always satisfactorily resolved by simple application of the overall level of scrutiny accorded to a given type of statute. Unfortunately, the Court is exceptionally inconsistent when deciding how much deference to accord congressional fact-findings, in cases that include but also go beyond the enforcement power. Consider two contexts: the enforcement power and abortion. As chapter 4 described, some of the Court's more extravagant applications of *Boerne*'s congruence and proportionality standard have featured remarkably skeptical review of the factual foundations for the challenged enforcement legislation. Yet in a 2007 case challenging a federal ban on so-called partial-birth abortions, the Court accorded significant deference to Congress's findings, even when other findings in that law were acknowledged to be completely and unambiguously mistaken.

Such inconsistencies present cause for concern. If the deference question really is as crucial as it seems to be, then it behooves the Court to develop more principled and transparent rules governing when it will defer and when it won't. Unfortunately, the Court's rhetoric is as unsatisfying as its practice. When it wishes to defer, the Court offers platitudes about Congress's superior fact-finding capabilities and the need to respect the judgments of a coordinate branch of government. When it doesn't, it offers equally vacuous bromides about courts' need to reach independent conclusions about the constitutional justifications for statutes.[3] Nor does this inconsistency track larger ideological divides on the Court. Both liberal and conservative justices are guilty of approaching the deference question inconsistently.

A First Cut at an Answer

Scholars have suggested one straightforward answer to the deference question: courts should defer to congressional findings that *increase* individual rights and not defer to those that *constrict* rights. Their argument is as straightforward as the approach itself. Congress, they note, is a majoritarian institution, and courts are countermajoritarian institutions. Thus, as a general matter, Congress cannot be trusted when it acts to limit rights—and when it does so, courts have a more important countermajoritarian role to play, through more searching judicial review. By contrast, the theory goes, when Congress acts to increase rights, there is less need for courts to perform their countermajoritarian, individual rights–protecting, role.[4]

As attractive as this theory sounds, we cannot simply accept it, pronounce the deference question settled, and move on. First, as we will see, facts differ on axes other than their impact on individual rights. Ignoring the nature of a type of fact, or its complexity, and basing the entire deference analysis on the finding's impact on individual rights erases from the analysis important considerations that should play a role in answering the deference question. Second, even on its own terms, this prescription raises sticky questions. While we may often know when a finding increases or decreases individual rights, in many cases we may not. Consider an abortion restriction that is defended as protecting the rights of the unborn. Even though the Court's Fourteenth Amendment doctrine unquestionably protects the right to an abortion, it also recognizes the state's interest in protecting the potentiality of life in the fetus. What happens if Congress defends an abortion restriction as protecting the rights of fetuses? Or consider the wave of state legislation in 2014 that sought to protect the rights of Americans who had religious objections to same-sex marriage, by allowing religiously based refusals to serve persons in public accommodations. If such legislation came out of Congress, would we describe it as legislation increasing those Americans' rights to religious liberty, or impairing the rights of gay and lesbian Americans to nondiscriminatory access to goods and services?

Broaden the scope now and consider the underlying logic for this prescription. How closely does reality fit with the picture in which Congress generally acts in a majoritarian, rights-limiting fashion? Consider the evidence over the past two decades. As I have written elsewhere, describing the last quarter century of federal individual-rights legislation:

> Congress may have enacted restrictions on partial-birth abortions, but it also enacted the Freedom of Access to Clinic Entrances Act (FACE Act). It may have codified the military's anti-gay policy, but in 2010 it reversed itself. . . . [It] has also enacted the Violence Against Women Act (VAWA), the Americans with Disabilities Act (ADA), and the Genetic Information Non-Discrimination Act (GINA); has extended the Voting Rights Act (VRA); and has come close to enacting the Employment Non-Discrimination Act (ENDA). Indeed, in something of a direct contradiction to the counter-majoritarian thesis, Congress has also amended civil rights statutes to overrule defendant-friendly judicial interpretations.[5]

There may be reasons for all of these apparent deviations from the standard picture of a rights-protecting Court confronting a rights-limiting Congress. But the sheer number of deviations suggests that maybe the picture needs adjusting—and, with it, our presumptions about when to defer.

A defender of this thesis might respond by claiming that the point is not the actual record of congressional action but the presumption that the Constitution itself provides. On this argument, because the Constitution is a rights-protecting document, we should grant Congress a wide berth when it acts in support of that fundamental thrust. But again there is reason to wonder. First, while the Constitution certainly aims at protecting rights, it also aims at creating a government structure. That structure includes states. Thus, at least in the Enforcement Clause context, when Congress legislates in ways that reduce state regulatory latitude, a countervailing value—state autonomy—pushes against an overarching rule according deference to congressional findings when they increase rights at the expense of that autonomy.

Indeed, to bring the matter full circle, defenders of our federal system often note that federalism was designed, and arguably still operates today, to increase liberty by dispersing power. One does not have to be grudging about the scope of power appropriately accorded Congress in order to also recognize the liberty-enhancing features of a system where states enjoy significant latitude to launch novel regulatory experiments free from federal intervention. Indeed, it was exactly that latitude—and the federal government's obligation to respect the results of those experiments—that led the Court in 2013 to insist that the federal government recognize same-sex marriages performed in states that had decided to legitimate them.[6]

Thus, while intuitive and outwardly attractive, this initial cut at answering the deference question comes up short. Its insights are valid—but they are not enough. The challenge to develop a more solid deference jurisprudence remains.

Why Defer? Expertise and Authority

Given the degree of inconsistency in the Court's deference decisions, it may help to begin confronting that challenge by asking a basic question: Why defer at all? Help on this question comes from perhaps a surprising source—the law governing administrative agencies. For decades administrative law has been preoccupied with a similar deference question: To what extent should courts defer to agencies' interpretations of their authorizing statutes (e.g., the EPA's interpretation of the Clean Air Act)? Of course, that context is significantly different from ours. It may be obvious, but it bears stating explicitly: agencies are not Congress, and an interpretation of a statute is not a finding of fact. Nevertheless, administrative law doctrine about the statutory interpretation deference question has broached some fundamental questions about deference more generally. That analysis provides insights useful to our examination of our particular deference question.[7]

The Supreme Court has identified two types of deference that might apply when an agency interprets its authorizing statute. The first (chronologically speaking) is so-called *Skidmore* deference, named after the 1944 case that enunciated it.[8] *Skidmore* deference instructs courts to defer to the extent the court is persuaded the agency correctly answered the interpretive question. Of course, *Skidmore* deference goes beyond that simple instruction, which by itself simply states the circular proposition that a court should "defer" to the agency to the extent the court is convinced the agency's answer is correct. Thus, *Skidmore* has been understood to factor into the deference decision the consistency of the agency's interpretation over time, the amount of experience the agency has had with the statute, and the care the agency took in reaching its decision.[9]

Forty years after *Skidmore*, the Court enunciated a second deference standard, which became known as *Chevron* deference.[10] *Chevron* also instructed courts to defer to agency statutory interpretations, requiring that courts affirm any reasonable agency interpretation of an ambiguous statute. However, *Chevron* deference is not triggered by the factors *Skidmore* identifies as relevant. While the Court has split sharply on when *Chevron* deference should apply, the majority view holds that *Chevron* deference is triggered not by *Skidmore*-type factors but instead by Congress's intent to give the agency authority to interpret the statute.[11]

Skidmore and *Chevron* reflect two very different theoretical justifications for deference. *Skidmore* deference is grounded in the Court's willingness to presume agency *expertise*, which justifies confidence that the agency likely answered the interpretive question correctly. Thus, Justice Jackson, the author of *Skidmore*, referred to the deference factors he identified as giving the agency the "power to persuade, if lacking power to control."

By contrast, *Chevron* deference rests heavily on that "power to control"—that is, the agency's *authority* to answer the interpretive question. While Justice Stevens's opinion in *Chevron* gave passing attention to the greater familiarity the agency had with the statute, his analysis focused almost exclusively on the argument that a gap in statutory language reflected a congressional decision to delegate interpretive authority to the agency charged with implementing that law. Indeed, in *Chevron* itself the Court deferred to an agency's interpretation that had been adopted and rescinded several times over the course of the previous few years. Under *Skidmore*, such inconsistency would have led the court to reduce its deference, given the damage that inconsistency would cause to any agency assertion of expertise.

The expertise and authority foundations of, respectively, *Skidmore* and *Chevron* deference reflect fundamental justifications for deference that extend beyond the subject of agency statutory interpretations. The expertise foundation of *Skidmore* responds to a basic truth: deference is appropriate when there is reason to think the institution receiving the deference likely answered the question correctly. This truth applies in real life: in a well-functioning classroom, for example, students defer to the instructor not just because the instructor has authority in the classroom (e.g., over grading) but also because students expect the teacher to know more than they do.

Just as intuitively, deference also flows from authority. As the classroom example in the prior paragraph illustrated, we naturally think that a grant of authority to an institution implies, among other things, the power to make decisions that are binding on others—that is, decisions that must be deferred to. Of course that authority—and hence that deference—need not be absolute: even *Chevron* deference provides that the agency's interpretation should prevail only when it is reasonable. But the agency's ability to prevail even when the reviewing court might have decided the matter differently results, in *Chevron*, from its presumed authority to answer the question.

Thus, expertise and authority provide potential entryways into a principled theory of deference. However, these theoretical justifications for deference are not enough to answer the deference question. Instead, we must examine an additional factor—the types of findings for which deference is claimed.

The Nature of Facts

The deference question cannot be resolved without considering the type of finding for which deference is claimed. This truth flows from the expertise and authority justifications for deference explained in the prior section. Simply put, legislatures (and, in particular, Congress) may have different expertise and authority to find different types of facts.

This insight requires that we make at least some attempt to categorize facts. Of course, the universe of facts is immensely wide. Indeed, the entire idea of a "fact" as opposed to, say, a belief or even a social artifact such as a law, is highly contested. For example, legal scholars have persuasively argued that the distinction between law and fact is difficult to maintain on a principled basis.[12] Nevertheless, the Court's Enforcement Clause doctrine assumes that distinction, by reserving to the Court the power to interpret the Fourteenth Amendment—that is, the power to find the law—while recognizing that Congress enjoys some degree of discretion to enforce that court-found law, based on Congress's conclusions about both the constitutional violations that occur in the world and the best means of preventing them. Thus, judicial doctrine, by allocating lawmaking power to the courts and (at least some) fact-finding power to Congress, assumes that a workable law-fact distinction exists. To work within the parameters of that doctrine, we need to make that same assumption.

Luckily, we can create some commonsense classifications between different types of facts (and, by extension, between facts and law). Most obviously, we can categorize some facts as empirical. These facts describe phenomena that objectively exist. To be sure, their objective existence does not necessarily make such facts easy to find. For example, the rate of climate change and the degree to which it is a human-induced phenomenon are empirical facts, but facts that are obviously difficult to find with any precision. Of course, not all empirical facts are that hard to uncover. To take just one notorious example, in banning "partial-birth" abortions in 2003, Congress found that the outlawed methods were not taught in American medical schools. That was simply not the case, as lower courts and indeed the Supreme Court recognized. Regardless of their difficulty or ease in discovery, and conceding that the category itself (like all fact categories) is not hermetically sealed from the others, one can identify a category of empirical facts, so defined by their susceptibility to objective determination.[13]

At the other end of the spectrum we can identify a category of facts that we can call "ideological" or "value-based" facts. These are facts that primarily reflect ideological precommitments; indeed, it would not be wrong to call these facts value judgments. Beliefs about the morality of abortion, or the fundamental efficacy of free markets, or even about whether eighteen-year-olds are mature enough to merit the franchise can be described as ideological or value-based facts.

One might legitimately question whether such beliefs are properly called "facts." But at the very least it seems clear that such judgments are not law—thus, they remain appropriate subjects for the deference inquiry, since the Court's Enforcement Clause doctrine concedes at least some congressional discretion to reach nonlegal conclusions. Nor is this identification purely instrumental—there are real reasons why calling them facts is defensible. These facts, even if grounded in belief and ideology rather than empiricism, are nevertheless views about real social phenomena rather than views about an abstraction such as a legal rule.

Of course, many facts Congress may find can be fairly described as combining elements of ideology and empiricism. For example, a congressional judgment that a particular financial policy will have a particular economic effect may rest on both empirical facts (e.g., the current balance sheets of American banks) and ideology (e.g., the belief that markets can fundamentally be trusted to self-correct). As this example suggests, such mixed or "evaluative" facts can relate to law, by taking the form of a prediction of a particular law's effects. As one might intuitively realize, such evaluations and predictions are composed of varying mixtures of empirical findings and ideological or value-based beliefs. Understanding these facts as mixtures of two theoretically pure fact types, and, indeed, understanding those two ideal types themselves, helps us sharpen our application of the expertise and authority justifications for deference.

Different Types of Facts/Different Justifications for Deference

How do the different types of facts discussed here relate to the expertise and authority justifications for deference? Begin with expertise. If expertise-based, "*Skidmore*-type" deference rests on confidence that the institution seeking deference has likely answered the question correctly, then such a deference justification would be more appropriate when the finding at issue was more empirical in nature. Empirical facts are defined by their grounding in objective reality—unlike value-based facts, they are susceptible to discovery as right or wrong. As such, it is coherent for institutions (e.g., Congress) to claim deference for such facts based on a claim that the institution is likely to have found them correctly.

On the other hand, an authority-based justification for deference to empirical findings is a more awkward fit. One can certainly envision an institution deciding empirical facts and then claiming deference based on the authority it has been granted. For example, a jury's fact-findings are largely unassailable not necessarily because we trust the jury to have likely gotten the facts right but because our system allocates a certain amount of fact-finding authority to juries. But if we consider the question on a blank slate, attempting to intuit justifications for deference, then expertise seems to be a far more natural reason to defer to a fact finder who has found empirical facts.

By contrast, authority better supports claims for deference to findings that lie at the ideological end of the spectrum. Authority-based deference claims focus not on the likelihood that the institution claiming deference has gotten the question right; instead, they focus on some broader privilege the institution enjoys to make the decision for which it claims deference. The privilege Congress can claim to find ideological facts flows primarily from its legitimacy in perceiving and reflecting the moral and ideological values of the American people. Those characteristics bestow legitimacy on Congress to find ideological facts because those facts rest ultimately on the ideological values of the American people—values that, because of Congress's popular election, numerosity, and national scope, Congress is best suited to discern and instantiate into legislation.[14]

Ideological facts nicely illustrate the difference between expertise- and authority-based justifications for deference. It makes little sense for Congress, or any institution, to state an expertise-based claim for deference to its findings of ideological facts because such facts, by definition, are not susceptible to objectively correct answers. Because the only criterion for correctness for these facts is their confluence with the ideological views of the American people, it makes much more sense for the deference claim to be based on Congress's assertion of authority to discern those ideological views and instantiate them into legislation. This latter claim is quite reasonable, given Congress's presumed representativeness.

A Word about Doctrine

Even if readers are persuaded by the analysis so far, at some point one might stop and ask what seems like an obvious question: Doesn't the underlying substantive law doctrine count for anything when answering the deference question? Indeed it does.

When thinking about this question, it may help to consider the example of Congress's power to regulate interstate commerce. In 1995 the Court held, for the first time since the 1930s, that a federal law exceeded that power.[15] However, in that case, which struck down federal regulation of gun possession in school zones, the Court suggested that the result might have been different had Congress found facts connecting gun possession to interstate commerce.

While this invitation to fact-finding did not help Congress in the guns case, it would seem to have helped it in the next major Commerce Clause case five years later, dealing with a federal law giving victims of gender-motivated violence a right to sue their attackers. When enacting that statute—the Violence Against Women Act (VAWA)—Congress made numerous findings detailing how gender-motivated violence affected interstate commerce. Those findings would appear to have immunized VAWA from a strike-down, based on the Court's statement in the guns case five years earlier.

VAWA put the Court in a bind. If it upheld the law based on those findings, it risked abandoning an important part of its decade-long effort to rein in federal power. The problem extended far beyond VAWA itself: if all Congress had to do to immunize a statute from a Commerce Clause challenge was to insert findings stating the effect the regulated conduct had on interstate commerce, then one would expect the winning legislative coalition to do just that—at least if one believes that Congress finds facts instrumentally or, as we will call it later in this chapter, "cynically." In today's interconnected world, it would have been easy for Congress to find such facts.

Thus, in the VAWA case,[16] the Court severely limited its own earlier suggestion about findings' usefulness. It explained that allowing Congress to successfully defend such laws by inserting such findings would allow it to regulate any crimes and, indeed, any human activity. Such "reasoning," the Court explained, had already been rejected by the Court as a matter of constitutional doctrine denying the federal government such an all-encompassing regulatory power. Thus, the Court rejected reliance on VAWA's findings.

Leaving aside the details, the point of this example is straightforward: legal doctrine, in this case the Court's view that the Constitution places some regulatory issues beyond congressional power, trumped statutory findings that otherwise brought the law within that power. In other words, the Court's doctrinal choice in favor of reserving some topics for state regulation mandated a refusal to defer to congressional findings that thwarted that choice.

The Commerce Clause example is a helpful reminder that deference decisions are made in the shadow of legal doctrine. Those decisions influence results under that doctrine, sometimes to the point where the amount of deference accorded a congressional finding effectively determines the result of the case. At the very least, such deference decisions may push the Court in a direction it might not otherwise take. For example, a congressional finding that a concededly critical government interest could not be effectively achieved in any way other than the method Congress enacted—that is, a finding that the statute was "narrowly tailored"—would push the Court toward upholding that statute, even if it infringed on a presumptively protected right that was subject to heightened judicial protection.

If the authority/expertise nature of the deference template sketched earlier suggested judicial deference to such a finding, then the Court might feel itself losing control of its doctrine—just as deference to VAWA's findings, by allowing Congress to demonstrate a connection between any activity, however local, and interstate commerce threatened the Court with loss of control over its federalism agenda. In that case, deference decisions would influence constitutional doctrine. But exactly because of this threat, such influence also runs in the opposite direction—that is, doctrine also influences deference choices. Indeed, in the VAWA case itself the threat such deference posed to the Court's federalism agenda pushed the Court away from deferring to congressional findings about an activity's effect on interstate commerce.

Thus, doctrine certainly matters when answering the deference question. But doctrine cannot be the only determinant. The competing expertise and authority justifications for deference, and their different applications to different types of facts, demand a more nuanced analysis. As noted earlier in this chapter, the Court has recognized this when, for example, it deferred to congressional findings about the cable television market even though those findings suggested the constitutionality of a presumptively disfavored speech restriction. The next section of this chapter explains how these factors—the nature of the deference claim, the type of the finding(s) involved, and the underlying legal doctrine—combine to provide several principles of deference that should guide the deference question, both as a general matter and, in particular, when the Court reviews enforcement legislation.

The Principles of Deference

The preceding analysis yields several deference principles applicable to enforcement legislation. These principles apply the insights gained by distinguishing between both the two different justifications for deference and the different types of facts. They also account for the role played by the substantive constitutional law doctrine lurking in the background of every deference decision. As applied to the Enforcement Clause context, these principles seek to more carefully delineate Congress's proper role in enforcing Court-made Fourteenth Amendment law. As such, they seek to ensure a meaningful role for Congress, within the context of the Court's insistence that it alone enjoys ultimate supremacy in stating constitutional meaning.

Principle 1: Courts Should Focus Their Scrutiny on Empirical Facts

This principle might seem odd. After all, doesn't Congress have an impressive capacity—literally, expertise—to discover complex empirical facts such as the rate of climate change? Indeed, it does. However, two considerations suggest that courts should in fact focus their scrutiny on just such findings.

First, not all empirical findings are complex. It may be difficult to determine facts about climate change, but it is not particularly difficult for a court to determine the content of the curriculum of American medical schools. Thus, when Congress mistakenly found in the Partial-Birth Abortion Ban Act of 2003 (PBABA) that the outlawed procedures were not taught in medical schools, courts—including the Supreme Court—were on solid ground in rejecting that finding.

Second, this principle speaks in relative terms. Even if some empirical facts are difficult for courts to uncover, evaluative and ideological facts present even more daunting challenges. Recall that deference demands for these latter types of findings rest, partially or fully, on an authority justification. It is difficult to see how nonelected judges possess the authority to discern the values of the American people, at least compared with the authority of legislatures (in particular, in the case of enforcement legislation, Congress).

At times, the Court itself has attempted to discern those values by examining trends in state laws. For example, one way the Court has applied the Eighth Amendment's prohibition on "cruel and unusual punishment" has been to examine whether states have reached a consensus rejecting a particular punishment as "cruel and unusual." That approach is open to criticism for lacking an objective methodology for evaluating the data and, thus, for its indeterminacy.[17] But when legislative findings are already presumed to reflect those values, there is a strong authority-based justification for courts to defer.

By contrast, empirical findings rest on an expertise grounding that is arguably more evenly shared between courts and Congress. Of course, Congress has impressive fact-gathering capabilities: specialized staffs and a much more straightforward process for seeking input from interested parties. By contrast, courts have a much more limited and generalist staff and are mostly limited to input via party submissions and amicus briefs.[18] Still, the relative ease with which at least some empirical facts can be uncovered militates in favor of a relatively greater judicial role in scrutinizing those types of findings.

In addition, the nature of the legislative process potentially militates against an expertise-based deference claim for empirical findings. As noted earlier, empirical facts are characterized by their theoretical susceptibility to accurate discovery. To put the matter simply, it may be hard to determine the extent to which the climate is changing, but, theoretically at least, if we study the question hard enough, we could find out. The objectivity of empirical facts may give us at least some reason to be concerned if Congress's process for uncovering them is influenced by political considerations. Commentators often suggest that Congress's fact-finding process is not of the "sincere" variety, in which legislators lacking preexisting views engage in a good-faith search for the truth based solely on the information provided in the formal legislative record. Instead, legislators have preexisting political preferences that motivate their search for favorable facts. Given that possibility, the more politically neutral judicial process appears more favorable to accurate discovery of objective facts, despite courts' relative lack of fact-finding tools.[19]

Principle 2: The More "Legal" the Finding, the Less Deference It Merits

Acceptance of the law-fact distinction implicit in the Court's Enforcement Clause doctrine means that congressional findings that shade into statements of law should receive less deference from the Court. Leave aside obvious cases where, for example, Congress "finds" that a particular law is a narrowly tailored means to satisfy a compelling government interest. Such findings clearly appear legal in nature, as they essentially announce the result of a legal test. Consider instead other, subtler examples. For example, in antidiscrimination legislation Congress sometimes "finds" that the group it wishes to protect is "a discrete and insular minority." This "finding" resonates deeply in constitutional law: recall from chapter 2 that *Carolene Products* cited "prejudice against discrete and insular minorities" as a reason for courts to scrutinize more closely discrimination against that group. Given the importance of "discrete and insular minority" status, a congressional finding that a particular group occupies that status comes close to dictating a certain result and, thus, essentially dictating constitutional law.

Unfortunately, the analysis is more complicated than that. Many findings Congress might make have similar legal implications yet refer to social phenomena where we might expect Congress to have some expertise or authority to support its judgment. For example, a finding that Americans have a reasonable expectation of privacy in their household garbage, while arguably grounded in perceptions of the social reality of contemporary American society, would also significantly influence the result of a Fourth Amendment challenge to a police search of such garbage. Indeed, when the Court considered that issue, the justices debated what Americans expected regarding the privacy of their garbage.[20]

A more detailed discussion of the garbage case can wait until chapter 10. For now all we need to acknowledge is the difficult truth that facts interact with law in myriad ways, some of which suggest a role for Congress even on matters that largely answer the constitutional law issue. Thus, *Boerne*'s implicit insistence on a distinction between law and fact requires courts reviewing enforcement legislation to do the hard work of breaking down findings into their empirical or value components, and their legal components.

Yet while this work is hard, courts should do it. Indeed, perhaps the more accurate statement is that courts already do this work but should do it more transparently. The alternative is to bury this analysis under platitudes about either the Court's superiority in interpreting the Constitution or, alternatively, Congress's role in finding facts. Those platitudes reflect important starting points, but they do not answer the question of how much deference a mixed law/fact-finding merits. Courts do more work than they let on when they either defer or refuse to defer to such mixed findings. They should be more up front about that work.

Principle 3: Precisely Targeted Findings Merit Closer Judicial Scrutiny

This principle calls for heightened judicial review of findings that are "precisely targeted"—that is, findings that precisely satisfy a court-made doctrinal test. For example, in the 2003 partial-birth abortion law, Congress found that the banned procedures were never medically necessary. That finding effectively removed the Court's abortion-rights doctrine—in particular that doctrine's insistence that abortion restrictions contain exceptions for maternal health—as an obstacle to the policy result Congress wanted

So understood, it is easy to see why a court might justifiably review such findings more closely. By precisely targeting the right at issue, such findings have a similar effect as the legal "findings" addressed by Principle 2. Nevertheless, caution is warranted before concluding that such findings merit skeptical judicial scrutiny. To the extent a precisely targeted finding otherwise warrants judicial respect because of either the nature of the facts thus found or its particular deference justification, this principle's suggestion for closer scrutiny reveals a tension among these deference principles. Such tension is inevitable, given the diverse characteristics of fact-findings, and the fact that those characteristics may point toward conflicting answers to the deference question. As frustrating as this might be, it bears repeating that a more transparent deference analysis, where these countervailing factors are identified and confronted rather than submerged under platitudes, seems superior as a methodology for courts to make these decisions.

Indeed, considering a finding's precisely targeted nature as one deference factor among several suggests an analogy to other parts of constitutional law. Recall from our discussion in chapter 3 that a plaintiff challenging an action as violating equal protection must show that the action reflects discriminatory intent rather than just exhibiting disparate impact.[21] For example, a woman alleging that a height requirement for prospective firefighters unconstitutionally discriminates on the basis of sex must show that that rule reflected an intent to classify based on sex. If the court concludes that the requirement's disparate impact on women constitutes merely a collateral result that government did not intend (e.g., because the department was acting based on a legitimate need that firefighters be of a certain height), the sex discrimination claim cannot proceed. However, in determining whether that discriminatory intent exists, a court will consider, among several factors, whether the action has a disparate impact on the alleged victims (here, women). This makes perfect sense: even if one agrees that an action's disparate impact is not enough to prove discriminatory intent, such disparate impact is surely probative of that intent.

Mapping this doctrine onto the deference question suggests that a finding's "disparate impact" on a particular constitutional value should be one factor in determining how much deference that finding merits. Return to the example of the abortion law's medical necessity finding. That finding surely impacts the robustness of the abortion right: as discussed earlier, it allowed Congress to avoid the Court's insistence that any abortion restriction contain an exception for maternal health. Indeed, that finding perfectly "checks" the maternal health "box": if the procedure is never medically necessary to protect women's health, then that part of the Court's doctrine imposes no limits on Congress's ability to restrict abortions. One can easily and intuitively analogize such a finding's impact on the effective scope of the abortion right to the disparate impact a particular government action might have on a group's equality rights. Such disparate impact may not prove the "fire" of either bad intent (in the equal protection context) or desire to wrest interpretive power from courts (in the deference context). But it surely constitutes "smoke" that warrants a closer look.

For these reasons, precisely targeted findings raise concerns that Congress is stepping beyond its *Boerne*-recognized authority and attempting to wrest interpretive power away from the Court. Indeed, such findings also raise an expertise-based concern: one may reasonably doubt whether Congress is using its fact-finding expertise properly when the challenged finding just happens to be exactly what Congress needs to find in order to avoid constitutional obstacles to achieving its policy goals.

This last point requires a bit more discussion, however, because it might elicit the objection that it unfairly penalizes Congress. A defender of such precisely targeted findings might argue that Congress has every incentive to focus on finding the facts that the Court's doctrine deems relevant to the constitutionality of a particular piece of legislation. To use a blunt analogy, if bank robbers rob banks because that's where the money is, why should Congress be subjected to heightened suspicion when it finds facts that the Court has deemed critical to the constitutionality of the policies Congress wants to enact?

This question raises a basic issue about our understanding of the legislative process. Very roughly speaking, we can view Congress's fact-finding process through one of two lenses. First, we can view that process as a "cynical" one—that is, as a purely instrumental one through which Congress seeks solely to vindicate its policy goals. On this understanding, legislators don't engage the fact-finding process with good faith and an open mind. Instead, to speak harshly, Congress seeks to ram through its preferred policies, using findings as nothing but tools to check the boxes judicial doctrine insists on. Alternatively, we can view the legislative process as a "sincere" one, in which legislators use the formal fact-finding process in good faith and rely on it to uncover the relevant facts.

Scholars of the legislative process often admit that they find it difficult to embrace one or the other of these archetypical views as the exclusive means by which Congress conducts its business. Our intuition suggests that the answer likely lies somewhere in the middle and varies with the legislator and the type of legislation and type of fact at issue. Happily, though, both the "sincere" and the "cynical" views of the process would benefit from the deference principle under consideration. If one assumes the "sincere" model, then most findings that precisely target constitutional rights will likely survive even heightened judicial review, given Congress's undisputed capabilities for finding facts. If, as the sincere model assumes, Congress uses those capabilities in good faith, in most cases the result would be an accurate finding, or at least one that is not so egregiously wrong as to warrant a judicial rejection. Conversely, if one assumes the "cynical" model, then review of precisely targeted findings becomes even more important. In that case, Congress's purely instrumental drive to evade constitutional objections to particular policies becomes especially problematic when it purports to find facts that just so happen to land exactly on the "delete" button that removes those objections.

Principle 4: If Congress Has a Record of Faulty Fact-Finding on an Issue, Less Deference Is Warranted

This principle reflects a straightforward intuition that Congress should be presumed to have less fact-finding expertise on a given issue when it has stumbled in its related fact-finding. In an area where reliable deference guideposts are few, surely a good indicator of the deference due a particular finding is the quality of Congress's related findings.

Like Principle 3, this principle leads to appropriate results regardless of one's understanding of the legislative process. If one adopts the "sincere" version of that process, then presumably congressional misfires triggering heightened review of related findings will be rare. Even when courts apply this principle to perform more careful scrutiny of a finding that is infected by its neighbors, that finding will likely survive if Congress really did use its impressive fact-finding capabilities in good faith. If one instead adopts the "cynical" view of the legislative process, then faulty findings should trigger judicial concerns that the majority faction has hijacked the fact-finding process in order to serve its goal of brushing aside constitutional objections to that statute. Application of this principle would incentivize even cynical legislators to create a better record, once they recognize the risk that a particularly aggressive (i.e., poorly supported) finding might prompt courts to more carefully scrutinize its neighbors.

Principle 5: If Congress Has Found Conflicting Empirical Facts in the Past, Then Its Current Finding on That Issue Merits Less Deference

This principle again reflects a straightforward intuition—in this case, that serial inconsistency in facts found by Congress damages its expertise-based claim for deference. So understood, this principle hearkens back to the *Skidmore*-based deference template explained earlier in this chapter, which considers (among other factors) the consistency of the agency's statutory interpretation when deciding how much deference that interpretation merits.

The *Skidmore* analogy also reveals this principle's basis in the expertise justification for deference. In turn, its expertise-based concern for consistency logically limits its applicability to empirical facts. Let's unpack that. If Congress grounds its deference claim on its authority to reflect Americans' values, no logic justifies insisting on congressional consistency. Indeed, one would *expect* Congress's findings to change as Americans' values change and find reflection in new legislators finding new value-based facts. By contrast, Congress's claim for deference in finding *empirical* facts must be grounded on its expertise in uncovering objectively verifiable facts about the world. There would be little substance to any expertise-based deference claim if Congress could freely contradict itself in finding facts about the world, and each time demand deference as the expert fact finder.

This principle, like earlier ones, should also incentivize careful congressional fact-finding regardless of the picture one holds of the legislative process. A "sincere" legislature would presumably take special care when finding a different fact than one found by an earlier Congress, given the respect it would accord its predecessor's work. Similarly, a "cynical" legislature aware of this rule would likely take special care buttressing a finding that contradicted an earlier one, to ensure that the new finding withstood the more careful review this principle calls for.

Of course, this principle is subject to the commonsense caveat that the world changes, as does our knowledge of it and ability to measure it. For example, a finding that racial discrimination in public accommodations hinders interstate commerce might demand deference in 1964, even if Congress might (hypothetically) have found the opposite a century earlier. Similarly, a finding detailing the human role in climate change might merit deference in 2015 even if (again hypothetically) a decade earlier Congress might have found the matter to be in doubt. Therefore, this principle should not be understood as freezing the first set of facts found by Congress, and thus setting off a race to the legislature to lay claim to those first findings and thus cement them in place permanently. To repeat, this principle simply reflects the commonsense idea that Congress can hardly demand deference as the expert fact finder in an area if it continually contradicts itself on what those facts really are. So understood, this principle constitutes a modest suggestion—but, nevertheless, one that may helpfully guide courts and tame any "cynical" congressional use of the fact-finding process.

Principle 6: If Courts Have Encountered Difficulty Finding the Relevant Facts, Then Congressional Findings on That Issue Merit More Deference

This principle also reflects common sense, in calling for courts to defer to congressional findings when courts themselves encounter difficulty finding the relevant facts. Indeed, this principle can be understood as a general gloss on the five more specific principles that came before it. In common parlance, if a court has a difficult time finding a fact, then it should get out of the way when Congress steps in to find it.

Of course, "getting out of the way" cannot be taken too literally. Courts' fundamental role includes serving as a check on legislatures. Performing that role requires at least some judicial review of legislative action, even when courts consider themselves not fully competent to second-guess legislative choices. To return again to the administrative law analogue that has shadowed much of this chapter's analysis, courts regularly (and appropriately) review the rationality of agency regulatory choices, even when those choices present highly complex technical issues beyond the ken of a generalist judiciary.[22]

These six deference principles provide guideposts for courts confronting congressional findings likely to be present in enforcement legislation. They can only be guideposts: as the discussion here makes clear, these principles, in reflecting the complexity of the deference question, do not purport to provide hard-and-fast rules capable of easy and always-consistent application. However, by digging past the surface platitudes that often accompany the Court's resolution of the deference question, they provide a transparency that makes deference decisions more credible. They may even make resolutions of that question more accurate, by explicitly focusing the justices' attention on the issues that matter to resolving the deference question in a given context. The next section applies these principles to situations that will likely face the Court when it confronts the next generation of enforcement power challenges.

Preliminary Applications

Detailed applications of these principles must await chapters 9 and 10, which combine these principles with the doctrinal approaches sketched in chapters 5 and 6. However, we can make some preliminary, general points about how these principles relate to the types of enforcement legislation we have considered in earlier chapters.

Animus

First, these principles suggest that courts should accord significant deference to many types of congressional findings that would likely be relevant to enforcement legislation targeting animus. Most notably, the value-based nature of findings that a particular type of discrimination reflects animus militates in favor of judicial deference. This conclusion follows from Principle 1's direction that courts focus their scrutiny on empirical facts and Principle 6's suggestion that courts defer to Congress when Congress possesses relatively more of the relevant fact-finding expertise or authority.

Nevertheless, this call for deference confronts a countervailing force. Principle 2 cautions against judicial deference to congressional findings that shade into legal conclusions. Similarly, Principle 3 cautions courts to review carefully findings that precisely target the constitutional value at issue. In our case, findings about a particular type of discrimination's basis in animus appear to reflect either bald legal conclusions or, at the very least, fact-findings that precisely target the right at issue.

So understood, application of these principles to an animus finding raises the difficult question of how the analysis should play out when these principles point in opposite directions. In such a case it helps to consider Principle 6, which calls for courts always to keep in mind the relative competencies and authorities of Congress and courts. In a case like this, where Congress makes legally resonant findings that are difficult for courts to legitimately review, this principle suggests that, ultimately, courts need to recognize congressional superiority in finding the particular facts at issue, simply as a matter of courts' recognition of their own relative incapacities.

This resolution of the issue may sound like a blunt preference for some principles (1 and 6) over others (2 and 3). However, this objection is mitigated by two considerations. First, the Court itself stated the legal rule—in this case, the anti-animus principle—that Congress seeks to enforce via the type of finding under discussion. It need not have stated that rule. It could have limited the scope of the equal protection guarantee in any number of ways that would have limited the force of congressional findings of animus. It could have restricted the Equal Protection Clause's scope to racial equality, or even to racial equality with regard to a discrete set of rights, most notably the rights protected by the Civil Rights Act of 1866. Indeed, it could have limited its scope to the "equal protection" of rights otherwise granted, rather than reading the clause as a "guarantee of equal laws."[23] At the very least, it could have limited the clause's scope to protection for groups, rather than extending its scope to include so-called classes of one.[24] It did none of these, even though credible arguments were available to the Court limiting the clause's scope in these ways. Instead, it read the clause as a broad guarantee of government fairness and reasonableness, applicable to all persons and all forms of government action. By thus expanding equal protection's scope, the Court has all but invited Congress to step in and apply, through enforcement legislation findings, the meaning that the Court itself has stated.

We can also be comfortable with this resolution of the conflict for a second reason: the residual control the Court retains over congressional findings. A finding that a particular type of discrimination reflects animus may merit deference, given Congress's superior authority to discern Americans' values and instantiate those values into legislation. However, it would still be appropriate for the Court to satisfy itself that Congress's judgment did in fact reflect those values. Recall that chapter 6 laid out a methodology by which courts could review the reasonableness of Congress's conclusions about animus. That methodology provides for courts reviewing the evidentiary support for Congress's conclusions, rather than reviewing those conclusions themselves.

Let's map chapter 6's proposal onto the template of our deference principles. When our proposal in chapter 6 calls for courts to refocus their scrutiny toward the *existence* of the social consensus Congress claims to be acting on, it calls for them to focus their review on an empirical fact—the existence (or not) of that consensus—rather than on the underlying moral truth of that consensus. Put bluntly, courts are far more capable of discerning the empirical fact whether *American society condemns* a particular type of discrimination as unfair than they are deciding, as an issue of values, whether such discrimination *is* unfair. By providing for meaningful judicial review of doctrinally resonant findings, this approach satisfies Principles 2 and 3, which call for more careful judicial review when congressional findings start to resemble legal conclusions. By recasting that review as a judicial check on the existence of the asserted social consensus, rather than on the ultimate truth of that consensus, it respects Principle 1's preference for judicial review of empirical facts and, by extension, Principle 6's admonition that courts deciding deference issues always keep in mind their and Congress's respective fact-finding capacities.

Deference to Policy Judgments

Chapter 5 set forth an additional problem with the Court's current approach to enforcement legislation—the problem that arises when courts review the effectiveness of or need for enforcement legislation. This problem is inherent in congruence and proportionality review, because that standard requires some relationship between the enforcement legislation and the constitutional problem it targets. Measuring that relationship necessarily requires considering the seriousness of the targeted problem and the effectiveness of the statute in remedying it. Both *Coleman* and *Shelby County* focused on the latter of these inquiries: as chapter 5 explained, *Coleman* concluded that the Family and Medical Leave Act's self-care provision was ineffective in furthering the asserted sex equality goal, while *Shelby County* concluded, among other things, that the coverage formula governing the VRA's preclearance provisions resulted in coverage decisions that were no longer necessary to further the goal of racial equality in voting.

How do the deference principles discussed earlier in this chapter apply to the deference issues posed by *Coleman* and *Shelby County*? Recall the relevant arguments made by the defenders of those statutes. The defenders of the FMLA's self-care provision argued that that law was necessary to counteract perceptions that FMLA family-care leave constituted a women's benefit that, perversely, made women less desirable as employees and thus even more prone to discrimination. The Court rejected that argument, finding it "overly complicated" and "unconvincing." For their part, the VRA's advocates argued, among other things, that the preclearance provisions continued to play a necessary role by deterring the covered jurisdictions from returning to their old discriminatory ways that, for purposes of argument, those advocates acknowledged had receded. The *Shelby County* Court rejected that argument, concluding essentially that such deterrence arguments proved too much, by seemingly justifying such legislation indefinitely and regardless of the visible improvements in the covered jurisdictions' minority voting climates.

To repeat, detailed application of this book's approach—including this chapter's deference principles—to these statutes must await chapter 9. However, as with the earlier brief discussion of enforcement legislation justified on an anti-animus ground, here too we can make some general points. Most important, the conclusions at issue in *Coleman* and *Shelby County* are what this chapter has called "mixed," or "evaluative," conclusions—that is, conclusions that include empirical and ideological components. This characterization follows from chapter 5's description of these conclusions as policy judgments, which in turn we defined as consisting of empirical findings filtered through the lens of the policy maker's worldview, or ideology.

Because such conclusions include significant ideological components, they merit judicial deference on a similar ground as legislation that targets animus. Recall from the previous subsection that findings about a state action's foundation in animus merit deference under Principle 1's call for courts to focus their scrutiny on empirical findings, and Principle 6's caution that they respect conclusions that they have little competence or authority to review closely. So too here: findings about the effectiveness of a given enforcement statute or the continued need for that statute merit deference on the ground that they reflect legislators' understandings of the significance of particular empirical facts—understandings that, because they are based in legislators' popularly ratified ideologies, courts lack the authority to second-guess.

To be sure, Principle 1's call to focus judicial review on the empirical components of findings supporting such legislation does offer courts a method for performing meaningful review of such statutes. And, indeed, our deference principles offer justifications for more careful judicial scrutiny of particular empirical findings—in particular, Principle 4, which calls for more careful scrutiny of findings when their neighboring findings are revealed as flawed, and Principle 5, which calls for more careful scrutiny in case of temporal inconsistency. Taken together, these principles point in the same direction: toward more careful scrutiny of the empirical components of Congress's findings, and less scrutiny of those findings' ideological components.

We can make one final general point about how these principles relate to the types of policy-inflected findings at issue in *Coleman* and *Shelby County*. Just as with the findings at issue in animus-targeting enforcement legislation, the policy-inflected findings at issue in these latter cases could be questioned as examples of Congress attempting to wrest interpretive power from the Court. On this theory, findings about a statute's need or effectiveness are so precisely targeted to the relevant legal test as to be the functional equivalent of legal conclusions. Here, the relevant legal test is *Boerne*'s insistence that enforcement legislation be congruent and proportional to the targeted constitutional violations. This final objection to these findings argues, for example, that a finding that the FMLA's self-care provision effectively combats sex discrimination ends, or at least heavily influences, the congruence and proportionality analysis before it starts, by essentially "finding" that the provision is effective, and thus a presumptively congruent response to that discrimination.

This objection takes us back to Justice Scalia's critique of the congruence and proportionality test. At the end of chapter 5 we noted how Justice Scalia eventually abandoned that test, concluding, among other things, that it involved the Court in disrespectfully checking Congress's "homework"—that is, second-guessing the factual and policy justifications for the challenged law. To be sure, his proposed response—to limit Congress (except in race cases) to simply crafting penalties for state violations of Court-announced law—is far too limited, as a matter of both historical understanding and logic. But when we consider the final objection lodged earlier—the objection that Congress's policy conclusions effectively determine the constitutionality of legislation under the congruence and proportionality test and thus effectively state the law—we can understand his frustration.

Again, though, the fault in this situation does not lie with Congress. The Court, by crafting a constitutional standard that turns in part on the policy efficacy of the challenged law, has put itself in a position where its judicial scrutiny includes such policy review. This chapter's deference analysis and its expression in its six deference principles suggest that such review must be deferential. The chapter's suggestion that empirical findings remain open to more careful judicial scrutiny attempts to preserve a role for meaningful judicial review of statutes that, like the FMLA and the VRA, are challenged fundamentally on policy grounds. But we should be clear that, fundamentally, judicial review of Congress's policy conclusions should be limited.

Nevertheless, before simply concluding that the Court should defer to such conclusions, it bears recalling the role substantive legal doctrine plays in our theory of deference. We haven't talked much about the role substantive Fourteenth Amendment doctrine should play in answering the deference question. Let's conclude the chapter by doing that.

First, the Constitution's concern for federalism requires at least some caution before simply concluding that the ideological foundation for Congress's predictions about the continuing need for the VRA justifies uncritical judicial deference to those predictions. Such a case presents the difficult situation where Congress's value-inflected findings risk impairing the constitutional law principle that places a high value on states retaining meaningful freedom from federal regulation.

Nevertheless, in the case of enforcement legislation that same constitutional law also points toward *less* state freedom. In several different ways the Court has suggested that the enforcement power is broader than Congress's other major domestic power—to regulate interstate commerce. The commerce power is limited by the so-called anticommandeering principle that prohibits commerce regulations that force states to alter their lawmaking or law-enforcing priorities; by contrast, the VRA illustrates that the enforcement power allows Congress to cut deeply into state sovereign prerogatives.[25] The commerce power is also limited by the Court's 1996 decision denying Congress the ability to make states liable for damages and other retrospective relief; by contrast, the enforcement power has been construed to allow plaintiffs to seek such relief from states.[26] Finally, a not-insignificant bloc of justices has expressed serious doubts about the proposition that the Commerce Clause by itself precludes state regulation—the so-called dormant Commerce Clause.[27] Again by contrast, the Fourteenth Amendment, by its own force completely apart from enforcement legislation, imposes serious prohibitions on state action.

Thus, the relevant Fourteenth Amendment doctrine is, at the very least, not implacably hostile to federal regulation of the states. In turn, Court-announced federalism principles are not as imperiled by enforcement legislation as appears at first glance. This is not to say that enforcement legislation does not risk impacting such principles. It does. However, judicial review of empirical findings, and of the empirical components of compound, evaluative findings, will go a long way toward ensuring review that is meaningful, adequate to prevent Congress's fact-finding power from devolving into a de facto interpretive power, and consistent with the Constitution's federalism.

Moreover, judicial review of even value-inflected predictive facts, to ensure that such predictions are at least reasonable, adds another layer of judicial control. The Court in *Shelby County* purported to find that Congress's predictive judgments were simply not rational. However, the Court's own exasperation at the dueling evidentiary claims made by the two sides[28] suggests that what the Court was engaging in was far more than mere rationality review. Had the Court limited itself to true rationality review of these predictive judgments, along with more searching review of those judgments' empirical foundations, it could have engaged in meaningful judicial scrutiny of Congress's choices—scrutiny that accommodated the Court's federalism concerns but was nevertheless appropriate to its institutional role in light of the deference principles this chapter has offered.

8

An Aside on State Action

So far we have talked about some very important issues relating to Congress's power to enforce the Equal Protection Clause. But up to now our analysis has assumed that the enforcement legislation at issue directly regulates state governments—for example, state legislation singling out a particular group, or lower-level state action, such as a manager in a state government workplace discriminating against an employee. Thus, so far we have not considered what the enforcement power allows Congress to do about *private* discrimination. This issue—what scholars sometimes call the "state action" issue—is the subject of this chapter.

This chapter's title describes the state action issue as an "aside." And for our purposes, it is, in the sense that our analysis of this issue takes us a bit off the track of our analysis up to now. So far, our focus has been on identifying the core meaning of equal protection, and considering how much deference Congress merits when it seeks to enforce that core meaning. As we will see, the state action issue requires us to delve more deeply into the core meaning not of equal protection but of the enforcement power itself.

That slight detour is worth it. The stakes in the state action question are high. Our working assumption up to now, that the enforcement legislation at issue directly regulates state government, excludes a lot of legislation we might intuitively think of as coming within the ambit of the enforcement power. When Congress regulates private discrimination, it almost always does so under its power to regulate interstate commerce. But, as the introduction to this book noted, recent cutbacks on the commerce power (and other Article I powers, such as the spending power) have given the enforcement power a new practical importance.

Moreover, one can be forgiven for thinking about even private discrimination as implicating constitutional guaranties, even if it is in some abstract way. For example, we normally don't think of statutes such as the Civil Rights Act of 1964 as being about the regulation of commerce. Instead, we think about such laws as vindicating, albeit indirectly, the promise the nation made to itself after the Civil War—the promise that we would all be equal. Thus, as the book's introduction noted, the enforcement power carries both a practical importance and an expressive resonance that merits our study—

and, of particular importance for this chapter, our study of its application to private conduct.

To be sure, the familiar prohibitions in Section 1 of the Fourteenth Amendment—against infringing privileges or immunities, equal protection, and due process rights—are directed at states. (This isn't true of the Thirteenth Amendment: the prohibition of slavery does apply to private persons. But while the Court has at times given an expansive reading to that prohibition and congressional power to enforce it,[1] those rulings, in addition to being controversial among scholars, stop short of allowing us simply to substitute the Thirteenth for the Fourteenth Amendment when we wish to think about congressional power to regulate private conduct.)[2] To speak colloquially, Section 1 of the Fourteenth Amendment is, for the most part,[3] a series of "thou shalt nots" directed at state governments. But we should stop and think before we quickly conclude that, as a matter of simple logic, the enforcement power should be limited to punishing states when they violate those commands, or deterring them from doing so.

Concede that, indeed, the relevant parts of Section 1 command states, and only states. Let's now consider the broadest argument for congressional power to regulate private parties—an argument that enjoyed significant support during the Reconstruction era.[4] Assume that states are defaulting on their obligation to guarantee, literally, the equal protection of the laws. Assume in particular that states are enforcing murder statutes only when the victim is white. Surely, we would say, the state is denying black victims the "equal protection" of its laws against murder. We would also surely agree that Congress can punish a state for such violations of equal protection. After all, the most limited understanding of the enforcement power would allow Congress to impose penalties for judicially enforceable state violations of the Fourteenth Amendment.[5]

That power would also presumably authorize Congress to enact legislation compelling states to act in conformance with the amendment. For example, Congress could make it a violation of federal law for states to enact or enforce any law that treated blacks and whites differently for purposes of criminal law enforcement. Such a law would be no different in form than a command that states not engage in employment discrimination based on race—a type of law the Court has had no constitutional difficulty with since at least the 1970s.[6] It is also largely accepted that Congress could attempt to deter such state violations, even if those deterrence mechanisms went beyond simple commands to states to cease violating the Fourteenth Amendment.[7] Again, current enforcement power doctrine makes it clear that Congress can prohibit conduct that itself is constitutional, in order to ensure that unconstitutional conduct is prevented.[8]

Consider how far this analysis has taken us. Under current doctrine, Congress may enact enforcement legislation that doesn't directly punish or prohibit unconstitutional conduct, by casting a liability net wider than the actual constitutional prohibition itself, as long as that "wider net" tends to reduce the instance of such unconstitutional activity. Of course, "tends to reduce" is a vague statement that elides difficult questions of degree. For example, how much benefit (in terms of reducing unconstitutional conduct) does such legislation provide, and at what cost (in terms of cramping legitimate state regulatory prerogatives)? Such questions of degree are picked up by the "congruence and proportionality" standard.

But leave aside those degree questions for the moment and focus instead on the big picture. If Congress has at least the theoretical right to cast a broader net, then why shouldn't it be able to cast that net over private parties? To repeat, private parties cannot violate Section 1 of the Fourteenth Amendment: we can start with the assumption that Section 1's series of "thou shalt nots" regulates only states. But if regulation of private parties constitutes a congruent and proportional response to unconstitutional state conduct—for example, if such regulation effectively deters states from violating the Fourteenth Amendment—then why can't Congress cast its liability net over private parties?

One answer is that such regulation can never be congruent and proportional, because regulating private parties is simply categorically different from regulating states themselves. The Court has at times suggested this, most recently in the 2000 case *United States v. Morrison.*[9] As we noted briefly in chapter 7, *Morrison* dealt with a provision of the Violence Against Women Act that gave victims of gender-motivated violence a federal law cause of action against (i.e., a right to sue) their attackers. As such, this provision regulated only private parties (the victim and the attacker), even though it did so in response to Congress's conclusion that states were violating equal protection by refusing to prosecute gender-motivated crimes as fully as other crimes.

After holding that that provision exceeded Congress's power to regulate interstate commerce, *Morrison* then concluded that it was also an invalid use of Congress's enforcement power. The Court relied heavily on cases from the early 1880s—when the last embers of Reconstruction were dying out—for the proposition that the enforcement power simply did not authorize regulation of private persons. Translating that supposed rule into its modern formula governing the enforcement power, the Court then concluded that the VAWA provision at issue was not congruent and proportional to the asserted discriminatory treatment imposed by states. According to the Court, the statute failed the congruence and proportionality test because "it [was] not aimed at proscribing discrimination by officials." Rather, "it [was] directed not at any State or state actor, but at individuals. . . ."[10] Let's map this analysis onto the template we've created for evaluating enforcement legislation. That template requires us to distinguish between statements of core Fourteenth Amendment law and subconstitutional decisional aids such as the Court's tiered scrutiny structure, with enforcement legislation required to be congruent and proportional only to the former. That template also calls for courts to accord substantial deference to Congress's judgments about the need for enforcement legislation, or such legislation's efficacy.

Applying this template thus requires us to begin our analysis of the state action question by asking about the constitutional status of the rule *Morrison* applied limiting the enforcement power to regulation of state actors. It is clear that the relevant text of Section 1 of the Fourteenth Amendment—the series of "thou shalt nots" we noted earlier—is in fact aimed only at states. But that undeniable fact doesn't fully answer our question. Section 5, after all, has its own meaning: to "enforce" a prohibition on state action such as a denial of equal protection might authorize more than simply restrictions on states themselves. Is there a core, court-stated meaning of Section 5 that restricts Congress to regulating only state actors when it attempts to enforce Section 1's restriction on state action?

The *Morrison* Court thought there was. As noted earlier, it relied heavily on two cases from the 1880s—*United States v. Harris*[11] and *The Civil Rights Cases*[12]—that it read as announcing a hard-and-fast rule against Congress using the enforcement power to regulate private activity. But the matter is not quite as clear as *Morrison* suggested. The *Harris* and *Civil Rights Cases* opinions are notably vague in their discussion of the state action requirement. Both contain language suggesting that the problem with the enforcement legislation they struck down was that it regulated private conduct *without any requirement that the state have engaged in unconstitutional conduct.*[13] Such language implies that, when states have in fact engaged in such unconstitutional conduct, the enforcement power might authorize regulation of private parties.

Yet, as *Morrison* noted, when those cases were decided it was well known that there was state action of some sort infringing the rights that Congress sought to protect with enforcement legislation. It observed that the statute struck down in *Harris*—which provided federal remedies for certain types of private violence committed against freed slaves—was motivated in part by Congress's recognition that states were not enforcing their own laws protecting freedmen. Similarly, the statute struck down in *The Civil Rights Cases*—a statute that prohibited racial discrimination in public accommodations such as theaters and railroads—acted against a backdrop of state nonenforcement of common-law and statutory requirements that such accommodations be open to all who could pay. But despite such state involvement, the Court in these two nineteenth-century cases still struck down the laws.

The debate about the meaning of these nineteenth-century cases—in particular, about the absoluteness of their bar on enforcement legislation's regulation of private parties—has absorbed scholars for decades. But even the brief discussion here suggests an ambiguity that renders them less than solid precedent for the absolutist principle for which *Morrison* cited them. Further, in 1966 the Court came tantalizingly close to overruling the state action requirement and allowing Congress to regulate private action in order to safeguard Fourteenth Amendment rights. (Indeed, a majority of justices in that case expressed significant doubt about the state action rule.)[14] It is possible even to read *Morrison* as expressing some ambiguity about the matter. After reading *Harris* and *The Civil Rights Cases* as imposing a rigid prohibition on Congress using its enforcement authority to regulate private parties, the *Morrison* Court went on to explain why the VAWA provision failed the congruence and proportionality test, even assuming that Congress had at least some Enforcement Clause authority to regulate private parties.

In light of the ambiguity in both those nineteenth-century cases and *Morrison* itself, and the Court's abortive 1966 embrace of congressional power to regulate private parties, it might be appropriate to consider this matter unsettled as a question of core constitutional meaning. And when we do, we find little to commend such a hard-and-fast rule.

The Evolution of the Enforcement Clause's Text

First, consider the clause's text, and how it evolved during the amendment's enactment process. Probably the strongest textual argument in favor of a state action limit on the enforcement power lies in the fact that, between Congressman John Bingham's original proposal and the amendment's ultimate version, Congress's enforcement power shifted. Bingham's original proposal—indeed, the entirety of his proposed amendment—provided that "[t]he Congress shall have power to make all laws which shall be necessary and proper to secure the citizens of each State all privileges and immunities of citizens in the several States, and to all persons in the several States equal protection in the rights of life, liberty, and property."[15]

One might immediately see how different this enforcement authority is from the one that was eventually enacted. Rather than the current familiar structure of Section 1 restricting state action and Section 5 authorizing Congress to enforce those restrictions, the Bingham proposal seemed to authorize Congress to enact laws to affirmatively ensure equality. As mentioned in chapter 3's brief tour of the Enforcement Clause's drafting history, the Bingham phraseology at least suggested the possibility that Congress could, for example, enact a complete code of property law for the states, in order to "secure to all persons" "equal protection in the right [] of . . . property." And indeed, as the *Boerne* Court noted, Bingham's amendment was tabled after a debate that featured criticisms that it centralized power too much in the federal government. Eventually, Congress adopted the proposal that was ratified, with its familiar structure of Section 1 prohibitions and Section 5 enforcement authorization.

Consider, then, the evidence: Bingham's original proposal appears to have provided Congress with power to regulate how persons engaged in private transactions with each other, then some congressmen objected to that proposal on federalism grounds, then his proposal was tabled, and, eventually, a seemingly more restrictive enforcement power was adopted. One can see how the *Boerne* Court confidently concluded that the evidence showed that those federalism concerns *caused* the failure of that earlier, broader enforcement authority.[16] If that story is accurate, then we have strong evidence that Congress considered, then shrank back from, authorizing itself to regulate private conduct such as property and contract relationships.

But scholars take issue with the Court's history. Professor Ruth Colker has argued that this change in the enforcement power did not convince a single conservative to switch his vote in favor of the amendment. She also found no evidence that pro-Reconstruction "Radical" Republicans' statements of disappointment at the proposed amendment's limited scope referred to the enforcement power; indeed, she observes that Radical critiques of the final version hardly mentioned the enforcement power. Instead, the real action during Congress's debates centered on Section 2, which considered voting and voting rights, and Section 3, which dealt with former Confederates' eligibility to hold political office.[17]

To this evidence that the shift in language was not intended to alter Congress's enforcement power we can add the very real political concerns Republicans faced in 1866. They knew that eventually the southern states would be readmitted to the Union, and thus to Congress. Indeed, they would return with increased political power, given the repeal of the Three-Fifths Clause that had previously limited the electoral power provided by the slave population. (It was for this reason that Republicans drafted Section 2 of the amendment, which reduced a state's congressional representation to the extent it disenfranchised voters, as southern states were expected to do to African Americans. Racial nondiscrimination in voting was not enacted until the Fifteenth Amendment, in 1870.) Had the Republicans stuck with the Bingham proposal, which did no more than authorize Congress to enact equality legislation, new majority coalitions of southerners and northern conservatives were thought likely simply to repeal any legislation the Reconstruction Congress enacted and block new legislation.

Thus, Republican leaders realized the importance of going beyond the Bingham proposal and enacting as part of the new Fourteenth Amendment concrete, judicially enforceable guarantees rather than simply an authorization to Congress to enact legislation that a later Congress could—and likely would—defeat. Given that dynamic, it makes sense for the enforcement provision to have shifted from Bingham's version to the eventually enacted version tying Section 5's enforcement power to Section 1's catalog of "thou shalt nots."

In sum, the story told by the *Boerne* Court, in which Congress considered but shied away from a broader enforcement authority that might have supported power to regulate private conduct, is plausible but hardly definitive. We need to look further at the issue.

The Logic of a State Action Requirement

The Basic Argument

When one looks further, one finds even more serious problems with a state action limit on the enforcement power. A power to "enforce" a given law is, nearly by definition, a flexible one. Law "enforcement" requires a great deal of discretion: police captains need to decide where to station officers and what crimes to investigate, and prosecutors must make similarly delicate yet practical choices when deciding which defendants to charge, and with what crimes. As we observed in chapter 5, when Congress uses its enforcement power, it must make similarly delicate and policy-infused judgments about how best to attack stubborn discrimination or discrimination that seems to have disappeared but may have simply gone temporarily dormant. These same sorts of practical judgments often attend a congressional decision to combat state discrimination by regulating private conduct.

The examples here are straightforward. Let's consider one. Hypothesize a state that refuses to desegregate its schools in response to a federal court order. All would agree that Congress could respond to such continued violations of equal protection by ordering the state to desegregate, on pain of some penalty Congress might impose. But assume now that, rather than simply refusing to begin the official process of desegregating, a state instead withdraws police protection from schools, despite knowing that gangs of thugs will prevent black students from attending formerly white schools.

Surely, one way Congress could respond to such "state action," and enforce the equal protection right to a desegregated education, would be to prohibit such state defaults on its constitutional obligations—here, for example, to ensure that black students enjoy equal educational opportunities as white students. But direct federal regulation of the state might constitute an awkward response, given the difficulties in judging when a state had in fact complied with a federal requirement that it provide adequate security to desegregated schools.[18] A more straightforward approach would be for Congress to respond to such state government defaults more directly, by providing that "equal protection" itself.[19]

This understanding of the power to "enforce" the Constitution is nothing new: scholars have argued in its favor for at least a generation.[20] Considering the logic of the enforcement power, doesn't it further make sense that Congress should be allowed significant discretion when deciding how best to enforce a clear constitutional right? After all, decisions to enforce a law in one way or another are, at base, policy decisions. The police captain, the prosecutor—and Congress, too—all have to make difficult judgments about the efficacy of particular approaches to enforcing law.

To be sure, there must be limits to such discretion. A policeman can't enforce a jaywalking law by arresting someone who hasn't yet entered the street. So too, Congress must show that its remedies are congruent and proportional to the underlying constitutional violations they target. But unless they are compelled by the text, hard-and-fast limits on particular remedies seem out of place. "Jurisdictional" limits on the enforcement power may be appropriate when, as with granting the franchise to eighteen-year-olds in *Oregon*, the right Congress seeks to enforce simply does not exist as a matter of Fourteenth Amendment law. Similarly, if we decided that "enforcing" Section 1's prohibition on state denials of equal protection necessarily means only ensuring that *states* provide equal protection, then a remedy that operates only on private parties might raise questions. By contrast, if the Equal Protection Clause ensures that persons *enjoy* the right to equal protection, with states mandated to provide (i.e., not withhold or "deny") that protection, then enforcement of this latter understanding of the right could easily accommodate regulation of private parties, particularly when the state defaults on that mandate. In that latter case, Congress's choice to enforce that right by regulating private parties would simply constitute a judgment about appropriate remedies.

The Example of Public Accommodations Laws

Unfortunately, the matter is even more complicated. Let's consider the Civil Rights Act of 1964. Among other things, that landmark law prohibited employment discrimination on the basis of race, sex, and religion and also banned those types of discrimination in public accommodations. Thus, the public accommodations provisions of the law set out to accomplish again what Congress had tried to do when it enacted the Civil Rights Act of 1875—the law that was struck down in *The Civil Rights Cases* of 1883.

The fascinating story is that the Kennedy and Johnson administrations and their congressional allies considered grounding what became the 1964 Civil Rights Act on the enforcement power.[21] Eventually, the political actors in Washington decided instead to rely primarily (though not exclusively) on Congress's power to regulate interstate commerce. But what if they had moved ahead with their plan to defend the statute primarily as enforcement legislation? Leave aside the inevitable clash that path would have caused with *The Civil Rights Cases*: knowledgeable insiders at the time were hopeful that the Court would have either overruled or distinguished that precedent.[22] (Recall that those cases may not have been as rigidly opposed to regulation of private parties as they are sometimes made out to be.) Instead, let's update by a half century the decision that Congress and the president had to make in 1964, and test that statute against the modern law of the enforcement power: the congruence and proportionality test. How would the public accommodations provisions of the 1964 act stack up against our proposed approach to the enforcement power in 2015?

Assume away the definitional difficulty noted earlier—that is, assume that, at least theoretically, Congress could use its enforcement power to regulate private conduct. Consider what the Court would have to conclude in order to decide that the 1964 law satisfied the congruence and proportionality test. It would have to conclude, after according Congress the appropriate amount of deference, that there was some reasonable connection (i.e., some congruence and proportionality) between the private discrimination and unconstitutional state action that Congress could attempt to target via enforcement legislation.

Here's where the difficulty starts. As scholars have long realized, searching for a hard-and-fast distinction between purely private conduct and state action is a fool's errand. If one looks hard enough—and usually it doesn't take that hard of a look—one can always find the state lurking in the shadows of private transactions. Consider our example, public accommodations. In the early 1960s the nation was roiled by sit-in protests in the South, where young

African Americans would sit at segregated lunch counters and request service. Assume that state law did not require lunch counter segregation; thus, the state would not be implicated in that obvious way. Would the state nevertheless be implicated in that discrimination? One might not think so. But what if, as usually happened, the proprietor called the police, who forcibly removed the protesters and arrested them for trespassing? Or what if the lunch counter was licensed by the health department? Or was required by state law to carry liability insurance? Or got its electricity from a municipal utility?

The point here is not that any of the state action mentioned earlier would constitute Fourteenth Amendment "state action." Instead, the point is simply that connections between private and public conduct are easy to find, if one looks. Thus, scholars considering the state action issue more generally have concluded that the key is not simply to find "state action" (which one can always do), but instead to determine whether the state action we inevitably find is in fact unconstitutional.[23]

Unfortunately, when the state's role is indirect and secondary, as it often is in these cases, determining whether the state's conduct is unconstitutional is highly contested. But the point is not just that such decisions are difficult. In addition, enforcement legislation predicated on conclusions about when the state's (inevitable) conduct crossed a constitutional line would entail Congress making legal judgments about the constitutionality of particular types of state conduct. For example, if Congress used its enforcement power to prohibit private racial discrimination in restaurants, it might argue that state court enforcement of such private racism implicated states in that discrimination. Such an argument necessarily involves a congressional judgment about when that state government conduct constitutes unconstitutional "state action."

Mapping that point onto our larger enforcement power template, we thus reach the conclusion that if Congress makes aggressive use of its enforcement power to pronounce as unconstitutional the inevitable state action that it finds, it would effectively be interpreting the Constitution. Such legislative constitutional interpretation, translated into enforcement legislation, would challenge the Court's insistence that it alone enjoys the ultimate authority to interpret the Constitution.

A Power to Regulate Private Conduct?

The concern noted in the prior sentence means that we should flash a yellow warning light at any congressional attempt to regulate private conduct under its enforcement power. But on the other hand, the analysis of VAWA earlier in this chapter provides a more straightforward explanation for why regulation of private conduct can constitute a completely reasonable means of enforcing Section 1's prohibition on state conduct that denies equal protection.

Harmonizing these seemingly contradictory conclusions, it appears that the proper answer to the state action question would allow Congress at least some leeway to enforce Fourteenth Amendment guarantees by regulating private conduct. This is especially true when Congress regulates private parties for the purpose of correcting or deterring obvious state misconduct.

However, like all examples of enforcement power discretion, the power to regulate private conduct must also be limited, lest this power morph into a power to redefine the underlying constitutional rule itself. Here, for example, unrestricted congressional leeway to regulate private conduct under its enforcement power would allow Congress effectively to make private parties subject to the Fourteenth Amendment itself—something that most scholars agree would go beyond the amendment's meaning. Indeed, as we discussed at the end of the prior section, even congressional regulation of private conduct justified on the ground that it is tied to some unconstitutional state action also threatens to give Congress a de facto power to interpret the Constitution, if the unconstitutionality of that state conduct is not reasonably clear.

The analysis may be intricate, but the principle is straightforward: given how contested the state action concept is, congressional regulation of private conduct justified on the theory that such conduct is tied to unconstitutional state action presents a real risk of congressional usurpation of interpretive power. If we are to remain faithful to our underlying assumption that courts enjoy ultimate supremacy in interpreting the Constitution, then such legislation must be subject to significant judicial scrutiny of the constitutionality of the underlying state action.

But there are easier cases, too—such as the VAWA case. When, as in VAWA, Congress regulates private party action that is tied to clearly unconstitutional state conduct, it would seem adequate, and within the judicial ken, for courts to confirm that Congress found adequate facts tying private conduct to those state constitutional violations, and that it appropriately concluded that regulating such private conduct would deter those violations. Chapter 7 laid out a series of deference principles guiding such judicial review, while respecting Congress's role in deciding what tools would best enforce the restrictions on unconstitutional state action.

Let's conclude this chapter by applying this theory to VAWA. The VAWA provision struck down in *Morrison* provided a federal-law cause of action for a victim of gender-motivated violence. Thus, under VAWA a victim could sue her attacker in federal court. The statute was defended on the theory that local criminal justice systems often downplayed gender-motivated violence, investigating and prosecuting such crimes less frequently and less intensively than they merited because of sexist assumptions about those crimes. Congress amassed what even the *Morrison* majority conceded was "a voluminous . . . record" revealing that state law enforcement officials were "perpetuating an array of erroneous [gender] stereotypes and assumptions."[24]

Given that record and the difficulty inherent in Congress ordering state law enforcement simply to do its job, it made sense for Congress to attempt to ensure some measure of vindication for crime victims who were subject to discriminatory investigation and prosecution by state authorities. To be sure, this conclusion implies that direct federal vindication of those victims' rights to equal protection of the state's criminal laws is not categorically (or "jurisdictionally") outside the boundaries of Section 5's authorization to Congress to "enforce" Section 1's mandate against states "depriv[ing]" persons of equal protection. But as noted earlier, the amendment's drafting history and its early judicial interpretations do not require the conclusion that Congress's enforcement power is so limited.[25] Given the difficulty inherent in directly regulating state law enforcement, the balance of the argument seems to rest against such a categorical limitation on Congress.

The only question then becomes one of Congress's choice of remedies. The Court rejected this provision of VAWA as failing the congruence and proportionality requirement because it acted on private parties, rather than on state officials themselves. As the Court noted, it "visits no consequence whatever" on any state official and is not "aimed at proscribing" any Fourteenth Amendment violation.

Again, by this point in the argument we've rejected *Morrison*'s claim that the enforcement power categorically excludes congressional regulation of private parties. Still, it is fair to ask, now simply as a matter of Congress's policy-based discretion over remedies, whether VAWA would likely influence state officials to start providing the equal protection the Fourteenth Amendment commands of them. One must concede that providing these crime victims with a federal civil remedy against their attackers constitutes a somewhat circuitous way of vindicating their rights to equal protection at the hands of state law enforcement authorities. Expressing his disagreement with the *Morrison* majority's enforcement power analysis, Justice Breyer suggested that the federal law might lead states to improve their own "remedial" systems, "primarily through example." While this may not be the most satisfying argument, before condemning it perhaps we should realize the difficult remedial task Congress faced when it confronted states' systemic unequal treatment of an entire class of crimes. Moreover, we should realize that civil liability may well play a deterrent role analogous to the role played by the criminal law (which, by hypothesis, is not doing its job in these cases).

So understood, a civil remedy may correct, in some measure, the state's denial of the equal protection of its laws to the victims of these crimes, either by encouraging states to stop discriminating or by furnishing (federal) protection when states fall down on their own obligations. To be sure, this remedy does not operate on the state itself. But it nevertheless corrects the effects of the state's misconduct. As such, such regulation of private conduct should remain a tool in Congress's enforcement power tool kit—even if that tool must be used with care.

PART IV

Applying the Fix

Equal Protection and Beyond

9

Irrationality, Animus, and Deference

It is time to consider real examples of how we can apply the reformulated enforcement power we've sketched out. This chapter applies the book's proposals to the equal protection situations we have discussed up to now. Chapter 10 applies it to the remaining areas of equal protection law and to other Fourteenth Amendment rights.

Suspect Classes and the Deference Question

A useful place to start is with legislation that enforces the equality rights of groups the Court has acknowledged merit heightened judicial protection—what the law calls "suspect" and "quasi-suspect" classes. Under current doctrine, legislation targeting such discrimination usually enjoys more relaxed judicial scrutiny. Nevertheless, such legislation has come to be marked by dynamics that have eroded the Court's previously hospitable reception. Chapter 5 discussed these dynamics: we will summarize them very briefly here. Recall that sometimes antidiscrimination legislation appears to succeed: the blatant discrimination the law targeted becomes less prevalent, and at least some indicators suggest the problem has been substantially or even fully resolved.

This phenomenon presents courts with two difficult problems when reviewing enforcement legislation for congruence and proportionality. First, and most obviously, it allows parties challenging such legislation to claim that the legislation has succeeded and has thus become unnecessary and hence invalid. In turn, defenders of such legislation argue that any such success relies on the continued existence of the statute as a deterrent to backsliding. The Court's invalidation of the coverage formula for the Voting Rights Act's preclearance provisions in *Shelby County* turned heavily on its rejection of the deterrence argument.

Second, this phenomenon leads equality advocates to worry that the targeted discrimination has morphed into subtler variants that are harder to spot than blatant, "first-generation" forms. That concern leads advocates to propose more indirect tools, which are grounded on more nuanced analysis and more intricate causation chains. In turn, such intricacies prompt arguments that the laws are insufficiently related to the underlying constitutional violations to satisfy the Court's requirement of congruence and proportionality. Defenders of such legislation respond with pleas for the court to defer to Congress's judgment on those issues. The Court's analysis of the FMLA's self-care provision in *Coleman* presents a version of this type of deference request.

The next two sections consider these two arguments. Before turning to them, though, it bears repeating chapter 5's warning that these problems are not confined to the VRA and the FMLA's self-care provision, the two examples of these dynamics that have reached the Court so far. Modern federal antidiscrimination law is maturing. The Civil Rights Act of 1964 turned fifty in 2014; the Voting Rights Act is only a year younger, and even the Pregnancy Discrimination Act, enacted in 1978,[1] is nearly a generation old. The age of these laws, while not a sufficient condition for triggering the dynamics discussed earlier, has nevertheless made them possible, both by giving credence to arguments that the laws have (finally) succeeded and, conversely, by convincing equality advocates that discriminatory attitudes have been driven into subtler manifestations, thus requiring more nuanced remedies. Of course, we can't know the precise contours of future claims of this sort. Still, we can expect to encounter them.

The Paradox of Success

Consider first the argument, which challengers successfully made to the Court in 2013, that the VRA's formula governing the geographic reach of the statute's preclearance provisions was obsolete, and thus "inappropriate" enforcement legislation, given the statute's success at reforming the covered jurisdictions' previous discriminatory habits. The Court's conclusion—and the dissent's protest—ranged over a variety of issues, but for our purposes the most relevant area of disagreement considered the statute's continued deterrent effect. Chief Justice Roberts's majority refused to engage the deterrence argument. Its entire analysis, which we quoted earlier in chapter 5, consisted of the following sentence: "Under [the deterrence argument], however, [the coverage formula] would be effectively immune from scrutiny; no matter how 'clean' the record of the covered jurisdictions, the argument could always be made that it was deterrence that accounted for the good behavior."[2] Recall also from chapter 5 the chief justice's mocking analogy of the government's deterrence argument to the story of the man who claimed to have a whistle that repelled elephants, and who offered as proof of its deterrent power the fact that whenever he blew on it, no elephants would be found. That analogy lurks just below the surface of the Court's quick and unambiguous rejection of the deterrence argument for these VRA provisions.

Whatever one might think of his dismissive (non)answer to the deterrence argument, one can still understand the chief justice's frustration: as chapter 5 explained, evaluating such arguments presents courts with daunting challenges. Yet by failing to seriously consider deterrence as a justification for the law, the Court in *Shelby County* denied Congress the use of a fundamental justification for many laws. The hard fact is that Congress—and legislatures more generally—often enacts laws in order to deter unwanted conduct. Frequently, that deterrent effect is difficult to measure. To be sure, courts considering constitutional challenges to legislation usually don't second-guess such deterrence judgments (much less rule such arguments out of bounds). But it did in *Shelby County*. The Court had its reasons for doing so: in particular, the VRA's preclearance provisions impose deep restrictions on states' sovereign prerogatives and do so only on some states rather than equally on all.[3]

Still, concern for federalism does not justify the Court's bald refusal to consider the deterrence argument. After all, the Fourteenth Amendment was *designed* to limit state power. As noted earlier, a refusal to credit such an argument robs Congress of an important justification for enforcement legislation that targets entrenched discrimination that is susceptible to resurfacing when the opportunity arises. A better approach—the approach suggested by chapter 7's examination of the deference question—would be to consider the support for the deterrence argument and apply the appropriate amount of deference to its components.

Let's apply chapter 7's deference principles to the deterrence argument in *Shelby County*. As a general matter, distinguishing between a law's success in eradicating a particular social evil and its deterrent effect in simply suppressing it requires, at the very least, a sophisticated understanding of the social dynamics of the given context. In the case of the VRA, for example, it requires a deep understanding of how politics and society have changed in the covered jurisdictions since the 1960s. In turn, that understanding requires a type of judgment that chapter 7 described as the application of ideology to the empirical facts of voting and political participation rates in the covered jurisdictions.

The role of personal ideology—understood here as a set of beliefs about the world that are not subject to empirical verification—surfaces in Chief Justice Roberts's elephant whistle analogy. The owner of the whistle (if sincere) truly believes that the whistle is effective in keeping away elephants. The empirical record (the lack of elephants in the vicinity) is consistent with that belief, although (of course) it is also consistent with the converse of that belief—it might just be that there are no elephants in the area for reasons that have nothing to do with the whistle.

Short of conducting a counterfactual experiment (putting the whistle away and seeing what happens), one cannot conclusively know who is right. Obviously, we have our intuitions—here, that the owner of the whistle is either lying or deluded. But we have that intuition only because we have our own views about how the world works. To be sure, our views are informed by our experience with the world: if we find ourselves in Antarctica, we doubt we will encounter elephants, whistle or not. So too with the VRA's deterrent effect. Our own experience of the world might suggest to us that the covered jurisdictions really have changed, and have done so permanently. Or that experience might suggest to us that the statute has only suppressed, not eradicated, discriminatory impulses.

So understood, decisions on these questions are fundamentally policy-based, in that they are founded on empirical facts (here, voting rates and the like), as filtered through the decision maker's own view of the world—what chapter 7 called (nonpejoratively) his "ideology." This description of these types of decisions strongly suggests that Congress should have significant latitude in making them, just as the federal legislature is given strong deference whenever it makes policy judgments.

But we cannot stop with a call for complete deference to Congress. Chief Justice Roberts has a point that unquestioning acceptance of a deterrence justification for a statute would render that law "effectively immune from scrutiny."[4] A judge on the lower court panel in the VRA case made the same point more colorfully: without a meaningful limit on such an argument, he said, "the supposed deterrent effect would justify continued VRA renewals out to the crack of doom."[5] Hence, the paradox. On the one hand, conclusions about a law's deterrent value are fundamentally based in policy, and thus merit substantial deference to the extent those policy judgments are based on lawmakers' ideologies. On the other hand, such arguments carry the potential for an indefinite extension of a law even when, on the face of things, it appears to have done its work successfully and thus rendered itself obsolete.[6]

Ideally, one would solve this paradox by adopting an approach to judicial review that both respects Congress's legitimacy and authority to make the decisions it was best suited to make and provides for meaningful judicial review of the questions that are most susceptible to judicial scrutiny. But no approach can be perfect: tough choices have to be made about which institution—Congress or the Court—should enjoy the ultimate advantage when deciding how far enforcement legislation can legitimately stretch when justified, even in part, on grounds that include an ideological component. The preceding discussion should make clear that judgments about a law's deterrent effect are best made by Congress.

This is not to deny a role for judicial review. As chapter 7 explained, at the very least a court in this situation may appropriately review the empirical component of such judgments. In the case of the VRA, the Court could have reviewed the accuracy of the empirical data about minorities' voting and political participation rates in the covered jurisdictions. If that review had uncovered serious inaccuracies, it might have been justified in demanding stronger evidence of the statute's deterrent effect. For example, if minority voting rates in those covered jurisdictions were sharply higher than asserted by Congress, then it might be less credible for Congress to argue that the VRA was the only thing preventing a return to the bad old days of Jim Crow. The same might be said if the statute's defenders has misstated or misanalyzed data about successful VRA Section 2 suits against covered jurisdictions, or Justice Department objections to those jurisdictions' preclearance requests.

Even without such empirical flaws, it would remain appropriate to test the deterrence argument against a reasonableness requirement. To be sure, any such judicial review would have to recognize courts' lesser competence to pass judgment on a congressional conclusion about a law's deterrent effect. Still, courts often impose nonarbitrariness requirements on government action, even in technically complex areas where they confess their lack of knowledge.[7]

Such review is difficult. Indeed, in *Shelby County* Chief Justice Roberts expressed something close to exasperation with the various arguments and counterarguments the parties made about the relevance of different parts of the empirical record allegedly supporting the statute.[8] As with the deterrence argument more generally, an argument about the relevance of a given set of facts to the statute's deterrence justification may be difficult for courts to evaluate, given the policy discretion inherent in any decision to consider one set of facts more probative than another. Again, though, courts could review those facts themselves, to ensure at least that Congress was weighing the relevance of *accurate* facts. This combination of deferential review of Congress's policy choices and more searching review of the choices' factual support constitutes a far superior option to what the Court actually did in *Shelby County*—namely, to simply refuse to consider the argument.

The Need for More Stringent Remedies: First- and Second-Generation Discrimination

Let's turn now to the second dynamic we identified at the start of this chapter—the dynamic that results in more nuanced legislative responses to discrimination. As discussed in chapter 5, this dynamic also begins with a straightforward story of success. It starts with Congress identifying blatant discrimination and enacting legislation prohibiting it. Eventually, the law begins to achieve its intended effect: such discrimination (e.g., employment ads stating "Men Only") becomes less prevalent.

So far, this story is very similar to the first one—antidiscrimination legislation is enacted and appears to succeed. But our new story then takes a slightly different path. Instead of a challenger claiming that the law has obsolesced itself by its very success, here interest groups concerned about the targeted discrimination begin to worry that that discrimination is simply taking on subtler forms. For example, rather than discriminating against women overtly, employers begin expressing concern that women are not reliable employees because of their presumed family-care responsibilities. Such attitudes, while they have the same effect as overt discrimination (women are disadvantaged in the workplace), may not strike judges as "discrimination because of sex." At the very least, they might not be amenable to detection by judges applying a general nondiscrimination mandate on a case-by-case basis. The dynamic completes its cycle when the legislature responds by enacting legislation that seeks to root out or counteract these subtler manifestations of discrimination.

This description characterizes the story of the FMLA's self-care provision. As chapter 5 discussed in more detail, in the 2012 case *Coleman v. Court of Appeals of Maryland*,[9] the Court held that that provision was not valid enforcement legislation, even though it was defended as a measure to ensure sex equality, and even though the Court had recognized sex as a quasi-suspect classification. In particular, the Court described as "overly complicated" and "unconvincing" the argument that that provision played a double prophylactic role by mitigating any sex-skewed impact caused by the statute's companion feature, which granted employees time off for *family* care. The dissent disagreed, arguing that the relationship was straightforward and logical.

For our purposes, the fact of this disagreement, and who gets the better of the argument, is less important than the more general question this debate poses for judicial review of enforcement legislation. If, as seems likely, many types of discriminatory attitudes linger on, given their often-durable foundation in deep-seated assumptions, stereotypes, and animus, then antidiscrimination advocates will likely press Congress to respond with more nuanced regulatory tools. The 2003 *Hibbs* case, discussed in chapter 4, recognized this dynamic. It recounted the story of sex equality legislation and noted that successive Congresses, starting in 1964 and continuing to the FMLA three decades later, recognized the persistence of sex discrimination in employment and attacked it with ever more nuanced remedies.[10]

So understood, the question for a reviewing court in a case like *Coleman* becomes similar to the question posed by *Shelby County*: How should a court review a congressional judgment about the particular policy effects of a given statute? As with our discussion of *Shelby County*, one response to the judicial review question in *Coleman* involves the Court deconstructing the congressional judgment into its component parts and focusing its review on the issues on which the Court is best able to scrutinize Congress's conclusion. Once again, courts may find themselves especially competent to review the empirical facts supporting Congress's policy judgment, rather than that judgment itself.

Let's apply this suggestion to the dispute over the self-care provision. The plurality opinion rejecting that provision as valid enforcement legislation observed that "Congress made no findings, and received no specific testimony, to suggest that the availability of self-care leave equalizes the expected amount of FMLA leave men and women will take."[11] It also noted Congress's conclusion that men and women would likely take approximately five days of self-care leave per year; based on that conclusion, the plurality expressed doubt that the self-care provision would do much to counteract the family-care provision's skew toward women.[12]

Consider now Justice Ginsburg's counterargument. She cited congressional testimony by business groups warning that provision of family-care leave alone would lead to increased discrimination against women. She also noted the evidence (also cited by the plurality) that men and women would likely take self-care leave in equal amounts. But she drew very different lessons from that evidence. Rather than expressing doubt about the equalizing effect of self-care leave, she instead stressed that self-care leave would "counter employers' *impressions*" about FMLA leave more generally and "blunt the force of *stereotypes*" about men's and women's reliability as employees.[13] The italicized words here (not Justice Ginsburg's italics) reveal her argument's focus on employer perceptions and stereotypes rather than on the actualities Justice Kennedy's plurality opinion focused on.

To repeat, determining who wins the Kennedy-Ginsburg debate is less important than grasping the lessons that debate reveals. Neither side took issue with Congress's facts themselves—unsurprisingly in Justice Ginsburg's case, since she was arguing to uphold the legislation. But Justice Kennedy didn't either. Instead, he criticized their implications. That should raise a red flag: as chapter 7's discussion of deference argued, interpreting facts as either supporting or not supporting a particular policy itself involves some measure of policy judgment appropriately reserved for Congress.

Still, one can sympathize with Justice Kennedy when, literally, he does the math and concludes that, at most, the self-care provision would lead to men taking five sick days per year, an amount that paled in comparison with the FMLA's twelve-week maximum for all leave put together. How would such a paltry equalization effect make a serious dent in the gender imbalance allegedly created by the statute's provision of family-care leave? Given these facts, one can understand the adjectives he used when evaluating this part of the employee's argument: "overly complicated" and "unconvincing."

But wait. Perhaps Justice Kennedy was evaluating the wrong argument. Consider again Justice Ginsburg's dissent. Her inquiry into whether the self-care provision would "counter employers' *impressions*" and "blunt the force of *stereotypes*" suggests a different congressional goal: not primarily to change the *actual* relative burdens men and women place on their employers but to change employers' *perceptions* of those burdens.

Justice Ginsburg's focus leaves us in essentially the same place as the deterrence argument in *Shelby County*. In both cases, we can understand Congress to be legislating to counteract phenomena (the potential for backsliding in voting rights and employers' sex stereotyping) that are difficult, if not impossible, to prove empirically. Yet surely Congress has a legitimate interest in attacking those phenomena. Thus, if legislation targets difficult-to-prove phenomena that can be perceived only through the filter of one's own ideologically colored view of the world, then it is hard to see how courts can legitimately scrutinize the need for such a law, or its success. As we acknowledged in the voting rights context, courts can legitimately strike down laws that truly have no conceivable connection to such goals. But beyond such necessarily deferential review, it seems appropriate for courts to confine their closest scrutiny to the empirical facts on which Congress has based its judgment—not on the use Congress makes of those facts.

Emerging Groups

Another type of enforcement legislation that would be impacted by this changed understanding of the enforcement power is legislation dealing with emerging groups. As noted in chapter 4, "emerging" groups are distinguished by the fact that their identifying trait—for example, sexual orientation or genetic makeup—has never been the subject of a Supreme Court decision about that trait's suspect status. These groups are an important part of our story about congressional enforcement power exactly because they (and we) will likely never learn whether they are a suspect class, given the Court's de facto abandonment of that analysis.

But the Court's unwillingness to decide these groups' suspect class status will not prevent Congress from legislating to protect them. Indeed, this book calls such groups "emerging" exactly because their equality demands have recently begun to command significant legislative attention. Some of that attention will take the form of federal legislation grounded in Congress's enforcement power. When determining the constitutionality of such legislation, the Court will be faced with a choice: either rely on its all-but-abandoned suspect class analysis, or adopt an alternative methodology. Chapter 6 presented and argued for just such an alternative—one that entails the Court reviewing Congress's judgment that the discrimination Congress targeted has been rejected by the American people as fundamentally unfair.

Let's consider in more detail an example that we touched on in chapter 6. At some point in the next several years Congress will likely enact the Employment Non-Discrimination Act, a bill that is designed to protect gays, lesbians, and transgendered people from employment discrimination. Support for the bill has gradually increased over the years and now includes both Republican and Democratic lawmakers. If enacted, ENDA will almost certainly apply to state government employers as well as employers in the private sector. In turn, this regulation of state governments will likely be grounded in part on the enforcement power, which provides the surest way of providing for damages and back pay awards when state employers engage in the prohibited job discrimination.

How would the Court evaluate ENDA as enforcement legislation under this book's proposed approach? Recall the fundamental question that approach would require the Court to answer: Was Congress reasonable in concluding that the American people had rejected sexual orientation employment discrimination as fundamentally unfair? That question requires a little unpacking. First, this inquiry requires the Court simply to ask whether Congress was *reasonable* in reaching its conclusion. This standard flows from our discussion, in chapter 7, of the deference question. More precisely, it flows from chapter 7's conclusion that the types of judgments implicit in a conclusion about fairness are those that Congress can make both more legitimately and more competently than courts. Courts' comparative lack of authority requires that any judicial review of such judgments be deferential.

Second, the Court's inquiry would not consider whether such discrimination *was* fundamentally unfair, but rather whether Congress had accurately determined that *the American people* had reached that conclusion. This is a very different question than what the Court has asked in its enforcement power cases up to now. This reframed question recognizes the fundamentally moral nature of judgments about discrimination. It also recognizes the authority of the American people, acting through their national representatives in Congress, to instantiate that moral judgment into enforcement legislation. Recognition of that authority transforms the enforcement power question into an inquiry into whether the challenged legislation accurately reflects the views of the American people. Third, the question posed here frames the relevant discrimination narrowly—in the case of ENDA, not simply as sexual orientation discrimination but as sexual orientation discrimination in employment. (Indeed, it is for this reason that this example ignores ENDA's potential protection for transgendered workers, as such discrimination would pose a different question that would have to be answered by its own distinct application of this methodology.)

Let's now consider how a court would answer this question. A court faced with this challenge would have to review the evidence indicating a social consensus condemning this type of discrimination. Of course, the most relevant data would concern employment discrimination against gays and lesbians. But note something important: a court performing this analysis would not simply, or even primarily, ask whether *states* were engaged in employment discrimination against gays and lesbians. Even less would it ask whether any such discrimination would fail the relevant doctrinal test if a gay employee challenged it as unconstitutional.

The Court's current approach to the enforcement power would ask such questions. However, information on that point is, at best, not fully responsive to the relevant question: what American society thinks about the fundamental fairness of sexual orientation employment discrimination. Of course such evidence is relevant: for example, if it was determined that a significant percentage of American state government units regularly engaged in such discrimination, that would suggest that American society does not reject that practice.

But note two points here. First, in this example the practices of those state government units would hardly tell the full story about what American society thinks. If the relevant inquiry ultimately concerns broader social attitudes, then state governments' practices tell only part of that story. Second, and even more fundamentally, consider the direction in which such discrimination would cut under the Court's current approach, as opposed to the approach suggested by this book. Under the Court's current approach, a record of such discrimination would militate in favor of the enforcement legislation's constitutionality, at least if that discrimination was so invidious as to fail whatever standard of review the Court would apply to sexual orientation discrimination. (Don't forget that in the ENDA example the standard of review question remains unanswered, given the Court's refusal to determine the suspect class status of sexual orientation.) But under this book's approach, such a record would suggest societal approval of this type of discrimination and refusal to condemn it as fundamentally unfair. If that is the question the enforcement power requires a court to ask, then the hard truth is that pervasive discrimination on that ground suggests no societal consensus condemning the practice.

At this point you may be tempted to put this book down and stop reading. After all, how can congressional power to enforce a constitutional guarantee of equal treatment be thwarted by the fact that states—and society more generally—persist in engaging in the type of discrimination Congress seeks to stamp out? This objection requires two quick responses before we return to our ENDA example. First, this approach should only apply when the relevant equal protection rule is the general one that states not engage in discrimination that is fundamentally unfair. As this book has demonstrated, that rule applies to a great deal of discrimination we might care about but not all of it. Most notably, the Court has made clear that racial equality is a particular concern of equal protection, based on the undeniable historical intent of the Fourteenth Amendment's framers to ensure racial equality. Thus, at least racial discrimination does not come under the approach we have sketched so far. (Congressional power to ensure racial equality is discussed in chapter 10.)

Second, with regard to the types of discrimination that *are* subject to this rule, it bears repeating that in the absence of suspect class analysis courts have very few tools with which to evaluate the fairness of a given type of discrimination. Sometimes, as with *Cleburne*, the government itself provides the evidence that, in a particular situation, it is acting in a fundamentally unfair way. But in most cases the court's task—to determine the fairness of an entire species of discrimination—is intensely difficult to perform. Given the fundamentally normative nature of the question to be answered, enforcement power questions need, at base, to be decided by reference to what the American people think constitutes fair treatment.

You still may not be moved. But hold on, and realize that this approach should not unduly cramp congressional power. It would be a highly unusual situation, especially in this politically polarized age, for Congress to muster the energy to enact enforcement legislation prohibiting discrimination that the American people had not yet already begun to condemn in other forums. If modern civil rights movements have taught us anything, it is that progress only comes when it is made on several fronts and in a variety of forums. Over a quarter of the states had fully extended the franchise to women before the Nineteenth Amendment was ratified, with the vast majority of the remainder according at least partial suffrage rights.[14] Before the Supreme Court issued its first opinions on same-sex marriage in June 2013, nearly a quarter of the states had approved full marriage rights for same-sex couples, and countless private companies had extended marital benefits to same-sex couples. More generally, LGBT people became an important political influence in the politics of liberal cities and states long before they began to win successes at the national level.[15] Even African Americans' campaign for equality—a campaign that, perhaps more than most, focused on action at the federal level—took place in a context where academic and popular opinion had decisively turned in favor of equality, at least as a theoretical matter.[16]

Today, it is even less likely that federal action—in particular, congressional action—would be forthcoming in the absence of at least some nationwide agreement on a particular group's equality claim. Thus, the potentially troubling situation described earlier—where Congress enacts enforcement legislation condemning discrimination that is still pervasively practiced across the nation—is unlikely to occur.

Return now to the ENDA example. So far we have been talking mainly about state government practices with regard to sexual orientation employment discrimination. But a court considering the enforcement power foundation for ENDA would not stop with that evidence. As we might expect from a court asking a broad question about American society's views on a given type of discrimination, a court applying this book's approach to ENDA would consider a wide range of evidence about Americans' attitudes toward employment and sexual orientation. Of course, employers' actual practices would be quite probative. Thus, the court would appropriately examine the policies of American employers, both public and private.

But employers are not the only Americans with opinions about employment discrimination. Broader measures of Americans' views, including those of everyday citizens and major civil society groups, should matter, too. Indeed, a court examining the views of those groups should not stop with considering their views about sexual orientation employment discrimination. Employment is a social context that is analogous to other contexts: admission into professional societies and affinity groups, and even into public accommodations. Thus, while Americans' views about gays' and lesbians' inherent right to nondiscrimination in these other forums are one or more steps removed from the employment context, they remain relevant. A court considering the reasonableness of Congress's conclusions about Americans' attitudes toward sexual orientation employment discrimination should consider this broader evidence as well.

This approach is fundamentally different from the Court's post-*Boerne* enforcement power doctrine. That current doctrine examines the extent to which *states* are *violating* a *judge-made doctrinal rule* about the *judicially de-*

termined constitutionality of a particular type of discrimination. By contrast, a court applying this book's methodology would examine the extent to which *American society* is *applying* a *societal consensus* about the *fundamental fairness* of such discrimination. This approach thus constitutes a fundamental refocusing of the enforcement power, away from searching for state government violations of a judge-made constitutional rule, and toward searching for the existence of a consensus among American citizens condemning a particular type of discrimination as violating a core equal protection principle.

Part II of this book attempted to justify this refocusing. To summarize that argument very briefly, this refocusing reflects the normative, nonlegal nature of most decisions about the fairness of a particular type of discrimination. Given the nature of those decisions, this book has argued that Congress is the institution best suited to instantiate those decisions, even while recognizing that the Court must do its best to decide direct constitutional challenges when Congress fails to enact enforcement legislation. But when Congress does enact such laws, it should be given a wide berth, subject only to a review of its supporting facts and a deferential judicial examination to ensure that Congress was in fact acting pursuant to a national consensus. How deferential that examination should be is treated below.

Note that this approach contains a built-in limiting mechanism. It is not easy to enact federal legislation. The framers deliberately made the process onerous; in recent decades heightened political partisanship has resulted in the erection of even more roadblocks and choke points. Earlier in this chapter we explained how these facts make it unlikely that under this book's approach significant enforcement legislation would be enacted that lacks a national consensus. Now we can add to that insight its mirror image: this approach's built-in limiting mechanism should give the Court comfort that any enforcement legislation that does manage to run the lawmaking gauntlet enjoys such a consensus. This observation further justifies the more deferential judicial review this approach calls for.

Indeed, we can make an additional point. States—the parties enforcement legislation targets—constitute an integral part of the nation whose consensus on an issue this approach requires in order for enforcement legislation to be upheld. Thus, as noted briefly earlier, it is unlikely that an interest group would succeed in gaining enactment of enforcement legislation when states have not already responded to such equality claims, either by enacting antidiscrimination legislation of their own or simply by refraining from engaging in that discrimination themselves. In this sense, then, this approach to the enforcement power, by examining enforcement legislation for support in a societal consensus that necessarily includes states in the relevant population, makes states key players in determining which enforcement legislation survives judicial review.

The ENDA example typifies this organic process for determining the constitutionality of enforcement legislation. The struggle for workplace equality for gays and lesbians began in earnest in the 1970s. While an early version of ENDA was introduced in 1974, the most rapid progress was made (as one might expect) at the state and local level. Starting in the mid-1970s, states, municipalities, and private entities slowly began adding employment protections for gays and lesbians.[17] By contrast, the momentum toward federal nondiscrimination law slowed as opponents organized at the national level. This dynamic should not be surprising: one would expect gay-friendly jurisdictions to respond more quickly to calls for such nondiscrimination laws, with the national effort lagging behind due to opposition from more conservative parts of the nation.[18]

Over time, however, as more states, localities, and private entities debated and approved such protections, public support grew. As of 2014, solid majorities of the American people support such measures, and congressional support for ENDA now extends into both parties. This is not to say its passage is assured in the near future: the power of congressional leaders to set Congress's agenda, and the existence of formal and de facto supermajority requirements may delay its enactment well past the point when actual majorities of both houses of Congress would support it. But it is exactly the existence of such roadblocks that should make the Court more comfortable when Congress does eventually act. And because such action would almost certainly result from preliminary work done in American society—at the level of state and local governments, but also with private employers and Americans more generally—enactment of such legislation likely reflects the existence of the consensus this book has identified as the ultimate prerequisite for valid enforcement legislation of this type.

Of course, states cannot fully control the constitutional fate of enforcement legislation. After all, the Fourteenth Amendment regulates states; thus, they can't be expected to play a conclusive role in determining Congress's lawful scope in enforcing that regulation. Nevertheless, by refocusing the Court's enforcement power review on the existence of a consensus among a national society that necessarily includes state governments, this approach recognizes states'—and their citizens'—roles in giving meaning to the Fourteenth Amendment's broad, but vague, equality mandate.

We can illustrate the superiority of this approach by contrasting it with how hard-line adherents of the Court's current approach analyzed the issue in the 2003 *Hibbs* case upholding the FMLA's family-care provision. In *Hibbs* the dissenters faulted the majority's decision partly on the ground that states had already recognized the problem and had begun providing such leave to their employees. Under the book's approach, state recognition of the problem—here, their recognition of the unfairness to women implicit in managers' assumptions about women's primary responsibility for family care—would militate *in favor* of the FMLA's constitutionality.[19] When one reflects on it, it is a strange argument that state recognition of a discrimination problem makes it harder for Congress to enact legislation targeting that problem. Yet that is the inevitable inference to be drawn from the Court's current approach to this issue. It is time for a new approach.

In 2014 a federal judge wrote the following in an opinion ruling against gay and lesbian couples who claimed a Fourteenth Amendment right to marry, and in favor of letting states decide the issue through the democratic process: "Better . . . , we think, to allow change through the customary political processes, in which the people, gay and straight alike, become the heroes of their own stories by meeting each other not as adversaries in a court system but as fellow citizens seeking to resolve a new social issue in a fair-minded way."[20] This book argues that such state-level resolutions of equality issues, when numerous and consistent enough to help reflect a national consensus as perceived by Congress, should help justify analogous action by the citizenry at the national level. After all, it is the *national* citizenry—acting through Congress—to whom the Constitution gives the power "to enforce" Fourteenth Amendment rights.

Beyond Animus: Newer Groups and Newer Equality Arguments

Underlying this book's approach is a recognition that courts are often not very good at reaching accurate conclusions about when discrimination is fundamentally unfair and thus violates equal protection. Some scholars' consideration of the phenomenon of discrimination suggests that the question is even harder than one might think at first glance. For example, Deborah Hellman argues that discrimination is wrong when it has the effect of demeaning a person by depriving that person of his equal moral worth.[21] Her argument matters for our present purposes because she further argues that determining whether particular rules are demeaning turns heavily on the social context.

Hellman provides two straightforward examples that suffice to make the point: the requirement in the Jim Crow South that blacks sit at the back of busses, and the apartheid-era requirement that black South African prisoners wear shorts, while white and mixed-race prisoners were required to wear pants. Neither riding in the back of a bus nor wearing shorts, she notes, is inherently demeaning. Instead, their demeaning effect flows from the social meaning accorded those requirements: respectively, the distaste many southern whites of the Jim Crow era felt for mixing with blacks, and the colonialist paternalism that infantilized black Africans, as expressed in the requirement that they wear short pants. (To be sure, the modern Supreme Court rejects such a socially infused understanding of the meaning of race classifications, viewing all uses of race to be highly suspect, whatever the social context. But at this point we are discussing the views of scholars, not the Court.)

This book's suggested framework for judicial review of enforcement legislation reflects this more social meaning–infused understanding of discrimination, by calling for judicial deference to congressional judgments that some classifications are in fact fundamentally unfair. So far, we have focused our analysis of such judgments by focusing particularly on sexual orientation. That focus reflects the reality that today the gay rights movement is probably the most active movement of emerging social groups. In 2015 if the evening news carries a discussion of a new civil rights battle, it probably involves gay rights.

But other groups are also clamoring for their equality rights, sometimes making arguments that are hard to analogize to arguments other groups made in prior years. Consider, for example, persons with genetic predispositions to particular diseases. In the course of enacting the Genetic Information Nondiscrimination Act (GINA) in 2008, members of Congress frequently expressed the view that discrimination on the basis of genetics was unfair.[22] Yet the type of unfairness characterizing such discrimination does not easily map onto other groups' claims of unfair discrimination. Thankfully, most animus-based condemnations of persons with genetic predispositions to diseases as "defective" have been relegated to the history books.[23] Yet congressmen debating GINA still condemned genetics discrimination as unfair. Indeed, one prominent journalist, commenting on GINA's passage, referred to what he called "the near total and uncontroversial agreement among Americans that genetic discrimination is wrong" in the course of concluding that "[we] Americans are a lot more radical about equality than we think."[24]

What is it about genetics that leads Americans to conclude that it is unfair to discriminate on that basis? A full answer to that question would take us far afield from our focus on congressional power to enforce equal protection. But it is important to flag the question because it forces us to confront the fact that our ideas of unfairness sometimes go far beyond straightforward arguments about the majority's simple dislike of a minority group. Genetics discrimination, for example, may strike Americans as unfair because it is based on a characteristic that, at least at our current state of science, is largely beyond our power to control.[25] So understood, "the near total and uncontroversial agreement among Americans that genetic discrimination is wrong" helps us understand what Americans think about equality, beyond the more straightforward stories that focus on animus and irrationality.

How could a court review the Enforcement Clause bona fides of legislation such as GINA? Of course, it could construct its own equal protection doctrine that takes into account discrimination based on characteristics beyond our control. Indeed, suspect class doctrine does just that, by asking, in part, whether the trait at issue is "immutable." But immutability is an ungovernable engine. Height is immutable—yet nobody thinks it is invidious when the Olympic basketball team picks tall people over short ones. More conceptually, attempting to describe a trait as immutable or not risks essentializing traits, such as race, sex, or genetic composition, as existing in the abstract, untethered to the particular society that defines that trait and categorizes according to it.

Scholars have attempted to make the immutability idea more precise by tying it to social context. For example, Samuel Marcosson has argued that immutability can be "constructed" as a description of a trait by considering the extent to which an individual in a particular social context feels, or is made to feel, as though that trait is a core part of his identity.[26] In other words, and to simplify Marcosson's complex argument, if society is constructed so that people with certain genetic predispositions feel as though those biological facts classify them in a socially meaningful way, then those people will experience that trait as immutable. On this theory, then, perhaps the Olympic basketball team's discrimination against short people appears no more morally troubling than discrimination based on a would-be player's possession of a particular skill, such as the ability to dribble. By contrast, discrimination based on one's genetic susceptibilities to illness appears to cut more to our sense of who we are as human beings.

To further complicate matters, these differing experiences of trait-based discrimination change as society changes. "Sexual orientation" did not exist as a category 200 years ago—the groups "homosexual" and "heterosexual" did not exist. "Genetic makeup" did not exist, either—because of our lack of scientific knowledge, that classification criterion would have been inconceivable to most people before the mid-nineteenth century. Moreover, once society calls such lines into existence, their salience changes as society evolves. "Irish" was once a label that carried serious implications for social acceptance in America; today, it is for the most part a benign expression of one's ethnic heritage.

If all this is true—if our perceptions of which lines matter and which don't (and, indeed, which lines "exist" and which don't) change along with society—

then at some point judge-made law will fall behind social understandings. Of course, the extent of this disconnect can be overstated: the changes we are discussing come about very slowly. But their pace may be accelerating, with both the increasing pluralism of American society and the increased opportunities today's communications media and networks provide for the construction of new identities. If Congress identifies such groups and provides them Enforcement Clause–based protections, then courts will have to determine how to respond.

The precise contours of such a response will vary with the details of the group's identity, as understood both by its members and by society at large. For example, employment protection for transgendered workers may force courts to determine whether such discrimination is best understood as a species of sex discrimination, or as its own analytically distinct category. (Indeed, courts have been struggling for at least three decades with the question whether employment discrimination based on transgender identity *is* employment discrimination based on sex.)[27] Similarly, if and when GINA comes to the Court as enforcement legislation, it will have to determine the relationship between, on the one hand, the objective fact that certain people possess genes that carry certain probabilities for physical outcomes and, on the other hand, the socially enmeshed meaning that comes along with that fact. Such meaning may include the sense that the perceived randomness and "unearned" qualities of genetic anomalies render discrimination on that ground problematic. Such meanings are highly contextualized and not susceptible to any general rule: height is similarly distributed more or less randomly (indeed, genetically!), but in most cases height discrimination by itself simply does not raise the same instinctive concerns.

Regardless of the details of the job facing them, a major component of courts' work when considering such new types of enforcement legislation will consist of uncovering the social (and thus socially contingent) meaning of the classification tool. Acknowledging the nature of that task inevitably suggests that politically responsive legislatures can play an important role in identifying new groups and determining the significance of their identity categories. In sum, if naming a category and determining its social salience constitute morally fraught tasks, then courts should give a broad berth to Congress's responses, in particular, its determinations about which categories exist in American society, and what their existence means for purposes of equal protection's fundamental command of fair and reasonable classification.

10

Beyond Irrationality and Animus

The Enforcement Power in Other Contexts

Even if you are convinced by all the analysis up to now, you may be wondering what relevance this book has to congressional enforcement of constitutional rights beyond the equal protection rights we have focused on thus far. Most notably, the Due Process Clause of the Fourteenth Amendment is the source of most of the nonequality constitutional rights we enjoy against state infringement. These include the familiar rights that are often referred to as "unenumerated due process rights": rights to sexual autonomy, family life, and privacy, including the right to abortion. They also include the rights in the Bill of Rights that have been "incorporated" via the Due Process Clause to apply against the states. These latter rights range, among others, from the First Amendment rights of free speech and religious exercise, to the Second Amendment right to gun possession, to the Fourth Amendment right against unreasonable searches and seizures. Indeed, the Equal Protection Clause itself protects rights that go beyond the rules we have discussed so far.

The sheer variety of these rights suggests that it might be difficult to offer a clean-cut approach for understanding Congress's role in enforcing them. And indeed it is, especially given the methodology this book has offered. As should be clear by now, that methodology acknowledges the Supreme Court's role in stating constitutional meaning. However, it also recognizes Congress's role in applying that meaning to the myriad situations where the vindication of constitutional rights requires translating abstract constitutional meaning into concrete rules. Given how broadly these substantive rights vary, application of our approach to the enforcement power will yield different results, depending on the character of the right at issue. Nevertheless, we can offer some examples that illustrate how this book's approach applies to due rights beyond equal protection's prohibitions on arbitrary and invidious classifications.

Legal Analysis versus Factual Analysis

Let's begin with due process. Perhaps the most basic point we can make about the difference between equal protection rights and due process rights is that due process rights rely relatively less on moral reasoning. As we have seen throughout this book, deciding what equality requires is difficult, if not impossible, without a set of judgments about which traits should matter in which particular situation. If we believe that they don't matter, or shouldn't matter, then we have concluded, essentially, that decisions to consider that trait for that decision are either irrational or invidious. As this book has tried to demonstrate, such judgments are often fundamentally moral. Because Congress is far better placed than courts to discern Americans' moral judgments, the book has in turn argued that Congress merits substantial deference when determining the fundamental fairness of a given classification tool in a given context.

Due process rights are different. Speaking at a high level of generality, the methodology by which such rights are applied to particular situations requires a relatively heavier dose of what we can loosely describe as legal reasoning—that is, reasoning that relies on the interpretation and application of principles that are the traditional stock-in-trade of lawyers. Of course this initial statement of the idea is circular. But when we flesh out the idea, it becomes less so.

We will examine this issue by focusing on three due process rights: the Fourth Amendment right to be free from unreasonable searches and seizures, the Second Amendment right to possess a firearm, and the First Amendment right to free religious exercise. Each of these rights poses a somewhat different challenge for applying this book's approach to the enforcement power. In addition, the free exercise right was the right at issue in the *Boerne* case: thus, selecting it as one of our test cases allows us to speculate how that case might have come out under our approach—or, at least, what the Court's analysis would have looked like. Still, the variation between different rights reminds us that these examples are only illustrative. Applying this approach to legislation enforcing particular due process rights would require a careful understanding of that particular right, and of the core constitutional content of whatever the Court has said about that right.

Rights-Enforcing Legislation and Congress's Legitimate Role

This book has argued that Congress enjoys an important role in applying the broad legal conclusions the Supreme Court has drawn when interpreting the Fourteenth Amendment. The scope of that role turns on the degree to which the Court's interpretations create room for congressional action, by acknowledging the relevance of determinations that are most competently or legitimately made by the national legislature rather than by the Court itself.

This book has argued in particular that the Court's interpretations of the Equal Protection Clause have created a significant role for Congress because those interpretations rely for their application on determinations of fairness that are fundamentally nonlegal in nature.

As a theoretical matter, this thesis maps neatly onto Congress's power to enforce the Due Process Clause. There is no reason one would not ask in this latter context the same questions about judicially declared constitutional meaning and the relative competence and authority of Congress and the Court to demarcate Congress's power to enforce Fourteenth Amendment rights. However, as a practical matter the variety of due process rights, the different tests the Court has crafted when vindicating those rights, and the different relationships those tests have to core constitutional meaning combine to make it challenging to transplant our thesis from laws enforcing equal protection to those enforcing due process.[1] Certainly, the variety of doctrinal tests governing due process adjudication makes it impossible to provide a comprehensive application of our thesis to due process enforcement legislation. What we can do, however, is explain the process by which courts should perform this task, and illustrate that process through some representative examples.

Let's begin by clearing away one piece of underbrush. When a Bill of Rights provision is held to apply against the states, that is because the Court has decided that that provision was "incorporated" by the Fourteenth Amendment's Due Process Clause. The idea of "incorporation" is simply one way of saying that the Due Process Clause includes within it the protections of that particular Bill of Rights provision. (Scholars often conclude that the Due Process Clause is the wrong home for such "incorporated" rights, arguing instead that the Fourteenth Amendment's Privileges or Immunities Clause was the intended vehicle for such incorporation. This academic debate need not detain us, as the Court has shown little inclination to revise its Fourteenth Amendment jurisprudence to accomplish this shift.) The Court began finding Bill of Rights provisions to have been incorporated in the late nineteenth century, with that process continuing slowly throughout the first half of the twentieth century and then picking up speed as the Warren Court of the 1950s and 1960s incorporated whatever criminal procedure provisions earlier Courts had failed to incorporate. Today, nearly all of the Bill of Rights has been incorporated.

During the incorporation process, various justices at times wondered whether the incorporated version of a given Bill of Rights provision provided the same protections as the original provision in the Bill of Rights itself. For example, when the First Amendment was deemed incorporated to apply against the states, did it have the same meaning that it had in its original version?[2] The justifications for reading the original version of a Bill of Rights provision differently from its incorporated version are complex, and beyond the scope of our discussion. But the outcome of this inquiry does matter for us, as it furnishes the actual constitutional rule to which congressional enforcement legislation must be congruent and proportional. Thankfully, this is one question we can readily answer. Despite individual justices' periodic protests,[3] the Court has almost uniformly construed the incorporated version of a given Bill of Rights provision to mean exactly the same thing as its original version.[4] However difficult it might be to determine the core meaning of an incorporated right for purposes of evaluating federal legislation seeking to enforce that right, one question we don't need to worry about is whether that incorporated right means something different from its original version. It does not.

But that's where the simplicity ends. As noted earlier, the Bill of Rights provisions the Due Process Clause incorporates cover a vast amount of state conduct. Compounding this variety, these rights take different forms, from seemingly absolute protections (such as the First Amendment's Free Exercise Clause stating that "no law" may be made prohibiting free religious exercise) to guarantees of reasonableness (as with the Fourth Amendment's guarantee against "unreasonable" searches and seizures) to the Second Amendment's gun possession right, which is prefaced by a statement setting forth the right's underlying purpose. Indeed, due process rights vary on an even more fundamental axis: while the Bill of Rights provisions that have been incorporated against the states are grounded in at least somewhat specific text, other rights are "unenumerated," in that they are based solely on the Due Process Clause's guarantee against deprivations of "liberty." These include the rights to sexual autonomy and abortion, among the most controversial of due process rights.

The disparate nature of these rights, both as to the social contexts they address and the character of the rights themselves, necessarily means that we face a difficult and constantly shifting task when evaluating legislation enforcing them. It also means that we will reach different outcomes when we bore down and identify the core constitutional rule to which a given piece of enforcement legislation must be congruent and proportional. As a theoretical matter this should not pose a serious problem: this book's thesis has always required, as a starting point for Enforcement Clause analysis, that the Court identify the core constitutional rule the enforcement legislation seeks to enforce. But the relative paucity of core equal protection law contrasts with the great variety of due process law, which, as described earlier, includes the core rules of each incorporated Bill of Rights provision, as well as the core of the unenumerated rights the Court has found in the Due Process Clause. That great variety means that enforcement legislation aimed at Due Process rights should generate analysis that leads in turn to a variety of results, depending on the right that Congress is seeking to enforce.

Illustrative Examples: Guns, Garbage, and God

Guns

Let's now consider three specific illustrations of the dynamic sketched out previously. Begin with the Second Amendment. In 2008 the Supreme Court held that the amendment's guarantee of "the right of the people to keep and bear Arms" was an individual right. The Court thus rejected the argument that that right existed only in connection with service in a militia, despite the amendment's prefatory clause stating that "[a] well regulated Militia [was] necessary to the security of a free State" before actually bestowing the right itself. In rejecting that argument, Justice Scalia's majority opinion used originalist methodology to determine how people in the framing era defined each relevant word in the operative clause: "the people," "keep," "bear," and "arms." Based on that examination, he concluded that the operative clause bestowed an individual right to possess weapons.

Justice Scalia's conclusion was controversial; four justices offered up a competing interpretation of the relevant language. For our purposes, however, what is important is not which side reached the right conclusion but, rather, the character of the majority's legal conclusion. The *Heller* Court's conclusion that the Second Amendment protects an individual right constitutes a statement of core constitutional law. One might disagree with that statement, just as one might disagree with the Court's statement that the Equal Protection Clause encodes a strong presumption against any government use of race as a classifying tool. But just as this latter statement reflects the Court's understanding of core constitutional meaning, so too does *Heller*'s statement about the individual nature of the firearms possession right.

We can know this by examining *Heller*'s methodology. In reaching its conclusion about the nature of the Second Amendment right, *Heller* did not apply mediating principles akin to the political-process reasoning the Court used to decide many equal protection cases during the 1970s and 1980s. It did not, for example, reach its conclusion based on concern that firearm possession rights were likely to be disfavored in the political process, or that firearms were likely to be used by persons who lacked meaningful access to that process. (By contrast, the dissent in the case incorporating the Second

Amendment cited *Carolene Products* in suggesting that the identification of new substantive due process rights should pay at least some attention to the political situation faced by the group claiming the right.)[5] Nor did it employ interest-balancing or a particular scrutiny level to determine the existence of the individual right. Rather, it examined what might be considered the most intensively core source of constitutional meaning—the text itself.[6] In particular, it examined that text through a particular prism—the prism of originalist methodology, which seeks to uncover and apply the original meaning of the provision at issue.

Originalist methodology has been heatedly criticized and just as passionately defended. We don't need to enter that debate. For our purposes, all we need to say is that conclusions reached through an originalist methodology—that is, conclusions about what the words of the constitutional text were understood to mean by the generation that ratified those words—yield conclusions that have to be understood as core constitutional law. Again, just to be clear, this conclusion takes no position on originalism as a methodology. It might be the right way or the wrong way to do constitutional law. Even if it makes sense as a theoretical matter, judges performing such analysis might be so prone to err as to make it inadvisable as a judicial methodology. Finally, other methodologies might also yield conclusions that merit that same status as statements of core constitutional law. But the methodology the Court used in *Heller* does yield such statements—regardless of what one thinks about those statements or about the methodology that produced them.

Thus, we know that the Second Amendment, as a matter of Court-announced core constitutional meaning, bestows an individual right "to keep and bear arms." But *Heller* went further in specifying the scope of the Second Amendment right. First, it identified self-defense as "the central component" of that right. Second, it held that the right was limited to the possession of weapons in "common use." Based on these components of the right, the Court invalidated not just the District of Columbia's ban on possessing a handgun in the home but also what the Court described as the District's "prohibition against rendering any lawful firearm in the home operable for the purpose of immediate self-defense."[7]

Drawing on our analysis of the *Cleburne* case in chapter 6, we should see that this strike-down of a law prohibiting home use of commonly available weapons for self-defense reflects core constitutional meaning. As we said in our discussion of *Cleburne*, the Court's decision to invalidate a law suggests that, at some point, the government crossed an actual constitutional line. When considered alongside the language quoted in the previous paragraph, *Heller*'s invalidation of the requirement that lawfully possessed weapons in the home be rendered inoperable for a self-defense use therefore strongly suggests that self-defense is part of the core constitutional right the Court discovered in that case. Indeed, when two years after *Heller* the Court incorporated the Second Amendment, it described the right in precisely these terms—even using the word "core" to describe it.[8]

Where does this analysis leave the enforcement power? One can imagine a future Congress seeking to enforce Second Amendment rights against states that prefer to regulate guns heavily. How much leeway would Congress have? A realistic answer to this question must concede that the Court will likely have more occasions to determine the core meaning of the Second Amendment.[9] After all, it has only decided two cases considering the scope of the individual gun possession right. But let's apply what we know for now. We know that the Second Amendment protects an individual right to possess commonly available weapons. We also know that self-defense in the home constitutes "the core" of that right. Thus, at least under the current state of the law, federal legislation enforcing the Second Amendment must aim at protecting an individual right with several components: the right to possess, in the home, commonly available weapons for self-defense purposes.

At first blush this appears to provide a satisfyingly clean rule. Unfortunately, it immediately becomes muddier once we begin considering laws Congress might enact to enforce that right. For example, could Congress enact legislation prohibiting states from banning possession of ammunition? Could it prohibit states from limiting the amount of ammunition an individual may possess? What about transporting guns: Could Congress enact legislation making it easier to carry concealed weapons in an automobile, on the theory that restrictions on guns' transport burdened the exercise of the core Second Amendment right by making it harder to get a gun into a home? What about restrictions on shooting ranges and other facilities where people learn to shoot? Does the Second Amendment right to possess a gun for self-defense include a right to access facilities where one learns how to use a gun for that purpose?[10]

These are difficult questions. But we need to consider how we would go about answering them because, as we have seen in the equal protection context, vindication of a constitutional right often requires protections that go beyond the borders of the core right itself. This book has suggested two basic principles when answering such questions in the context of equal protection enforcement legislation. First, it has argued that courts should distinguish between core constitutional meaning and decisional aids when identifying the right to which the legislation must be congruent and proportional. Second, it has argued that the Court should be more principled and transparent when deciding when and how much to defer to congressional fact-findings supporting enforcement legislation.

Let's apply these principles to two of the hypothetical Second Amendment enforcement statutes offered earlier. Consider first a prohibition on state laws banning the possession of ammunition in the home. The Court should have no difficulty upholding such an enforcement statute. The analysis would be straightforward: the core Second Amendment right consists of home possession, for self-defense purposes, of a gun. And not just any gun. Remember that *Heller* struck down a District of Columbia ordinance requiring that guns kept at home be rendered inoperable. Thus, the core right seems to consist of possession of a gun *that works*. Thus, a federal ban on state laws outlawing ammunition would presumably be understood as enforcing the core Second Amendment right.

More difficult issues emerge once we get to more indirect protections for the core right. Consider, for example, a hypothetical enforcement statute making it easier to transport guns. While such a law could be defended as making it easier to exercise the core right of home possession of a weapon, one could just as easily understand it as expanding the right from home possession to possession outside the home. Applying chapter 7's deference principles, one might object that such a law effectively enlarges the scope of the right, and thus wrests from the Court the power to interpret the Constitution.[11] That objection, in turn, might justify more careful scrutiny of the factual foundations supporting that law.

The conflict posed by this hypothetical statute—between, on the one hand, the argument that broader gun rights enforce the core Second Amendment right and, on the other, the argument that such laws simply (and inappropriately) expand the underlying right—goes with the territory when one considers the enforcement power. Despite this difficulty, in one way the enforcement power analysis is more straightforward in the Second Amendment context than when Congress sets out to enforce the Equal Protection Clause. As identified in *Heller*, the Second Amendment right is far less dependent for its application on contested value judgments. Of course, *Heller*'s recognition of an individual right to possess guns was controversial, and remains so today. But taking *Heller* as a given—that is, assuming that *Heller*, right or wrong, represents the Court's authoritative statement of the Second Amendment's meaning—the right that case announced can be applied without making value-inflected judgments. Difficult decisions might still have to be made—for example, about the constitutionality of state ammunition laws, or attempts to regulate certain types of handguns. But those decisions do not turn on the sort of explicitly moral judgments that confront courts in equal protection cases—for example, judgments about the fundamental fairness of a particular type of discrimination.

Because Second Amendment rights—and potentially other due process rights—do not require the sort of explicitly normative judgments that attend decisions on equal protection issues, congressional enforcement power may not be as robust as in the equal protection context. To be sure, even in due process cases Congress might be able to make a persuasive argument for strong enforcement legislation. But the argument would have to rest on a different foundation than the one that chapter 6 argued animates much modern equality-enforcing legislation. Recall that chapter 6 argued that equality-enforcing legislation merited special deference because of the fundamentally normative, value-inflected nature of the key judgments underlying such laws. By contrast, decisions about the scope of the Second Amendment right turn more heavily on analysis, such as *Heller*'s historical analysis, that is relatively more accessible to courts.

Of course the Court should respect Congress's policy judgments about the need for particular laws enforcing core constitutional rights, even when, as with the guns example, courts can apply the constitutional rule reasonably competently. Earlier chapters made this argument when they critiqued the Court's second-guessing of the analogous policy judgments underlying the FMLA and the VRA. But such respect is different from the type of deference that would be due Congress's judgments about the moral sensibilities of the American people. These latter judgments simply play less of a role when, as with the Second Amendment, the right is identified in a way that its application turns less on such moral evaluations.

But we're not done. We can't pronounce this analysis to apply each and every time Congress enforces a due process right. As we noted earlier in this chapter, due process rights come in all shapes and sizes. Most important for our current purposes, they rest on different types of judgments. As with the Second Amendment example, some of those judgments may be accessible to courts using commonly accepted tools of legal reasoning. But others not so much.

Garbage

Consider, for example, the Fourth Amendment. Among its other provisions, the Fourth Amendment prohibits "unreasonable searches and seizures." For almost fifty years, the Supreme Court has understood this provision as presumptively prohibiting warrantless police searches of tangible items or eavesdropping on conversations in which the individual has a reasonable expectation of privacy.[12] This rule draws a line that in many cases is quite easy to apply: for example, a person who secures items in a locked suitcase has a reasonable expectation of privacy in those items, while a person who leaves them open for all to see in a public place does not.

But difficult cases remain. One example is, literally, garbage. In *California v. Greenwood*,[13] the Court concluded that a person did not have a reasonable expectation of privacy in the household garbage he wrapped in an opaque plastic bag and left out for collection by city sanitation workers. Justice White's six-justice majority sparred with Justice Brennan's dissent (for himself and Justice Marshall) on the question of how American society viewed the privacy of garbage placed out for collection.

As with *Heller*, for us the important issue in *Greenwood* is not who got the better of this argument. Instead, the point is that both justices based their legal conclusions on understandings about Americans' social attitudes toward garbage. Justice White argued that it was "common knowledge that plastic garbage bags left on or at the side of a public street are readily accessible to animals, children, scavengers, snoops, and other members of the public."[14] He also found it probative of the expectations issue that many lower courts had rejected similar claims of a privacy interest in garbage. He further rejected the defendant's argument that California state law's protection against such searches gave him (a resident of California) a reasonable expectation of privacy.[15]

Justice Brennan disputed this reading of Americans' attitudes. He relied heavily on sociological evidence about what garbage reveals about the person who discarded it, cited the public outrage when a reporter rifled through the garbage of a prominent public official (former secretary of state Henry Kissinger), and noted that municipalities often require that garbage be placed in sealed containers and prohibit private rummaging. He concluded with an eloquent flourish, accusing the majority of painting "a grim picture" of "a society that is not prepared to recognize as reasonable an individual's expectation of privacy in the most intimate of personal effects sealed in an opaque container and disposed of in a manner designed to commingle it imminently and inextricably with the trash of others."[16]

Greenwood reveals how thoroughly some Fourth Amendment questions turn on social understandings, such as the extent to which Americans expect privacy in particular items and contexts. To use chapter 7's schema, the justices' differing conclusions in that case reflect different understandings of Americans' values. Thus, there would be good reason for the Court to accord Congress significant latitude if Congress, acting on its own reading of those values, enacted a law expanding the range of situations protected by the Fourth Amendment.

As with the parallel analysis in the equal protection context, this deference would come with caveats. A statute that *reduced* the places protected by the Fourth Amendment might be problematic, to the extent earlier judicial decisions protecting those places could be said to state and apply core constitutional law. Some of those decisions surely do state such core law. Most notably, the text of the Fourth Amendment protects "persons, houses, papers, and effects." Dissenting in *Katz v. United States*, the case that has come to be seen as the foundation for the reasonable expectations of privacy idea, Justice Black protested that the scope of the amendment could not be stretched beyond the four terms quoted here.[17] On this view he was in the minority; nevertheless, his argument supports the idea that the textual core of the Fourth Amendment protects an irreducible minimum of places that cannot be excluded from protection, even if Congress so decrees in an enforcement statute.

Even if Congress seeks to *expand* the list of protected situations, there remains room for judicial review. The nature of the relevant question—where do Americans believe an expectation of privacy is reasonable?—suggests that Congress's enforcement authority should rest on its conclusion that a national consensus supports the expansion of such protected contexts. As chapter 6 made clear in the equal protection context, courts remain able to review such congressional conclusions, albeit deferentially given Congress's superior authority to discern Americans' normative judgments on questions such as this one.

Indeed, one can take this example further. In addition to citing federal cases rejecting the privacy-in-garbage argument, *Greenwood* also cited state cases, some of which rested on state constitutional law rather than the Fourth Amendment.[18] This aspect of *Greenwood* illustrates how Congress might determine the existence of a social consensus supporting more expansive Fourth Amendment rights. As with equality-enforcing legislation, the actions of state governments themselves, in this case recognizing or rejecting a particular privacy expectation (and, in particular, grounding that decision on state law), should be an important input in the decision whether a national consensus supports Congress's judgment.[19]

Recall chapter 6's observation that this approach is inconsistent with—indeed, antithetical to—the Court's current approach to enforcement legislation. Under the current approach, state recognition of a particular equality (or, here, privacy) interest would suggest a lack of need for enforcement legislation. But consider how backward that approach is. If the relevant Fourth Amendment law requires that a social consensus must exist that a particular place or context is expected to be private, then it makes perfect sense for enforcement legislation to rest on Congress's conclusion that such a consensus exists. But, if the Court were to review that legislation under its current approach, the very existence of that consensus, as reflected in state law, would cut *against* the law's constitutionality, on the theory that the constitutional right at issue was not being broadly violated. This is as illogical a result in the Fourth Amendment context as chapter 6 argued it was in the equal protection context.

God

Let's now consider the final due process example: the First Amendment right of free religious exercise. This example brings our analysis full circle, as it was this right that Congress sought to enforce via the Religious Freedom Restoration Act, the statute the Court struck down in the *Boerne* case introducing the congruence and proportionality test. Using the free exercise right as our final example thus allows us to examine how our approach would apply to the facts that caused the Court to introduce its modern, more restrictive approach to the enforcement power.

Recall RFRA's basics from chapter 3. In the 1990 case *Employment Division v. Smith*,[20] the Court rejected the free exercise claims of Alfred Smith and Galen Black, two members of a Native American church who were fired from their jobs at a private drug rehabilitation organization because they had used peyote as part of a Native American religious ritual, in violation of a state law that included peyote on its schedule of banned substances. When Smith and Black applied for unemployment compensation, the state denied their claims on the ground that they had been fired for work-related misconduct. As framed by the Supreme Court, the question on appeal was whether the Free Exercise Clause "permits . . . Oregon to include religiously inspired peyote use within the reach of its general criminal prohibition on use of that drug, and thus permits the State to deny unemployment benefits to persons dismissed from their jobs because of such religiously inspired use."[21]

The Court, speaking through Justice Scalia, held that the Free Exercise Clause allowed Oregon to deny unemployment benefits to Smith and Black. Justice Scalia began by rejecting the plaintiffs' claim that the First Amendment's text ("Congress shall make no law respecting an establishment of religion, or prohibiting the free exercise thereof . . ."), as incorporated via the Due Process Clause, compelled the Court to invalidate any law that merely had the effect of hindering religiously motivated conduct. Instead, he characterized a narrower reading, under which the Free Exercise Clause allowed laws that impacted religious conduct merely as an incidental effect, as a "permissible" reading of the text. He then stated: "Our decisions reveal that the latter reading [of the clause] is the correct one."[22]

For our purposes, the most important difficulty Justice Scalia faced lay in the fact that several of those earlier decisions had balanced the plaintiff's free exercise rights against the state's interest, rather than simply rejecting the plaintiff's claim outright, as he proposed to do. After arguing why those cases' factual contexts were sufficiently different from the criminal law prohibition at issue in *Smith* as to make them not binding, he launched into an argument why such balancing was unsound—in his words, "contradict[ing] both constitutional tradition and common sense."[23] He argued that such balancing would "court[] anarchy," as government action would have to satisfy careful judicial scrutiny every time such action impacted a believer's religiously motivated conduct. Given the extraordinary diversity of Americans' religious beliefs, Justice Scalia cautioned that such an approach would "open the prospect of constitutionally required religious exemptions from civic obligations of almost every conceivable kind," from the military draft to vaccination, child labor, racial equality, and animal cruelty laws.[24]

What does Justice Scalia's analysis tell us about congressional power to enforce the free exercise right—for example, through the RFRA statute? At times, Justice Scalia seems to suggest that the core Free Exercise Clause rule permits governments to enact laws burdening religious conduct as long as those laws do not specifically target religion. Indeed, as noted two paragraphs earlier, he explicitly stated that such a reading of the Free Exercise Clause "is the correct one." If this is the right way to read *Smith*, then the rule it lays down is in fact a statement of core constitutional meaning.

At other times, though, Justice Scalia hedges. In particular, his argument rejecting judicial balancing of believers' free exercise rights against the government's interests sometimes sounds more like a concern about judicial competence. For example, he worried that, given the diversity of Americans' religious beliefs, a rule requiring balancing would immerse the courts in second-guessing the need for nearly every type of government action—as he stated, from military draft laws to vaccination, nondiscrimination, and animal cruelty laws, among others. Reading his argument, one can hear the distant echo of the Court's concern five years earlier, in the *Cleburne* case, that according heightened scrutiny to intellectual disability classification would open up the floodgates to claims from other groups—claims that courts could not reject on any principled ground. Recall that we identified that concern as one that might well justify the *Court's* rejection of the plaintiffs' suspect class argument, even while leaving the door open to more generous antidiscrimination protection from *Congress*.

So too with Justice Scalia's analysis in *Smith*. One could interpret his anxiety about courts' ability to balance believers' and the government's interests as a confession of judicial inability to apply the full measure of the free exercise right. Mapping our analysis of *Cleburne* onto *Smith*, that confession would leave room for Congress to supply the additional protection the Constitution provided but that courts could not vindicate—or, literally, "enforce."

Indeed, Justice Scalia finished his opinion in *Smith* by noting the possibility that legislatures might go further than the Court in protecting religious practice. He began the last substantive paragraph of his opinion with the following two sentences:

> Values that are protected against government interference through enshrinement in the Bill of Rights are not thereby banished from the political process. Just as a society that believes in the negative protection accorded to the press by the First Amendment is likely to enact laws that affirmatively foster the dissemination of the printed word, so also a society that believes in the negative protection accorded to religious belief can be expected to be solicitous of that value in its legislation as well.[25]

After an intervening sentence, he then continued: "But to say that a nondiscriminatory religious-practice exemption is permitted, or even that it is desirable, *is not to say that it is constitutionally required, and that the appropriate occasions for its creation can be discerned by the courts*."[26] In the italicized phrase that finishes this quote, we find an almost explicit summation of the ambiguity at the heart of Justice Scalia's analysis. On the one hand, he says that the type of accommodation Smith and Black requested from the Court is not constitutionally required—that is, the more restrictive reading of the Free Exercise Clause is, to quote Justice Scalia, "the correct one." On the other hand, he also suggests that the problem with claims for such accommodations is that courts cannot competently judge them.

Let's return to our enforcement power template and see how *Smith* maps onto it. Recall that our template requires the Court evaluating enforcement legislation to parse its own jurisprudence to determine the content of the true constitutional rule to which that legislation must be congruent and proportional. Applying that approach to *Smith* leads to an ambiguous result. On the one hand, the Court appears to state clearly that the Free Exercise Clause permits incidental, or collateral, infringements on religiously motivated conduct—for example, a generally applicable drug law that has the effect of prohibiting worshippers from ingesting drugs as part of a sacred ritual. On the other hand, Justice Scalia's rejection of the "balancing" approach adopted in a number of earlier cases turns heavily—although not exclusively—on the difficulties courts would experience in applying that approach every time a generally applicable law made it harder for someone to practice her religion.[27] This latter reasoning suggests that a deeper constitutional value lurks in the Free Exercise Clause. Courts may not be able to vindicate that deeper value. But, as he suggests at the end of his opinion, legislatures—including Congress—might.

Of course, Congress *did* attempt to vindicate that deeper value, in RFRA. And the Court struck it down in *Boerne*. How does that case's Enforcement Clause analysis stack up against the approach this book offers? First, note how RFRA responded to *Smith*. In particular, recall one of RFRA's findings, which we mentioned in chapter 3, in which Congress "found" that the pre-*Smith* balancing regime was a "workable test" for reconciling religious freedom claims with legitimate government needs.[28] Now that we've investigated *Smith* more, we can see how Congress could reasonably be read as attempting to assuage (or, perhaps more cynically, to leverage) *Smith*'s worry about courts' ability to balance, by "finding" that courts could in fact do so competently.

Now consider *Boerne*'s analysis of RFRA. Justice Kennedy began that analysis by identifying "the free exercise of religion as *defined* by *Smith*": "laws which are enacted with the unconstitutional object of targeting religious beliefs and practices."[29] Thus, here and elsewhere in the opinion,[30] he attempted to shift the focus away from *Smith*'s concerns about courts' competence to apply a more religion-protective rule, and toward that case's definition of the core free exercise rule—that government not single out religion for burdensome treatment. In effect, he read *Smith* as stating that principle as a core constitutional rule. From there, the stage was set for his conclusion that Congress had failed to demonstrate a record of state violations of that rule, and in turn, his argument that RFRA's broad coverage and harsh liability rule failed his newly announced "congruence and proportionality" requirement.[31]

Thus, our ultimate verdict about *Boerne* should turn, not just on its analysis of RFRA but on the correctness of its analysis of *Smith*. If Justice Kennedy was correct that *Smith* was fundamentally a case about the application of the core free exercise rule against intentional government burdening of religion, then he was on solid ground in insisting on at least some congressional evidence, reviewed under the appropriate deference standard, that states were violating that rule and that RFRA's broader liability rule helped deter those violations. By contrast, if Justice Kennedy misread *Smith*—if, instead, *Smith* was better read as simply a confession of judicial incompetence to protect a constitutional rule that protected religious exercise more deeply—then he should have given more deference to Congress's contrary determination. In this latter case, RFRA would have been better read as Congress insisting that courts overcome their nervousness about applying that deeper protection—in other words, that courts take to heart RFRA's finding that the pre-*Smith*, more religion-protective, rule was "workable."

* * *

It may sound ironic that the correctness of *Boerne* turns largely on the correctness of the Court's understanding of *Smith*. But on reflection this makes perfect sense. One cannot know whether legislation is congruent and proportional to the underlying right until one knows what that underlying right is. Indeed, all three of these examples—gun rights, search and seizure rights, and religious exercise rights—illustrate this same idea.

Where these examples diverge is in how the meaning of that underlying right influences the scope of Congress's enforcement power. If, as with the search and seizure right discussed in *Greenwood*, the right can only be applied based on an understanding of social reality (such as what privacy expectations Americans have), then Congress should have a great deal of latitude to enforce the right given its superior claim to discerning that reality. At the other extreme, if, as with the gun possession right, the core right at issue appears to be relatively clearly stated, then as a practical matter Congress's enforcement power should be more limited. In such a case, Congress's power should extend primarily to determining what subsidiary rights are appropriate to ensuring that the core right is protected.

The religious freedom example makes clear that this approach would require the Court to make difficult judgments about the meaning of the core constitutional right at issue. In particular, this approach would require the Court to examine carefully its own jurisprudence, to determine that core right. As exemplified by *Smith*, that examination may sometimes reveal decisions that rest on a mixture of core constitutional rules and subconstitutional decisional aids appropriate to a court with limited competence and authority. In that sense *Smith* parallels *Cleburne*.

Analogously, our insights about RFRA's validity as enforcement legislation hearken back to our earlier application of our proposed approach to equal protection enforcement. Recall that our earlier discussion concluded that the Court must read its own decisions carefully to distinguish core equal protection law from decisional aids, such as suspect class analysis, that help the Court uncover that core law but do not itself constitute it. Our discussion of RFRA's relationship to the constitutional rule of the Free Exercise Clause reveals the need for that same sort of careful analysis.

Equal Protection beyond Irrationality and Animus

The prior paragraph's reference to equal protection takes us back to one last issue we need to resolve concerning congressional power to enforce the Equal Protection Clause. Up to now, most of this book has considered legislation enforcing that clause. Despite the attention we've given that subject, there remain two aspects of that question that we have not yet considered. Recall that in chapter 6 we defined the core law of equal protection as consisting of four legal rules. We have discussed two of these—the prohibition on legislation that reflects animus and the similar prohibition on irrationality.

But we have only identified the two others, while deferring consideration of their enforcement power implications. These latter two principles consist of, first, the presumptive rule against race classifications and, second, the presumptive rule against unequal distribution of rights the Supreme Court has identified as particularly important. (This latter rule has been shorthanded as "the fundamental rights strand" of equal protection.) When chapter 6 sketched out our reformulated conception of Congress's power to enforce equal protection, we bracketed these latter two rules because their content raised different enforcement power issues than the anti-animus and rationality requirements. This chapter's discussion of substantive rights is the place to consider congressional enforcement power in these two final equal protection contexts.

Let's begin with the fundamental rights strand. This component of equal protection shares important similarities with the Court's due process jurisprudence.[32] Most notably, the Court has used similar reasoning in identifying both types of fundamental rights.[33] To be sure, practical differences distinguish a due process claim from an equal protection claim based on the fundamental rights strand. Most notably (and as one might guess), an equal protection claim is unavailable when the government has deprived all persons of the asserted right, thus effecting an "equal," if complete, deprivation of the right.[34] In such circumstances, a due process claim would still be available. But for our purposes, the key question is whether the Court uses similar methodologies to identify both types of rights. Because the Court does in fact use similar methodologies, we can analyze enforcement power issues similarly in both cases.

That methodology may create a right whose application in particular cases relies heavily on social meaning. Our earlier discussion of reasonable expectations of privacy for Fourth Amendment purposes should make that clear. But there is nothing about *equal protection* fundamental rights as a category that distinguishes the methods by which they are adjudicated—and, thus, the appropriate congressional role in vindicating them—from the analogous methods used to adjudicate *due process* fundamental rights.

Let's now consider equal protection's rule presumptively invalidating any race classification. As chapter 2 explained, this rule is not the product of an indirect, political process–based, analysis of equal protection. Instead, both the Court's rhetoric (identifying race as a particularly pernicious classification tool) and its analysis (giving close scrutiny to all race classifications, regardless of the justification or social context, and regardless of the majority or minority status of the benefited racial groups) reveal this rule's foundation in the Court's understanding of core constitutional law. To repeat a point made when we first introduced this rule in chapter 2: one may agree or disagree with the Court's reasoning, but that reasoning itself appears grounded in the Court's precise understanding of what the Constitution requires.

The Court's understanding of the core constitutional rule about race necessarily cabins congressional enforcement power on this topic. In particular, the core constitutional status of the presumptive color blindness rule means that congressional findings about a race classification's benign or invidious nature cannot carry substantial weight in allowing (much less mandating) race-conscious action by state governments. Even assertedly benign uses of race, such as set-asides for historically disadvantaged racial groups, have been condemned by the Court as resting on demeaning stereotypes, stigmatizing beneficiaries, and encouraging race-based thinking and race-based politics. It has identified color blindness as equal protection's central aspiration. Essentially, the Court has determined—as a matter of law, not a matter of fact or social context susceptible to contradictory congressional fact-finding, or even moral judgment susceptible to countermanding by popular consensus—that race classifications are invidious.

This is not to say that Congress is powerless to enact enforcement legislation addressing race. Of course, it remains able to enact enforcement statutes that are consistent with the Court's constitutional vision. That power includes the authority to make it easier to bring race discrimination claims. For example, in *Fitzpatrick v. Bitzer*,[35] a 1976 case discussed in chapter 3, the Court upheld as valid enforcement legislation a law that wiped away a plaintiff state employee's obligation to prove that the defendant state government employer had acted with the intent to discriminate on the basis of race. To the extent such legislation relies on policy judgments, such as those about the efficacy of or need for strong remedies, this book has argued that judicial review should be modest and focused on the statute's empirical support. Most notably, it has argued that the Court made a mistake in *Shelby County* when it failed to defer to Congress's conclusions about the continued need for certain jurisdictions to be subject to the Voting Rights Act's preclearance provisions.

By contrast, laws that *conflict* with the Court's own core vision of what the Fourteenth Amendment says about race would face a tougher road. Of course, Congress could attempt to enact a racial preferences enforcement statute that, based on its fact-finding, satisfies the Court's stringent test for race-conscious government action. However, the deference principles set forth in chapter 7—in particular Principle 3's call for more careful judicial evaluation of findings that precisely target a constitutional right—suggest that such findings would be subject to significant judicial scrutiny.

Congress might also argue that its Enforcement Clause power vests it with special authority to make findings supporting a policy of race-consciousness. In past decades the Court appeared amenable to this idea, but in more recent cases it has rejected it.[36] And it would certainly be the case that Congress would be powerless to simply disagree with the Court about the ultimate constitutionality of race-conscious government action. In both of these latter cases, one has to conclude that the Court, for better or worse, has stated the constitutional rule: race-conscious government action is strongly disfavored, and that rule applies as much to Congress as to the states. In light of that reality, our approach to the enforcement power would require rejecting such legislation.

Conclusion

An Enforcement Power for a Twenty-First-Century Constitutional Democracy

Books like this often conclude with chapters featuring high-sounding, eloquent titles. Whether or not you think the title of this particular concluding chapter hit that mark, a reader might dismiss it as yet another (attempted) eloquent but vague statement that says very little and does not much relate to the actual analysis in the rest of the book. In this short conclusion I hope to prove you wrong, by taking apart and thinking about the object ("a twenty-first-century constitutional democracy") for which I've hoped to construct a new enforcement power.

"A Twenty-First-Century . . ."

Everyone wants to be modern. Nobody wants to build "the car of yesterday"; similarly, nobody would want to construct an enforcement power for the nineteenth century. (An originalist might insist that that's what we have, and if we want to update it, we need to formally amend the Constitution. But that's different from the normative project of self-consciously creating an enforcement power to respond to twenty-first-century needs.)[1] Assume, then, that it is legitimate to want to build a modern enforcement power. What does modernity imply? What is it about America today that influences that power? There appear to be at least two answers, which push in the same direction.

First, American society is increasingly pluralistic. On nearly whatever axis one measures it, as a society today we are more diverse than we've been in a very long time—ethnically, religiously, and culturally. It would probably be impossible to meaningfully compare our level of diversity today with that of 200 years ago, and of course we have to remember that earlier eras witnessed massive migrations of persons to America, often from parts of the world that before then had not contributed threads to the fabric of American society. But we don't need to make an extreme claim. It is enough to observe what should be obvious: today people are increasingly hailing from more parts of the world, speaking more languages, adhering to more religions, and adopting more different ways of life. And there is no indication that this phenomenon is slowing down, much less reversing.

Second, and relatedly, Americans are defining themselves in more different ways than ever before. Broad-based affinity groups such as unions, mainstream religions, and political parties may be suffering declines in membership, but those losses are being at least partially balanced by the increased variety of affinity groups. The growth of easy mass communication, especially with the advent of first the Internet and then social media, allows persons who before might have been alone in their difference to reach out and find like-minded persons. The phenomenon of the lonely gay teenager who finds a social media site where he can speak with others like him, or of the person with a rare medical condition who is able to find an online support group, is repeated every day across a wide variety of traits and preferences.[2]

Together, these phenomena suggest that "groups" will continue to multiply in America. To the extent such groups center on new types of traits such as sexual identity or genetic makeup, this pluralism will require both courts and legislatures to determine what is required for members of those groups to enjoy "equal protection." To the extent such groups simply increase the number of preexisting social groupings (e.g., the number of ethnic groups or religions represented in the nation), the challenges will not be so fundamental. But they won't be easy, either, as we are starting to learn as we consider the equal protection implications of the fact that white Americans are expected to lose their numerical majority by the middle of the century. And to the extent such groups differ not just in degree or numerosity from what we've experienced before, but instead differ on more fundamental grounds, the challenge will be even more profound.

Let's put these ideas together to ask several questions about the modern relevance of Justice Stone's phrase from Footnote 4 of *Carolene Products*—"discrete and insular minority." First, what does it mean to be a minority in a nation where no ethnic group represents a majority? What does it mean for the notion of "discreteness" when many groups, such as gays and lesbians, are marked by a trait that is concealable? And, indeed, as Bruce Ackerman presciently asked several decades ago, what does it mean for the idea of "insularity" when modern communications (in particular today, social media) make it easier for members of a minority group to find each other and organize?[3] This conclusion is no place to resolve these fascinating questions. But we do need to raise them. And, in particular, we need to consider how an enforcement power "for the twenty-first century" should respond to these phenomena.

After progressing this far into the book, perhaps you'll be able to guess the outlines of our answer. If nothing else, Congress's superior authority to understand not just what types of discrimination Americans think is wrong, but what types of groups exist and thus what types of discrimination might exist, should endow it with increased power to enforce equal protection's promise. That promise is a resonant but vague one: as we've said throughout this book, it essentially reduces to a requirement not to engage in arbitrary or animus-based classifications. As this book has extensively discussed, Congress is usually better than courts at determining what types of discrimination the American people believe fail those fundamental requirements. But we have gone further. Chapter 9's discussion of emerging groups adds to this point the idea of Congress's authority to determine what groups even *exist* as meaningful social entities that might be subject to unconstitutional discrimination. That congressional authority will only grow more significant as Americans find new axes of commonality and difference, and create not just more groups but new categories of groups.

. . . Constitutional . . .

As a nation we live under a constitution. Regardless of one's views about what that constitution means or who has the power to interpret it, the fact that we have one indicates that we have made certain commitments to ourselves. Those commitments may or may not be judicially enforceable: one doesn't have to believe in judicial supremacy or indeed in any judicial interpretive role to accept the basic truth that any constitution worth the name necessarily contains principles that constrain the nation, even if those constraints operate only on the hearts and minds of the people themselves.

But even though a constitution constrains, its operation on the citizenry's collective decision making has the paradoxical effect of opening up space for democratic deliberation about the meaning and scope of those constraints. In this country, appeals to the Constitution permeate our political discourse. Conservatives call for decentralizing power and increasing (one understanding of) individual liberty in the name of a Constitution that has supposedly been ignored and subverted.[4] Similarly, liberals wield the Constitution to call for protections of rights (often a different set than conservatives); indeed, they cite the Reconstruction Amendments in particular as a justification for restricting state action alleged to abridge those rights. The correctness of any of these calls, as a matter of history or any other criterion, is not the point. The point, rather, is that our political discourse self-consciously seeks to faithfully apply the Constitution as Americans understand it.

. . . Democracy"

In other words, we make use of the Constitution as part of our democracy. This fact should disabuse us of the idea that the Constitution is nothing more than a lawyer's legal document. It surely *is* a lawyer's legal document, and has been since the start. But any realistic appraisal of its role in American life shows that it is much more.

Thus, the question—the final question posed by this book: Is it possible to harness that constitutional discourse in ways that go beyond political rhetoric? This book has argued that Americans' thinking about the Constitution can in fact influence, if not the document's legal meaning, then at least its enforceable application in concrete contexts. The enforcement power is ideally suited to facilitate that process.

The Enforcement Clause gives the people's representatives in Congress the power to make real—literally, to "enforce"—the individual rights provisions that account for the vast majority of rights the Constitution provides us against states. In particular, the power to enforce the equal protection guarantee gives Americans, through their congressional representatives, the authority to apply perhaps both the vaguest but also the most majestic of those rights: the right to be treated equally by government. As this book has argued, that right is deeply ingrained in American law and Americans' consciousness, extending back well before the enactment of the Equal Protection Clause itself. (Just think of the Declaration of Independence's ringing statement that "all men are created equal.") Thus, perhaps unsurprisingly, the idea of equality constitutes a fundamental component of Americans' constitutional identity.

Yet at the same time, the equality guarantee is remarkably open-ended and also dependent on social context. That fact helps answer the question about the proper respective roles of courts and the people in stating constitutional meaning. Simply put, the right to equality, perhaps uniquely among the rights we enjoy, cannot be conclusively and authoritatively delineated by judges. Subject to the few constraints that courts have been able to identify, the people must decide what constitutional equality means in any given context and in any particular generation—particularly our generation, with its increased pluralism and focus on group identity. The law—and the Court—should recognize the people's indispensable and legitimate role in making those decisions.

NOTES

PREFACE

1 This phrase is a play on a prominent scholar's call for popular constitutionalism. *See* Mark Tushnet, *Taking the Constitution Away from the Courts* (Princeton University Press, 1999).

INTRODUCTION

1 5 U.S. (1 Cranch) 137, 177 (1803).

2 *See, e.g.*, McConnell, "Institutions and Interpretation," 153, 182 (quoting a framer of the Fourteenth Amendment as emphasizing the importance of Congress's role in vindicating the rights it provided).

3 *See* New York v. United States, 505 U.S. 144 (1992) (holding that Congress lacks the power to commandeer states' legislative apparatus); Printz v. United States, 521 U.S. 898 (1997) (extending *New York* to prohibit federal commandeering of states' law enforcement apparatus).

4 *See* Garcia v. San Antonio Trans. Authority, 469 U.S. 528 (1985) (holding that the Constitution's general federalism principles did not prevent Congress from regulating states in their capacity as economic actors whose activities otherwise are regulable under the Interstate Commerce Clause).

5 *See* Seminole Tribe of Florida v. Florida, 517 U.S. 44 (1996) (holding that Congress's power to regulate interstate commerce does not allow it to make states liable for retrospective relief for violations of such regulation). *Seminole Tribe* dealt specifically with Congress's power to regulate commerce with the Indian tribes—that is, Congress's power under the Indian Commerce Clause. However, the Court understood the issue more broadly, to apply as well to Congress's power to regulate interstate commerce—an understanding that required it to overrule an earlier case, Pennsylvania v. Union Gas, 491 U.S. 1 (1989), which understood the Interstate Commerce Clause as authorizing retrospective relief against states.

6 For example, a prominent disability law and constitutional law scholar has stated that denying plaintiffs a cause of action for damages under the public services provisions of the Americans with Disabilities Act "would strike at the heart of [those provisions'] effectiveness," given the financial incentive it gives plaintiffs to sue, and her claim that "a remedial scheme consisting exclusively of injunctive relief . . . has proven to be ineffective." Colker, "Section 5 Quagmire," 653, 660.

7 *See, e.g.*, Nicole Huberfeld et al., "Plunging into Endless Difficulties: Medicaid and Coercion in *National Federation of Independent Business v. Sebelius*," 93 *B.U. L. Rev.* 1, 30 (2013).

8 Bond v. United States, 134 S.Ct. 2077 (2014).

9 *See, e.g.*, Katzenbach v. Morgan, 384 U.S. 641 (1966) (upholding the VRA provision prohibiting certain English literacy tests as conditions for voting, as valid legislation enforcing the Fourteenth Amendment); South Carolina v. Katzenbach, 383 U.S. 301 (1966) (upholding other VRA provisions as valid legislation enforcing the Fifteenth Amendment). The Fifteenth Amendment prohibits racial discrimination in voting.

10 Edwards v. California, 314 U.S. 160, 177 (1941) (Douglas, J., concurring); *id.* at 181 (Jackson, J., concurring).

11 Edwards (Douglas, J., concurring). Justice Douglas repeated this concern nearly a quarter century later, when he argued that the public accommodations provisions of the 1964 Civil Rights Act should be upheld as legislation enforcing the Fourteenth Amendment, rather than legislation regulating interstate commerce. *See* Heart of Atlanta Motel v. United States, 379 U.S. 241, 279 (1964) (Douglas, J., concurring).

12 Some scholars have argued that legislation regulating private parties in this way can be justified as legislation enforcing the Thirteenth Amendment's prohibition on slavery or involuntary servitude. *See, e.g.*, Rebecca Zietlow, "Free at Last! Anti-subordination and the Thirteenth Amendment," 90 *B.U. L. Rev.* 255 (2010); Alexander Tsesis, "A Civil Rights Approach: Achieving Revolutionary Abolitionism via the Thirteenth Amendment," 39 *U.C. Davis L. Rev.* 1773 (2006). This book does not engage that argument, confining itself to laws enforcing the Fourteenth Amendment.

13 521 U.S. 507 (1997).

14 *See* Kimel v. Board of Regents, 528 U.S. 62 (2000). "Suspect class" analysis is discussed in chapter 2.

15 29 U.S.C. §§ 2601–2654 (2006). *See* Coleman v. Court of Appeals of Maryland, 132 S.Ct. 1327 (2012). Chapter 5 discusses *Coleman* in more detail.

16 *See* Craig v. Boren, 429 U.S. 190 (1976) (holding that sex classifications merit "intermediate" scrutiny).

17 The post-*Boerne* Court has been unclear about whether that parallelism survives in the modern, post-*Boerne* world. *See* Northwest Austin Municipal Utility District No. 1. v. Holder, 557 U.S. 193, 204 (2009) (noting, but declining to resolve, the disagreement over whether the same standard of review applies to legislation enforcing the Fourteenth and the Fifteenth Amendments).

18 *See* Shelby County v. Holder, 133 S.Ct. 2612 (2013). Chapter 5 discusses *Shelby County* in more detail.

19 I have previously discussed how new groups' equality claims may impact Enforcement Clause doctrine. *See* William D. Araiza, "New Groups and Old Doctrine: Reconsidering Congressional Power to Enforce the Equal Protection Clause," 37 *Fla. State U. L. Rev.* 451 (2010).

20 *See, e.g.*, Jane Korn, "Fat," 77 *B.U. L. Rev.* 25 (1997); Anna Kirkland, *Fat Rights: Dilemmas of Difference and Personhood* (NYU Press, 2008) (both discussing obesity);

Constantina Safilios-Rothschild, "Prejudice against the Disabled and Some Means to Combat It," in *Social and Psychological Aspects of Disability* 261, 265 (Joseph Stubbins ed., University Park Press, 1977) (discussing disability); Roberts, "Preempting Discrimination," 439 (discussing genetics).

21 *See, e.g.*, Campbell Robertson, "A Divide on Voting Rights in a Town Where Blood Was Spilled," *New York Times*, March 1, 2013, *available at* http://www.nytimes.com/2013/03/02/us/politics/a-divide-on-voting-rights-where-blood-spilled.html?pagewanted=all&_r=0 (noting public disagreement on whether the VRA had entirely succeeded in stamping out racial discrimination in voting, and hence was no longer necessary). The Court discussed this issue in 2013 in *Shelby County v. Holder*, 133 S.Ct. 2612 (2013). Chapter 5 considers the Court's resolution of this issue.

22 For a classic statement of the "emptiness" of the idea of equality in the absence of a recognition of a particular substantive right, see Westen, "The Empty Idea of Equality," 537.

23 *See, e.g.*, Allegheny Pittsburgh Coal Co. v. County Commission, 488 U.S. 336 (1989).

24 304 U.S. 144, 152 n. 4 (1938).

25 *See, e.g.*, Grutter v. Bollinger, 539 U.S. 306 (2003) (ostensibly applying strict scrutiny to a state law school's use of race in its admissions decisions, but nevertheless deferring to the school's pedagogical decisions about the need for a racially diverse student body); Parents Involved in Community Schools v. Seattle Sch. Dist. No. 1, 551 U.S. 701, 782–798 (2007) (Kennedy, J., concurring in part and concurring in the judgment) (agreeing that a school district's use of race in student assignment decisions was unconstitutional, but acknowledging the legitimacy of school officials' awareness of racial impacts when making their decisions).

26 City of Richmond v. J. A. Croson Co., 488 U.S. 469 (1989).

27 *See, e.g.*, Reynolds v. Sims, 377 U.S. 533 (1964) (holding that the Equal Protection Clause presumptively mandates the equal distribution of the right to vote, when governmental offices are staffed by election).

28 *See* Massachusetts Bd. of Retirement v. Murgia, 427 U.S. 307 (1976) (upholding state law requiring retirement of police troopers when they turn fifty).

29 *See* Williamson v. Lee Optical, 348 U.S. 483 (1955) (upholding law limiting opticians' ability to fit corrective lenses without a prescription from an optometrist or ophthalmologist).

30 Other scholars have different views about how best to define "animus." *See, e.g.*, Susannah Pollvogt, "Unconstitutional Animus," 81 *Fordham L. Rev.* 887 (2012) (arguing that animus consists of biases and stereotypes that create castes).

31 531 U.S. 98 (2000).

32 384 U.S. 436 (1966).

33 Dickerson v. United States, 530 U.S. 428 (2000).

34 130 S.Ct. 876, 910 (2010) (concluding that elected officials' feelings of gratitude to larger spenders on their behalf did not constitute corruption or give rise to the appearance of corruption).

35 *See, e.g.*, Barry Friedman, *The Will of the People* (Farrar, Straus and Giroux, 2009).

36 Fay v. Noia, 332 U.S. 261, 282 (1947).

37 *See, e.g.*, Tsesis, *Promises of Liberty.*

38 *See* Tennessee v. Lane, 541 U.S. 509, 554, 561–565 (2004) (Scalia, J., dissenting) (arguing for a more limited enforcement power when congressional action aims at classifications other than racial ones).

39 Hellman, *When Is Discrimination Wrong?*

CHAPTER 1. EQUAL PROTECTION BEFORE THE MODERN ERA

1 For brevity's sake, this history also draws heavily on the conclusions reached by other scholars.

2 *See* Federalist No. 10 (Madison), *reprinted in* Rossiter, *The Federalist Papers*, at 82–83.

3 *See, e.g.*, Novak, *The People's Welfare.*

4 Scholars have sometimes referred to this concern as one grounded in fears about "corruption." *See, e.g.*, Zephyr Teachout, "The Anti-corruption Principle," 94 *Cornell L. Rev.* 341 (2009).

5 *See, e.g.*, Warsoff, *Equality and the Law*, 158–164.

6 *See* Andrew Jackson, Veto Message (July 10, 1832), in 2 *A Compilation of the Messages and Papers of the Presidents 1789–1897*, at 576 (James D. Richardson ed., Bureau of National Literature, 1911).

7 *See, e.g.*, Tushnet, "Thayer's Target," 9, 12.

8 *See, e.g.*, Stephen Calabresi and Larissa Leibowitz, "Monopolies and the Constitution: A History of Crony Capitalism," 36 *Harv. J. L. & Pub. Pol'y* 983, 1068–1073 (2013) (discussing the relationship between the class legislation idea and the transition away from particularized grants of corporate charters and toward general incorporation laws).

9 *See, e.g.*, Vanzant v. Waddel, 10 Tenn. 260 (1829); *see also* Corwin, *Liberty against Government*, 91–94 (tracing the evolution of the due process of law idea into a requirement that laws apply generally and equally).

10 *See id. at* 91 (noting the early equation of these two concepts in English law).

11 *See, e.g.*, Wilder v. Lumpkin, 4 Ga. 208, 219–220 (1848).

12 While space reasons preclude discussing it, it should be noted that the period before the Civil War was also marked by the beginnings of the women's rights movement, which in many ways was closely tied to the antislavery movement.

13 Article V prohibited until 1808 any amendments affecting states' freedom to engage in the slave trade.

14 *See, e.g.*, Foner, *Free Soil, Free Labor, Free Men*, 295–296.

15 *See, e.g., id.* at 261–300.

16 *See generally* Foner, *Free Soil, Free Labor, Free Men*, 87–102; *see also, e.g.*, Richards, "Abolitionist Political and Constitutional Theory," 1187, 1193–1194 (discussing antislavery advocates' claim that "the Slave Power" constituted a faction of the sort condemned by Madison); Leonard Richards, *The Slave Power: The Free North and Southern Domination 1780–1860* 4 (Louisiana State University Press, 2000) (dating the Slave Power argument to at least 1800). *See also* Cong. Globe, 32d Cong., 1st Sess. app. 713 (1852) (statement of Rep. Norton S. Townshend) (antislavery congressperson stating that "slavery is but the extreme of class legislation.").

17 *See, e.g.*, Amar, "The Supreme Court 1999 Term," 26, 58 (2000) (attacks on free speech and political association in the antebellum South); Matthew Raffety, *The Republic Afloat: Law, Honor, and Citizenship in Maritime America* 72 (University of Chicago Press, 2013) (noting the southern laws that required imprisonment of northern seamen of color when their ships docked in southern ports).

18 *See* Maltz, *Civil Rights*, at 13–28 & particularly 27.

19 *See, e.g.*, Tsesis, *Thirteenth Amendment and American Freedom*, 37–57; Rebecca Zietlow, "Free at Last! Anti-subordination and the Thirteenth Amendment," 90 *B.U. L. Rev.* 255, 272–294 (2010).

20 Civil Rights Act of 1866, Section 1, 14 Stat. 27.

21 *See, e.g.*, Oregon v. Mitchell, 400 U.S. 112, 152 (1970) (Harlan, J., concurring in part and dissenting in part) (arguing that Section 2 demonstrates that the Fourteenth Amendment does not speak to voting rights); Richardson v. Ramirez, 418 U.S. 24 (1974) (relying on Section 2 to uphold laws disenfranchising felons).

22 The 2013 debt limit standoff between President Obama and congressional Republicans did, for a moment, revive interest in Section 3, when it was suggested that that provision authorized or even mandated unilateral presidential action to guarantee the sanctity of the national debt. But the political resolution of the standoff mooted that discussion.

23 *See* Harrison, "Reconstructing," 1385, 1433–1451 (generally) & 1448 (with regard to government's latitude to deny protection to all).

24 *See* tenBroek, *Equal under Law*, 237.

25 *Yick Wo v. Hopkins*, 118 U.S. 356, 369 (1886).

26 Cong. Globe, 39th Cong., 1st Sess. 2766 (1866) (statement of Senator Jacob Howard); *id.* at 174 (statement of Representative James Wilson) (stating that in republican government, there can be "no class legislation" and no laws that "legislate against [one class] . . . for the purpose of advancing the interests" of another class). For a more comprehensive survey of the evidence in favor of this class legislation reading, *see* Melissa Saunders, "Equal Protection, Class Legislation, and Colorblindness," 96 *Mich. L. Rev.* 245, 285–293 (1997).

27 *See, e.g.*, Harrison, "Reconstructing," at 1410 & 1438–1440 (arguing that a prominent proponent of the class legislation idea also denied Section 1's relevance to voting, thus undercutting the idea that he saw Section 1 as applicable to all government action).

28 Slaughter-House Cases, 83 U.S. (16 Wall.) 36, 81 (1873) ("We doubt very much whether any action of a State not directed by way of discrimination against the negroes as a class, or on account of their race, will ever be held to come within the purview of [the Equal Protection Clause]. [The clause] is so clearly a provision for that race . . . that a strong case would be necessary for its application to any other.").

29 304 U.S. 144 (1938).

30 Many fine and more comprehensive studies of the Fourteenth Amendment exist. For just a few notable examples, *see* Curtis, *No State Shall Abridge*; Nelson, *Fourteenth Amendment*; Amar, *Bill of Rights*, 137–294.

31 83 U.S. 36 (1873).

32 U.S. Const. Art IV § 2 cl. 1; Corfield v. Coryell, 6 F.Cases 546, 552 (E.D. Pa. 1823).

33 83 U.S. at 81.

34 *Id.* at 61.

35 *See id.* at 62.

36 *See, e.g.*, Labbe and Lurie, *Slaughter House Cases*, 157 (suggesting that Justice Field's dissent on this point conflated the trade of butcher with the ability to own one's own slaughtering facility).

37 Justices Bradley and Swayne, while joining Justice Field's dissent, also wrote separate dissenting opinions. Chief Justice Chase, by then terminally ill, simply joined Justice Field's dissent without writing separately. *See id.* at 156 (noting the deterioration of Chase's health).

38 *See* 83 U.S. at 100–101 (Field, J., dissenting). To be sure, Justice Field might have been concerned if the state equally denied basic rights to all its citizens. But he focused his *Slaughter-House* dissent on the Louisiana monopoly law's asserted unequal treatment of the butchers who were not owners of the corporation.

39 94 U.S. 113 (1877).

40 *See, e.g.*, Powell v. Pennsylvania, 127 U.S. 678, 683 (1888) ("It is scarcely necessary to say that if this statute is a legitimate exercise of the police power of the state for the protection of the health of the people, and for the prevention of fraud, it is not inconsistent with [the Fourteenth] amendment; for it is the settled doctrine of this court that, as government is organized for the purpose, among others, of preserving the public health and the public morals, it cannot divest itself of the power to provide for those objects, and that the fourteenth amendment was not designed to interfere with the exercise of that power by the states."). *See also, e.g.*, Fiss, *Troubled Beginnings*, 159 (describing the liberty of contract as "not a principle from which limits on state power were derived, but rather the space or area left to the individual after the reasons for the creation of state power were exhausted. Liberty of contract was what remained to the individual after the state reached the outer bounds of its authority.").

41 *See* Macedo, *The New Right v. the Constitution*, 32.

42 Thomas v. Collins, 323 U.S. 516, 529 (1945).

43 Cooley, *Constitutional Limitations*, 36 (State constitutions "measure the powers of rulers, but they do not measure the rights of the governed.").

Even scholars who focus more on how courts understood the equal protection right have identified the police power as a fundamental component of the analysis. For example, Richard Kay identified one of two major theories of equal protection law during that period as the theory of "unjustifiable classifications"—the unjustifiability based on the lack of a valid police power explanation for the classification. *See* Kay, "Equal Protection Clause," 667.

44 *See* Fiss, *Troubled Beginnings*, at 85.

45 Recall from earlier in this chapter that the third source of rights in the Fourteenth Amendment—the Privileges or Immunities Clause—was early on construed in the *Slaughter-House Cases* so as to have very little actual significance.

46 *See, e.g.*, Bernstein, "*Bolling*," 1253, 1262–1263 (2005) (noting that during the late nineteenth century due process and equal protection doctrine often overlapped substantially).

47 See Nourse, "A Tale of Two *Lochners*," 751, 797–798.

48 *See* Gillman, "Preferred Freedoms," 623.

49 198 U.S. 45 (1905).

50 *See* Bernstein, "*Lochner* Era Revisionism, Revised," 1, 35–51.

51 *See, e.g.*, Kay, "Equal Protection Clause," at 679–680.

52 *See, e.g.*, Bernstein, "*Lochner* Era Revisionism, Revised" at 15–18 (arguing that the U.S. Supreme Court applied the class legislation test deferentially).

53 165 U.S. 150 (1897).

54 174 U.S. 96 (1899).

55 See Kay, "Equal Protection Clause," at 709–713. *See also* Wiecek, *Birth of the Modern Constitution*, at 27 ("[Constitutional adjudication during this period] could not deliver objective, neutral, and principled criteria for trial judges to apply and legislatures to follow. In cases involving both federal and state police power, the Court developed two inconsistent streams of precedent, some cases upholding regulation and others, on facts closely similar, striking them down.").

56 *See, e.g.*, Gundling v. Chicago, 177 U.S. 183, 188 (1900) ("Regulations respecting the pursuit of a lawful trade or business are of very frequent occurrence [across] the country, and what such regulations shall be and to what particular trade, business, or occupation they shall apply are questions for the state to determine, and their determination comes within the proper exercise of the police power by the state, and unless the regulations are so utterly unreasonable and extravagant in their nature and purpose that the property and personal rights of the citizen are unnecessarily, and in a manner wholly arbitrary, interfered with or destroyed without due process of law, they do not extend beyond the power of the state to pass, and they form no subject for Federal interference."). The plaintiff in *Gundling* alleged violations of both due process and equal protection, but the Court, consistent with the non-clause-specific nature of judicial review at this time, did not separate out its analysis by clause.

57 *See, e.g.*, Fallon, *Implementing the Constitution*, 61 ("[T]he American constitutional tradition has long recognized a judicial authority, not necessarily linked to any specifically enumerated guarantee, to invalidate truly arbitrary legislation.").

58 Meyer v. Nebraska, 262 U.S. 390 (1923) (striking down, as violating the liberty protected by the Due Process Clause, a state law forbidding the teaching of German); *see also* Pierce v. Society of Sisters, 268 U.S. 510 (1925) (striking down, as violating that same liberty, a state law restricting private education).

59 *See* Truax v. Corrigan, 257 U.S. 312 (1921).

60 127 U.S. 678 (1888).

61 270 U.S. 402 (1926).

62 While the Court stopped at the due process issue, finding a violation and thus declining to consider the equal protection claim, the Court, reflecting the overlap between due process and equal protection, nevertheless noted as relevant "the number and character of the things permitted to be used in [bedding] manufacture," thus making the comparison to *Powell* relevant. Recall that only five years earlier Chief Justice Taft, in the course of trying to distinguish due process from equal protection, conceded that the two rights overlapped in their insistence on at least some level of equal government treatment. *See* Truax, 257 U.S. 312 (1921).

63 304 U.S. 144 (1938).

64 A notable example of this dynamic was in the area of sex discrimination. After a long history of according sex classifications minimal judicial scrutiny, in 1971 the Court found a sex classification to violate equal protection in *Reed v. Reed*, 404 U.S. 71 (1971). *Reed* claimed to be applying the same rationality test that it had always applied to sex classifications, simply concluding that the statute at issue was irrational. In the very next term, Justice Brennan, writing for a plurality of the Court, called for according heightened scrutiny to sex classifications. In support of that call, he cited *Reed*, where he claimed that the Court had in fact accorded such heightened scrutiny, even though it did not say that. *See* Frontiero v. Richardson, 411 U.S. 677 (1973). Chapter 2 discusses *Reed* and *Frontiero* in more detail.

65 304 U.S. 144, 152 n. 4 (1938).

66 Pace v. Alabama, 106 U.S. 583 (1883).

67 163 U.S. 537 (1896).

68 Berea College v. Kentucky, 211 U.S. 45 (1908).

69 Gong Lum v. Rice, 275 U.S. 78 (1927).

70 Cumming v. Bd. of Education, 175 U.S. 528 (1899).

71 189 U.S. 475 (1903).

72 *E.g.*, Buchanan v. Warley, 245 U.S. 60 (1917) (striking down a city ordinance prohibiting African Americans from moving into predominantly white neighborhoods, and vice versa); McCabe v. Atchison, Topeka, and Santa Fe Ry., 235 U.S. 151 (1914) (rejecting the argument that blacks' lesser demand for first-class railroad accommodations justified making such accommodations unavailable when state law required segregation on railroads).

73 The heading for this subsection is taken from Harvard Sitkoff's book detailing the evolution of the black civil rights movement in the 1930s. Sitkoff, *A New Deal for Blacks*.

74 *See* Victoria Nourse, *In Reckless Hands:* Skinner v. Oklahoma *and the Near Triumph of American Genetics* 126–132 (Norton, 2008).

75 *See generally* Sitkoff, *A New Deal for Blacks*; *id.* at 44–62 (discussing the New Deal in particular).

76 *See generally* David Margolick, *Beyond Glory: Joe Louis vs. Max Schmelling and a World on the Brink* (Random House, 2010).

77 United States v. Carolene Products, 304 U.S. 144, 152 n. 4 (1938).

78 304 U.S. 144, 152 n. 4 (1938).

79 Lewis F. Powell, "*Carolene Products* Revisited," 82 *Columbia L. Rev.* 1087, 1087 (1982).

80 To be sure, because *Carolene Products* involved *federal* legislation, the relevant constitutional provision was the Fifth Amendment's Due Process Clause. Nevertheless, the deference *Carolene Products* announced was appropriate under the Fifth Amendment was clearly intended to apply as well to state regulation challenged under the Fourteenth, as evidenced both by the fact that many of the cases Footnote 4 cited were Fourteenth Amendment cases, as well as by the fact that the footnote's caution about "prejudice against discrete and insular minorities" clearly spoke in terms of discrimination and equality of the sort relevant to equal protection.

81 304 U.S. at 152 n. 4 ("It is unnecessary to consider now whether" other types of legislation would be subject to similarly nondeferential review.).

82 *Ibid.* ("Nor need we enquire whether similar considerations enter into the review of" certain other types of legislation.).

83 The ninth defendant, Roy Wright, was either twelve or thirteen years old, and thus considered by the prosecutor to be too young for execution. Despite his failure to seek that penalty, a majority of jurors voted for his execution, thus triggering a mistrial. But all the jurors agreed on his guilt.

84 *See, e.g.*, Justin Driver, "Recognizing Race," 112 *Columbia L. Rev.* 404, 419–420 (2012). For a complaint from the presumed author of Footnote 4 that the Court's 1930s criminal procedure cases gave insufficiently explicit notice to their racial aspects, *see* Lusky, "Minority Rights," 1, 26.

85 287 U.S. 45 (1932).

86 287 U.S. at 50–58 (sources for quotes in this paragraph) (emphasis added).

87 294 U.S. 587 (1935).

88 *See* 294 U.S. at 589.

89 As the Court noted, the requirement of real, and not just ostensible, equality was already well established by 1935. *See* 294 U.S. at 589 (citing earlier cases for the proposition that unequal administration of fair laws constitutes a denial of equal protection).

90 294 U.S. at 590.

91 *See* 294 U.S. at 592–593 & n. 1 (explaining the Court's evaluation of marks made in the jury roll); *see also New York Times*, February 16, 1935, 2.

92 294 U.S. 600 (1935).

93 *See* 294 U.S. at 602.

94 *See, e.g.*, Michael Klarman, "The Racial Origins of Modern Criminal Procedure," 99 *Mich. L. Rev.* 48 (2000); I. Bennett Capers, "Rethinking the Fourth Amendment: Race, Citizenship, and the Equality Principle," 46 *Harv. Civil Rights–Civil Liberties L. Rev.* 1, 4–6 (2011).

95 *Compare Norris with, e.g.*, New York Times v. Sullivan, 376 U.S. 254 285 (1964) (insisting on de novo review of the facts underlying a state court libel judgment); *compare also Patterson with* Fay v. Noia, 372 U.S. 391 (1963) (broadening federal district court authority to overcome state law procedural hurdles to federal habeas petitions). *See generally* Burt Neuborne, "The Gravitational Pull of Race on the Warren Court," 2010 *Sup. Ct. Review* 59 (discussing how concerns about racial inequality influenced Warren Court decisions across a broad variety of issues); *id.* at 68–69 (discussing how race equality concerns drove the Court's habeas doctrine, and in particular its doctrine about federal court power to ignore state law procedural defaults). *Sullivan*, while a First Amendment case, had clear racial overtones given that the alleged libel related to reports of official misconduct during civil rights protests. *See id.* at 79 (discussing *Sullivan* in racial terms).

96 297 U.S. 278 (1936).

97 *See, e.g.*, Allen, "Judicial Quest," 518, 522 (suggesting this connection).

98 297 U.S. at 281 and 282.

99 *See* Lusky, "Minority Rights," at 26 n. 73.

100 262 U.S. 390 (1923).

101 *See, e.g.*, David Bernstein, *Rehabilitating* Lochner*: Defending Individual Rights against Progressive Reform* 104 (University of Chicago Press, 2011).

102 Indeed, two years later he described those cases the same way in his solitary dissent in the first flag salute case, Minersville School Dist. v. Gobitis, 310 U.S. 586, 606 (1940). *Gobitis* is discussed in chapter 2.

103 I have made this argument in an essay reviewing Professor Bernstein's book, cited above in note 101. William D. Araiza, "Back to the Future," 28 *Const. Comm.* 111, 125–126 (2012).

104 *See* Nourse, "Tale of Two *Lochners*"; Allen, "Judicial Quest."

105 Indeed, the day after *Carolene Products* was handed down, Justice Stone wrote to another federal judge expressing concern about what he described as "the increasing racial and religious intolerance which seems to bedevil the world, and which I greatly fear may be augmented in this country." *See* Alpheus Mason, *Harlan Fiske Stone: Pillar of the Law* 515 (Viking, 1956) (quoting April 26, 1938, letter from Stone to Judge Irving Lehman).

106 *See* Nourse, "Tale of Two *Lochners*," at 797–798.

107 *See* Sitkoff, *A New Deal for Blacks*, at 143–162.

108 *See* Johnson v. Virginia, 373 U.S. 61, 62 (1963) ("[I]t is no longer open to question that a State may not constitutionally require segregation of public facilities"); Loving v. Virginia, 388 U.S. 1 (1967) (striking down the antimiscegenation laws that remained in force).

109 In McCleskey v. Kemp, 481 U.S. 279 (1987), the Court narrowly rejected the proposition that racial discrimination in a criminal justice system could be established by statistical evidence showing that blacks were more likely than whites to be sentenced to death for the same type of crime, and that crimes featuring white victims tended to yield death sentences more frequently than identical crimes featuring black victims. Several years ago North Carolina passed a bill allowing criminal defendants to base discrimination arguments on such statistical showings. That bill was subsequently weakened and was eventually repealed in 2013.

110 PBGC v. R. A. Gray, 467 U.S. 717, 729 (1984).

CHAPTER 2. THE RISE AND FALL OF *CAROLENE PRODUCTS*

1 Indeed, a former law clerk of Chief Justice Stone compared the justice's use of footnotes to that of a squirrel burying nuts for recovery and use at a future time. *See* Wiecek, *Birth of the Modern Constitution*, at 123 & n. 41.

2 310 U.S. 586 (1940).

3 *See* 310 U.S. at 602 (Stone, J., dissenting). On incorporation, see Cantwell v. Connecticut, 310 U.S. 296 (1940).

4 *See id.* at 600.

5 *See id.* at 605–607 (Stone, J., dissenting).

6 *See* Wiecek, *Birth of the Modern Constitution*, at 128 (discussing Frankfurter's reliance in *Gobitis* on paragraph two of the *Carolene Products* footnote); *id.* at 221–222 (noting the world situation and the "Fall-of-France" nickname).

7 *See* 310 U.S. at 603.

8 *See* Jones v. Opelika, 316 U.S. 584, 608 (1942) (Stone, C.J., dissenting) ("The First Amendment is not confined to safeguarding freedom of speech and freedom of religion against discriminatory attempts to wipe them out. On the contrary the Constitution, by virtue of the First and the Fourteenth Amendments, has put those freedoms in a preferred position.").

9 *See* Wiecek, *Birth of the Modern Constitution*, at 128 ("[In *Gobitis* Justices Frankfurter and Stone] were talking past each other. Frankfurter . . . saw the issue in paragraph 2 terms, whereas for Stone, it was a matter of paragraphs 1 and 3 in some combination.").

10 For a discussion of the decline of the "preferred position" idea, *see* Wiecek, *Birth of the Modern Constitution*, at 133–136.

11 *See, e.g.*, Reynolds v. Sims, 377 U.S. 533 (1964).

12 Paragraph three's concern for religious minorities found expression in the Court's increased attention to the First Amendment's Free Exercise Clause, particularly during the Warren Court.

13 323 U.S. 214, 216 (1944).

14 347 U.S. 497 (1954).

15 347 U.S. 483 (1954).

16 *See* Klarman, "Interpretive History," 213, 235–238.

17 *See, e.g.*, tenBroek, *Equal under Law*, at 201.

18 One prominent scholar contests this idea, arguing that the original meaning of the Fourteenth Amendment was broad enough to encompass *Brown*'s rule against segregated schools. *See* Michael McConnell, "Originalism and the Desegregation Decisions," 81 *Va. L. Rev.* 947 (1995). Professor (and former judge) McConnell concedes that his view is contrary to accepted wisdom. *See id.* at 951–952.

19 *See, e.g.*, Klarman, "Interpretive History," at 241–243 (expressing partial agreement with this argument but suggesting that precedent and other considerations also mattered).

20 Naim v. Naim, 197 Va. 80 (1955), *vacated*, 350 U.S. 891 (1956), *on remand*, 197 Va. 734, *appeal dismissed*, 350 U.S. 985 (1956).

21 *See, e.g.*, Herbert Wechsler, "Toward Neutral Principles of Constitutional Law," 73 *Harv. L. Rev.* 1, 34 (1959) (describing the Court's actions in *Naim* as "wholly without basis in the law"). For a reappraisal of the Court's conduct in *Naim*, see Gregory Michael Dorr, "Principled Expediency: Eugenics, *Naim v. Naim*, and the Supreme Court," 42 *Am. J. Legal Hist.* 119 (1998).

22 *See, e.g.*, Johnson v. Virginia, 373 U.S. 61, 62 (1963) ("it is no longer open to question that a State may not constitutionally require segregation of public facilities"). As support for that statement the Court cited *Brown* and two of the post-*Brown* per curiam opinions, *Mayor and City Council of Baltimore v. Dawson*, 350 U.S. 877 (1955) (striking down segregation of city-owned beaches and swimming pools, and providing no analysis and citing no authority for its conclusion), and *Turner v. Memphis*, 369 U.S. 350 (1962) (striking down segregation in a restaurant located in a city-owned airport, and citing *Brown* and several of the post-*Brown* per curiam opinions).

23 *See, e.g.*, Klarman, "Interpretive History," at 226–227 (quoting a letter Stone wrote to a fellow judge the day after the Court handed down *Carolene Products*, expressing concern about racial intolerance around the world); *ibid.* (concluding that Stone had protection for blacks in mind when he wrote Footnote 4).

24 *See, e.g.*, New York Times v. Sullivan, 376 U.S. 254 (1964) (rights of newspapers to be free of libel liability based on criticism of public officials); Reynolds v. Sims, 377 U.S. 533 (1964) (requiring that legislative districts be apportioned according to population under the "one man, one vote" principle); Harper v. Va. Bd. of Elections, 383 U.S. 663 (1966) (striking down the poll tax and suggesting that state classifications based on wealth are constitutionally suspect).

25 *See, e.g.*, Levy v. Louisiana, 391 U.S. 68 (1968) (holding that a law denying children the right to sue for the wrongful death of their mother violated equal protection, but failing to provide any broad justification for heightened review of such classifications).

26 Hoyt v. Florida, 368 U.S. 57, 62 (1961). Three justices concurred in part.

27 For an early identification of the then-new Burger Court's interest in halting several of its predecessor's projects, *see* Gerald Gunther, "The Supreme Court, 1971 Term: Foreword: In Search of Evolving Doctrine on a Changing Court: A Model for a Newer Equal Protection," 86 *Harv. L. Rev.* 1, 1 (1972) ("The Burger Court continues more confident about stopping further extensions of some Warren Court paths than about charting roads of its own.").

28 For an example of such an argument couched at a high level of generality, see Steven Calabresi and Julia Rickert, "Originalism and Sex Discrimination," 90 *Tex. L. Rev.* 1 (2011) (concluding that the Fourteenth Amendment prohibited any sort of caste system and that it should be read in light of the Nineteenth Amendment, giving women the franchise, with the result that the Court's current sex equality jurisprudence is defensible on originalist grounds).

29 *See, e.g.*, Graham v. Richardson, 403 U.S. 365, 372 (1971) ("aliens are a prime example of a 'discrete and insular' minority for whom . . . heightened judicial solicitude is appropriate") (citing Footnote 4).

30 404 U.S. 71 (1971).

31 411 U.S. 677 (1973).

32 *See, e.g.*, Hellman, *When Is Discrimination Wrong?*, 119 (suggesting that the military's presumption in *Frontiero* was likely at least rational).

33 The qualifier "essentially" is necessary because in 1954 the Court held that racial discrimination claims could be raised by persons claiming discrimination on a basis other than simply being black or white. Hernandez v. Texas, 347 U.S. 475 (1954) (recognizing that in Texas, Mexican Americans were recognized as a socially distinct group that could suffer racial discrimination).

34 411 U.S. at 685.

35 *See* 411 U.S. at 686 n. 17.

36 "Few," but perhaps not "nobody." *See* Craig Lerner, "Legislators As the 'American Criminal Class': Why Congress (Sometimes) Protects the Rights of Defendants," 2004 *U. Ill. L. Rev.* 599, 606 (noting that scholars sometimes apply the "discrete and insular" minority analysis to protection for criminals).

37 411 U.S. at 686 (internal quotations omitted).

38 Ely, *Democracy and Distrust*, at 158–160.

39 411 U.S. at 686.

40 *See* Michael Klarman, "The Puzzling Resistance to Political Process Theory," 77 *Va. L. Rev.* 747, 787 (1991) (using similar terminology).

41 Watkins v. U.S. Army, 837 F.2d 1428, 1444 (9th Cir. 1988).

42 Watkins, 837 F.2d at 1444–1445.

43 *See Watkins,* 837 F.2d 1428 (9th Cir. 1988).

44 High Tech Gays v. Defense Indus. Sec. Clearance Office, 895 F.2d 563, 574 (9th Cir. 1990).

45 The first of these two opinions, *Watkins*, was reviewed by the appellate court *en banc* and affirmed on a narrower, nonconstitutional ground. Thus, the later of these two opinions, *High Tech Gays*, did not have to follow the *Watkins* panel's suspect class analysis.

46 *See* United States v. Virginia, 518 U.S. 515, 575 (1996) (Scalia, J., dissenting).

47 *See* Ackerman, "Beyond *Carolene Products*," 713.

48 Ely, *Democracy and Distrust*, 152.

49 *See* Craig v. Boren, 429 U.S. 190 (1976).

50 Mathews v. Lucas, 427 U.S. 495, 505 (1976). In previous cases the Court had suggested that legitimacy classifications were irrational and thus unconstitutional. *See, e.g.*, Levy v. Louisiana, 391 U.S. 68 (1968).

51 427 U.S. at 506.

52 Clark v. Jeter, 486 U.S. 456, 461 (1988).

53 *See* Graham v. Richardson, 403 U.S. 365 (1971). However, the Court has exempted from strict scrutiny both alienage classifications drawn by the *federal* government (based on Congress's plenary power over immigration) and classifications drawn by states that relate to what one scholar describes as "self-government and the democratic process." Chemerinsky, *Constitutional Law*, 772.

54 *See, e.g.*, Craig v. Boren, 429 U.S. 190, 214 (Stewart, J., concurring in the judgment); *id.* at 211 (Stevens, J., concurring). In particular, Justice Stevens explicitly rejected the idea that courts should apply different levels of scrutiny to different types of discrimination. *See, e.g., id.* at 211–212. In other writing I have linked Justice Stevens's approach to equal protection to the pre-1937 class legislation approach. See William D. Araiza, "Justice Stevens and Constitutional Adjudication: The Law behind the Rules," 44 *Loyola L.A. Law Rev.* 889, 905 (2011).

55 473 U.S. 432 (1985).

56 *Craig*, 429 U.S. at 217 (1976) (Rehnquist, J., dissenting).

57 450 U.S. 464 (1981).

58 458 U.S. 718 (1982).

59 *See* Nguyen v. INS, 533 U.S. 53 (2001).

60 *See, e.g.*, Franklin, "Anti-stereotyping," 83 (arguing that since the mid-1970s the Court's sex discrimination jurisprudence has reflected a fundamental concern about sex-role stereotyping that limited life options for both men and women).

61 *See ibid.*

62 518 U.S. 515 (1996).

63 *See, e.g.*, Clark v. Jeter, 486 U.S. 456 (1988) (relying on precedent to apply intermediate scrutiny to classifications based on legitimacy).

64 473 U.S. 432 (1985).

65 473 U.S. at 442.

66 473 U.S. at 443.

67 473 U.S. at 444.

68 473 U.S. at 444.

69 473 U.S. at 445–446.

70 Williamson v. Lee Optical, 348 U.S. 483, 489 (1955).

71 473 U.S. at 448.

72 The city also expressed concerns about legal liability, which the Court rejected on the same grounds as its rejection of the flood evacuation justification.

73 *See* Cleburne Living Center v. City of Cleburne, No. CA 3-80-1576-F, slip op. at 9010, Finding 34 (N.D.Tex. April 16, 1982) (trial court finding that the city based its decision in part on some neighborhood residents' fear of and other negative attitudes toward intellectually disabled persons).

74 *See, e.g.*, Fallon, *Implementing the Constitution*, at 61 ("[T]he American constitutional tradition has long recognized a judicial authority, not necessarily linked to any specifically enumerated guarantee, to invalidate truly arbitrary legislation."); Powell, "Reasoning about the Irrational," 217, 228 ("Rational-basis scrutiny, as traditionally understood, flows from a presupposition of American constitutionalism so basic and pervasive that it is easy to overlook: in its dealings with persons, the American government is under a constitutional obligation to act rationally. Rationality in turn requires both that public actions make sense and that they make good sense, that they have some legitimate purpose."); *id.* at 274 ("Although the Constitution's text does not demand, in so many words, that government act rationally, the dominant assumption has long been that irrational official decisions are inconsistent with the constitutional norms of due process and equal protection. Furthermore . . . the rationality necessary to affirm the validity of a law or other public action turns on the presence in official decisions of independent considerations in the public interest, independent of sheer caprice or the desire to use public authority to pursue private or malicious ends."); *see also* Webster v. Doe, 486 U.S. 592, 608 (1988) (Scalia, J., dissenting) (noting the fundamental nature of the rule against government action in pursuit of purely private interests).

75 473 U.S. at 456 (Marshall, J., concurring in the judgment in part and dissenting in part) ("[B]ecause the Court invalidates Cleburne's zoning ordinance on rational-basis grounds, the Court's wide-ranging discussion of heightened scrutiny is wholly superfluous to the decision of this case. This 'two for the price of one' approach to constitutional decisionmaking—rendering two constitutional rulings where one is enough to decide the case—stands on their head traditional and deeply embedded principles governing exercise of the Court's Article III power.").

76 473 U.S. at 446.

77 473 U.S. at 450. Justice Stevens, who joined the majority but also wrote a concurrence for himself and Chief Justice Burger, agreed that those illegitimate neighborhood fears lay behind the city's action. *See* 473 U.S. at 455 (Stevens, J., concurring).

78 *See* City of Richmond v. J. A. Croson Co., 488 U.S. 469 (1989) (race); United States v. Virginia, 518 U.S. 515 (1996) (sex); Romer v. Evans, 517 U.S. 620 (1996) (sexual orientation); Allegheny Pittsburgh Coal Co. v. Cnty. Comm'n. of Webster Cnty., 488 U.S. 336 (1989) (land valuation); Village of Willowbrook v. Olech, 528 U.S. 562 (2000) (class of one).

79 488 U.S. 469 (1989).

80 *See, e.g.*, Johnson v. Virginia, 373 U.S. 61, 62 (1963) ("it is no longer open to question that a State may not constitutionally require segregation of public facilities").

81 *Bakke* dealt with the University of California–Davis's reservation of some of its medical school class seats for educationally or economically disadvantaged students or members of racial minorities—a program under which many white students apparently applied but none was accepted. *See* Regents of the Univ. of California v. Bakke, 438 U.S. 265, 273–276 (1978). A fractured Court struck down the university's admissions plan but did not agree on a rationale or standard of review.

82 *See* Bakke, 438 U.S. 265, 324, 357, 359 (1978) (Brennan, J., concurring in the judgment in part and dissenting in part). The question of these justices' embrace of a particular standard of review is muddied by their own description of that standard as "strict scrutiny." *See* 438 U.S. at 361–362. However, Justice Brennan (and the justices who joined his opinion) described that standard in a way rendering it identical to the intermediate scrutiny standard that had recently been adopted for sex discrimination. *See* Bakke, 438 U.S. at 359.

83 *See, e.g.*, Fullilove v. Klutznick, 448 U.S. 448, 517, 518–519 (Marshall, J., concurring in the judgment).

84 *See* Ely, "Constitutionality of Reverse Racial Discrimination," 723.

85 Other parts of her opinion gathered the votes of a majority of the justices. This part, however, only spoke for four justices.

86 488 U.S. at 493.

87 *See, e.g.*, Brief Amicus Curiae of the ACLU, et al., in No. 87-998, City of Richmond v. J. A. Croson Co., at 9–15 (using political process reasoning to argue for a less-than-strict level of judicial review of affirmative action plans designed to assist politically powerless minorities); Ely, "Reverse Discrimination" (same).

88 *See* 488 U.S. at 495 (following its discussion of the harms of race-conscious government action with the following sentence: "*Even were we* to accept a reading of the guarantee of equal protection under which the level of scrutiny varies according to the ability of different groups to defend their interests in the representative process, heightened scrutiny would still be appropriate in the circumstances of this case.") (emphasis added).

89 *See, e.g.*, Watkins, 837 F.2d 1428 (9th Cir. 1988).

90 Klarman, "Interpretive History," at 309.

91 *See, e.g.*, Grutter v. Bollinger, 539 U.S. 306 (2003) (applying what the majority called strict scrutiny but deferring to the defendant-university's argument that a racially diverse class serves important pedagogical interests justifying some use of race in its admissions decisions). *Compare id.* at 362 (Thomas, J., concurring in part and dissenting in part) (accusing the majority of watering down its strict scrutiny analysis).

92 *See* Fisher v. University of Texas, 133 S.Ct. 2411, 2418 (2013) (race classifications "are odious to a free people" and "contrary to our traditions" and "seldom . . . provide a relevant basis for disparate treatment").

93 518 U.S. 515 (1996).

94 Recall from earlier in this chapter that in her work before ascending to the bench, Justice Ginsburg developed the ACLU's sex discrimination litigation strategy.

95 *See* 515 U.S. at 566, 575–576 (Scalia, J., dissenting).

96 518 U.S. at 535.

97 517 U.S. 620 (1996).

98 *See* Rowland v. Mad River Local Sch. Dist., 470 U.S. 1009 (1985) (Brennan, J., dissenting from denial of *cert.*).

99 *See* 473 U.S. at 456.

100 To be clear, this reference to "gay rights claims" includes only claims under the Due Process and Equal Protection Clauses, not, for example, statutory claims or First Amendment claims.

101 517 U.S. at 635.

102 These two cases both relied on an earlier case that had reached a similar conclusion. *See* Dept. of Agriculture v. Moreno, 413 U.S. 528, 534 (1973) (concluding that a federal law denying food stamp assistance to unrelated members of a single household was motivated by unconstitutional animus against "hippie communes").

103 539 U.S. 558 (2003).

104 *See* 539 U.S. at 579 (O'Connor, J., concurring in the judgment).

105 133 S.Ct. 2675 (2013).

106 *See* William D. Araiza, "After the Tiers: *Windsor*, Congressional Power to Enforce Equal Protection, and the Challenge of Pointillist Constitutionalism," 94 *B.U. L. Rev.* 367 (2014).

107 For a critique of such accusations, *see* Smith, "Jurisprudence of Denigration."

108 134 S.Ct. 1623, 1644–1645 (2014) (Scalia, J., concurring in the judgment).

109 Only seven justices participated in *Carolene Products*; thus, Justice Stone's opinion was an opinion for the Court even though only four justices joined it.

CHAPTER 3. A HISTORICAL INTRODUCTION TO THE ENFORCEMENT POWER

1 521 U.S. 507 (1997).

2 32 U.S. 243, 247 (1833).

3 *See* Amar, *Bill of Rights*, 145–156.

4 For a discussion of the rise of legal positivism after the Civil War, see Stephen Feldman, *American Legal Thought from Premodernism to Postmodernism* 90–105 (Oxford University Press, 2000).

5 *See, e.g.*, Michael Schoeppner, "Peculiar Quarantines: The Seamen Acts and Regulatory Authority in the Antebellum South," 31 *Law & History Rev.* 559 (2013).

6 *See* Amar, *Bill of Rights*, 159–162 (noting the mails issue and the larger impact slavery had on state governments' lack of respect for basic rights).

7 41 U.S. 539 (1842).

8 *See* Robert J. Kaczorowski, "The Supreme Court and Congress's Power to Enforce Constitutional Rights: An Overlooked Moral Anomaly," 73 *Fordham L. Rev.* 153 (2004).

9 *See* Maltz, *Civil Rights*, at 53.

10 *See, e.g.*, Frederick Mark Gedicks, "Incorporation of the Establishment Clause against the States: A Logical, Textual and Historical Account," 88 *Indiana L.J.* 669, 716–717 (2013) ("An early version of Section 1 proposed by Bingham would have provided Congress with the power to legislatively enforce the rights guaranteed by Article IV and the Fifth Amendment. The proposal did not contain a self-executing enumeration of such rights, however, because Bingham, like many other Reconstruction Republicans, believed that the Privileges and Immunities Clause of Article IV already imposed the Bill of Rights and unenumerated natural and customary rights on the states. In Bingham's mind, the constitutional deficiency was lack of a federal enforcement mechanism for Article IV rights; state officials were constitutionally obligated by their oaths of office to protect these rights, but no provision of the Constitution empowered the federal government to enforce them."); *see also* Curtis, *No State Shall Abridge*, 59–63 (explaining Bingham's view); Maltz, *Civil Rights*, at 55.

11 For a thorough discussion of the details of the committee's changes to what became the proposed Fourteenth Amendment, *see* Maltz, *Civil Rights*, at 82–92.

12 Section 2 addressed congressional representation from states that denied universal male suffrage. Section 3 limited the right of former Confederates to hold governmental offices. Section 4 repudiated the Confederate war debt.

13 At least some indirect support for this understanding can be found in the statement of then representative James Garfield, who in a debate on enforcement legislation in 1871 contrasted the ultimate form of the amendment with the "congressional power only" version, concluding that the latter, rejected version, would have clothed Congress with significantly greater power. *See* Maltz, *Civil Rights*, at 103 (quoting Garfield); *id.* at 105 (supplying other evidence that this switch had this effect and perhaps made the amendment more attractive). *But see* Colker, "Historical Errors," 783 (disagreeing with this interpretation).

14 *See* Cox, "Constitutional Adjudication," 91, 110–111 (1966) (conceding that the language suggests this narrower reading, but arguing that the linguistic argument "lost much of its force" after the then-recent enforcement power cases he was commenting on).

15 For example, in her analysis of Congress's consideration of the enforcement power, Ruth Colker suggests that Thaddeus Stevens, a leading Radical Republican, considered Section 1's self-executing grant of rights to be more important than Section 5's grant of congressional enforcement power, because the inevitable reseating of southern congressional delegations would likely defeat significant enforcement legislation. *See* Colker, "Historical Errors," at 803.

16 *See, e.g.*, Steven Engel, "Note—The *McCulloch* Theory of the Fourteenth Amendment: *City of Boerne v. Flores* and the Original Understanding of Section 5," 109 *Yale L.J.* 115, 140–145 (1999).

17 Other scholars have suggested the significance of other Reconstruction-era legislation as relevant to the proper meaning of the Reconstruction Amendments and congressional power to enforce them. *See, e.g.*, James W. Fox, "Re-readings and Misreadings: *Slaughter-House*, Privileges or Immunities, and Section Five Enforcement Powers," 91 *Ky. L. Rev.* 67 (2002–2003) (focusing on the Freedmen's Bureau Act). It seems clear that at least some of these statutes regulated private conduct. *See, e.g.*, United States v. Harris, 106 U.S. 629, 639 (1883) (interpreting the 1871 Ku Klan Act as regulating private conduct).

18 *See, e.g.,* Wilson R. Huhn, "The Legacy of *Slaughterhouse*, *Bradwell* and *Cruikshank* in Constitutional Interpretation," 42 *Akron L. Rev.* 1051, 1075–1076 (2009); Scaturro, *Supreme Court's Retreat from Reconstruction*, 78–79.

Today these statutes tend to be upheld on bases other than Section 5. For example, the Civil Rights Act of 1866 has been interpreted to apply to private, not just state, contracting and, as so interpreted, has been upheld as legislation enforcing the *Thirteenth* Amendment. *See* Jones v. Alfred H. Mayer Co., 392 U.S. 409 (1968). A careful reader may recognize the irony: it was Reconstruction legislators' concerns about whether the Thirteenth Amendment adequately supported that statute that led those legislators to begin work on what became the Fourteenth Amendment. Similarly, the 1871 Klan Act was upheld as legislation enforcing both the Thirteenth Amendment and the national right of interstate travel. See Griffin v. Breckenridge, 403 U.S. 88, 104–105 (1971) (upholding the statute's Thirteenth Amendment foundation); *id.* at 105–106 (upholding its foundation in the national right of interstate travel). Still, statutes such as the Klan Act strongly suggest their intended foundation in Congress's power to enforce the Fourteenth Amendment. See 42 U.S.C.§ 1985(3) (' If two or more persons conspire . . . for the purpose of *depriving any person . . . of the equal protection of the laws* . . . the party so injured or deprived may have an action for the recovery of damages . . . against any one or more of the conspirators.") (emphasis added).

19 92 U.S. 542 (1875).

20 92 U.S. at 555.

21 109 U.S. 3 (1883).

22 106 U.S. 629 (1883).

23 *See, e.g.*, Ellen Katz, "Reinforcing Representation: Congressional Power to Enforce the Fourteenth and Fifteenth Amendments in the Rehnquist and Waite Courts," 101 *Mich. L. Rev.* 2341, 2355 n. 83 (2003); Frantz, "Congressional Power," 1353, 1377–1381.

24 For a discussion of the various justices' views on the state action requirement during the 1960s, *see* Christopher Schmidt, "The Sit-Ins and the State Action Doctrine," 18 *Wm. & Mary Bill of Rights J.* 767, 806–809 (2010).

25 *See* Colker, "Historical Errors," at 815 (identifying state action as the issue that most concerned framing-era statesmen).

26 Strauder v. West Virginia, 100 U.S. 303 (1880) (removal); Ex parte Virginia, 100 U.S. 339 (1880) (juror selection).

27 *See* Virginia, 100 U.S. at 340.

28 *See, e.g.*, Virginia, 100 U.S. at 345–346 ("Whatever legislation is appropriate, that is, adapted to carry out the objects the amendments have in view, whatever tends to enforce submission to the prohibitions they contain, . . . if not prohibited, is brought within the domain of congressional power."). *Compare* McCulloch v. Maryland, 17 U.S. 316, 421 (1819) (interpreting Article I's Necessary and Proper Clause by stating, "Let the end be legitimate, let it be within the scope of the constitution, and all means which are appropriate, which are plainly adapted to that end, which are not prohibited, but consist with the letter and spirit of the constitution, are constitutional.").

29 For a rare example of Congress using its Reconstruction Amendment enforcement power during this period, see the 1948 amendments to the Anti-peonage Act, discussed in Rebecca Zietlow, "Free at Last! Anti-subordination and the Thirteenth Amendment," 90 *B.U. L. Rev.* 255, 299–300 (2010).

30 265 U.S. 545 (1924).

31 Other amendments including enforcement provisions are the Nineteenth (female suffrage), Twenty-Third (District of Columbia presidential suffrage), Twenty-Fourth (poll tax), and Twenty-Sixth (eighteen-year-old suffrage). These enforcement provisions were nearly identically worded to those in the Thirteenth, Fourteenth, and Fifteenth Amendments. The Prohibition Amendment's enforcement provision contained different wording, as explained in the text.

32 *See* 265 U.S. at 559. Following the Court's established jurisprudence governing the Necessary and Proper Clause, it noted that Congress had to use means that were not prohibited to it, and that were calculated to achieve its goal. *See ibid.*

33 The Court split on a subsequent Prohibition enforcement statute that was arguably somewhat further removed from the amendment's purpose to prohibit the use of intoxicating liquors for beverage purposes. *See* Lambert v. Yellowley, 272 U.S. 581 (1926) (upholding, on a five-to-four vote, a federal statute limiting the amount of intoxicating liquor a physician could prescribe a patient for medicinal uses).

34 *See, e.g.*, South Carolina v. Katzenbach, 383 U.S. 301, 327 (1966) (citing *James Everard's*); Brief for the United States in South Carolina v. Katzenbach, 1966 WL 100406 at 30 & 47 (same).

35 383 U.S. 301 (1966).

36 For an examination of the ambiguity arising from the existence of two different amendments with two distinct (though identically worded) enforcement clauses, see chapter 5's discussion of the *Shelby County v. Holder* case. For a statement of the rule that the same standard governed legislation enforcing both amendments, see Katzenbach v. Morgan, 384 U.S. 641, 650–651 (1966); Fullilove v. Klutznick, 448 U.S. 448, 500 n. 2 (1980) (describing the enforcement provisions of all three Reconstruction Amendments as "virtually identical"); *see also* Michael Pitts, "Section 5 of the Voting Rights Act: A Once and Future Remedy?," 81 *Denv. U. L. Rev.* 225, 275 & 275 n. 254 (2003). *But see* Northwest Austin Mun. Util. Dist. No. 1 v. Holder, 557 U.S. 193, 204 (2009) (suggesting openness to applying different standards to Congress's Fourteenth and Fifteenth Amendment enforcement powers).

37 *See* 383 U.S. at 355 (Black, J., concurring and dissenting).

38 *See* 383 U.S. at 310–311.

39 "Let the end be legitimate, let it be within the scope of the constitution, and all means which are appropriate, which are plainly adapted to that end, which are not prohibited, but consist with the letter and spirit of the constitution, are constitutional." McCulloch, 4 Wheat. 316, 421 (1819), *quoted in* South Carolina, 383 U.S. at 326; *see also* South Carolina, 383 U.S. at 327 (citing *James Everard's* to that same effect).

40 Cox, "Constitutional Adjudication," at 102.

41 384 U.S. 641 (1966).

42 *See* 384 U.S. at 645 n. 3.

43 The Court concluded that, in addition to the Fifteenth Amendment's explicit ban on racial discrimination in voting, the Fourteenth Amendment, and the Equal Protection Clause in particular, spoke to at least some voting restrictions. *See* 384 U.S. at 647 & 647 n. 6.

44 360 U.S. 45 (1959).

45 *See* 384 U.S. at 654.

46 In particular, chapter 5 will discuss the Court's skepticism about the multistep reasoning used to defend the self-care provision of the FMLA in Coleman v. Court of Appeals of Maryland, 132 S.Ct. 1327 (2012).

47 *See* 384 U.S. at 651 n. 10; *id.*at 668 (Harlan, J., dissenting) (registering his disagreement with this argument); *see also, e.g.*, William Cohen, "Congressional Power to Interpret Due Process and Equal Protection," 27 *Stan. L. Rev.* 603, 606 (1975) (early use of the "ratchet" idea); Samuel Estreicher, "Congressional Power and Constitutional Rights: Reflections on Proposed 'Human Life' Legislation," 68 *Va. L. Rev.* 333, 419 n. 290 (1982) (identifying Professor Cohen's article as the first use of the ratchet concept).

48 *See, e.g.*, Cox, "Constitutional Adjudication"; Robert Burt, "*Miranda* and Title II: A Morganatic Marriage," 1969 *Sup. Ct. L. Rev.* 81, 83.

49 *See, e.g.*, Fay v. New York, 332 U.S. 261, 282 (1947) (referring to "the majestic generalities of the Fourteenth Amendment").

50 Morgan, 384 U.S. at 666 (Harlan, J., dissenting).

51 384 U.S. at 667.

52 384 U.S. at 668.

53 For an example of a scholar who agrees that congressional fact-finding played a crucial role in *Morgan*, see Colker, "Section 5 Quagmire," at 668 ("Congress's factual record was central to the Court's willingness [in *Morgan*] to tolerate Congress's creating standards beyond those previously established by the Court pursuant to Section 1 [of the Fourteenth Amendment].").

54 384 U.S. at 655.

55 392 U.S. 409 (1968).

56 42 U.S.C. § 1982.

57 *See* 392 U.S. at 439 ("By its own unaided force and effect, the Thirteenth Amendment abolished slavery, and established universal freedom. Whether or not the Amendment *itself* did any more than that—a question not involved in this case—it is at least clear that the Enabling Clause of that Amendment empowered Congress to do much more.") (italics in original; internal quotation and citation omitted).

58 392 U.S. at 439 (internal quotation and emphasis omitted).

59 The interpretation of that statute to cover private refusals to contract is itself controversial. *See* Maltz, *Civil Rights*, at 70–78 (presenting arguments on both sides of the issue).

60 *See* McAward, "Congressional Authority to Interpret the Thirteenth Amendment," 60, 61 (describing this understanding of *Jones*).

61 400 U.S. 112 (1970).

62 *See* 400 U.S. at 200.

63 *See id.* at 129–130 (Black, J.) (suggesting that Congress's enforcement authority allowed interference with state election rules only in the context of racial discrimination); *id.* at 294–296 (Stewart, J.) (arguing that age discrimination in voting did not violate equal protection, and thus could not be regulated by Congress under its enforcement power).

64 In his classic 1978 article on underenforced constitutional norms, Professor Sager provided another example of this phenomenon when he discussed the Court's 1974 decision that Section 2 of the Fourteenth Amendment permitted states to disenfranchise felons. As Professor Sager explained, that decision "fixed a boundary of the Court's equal protection construct on a purely analytical basis," with the result that "[a] congressional attempt to prohibit the exclusion of felons from the franchise which depended upon [Congress's enforcement power], accordingly, would not be valid." Sager, "Fair Measure," 1212, 1241.

65 427 U.S. 445 (1976).

66 The Court did not engage this question because the state government defendant did not argue that the statute exceeded Congress's enforcement power. *See* 427 U.S. at 456 n. 11. Still, the Court was aware of this issue, given Justice Stevens's separate opinion questioning the statute's enforcement power foundation. *See* 427 U.S. at 458 (Stevens, J., concurring in the judgment). Moreover, four days before the Court decided *Fitzpatrick*, it decided that the Commerce Clause did not authorize Congress to impose similar types of employment regulation on states. *See* National League of Cities v. Usery, 426 U.S. 833 (June 24, 1976). Thus, the *Fitzpatrick* Court was surely aware that the question of Congress's enforcement authority to regulate state employers was an important issue.

67 *See* Griggs v. Duke Power Co., 401 U.S. 424 (1971) (requiring that employers justify employment practices that disparately impact women and minorities).

68 Washington v. Davis, 426 U.S. 229 (1976). *Davis* was decided on June 7. *Fitzpatrick* was decided three weeks later, on June 28.

69 446 U.S. 156 (1980).

70 City of Mobile v. Bolden, 446 U.S. 55 (1980).

71 *See* 446 U.S. at 177–178.

72 *See* Laurence Tribe, *American Constitutional Law* § 5–14, at 338 (2d ed. Foundation Press, 1987).

73 *See ibid.*

74 494 U.S. 872 (1990).

75 To be sure, that precedent, even while purporting to require careful scrutiny of such generally applicable restrictions, usually resulted in the Court upholding the law. *See* Smith, 494 U.S. at 882–884 (1990) (discussing cases).

76 RFRA applied to both the federal and state governments. As a matter of enforcement power doctrine, *Boerne* only considered RFRA's applicability to state governments.

77 42 U.S.C. § 2000bb-1.

78 To be sure, often the Court expresses the strict scrutiny test as requiring that a law be "narrowly tailored" to meet a compelling government interest, rather than the "least restrictive means" of doing so. Nevertheless, *Boerne*'s description of RFRA's test as "the most demanding test known to constitutional law," 521 U.S. at 534, reflects its view that the statute did in fact mandate strict scrutiny.

79 *Ibid.*

80 42 U.S.C. § 2000bb(a), *quoted in* Boerne, 521 U.S. at 515.

81 At the Court, RFRA's defenders made exactly this point. *See* Brief of Respondent Flores in No. 95-2074, 1997 WL 10293, at 13–16.

82 508 U.S. 520 (1993).

83 For a comprehensive description of the controversy that gave rise to *Boerne, see* Waltman, *Congress, the Supreme Court, and Religious Liberty.*

84 400 U.S. 112 (1970).

85 The most notable exception is New York v. United States, 505 U.S. 144 (1992), which, on a six-to-three vote, struck down a federal law commanding states to consider particular regulatory actions.

86 *See* Boerne, 521 U.S. at 524 ("th[e] separation-of-powers aspect [of the original proposal to word the Fourteenth Amendment as a simple grant of power to Congress] did not occasion the widespread resistance which was caused by the proposal's threat to the federal balance" but "nonetheless attracted the attention of various Members [of Congress]").

87 521 U.S. at 528.

88 For an explanation of incorporation, *see* chapter 1.

89 According to one source, this test derived from the oral argument presentation for *Boerne*'s lawyer. *See* Waltman, *Congress, the Supreme Court, and Religious Liberty*, at 106; *see also* Oral Arg. in No. 95-2074, at 6 (argument of Marci Hamilton, arguing that "[t]here must be some kind of proportional fit between the means and the end [in order for enforcement legislation] to be appropriate.").

90 *See* 521 U.S. at 534–535.

91 521 U.S. at 532 (citing Rome, 446 U.S. at 177).

92 521 U.S. at 534 (internal quotation omitted).

93 521 U.S. at 534.

94 *See, e.g.*, Colker, "Historical Errors," at 785.

CHAPTER 4. THE MODERN ENFORCEMENT POWER

1 Justice Scalia did not join Justice Kennedy's historical analysis of Section 5, but he did join his announcement and application of the congruence and proportionality test.

2 The one exception to this statement was Justice Souter's vote with the conservatives in a case early in this period, which struck down a federal law that required states to put a particular issue on their legislative agendas. New York v. United States, 505 U.S. 144 (1992).

3 The first post-*Boerne* case on which the Court split on the scope of the enforcement power concerned Congress's power to enforce the Due Process Clause. *See* Florida Prepaid Post-secondary Education Expense Board v. College Savings Bank, 527 U.S. 627 (1999). Chapter 10 discusses congressional power to enforce substantive rights under that clause.

4 528 U.S. 62 (2000).

5 Reflecting the influence of federalism concerns on this case, the four dissenters—the Court's liberal bloc—ignored the majority's enforcement power analysis, focusing instead on attacking the 1996 decision holding that the Commerce Clause did not authorize Congress to make available monetary relief against states. *See* 528 U.S. at 92 (Stevens, J., dissenting).

6 531 U.S. 356 (2001).

7 473 U.S. 432 (1985).

8 538 U.S. 721 (2003).

9 538 U.S. at 736.

10 Other evidence he cited did tie private employer leave policies to those of state government employers but only in a general, conclusory fashion that likely would have been considered inadequate in *Garrett. See* Hibbs, 538 U.S. at 730 n. 3 & 731.

11 *See* 538 U.S. at 729–730 & 736–737.

12 *See, e.g.*, Reva Siegel, "You've Come a Long Way, Baby: Rehnquist's New Approach to Pregnancy Discrimination in *Hibbs*," 58 *Stan. L. Rev.* 1871, 1882–1883 (2006) (noting this speculation about his seeming new understanding of the severity of the burdens parental care responsibilities placed on female employees).

13 541 U.S. 509 (2004).

14 42 U.S.C. § 12132.

15 *See* 541 U.S. at 551 (Rehnquist, C.J., dissenting) ("The effect [of the majority's approach] is to rig the congruence-and-proportionality test by artificially constricting the scope of the statute to closely mirror a recognized constitutional right.").

16 541 U.S. at 532 (quoting Boddie v. Connecticut, 401 U.S. 371, 379 (1971)).

17 *See* Lewis F. Powell, "*Carolene Products* Revisited," 82 *Columbia L. Rev.* 1087, 1087 (1982) (describing Footnote 4 as "the most celebrated footnote in constitutional law").

18 Lochner v. New York, 198 U.S. 45 (1905).

19 *See, e.g.*, Nourse, "Tale of Two *Lochners*," at 754.

CHAPTER 5. CONSTITUTIONAL LAW AND LEGISLATIVE POLICY

1 *See, e.g.*, Kimel, 528 U.S. at 88 ("Difficult and intractable problems often require powerful remedies"); Hibbs, 538 U.S. at 737 (recounting the story of the stubbornness of sex discrimination). Indeed, this recognition goes even further back, to the Court's recognition of Congress's power to counteract southern states' stubborn attempts to frustrate African Americans' voting rights. *See* South Carolina, 383 U.S. at 309.

2 132 S.Ct. 1327 (2012).

3 *See, e.g.*, Reva Siegel, "Equality's Frontiers: How Congress's Section Five Power Can Secure Transformative Equality (As Justice Ginsburg Illustrates in *Coleman*)," 122 Yale L.J. Online 267, 271 (2013) ("Where the Justices who would deny Congress Section 5 power can see no connection between selfcare leave and constitutional equality values, the dissenters recognize in Congress's decision to bundle family-care and self-care leave a commitment to provide employees family leave in a form that would not exacerbate employers' tendency to discriminate against young women of childbearing age in hiring and promotion. Congress decided it could promote work-family balance without triggering discrimination by coupling a form of leave employers would expect women to take (family leave) with a form of leave employers would expect employees of both sexes to take (sick leave).").

4 The Court also rejected the argument that the self-care provision assisted single parents, an effect that enforced sex equality on the theory that most single parents were women. *See* 132 S.Ct. at 1337.

5 417 U.S. 484 (1974).

6 *See, e.g.*, Sylvia Law, "Rethinking Sex and the Constitution," 132 *U. Pa. L. Rev.* 955, 983 (1984) ("Criticizing [*Aiello*] has . . . become a cottage industry").

7 Indeed, Justice Ginsburg's discussion of the self-care provision's justification in eradicating pregnancy discrimination relied heavily on her call to reconsider *Aiello* and hold that pregnancy discrimination constitutes sex discrimination. *See* 132 S.Ct. at 1344–1345.

8 132 S.Ct. at 1355.

9 *See* 132 S.Ct. at 1347 (Ginsburg, J., dissenting) (beginning her discussion of the second argument for the self-care provision by stating, "But even if *Aiello* senselessly holds sway . . . I would nevertheless conclude that the [self-care provision is] valid § 5 legislation").

10 *See, e.g.*, Michael Selmi, "The Evolution of Employment Discrimination Law: Changed Doctrine for Changed Social Conditions" 4, *available at* http://papers.ssrn.com/sol3/papers.cfm?abstract_id=2430378 ("Although . . . discrimination has sharply receded since the 1970's, . . . the discrimination that remains has changed in character, becoming more subtle, more entrenched, and more systemic in nature which in turn means more difficult to identify or prove.").

11 Suk, "'A More Egalitarian Relationship at Home and at Work,'" 473, 476.

12 133 S.Ct. 2612 (2013).

13 *See* Shelby County, 133 S.Ct. at 2622 n. 1.

14 *See* Price Waterhouse v. Hopkins, 490 U.S. 228 (1989).

15 132 S.Ct. at 1336.

16 *See, e.g.*, Richard Ford, "Bias in the Air: Rethinking Employment Discrimination Law," 66 *Stan. L. Rev.* 1381 (2014).

17 Tr. of Oral Arg. at 28, Northwest Austin Municipal Utility Dist. No. One v. Holder, 557 U.S. 193 (2009) (No. 08-322) (statement of Chief Justice Roberts) ("Well, that's like the old—you know, it's the elephant whistle. You know, I have this whistle to keep away the elephants. . . . Well, there are no elephants, so it must work.").

18 *See, e.g.*, Feeley and Rubin, *Judicial Policy Making*, 5 (1998) (defining "policymaking" as "the process by which officials exercise power on the basis of their judgment that their actions will produce socially desirable results.").

19 *See* 132 S.Ct. at 1347–1349 (Ginsburg, J., dissenting) (discussing this argument).

20 For a short, helpful discussion of the difficulties these issues pose, *see* Claire Cain Miller, "Can Family Leave Policies Hurt Women's Careers? It Seems So," *N.Y. Times*, August 9, 2014, SR3.

21 133 S.Ct. at 2627.

22 Feeley and Rubin, *Judicial Policy Making*, at 5.

23 Lane, 541 U.S. at 558 (Scalia, J., dissenting). In its place, Justice Scalia argued for a rule giving Congress significant latitude to enforce the clause's prohibition on race discrimination, but reducing its power to enforce against other types of discrimination to simply prescribing remedies for actual court-found constitutional violations.

24 Even Justice Scalia agrees with this principle, but only limited to enforcement legislation targeting racial discrimination. *See ibid.*

CHAPTER 6. REFOCUSING CONGRUENCE AND PROPORTIONALITY

1 Sager, "Fair Measure."

2 *Id.* at 1214.

3 United States v. Windsor, 133 S.Ct. 2675, 2716 (2013) (Alito, J., dissenting) (internal quotations omitted).

4 *See* Village of Willowbrook v. Olech, 528 U.S. 562 (2000) (endorsing the idea that a "class of one" can state an equal protection claim).

5 *See, e.g.*, Romer v. Evans, 517 U.S. 620 (1996) (declining to decide whether sexual orientation is a suspect classification but nevertheless ruling for the plaintiffs on the ground that the law failed rational basis scrutiny).

6 Indeed, the *Garrett* Court thought the matter sufficiently trivial as to engage it fully only in a footnote. *See* 531 U.S. at 366 n. 4.

7 *See* Cleburne Living Center v. City of Cleburne, 726 F.2d 191, 194 (5th Cir. 1984) (citing the trial court opinion).

8 *See* 473 U.S. at 450 ("The short of it is that requiring the permit in this case appears to us to rest on an irrational prejudice against the mentally retarded, including those who would occupy the [planned] facility."); *id.* at 455 (Stevens, J., concurring) (concluding that the city's decision rested on the neighbors' irrational fears).

9 *See* 473 U.S. at 445–446.

10 For a fuller discussion of the concept of a "doctrinal gap," *see* Powell, "Reasoning about the Irrational."

11 *See* Cass Sunstein, "Homosexuality and the Constitution," 70 *Ind. L.J.* 1, 4 (1994) ("Under the Equal Protection Clause, the Supreme Court has invalidated certain forms of discrimination on the ground that they are irrational or unconnected with any legitimate public purpose. This idea is connected with an interesting conception of democracy: the distribution of benefits or the imposition of burdens must reflect a conception of the public good. The Court has also disqualified, as justifications of legislation, certain ideas on the ground that they reflect 'prejudice' or 'hostility.' A statute based on 'prejudice' cannot qualify as rational."); *see also* Fallon, *Implementing the Constitution*; Powell, "Reasoning about the Irrational."

12 *See* Brown v. Bd. of Education, 347 U.S. 483 (1954) (racial segregation in schools); Johnson v. California, 543 U.S. 499 (2005) (racial segregation in prisons); Village of Willowbrook v. Olech, 528 U.S. 562 (2000) (discrimination in petty bureaucratic decisions).

13 *See* William D. Araiza, "New Groups and Old Doctrine: Rethinking Congressional Power to Enforce the Equal Protection Clause," 37 *Fla. State L. Rev.* 451, 478–480 (2010).

14 531 U.S. at 367–368.

15 517 U.S. 620 (1996).

16 449 U.S. 166 (1980).

17 At least since 1954 the Court has read into the Fifth Amendment's Due Process Clause a requirement of equal treatment that mirrors the requirement imposed on the states by the Fourteenth Amendment's Equal Protection Clause. *See* Bolling v. Sharpe, 347 U.S. 497 (1954). The challenge in *Fritz* was decided on the basis of that equality guarantee.

18 *See, e.g.*, Jay Wexler, "Defending the Middle Way: Intermediate Scrutiny as Judicial Minimalism," 66 *Geo. Wash. L. Rev.* 298, 317 n. 123 (1998); Cleburne, 473 U.S. at 458–460 (Marshall, J., concurring in the result).

19 *See* 449 U.S. at 194 (Brennan, J., dissenting).

20 *See* 449 U.S. at 180–181 (Stevens, J., concurring in the judgment).

21 For one attempt to grapple with this problem, *see* Jones v. Bates, 127 F.3d 839, 861–863 (9th Cir. 1997) (considering the intent behind a popularly enacted referendum based on the information provided to voters in a voter information pamphlet).

22 *See* Garrett, 531 U.S. at 367–368.

23 *See* R. George Wright, "Michael Perry, Peter Singer and Quasimodo: Persons with Disabilities and the Nature of Rights," 14 *J. L. & Religion* 113 (1999–2000) (discussing the Quasimodo story in the context of society's views of the disabled).

24 *See, e.g.*, Constantina Safilios-Rothschild, "Prejudice against the Disabled and Some Means to Combat It," in *Social and Psychological Aspects of Disability* 261, 265 (Joseph Stubbins ed., University Park Press, 1977) (noting public feelings of disgust for the disabled). The philosopher Martha Nussbaum also makes this argument with regard to public attitudes toward homosexuality. *See* Martha Nussbaum, *From Disgust to Humanity: Sexual Orientation and Constitutional Law* (Oxford University Press, 2010).

25 *See* Garrett, 531 U.S. at 381–382 (Breyer, J., dissenting).

26 *See* Romer v. Evans, 517 U.S. at 636 (Scalia, J., dissenting) ("The Court has mistaken a *Kulturkampf* for a fit of spite.").

27 *See, e.g.*, William D. Araiza, "Deference to Congressional Factfinding in Rights-Enforcing and Rights-Limiting Legislation," 88 *N.Y.U. L. Rev.* 878, 909 (2013).

28 Hand, *The Bill of Rights*, 73.

29 *See, e.g.*, Richard Burt, "*Miranda* and Title II: A Morganatic Marriage," 1969 *Sup. Ct. L. Rev.* 81, 113–114 (noting Congress's superiority over courts, based in part on its electoral legitimacy, in distinguishing between various groups for purposes of allocating benefits and burdens).

30 500 U.S. 44 (1991).

31 *Id.* at 56.

32 *Id.* at 56.

33 In particular, a candidate carrying California (55 votes), Texas (38), New York (29), Florida (29), Illinois (20), Pennsylvania (20), Ohio (18), Michigan (16), Georgia (16), North Carolina (15), and New Jersey (14) would amass 270 votes.

34 488 U.S. 469, 495–496 (1989).

35 *See* Parents Involved in Community Schools v. Seattle Sch. Dist. No. 1, 551 U.S. 701, 744–745 (2007).

36 Fisher v. University of Texas, 133 S.Ct. 2411 (2013).

37 *See* Klarman, "Interpretive History," at 226.

38 *See, e.g.*, Ely, "Reverse Discrimination."

39 *See* Klarman, "Interpretive History," at 285 & 309.

40 *See, e.g.*, Daniel Farber and Philip Frickey, "Is *Carolene Products* Dead? Reflections on Affirmative Action and the Dynamics of Civil Rights Legislation," 79 *Cal. L. Rev.* 685, 692 (1991).

41 *See, e.g.*, Grutter v. Bollinger, 539 U.S. 306, 349–350 (2003) (Thomas, J., concurring in part and dissenting in part) (quoting from Frederick Douglass); Croson, 488 U.S. at 527 (Scalia, J., concurring in the judgement) (quoting approvingly legal scholar Alexander Bickel's moral argument against racial quotas); Croson, 488 U.S. at 518 (Kennedy, J., concurring in part and concurring in the judgment) ("The moral imperative of racial neutrality is the driving force of the Equal Protection Clause."); Metro Broadcasting v. FCC, 497 U.S. 547, 602 (1990) (O'Connor, J., dissenting) ("[T]he Constitution provides that the Government may not allocate benefits and burdens among individuals based on the assumption that race or ethnicity determines how they act or think.").

42 *See* 528 U.S. at 78–79.

43 *See* 528 U.S. at 79 ("Under our firmly established precedent . . . if the ADEA rests solely on Congress' Article I commerce power, the private petitioners in today's cases cannot maintain their suits against their state employers" in which they requested damages and back pay.).

44 *See* 531 U.S. at 380–381 (Breyer, J., dissenting) (noting this evidence).

45 *See, e.g.*, Michael Stein, "The Law and Economics of Disability Accommodations," 53 *Duke L.J.* 79, 128 (2003) (explaining how nonprejudiced employers can nevertheless misestimate the cost of disability accommodations). For an analysis of a similar dynamic in the context of genetics discrimination, *see* Anita Silvers and Michael Stein, "An Equality Paradigm for Preventing Genetic Discrimination," 55 *Vand. L. Rev.* 1341, 1382 (2002).

46 *See* United States v. Windsor, 133 S.Ct. 2675 (2013). *Windsor*'s approach is discussed, and critiqued, in chapter 2.

47 *See, e.g.*, Romer v. Evans, 517 U.S. 620 (1996) (concluding that a challenged state law reflected animus against the burdened group when no legitimate justification plausibly fit the statute).

48 *Cf.* Smith, "Jurisprudence of Denigration."

49 *See* William Eskridge, "Some Effects of Identity-Based Social Movements on Constitutional Law in the Twentieth Century," 100 *Mich. L. Rev.* 2062 (2002).

50 *See, e.g.*, Barry Friedman, *The Will of the People* (Farrar, Straus and Giroux, 2009).

51 *See* Ely, *Democracy and Distrust*, at 164.

52 *See, e.g.*, Franklin, "Anti-stereotyping" (finding stereotyping to be a connecting thread in the Court's sex equality jurisprudence).

53 518 U.S. at 533 n. 7 (quoting Brief for Twenty-Six Private Women's Colleges as Amici Curiae 5).

54 *See* Metro Broadcasting v. FCC, 497 U.S. 547, 602, 621 (1990) (O'Connor, J., dissenting). *Metro Broadcasting* was a case about race; however, the statement quoted in the text referred (in part) to sex and was followed by citations to sex discrimination cases. *Compare* Rostker v. Goldberg, 453 U.S. 57, 72 (1981) (upholding the federal government's requirement that men but not women register for a possible draft, in part because the government's decision was considered rather than unthinking or reflexive).

55 *See* Franklin, "Anti-stereotyping," at 132–137.

56 420 U.S. 636 (1975).

CHAPTER 7. THE DEFERENCE QUESTION

1 Other scholars have also noted this relationship. *See, e.g.*, Berger, "Deference Determinations," 465, 492–494.

2 *See* Turner Broadcasting System, Inc. v. FCC, 512 U.S. 622, 665–666 (1994).

3 *See* Berger, "Deference Determinations," at 469 ("[The Court's] deference determinations are often poorly justified, resting less on careful consideration and more on pithy platitudes about each political branch's strengths and weaknesses.").

4 William D. Araiza, "Deference to Congressional Fact-Finding in Rights-Enforcing and Rights-Limiting Legislation," 88 *N.Y.U. L. Rev.* 878, 903 & nn. 95–96 (2013) (citing scholars making this argument).

5 *Id.* at 931–932.

6 United States v. Windsor, 133 S.Ct. 2675 (2013).

7 For more about this relationship, *see* Berger, "Deference Determinations," at 498–520; Eric Berger, "Individual Rights, Judicial Deference, and Administrative Law Norms in Constitutional Decision Making," 91 *B.U. L. Rev.* 2029, 2058–2074 (2011).

8 Skidmore v. Swift & Co., 323 U.S. 134 (1944).

9 *See, e.g.*, Jamie A. Yavelberg, "Revival of *Skidmore v. Swift:* Judicial Deference to Agency Interpretations after *EEOC v. Aramco*," 42 *Duke L.J.* 166, 172 (1992).

10 Chevron USA v. Nat. Res. Def. Council, 467 U.S. 837 (1984).

11 Justice Scalia's is the primary—indeed, fundamentally, the only—voice dissenting from this consensus. *See, e.g.*, United States v. Mead Corp., 533 U.S. 218 239 (2001) (Scalia, J., dissenting) (arguing that congressional intent is not the proper touchstone for application of *Chevron* deference).

12 *See, e.g.*, Ronald Allen and Michael Pardo, "The Myth of the Law-Fact Distinction," 97 *Nw. U. L. Rev.* 1769 (2003).

13 *See, e.g.*, 5 *Oxford English Dictionary* 188 (2d ed. 1989) (defining "empirical" as "pertaining to, or derived from, experience").

14 *See, e.g.*, Neal Katyal, "Legislative Constitutional Interpretation," 50 *Duke L.J.* 1335 (2001) (arguing that Congress may have superior legitimacy to courts when discerning Americans' values).

15 United States v. Lopez, 514 U.S. 549 (1995).

16 United States v. Morrison, 529 U.S. 598 (2000).

17 *Compare, e.g.*, Thompson v. Oklahoma, 487 U.S. 815 (1988) (plurality opinion) (canvassing state law and jury verdicts to determine that executing a criminal who was less than sixteen years old at the time of the crime violated the Eighth Amendment); *with id.* at 848, 853 (O'Connor, J., concurring in the judgment) (questioning the reliability of the plurality's data); *and id.* at 859 (Scalia, J., dissenting) (reaching an opposite conclusion based on that same data).

18 Allison Orr Larsen has examined the problem posed by the Supreme Court's review of facts presented in amicus briefs, and by the Court's own independent search for facts. *See* Allison Orr Larsen, "The Trouble with Amicus Facts," *available at* http://papers.ssrn.com/sol3/papers.cfm?abstract_id=2409071 (reliance on amicus briefs); Allison Orr Larsen, "Confronting Supreme Court Factfinding," 98 *Va. L. Rev.* 1255 (2012) (independent fact-finding).

19 *See, e.g.*, John McGinnis and Charles Mulaney, "Judging Facts Like Law," 25 *Const. Comm.* 69, 90–116 (2008).

20 *See* California v. Greenwood, 486 U.S. 35 (1988) (holding that Americans do not have a reasonable expectation of privacy in the household garbage they put out for collection).

21 *See* Washington v. Davis, 426 U.S. 229 (1976), discussed in chapter 3.

22 *See, e.g.*, Sierra Club v. Costle, 657 F.2d 298, 410 (D.C. Cir. 1981) (reviewing an agency's decision for arbitrariness while recognizing that some parts of the technically complex record were "impenetrable").

23 *See, e.g.*, Harrison, "Reconstructing," at 1390 (arguing for this narrower understanding of the Equal Protection Clause and describing the broader version as the result of a "textual sleight of hand" from the Supreme Court).

24 *See* Village of Willowbrook v. Olech, 528 U.S. 562 (2000) (recognizing the equal protection "class of one" concept).

25 *Compare* New York v. United States, 505 U.S. 144 (1992) (announcing the anticommandeering principle and applying it to protect state legislatures) *and* Printz v. United States, 521 U.S. 898 (1997) (applying that principle to protect state law enforcement) *with* South Carolina v. Katzenbach, 383 U.S. 301 (1966) (upholding the preclearance provisions of the Voting Rights Act, despite their deep intrusion into state sovereignty).

26 *Compare* Seminole Tribe of Florida v. Florida, 517 U.S. 44 (1996) (prohibiting Congress from using its Commerce Clause power to make states liable for retrospective relief) *with* Fitzpatrick v. Bitzer, 427 U.S. 445 (1976) (holding that the Enforcement Clause allows Congress to make states liable for such relief).

27 *See, e.g.*, Camps Newfound/Owatonna v. Town of Harrison, 520 U.S. 564, 610–20 (1997) (Thomas, J., dissenting) (joined by Rehnquist, C.J., and Scalia, J.) (criticizing the entire idea of a "dormant" Commerce Clause); Bendix Autolite Corp. v. Midwesco Enterprises, 486 U.S. 888, 897 (1988) (Scalia, J., concurring in the judgment) (criticizing the doctrine).

28 *See* Shelby County, 133 S.Ct. at 2629 ("The court below and the parties have debated what [Congress's] record shows—they have gone back and forth about whether to compare covered to noncovered jurisdictions as blocks, how to disaggregate the data State by State, how to weigh § 2 cases as evidence of ongoing discrimination, and whether to consider evidence not before Congress, among other issues.").

CHAPTER 8. AN ASIDE ON STATE ACTION

1 *See, e.g.*, Jones v. Alfred E. Mayer Co., 392 U.S. 409 (1968) (holding that Congress's power to enforce the Thirteenth Amendment authorized it to enact the Civil Rights Act of 1866's prohibition on private discrimination in the sale of real property).

2 For an example of scholars' disagreement about the scope of Congress's Thirteenth Amendment enforcement power, *compare* Jennifer Mason McAward, "The Scope of Congress's Thirteenth Amendment Enforcement Power after *Boerne v Flores*," 88 *Wash. U. L. Rev.* 77 (2010) (arguing for relatively limited congressional power) *with* Tsesis, "Congressional Authority to Interpret the Thirteenth Amendment," 71 *Md. L. Rev.* 40 (2011) (responding, and arguing for broader power). Given that even proponents of broad congressional power to enforce the Thirteenth Amendment describe that power as the power to abolish the "badges and incidents" of slavery, it is doubtful whether that power would extend over the entire breadth of legislative classification decisions that are covered by the Equal Protection Clause.

3 The Citizenship Clause of Section 1, which affirmatively confers national and state citizenship on all persons born in the United States and subject to its jurisdiction, is the one exception to Section 1's "negative" format. It is perhaps not surprising that in one of the seminal nineteenth-century cases considering the state action issue, the dissenting opinion, which argued in favor of congressional enforcement power to regulate private persons, relied heavily on the Citizenship Clause. *See* The Civil Rights Cases, 109 U.S. 3, 46–51 (1883) (Harlan, J., dissenting).

4 *See, e.g.*, Curtis, *No State Shall Abridge*, 158 (discussing similar arguments as made by Reconstruction-era congresspersons).

5 *See* Tennessee v. Lane, 541 U.S. at 557–559 (Scalia, J., dissenting) (arguing that, except in the case of legislation enforcing racial equality, Congress should be limited to imposing penalties for court-determined violations of the Fourteenth Amendment).

6 *See* Fitzpatrick v. Bitzer, 427 U.S. 445 (1976) (assuming the constitutionality of Congress's extension of employment discrimination protections to state government employees, as valid legislation enforcing the Equal Protection Clause).

7 *But see* Lane, 541 U.S. at 557–559 (Scalia, J., dissenting) (noting Justice Scalia's disagreement with this expanded understanding of the enforcement power). Even Justice Scalia would uphold broader enforcement legislation in the race context.

8 *See, e.g.*, Kimel v. Bd of Regents, 528 U.S. 62, 81 (2000).

9 529 U.S. 598 (2000).

10 The Court also observed that Congress's findings indicated that state officials discriminated on the basis of sex in twenty-one states, not all or even a majority of them. *See* 529 U.S. at 626–627.

11 106 U.S. 629 (1883).

12 109 U.S. 3 (1883).

13 *See* Harris, 106 U.S. at 639; Civil Rights Cases, 109 U.S. at 14.

14 In United States v. Guest, six justices, in two different opinions, concluded that the Fourteenth Amendment allowed Congress to regulate private action. 383 U.S. 745, 774 (1966) (opinion of Brennan, J., for three justices); *id.* at 762 (opinion of Clark, J., for three justices). In *Morrison*, Chief Justice Rehnquist refused to accept these opinions as constituting a majority of the Court for that proposition, on the ground that Justice Clark's opinion was too cursory and unreasoned to reflect a conscious decision to overrule the state action requirement. *See* 529 U.S. at 624.

15 Cong. Globe, 39th Cong., 1st Sess., 1034 (1866).

16 *See* Boerne, 521 U.S. at 521–522.

17 *See, e.g.*, Maltz, *Civil Rights*, at 93; Curtis, *No State Shall Abridge*, 85–86 (Duke University Press, 1986) (explaining the view of Thaddeus Stevens); *see also* Mark Graber, "Constructing Constitutional Politics: Thaddeus Stevens, John Bingham, and the Forgotten Fourteenth Amendment," *available at* http://papers.ssrn.com/sol3/papers.cfm?abstract_id=2483355 (arguing that Republican congressional leaders cared the most about Sections 2 and 3 of the amendment).

18 *See, e.g.*, Kermit Roosevelt, "Bait and Switch: Why *United States v. Morrison* Is Wrong about Section 5," *available at* http://papers.ssrn.com/sol3/papers.cfm?abstract_id=2393649, at 20–21 (noting the difficulty Congress might encounter in attempting to directly require states to enforce its laws equally).

19 Indeed, this is the path the executive branch took in 1958 during the school desegregation crisis in Little Rock: rather than commanding the governor to protect black students attending Central High School, President Eisenhower called out federal troops to provide that protection.

20 *See, e.g.*, Frantz, "Congressional Power."

21 For a discussion of the White House and congressional deliberations on the proper foundation for the law, *see* Joel Goldstein, "Constitutional Dialogue and the Civil Rights Act of 1964," 49 *St. Louis U. L. Rev.* 1095 (2005).

22 *See* Christopher Schmidt, "The Sit-Ins and the State Action Doctrine," 18 *Wm. & Mary Bill of Rights J.* 767, 807–809 (2010).

23 *See, e.g.*, Laurence Tribe, *American Constitutional Law* § 18-1, at 1689 (2d ed. Foundation Press, 1988).

24 529 U.S. at 620.

25 Indeed, more extensive examination of both the congressional debates and the early judicial precedent only supports avoiding this stringent limitation on Congress's power. *See generally* Frantz, "Congressional Power."

CHAPTER 9. IRRATIONALITY, ANIMUS, AND DEFERENCE

1 Pregnancy Discrimination Act of 1978, Pub. L. No. 95-555, 92 Stat. 2076.

2 133 S.Ct. at 2627.

3 To state these arguments, in particular, the argument flowing from the VRA's imposition of unequal burdens on the states, is not to agree with them. In particular, the "unequal burdens" argument is open to serious critique. *See* Shelby County, 133 S.Ct. at 2648–2650 (Ginsburg, J., dissenting) (critiquing that argument).

4 133 S.Ct. at 2627.

5 Shelby County, Alabama v. Holder, 679 F.3d 848, 898 (D.C. Cir. 2012) (Williams, J., dissenting).

6 To be clear, the obsolescence argument does not amount to a criticism of the original motivations for the law. Indeed, justices accepting the obsolescence argument against the preclearance provisions' coverage formula acknowledged the important work those provisions did in eradicating (as they saw it) racial discrimination in voting in the South. *See* Shelby County, 133 S.Ct. at 2626; Northwest Austin Mun. Util. Dist. No. 1 v. Holder, 557 U.S. 193, 229 (2009) (Thomas, J., concurring in the judgment in part and dissenting in part).

7 *See, e.g.*, Sierra Club v. Costle, 657 F.2d 298, 410 (D.C. Cir. 1981) (reviewing an administrative agency's decision for rationality despite the denseness and complexity of the record).

8 *See* Shelby County, 133 S.Ct. at 2629 ("Congress compiled thousands of pages of evidence before reauthorizing the Voting Rights Act. The court below and the parties have debated what that record shows—they have gone back and forth about whether to compare covered to noncovered jurisdictions as blocks, how to disaggregate the data State by State, how to weigh [VRA] § 2 cases as evidence of ongoing discrimination, and whether to consider evidence not before Congress, among other issues."). After making this statement, he failed to reach a conclusion on this debate, moving on to other questions.

9 132 S.Ct. 1327 (2012).

10 *See* 538 U.S. at 729–730 & 736–737.

11 Coleman, 132 S.Ct. at 1335.

12 *See ibid.*

13 132 S.Ct. at 1348 (Ginsburg, J., dissenting) (italics added). In the second of these quoted phrases Justice Ginsburg is herself quoting from an amicus brief. *See ibid.*

14 *See* http://en.wikipedia.org/wiki/File:Map_of_US_Suffrage,_1920.svg.

15 *See, e.g.*, Eskridge, "Channeling," 419, 461–462.

16 *See, e.g.*, *id.* at 464 (2001) (national focus of African American rights activity); Sitkoff, *A New Deal for Blacks*, at 143–162 (academic opinion). Indeed, Professor Eskridge notes the local activism of groups such as the Southern Christian Leadership Conference in raising the civil rights movement's profile in the 1950s. *See* Eskridge, "Channeling," at 446–447 & 463 n. 164.

17 *See* Jerome Hunt, "A State-by-State Examination of Nondiscrimination Laws and Policies," *available at* http://www.americanprogress.org/issues/lgbt/report/2012/06/11/11696/a-state-by-state-examination-of-nondiscrimination-laws-and-policies/ (noting dates of state enactment of LGBT nondiscrimination laws).

18 *See, e.g.*, Eskridge, "Channeling," at 471–474 (describing countermovements triggered by the initial success of emerging groups' civil rights claims).

19 Readers may note that this argument parallels Justice Brennan's argument in the *Frontiero* case that legislatures' recognition of a discrimination problem strengthens, rather than weakens, the argument for judicial protection of the equality right at issue. *See* chapter 2. In this case, *state* legislatures' recognition of a problem strengthens the argument for *federal* enforcement legislation on that issue.

20 DeBoer v. Snyder, 772 F.3d 388, 421 (6th Cir. 2014).

21 *See* Hellman, *When Is Discrimination Wrong?*

22 *See* Roberts, "Preempting Discrimination," at 475–479.

23 For a chilling counterexample, *see* J. David Smith, *Ignored, Shunned, and Invisible: How the Label "Retarded" Has Denied Freedom to Millions* 120 (Praeger, 2009) (reporting on the reaction of an Aryan Nation leader to news that the child of a member had a cleft palate, that the child was "a genetic defect" who would "have to be euthanized" after the movement came to power).

24 http://content.time.com/time/magazine/article/0,9171,1738513,00.html (quoted at http://economistsview.typepad.com/economistsview/2008/05/genetic-discrim.html) (article by Michael Kinsley).

25 *See* Roberts, "Preempting Discrimination" (collecting arguments that the inherited nature of our genetic makeup renders genetic discrimination unfair).

26 Samuel Marcosson, "Constructive Immutability," 3 *U. Pa. J. Const. L.* 646 (2001).

27 *Compare, e.g.*, Ulane v. Eastern Airlines, 742 F.2d 1081 (7th Cir. 1984) (holding that discrimination on the basis of transgender status does not constitute sex discrimination under the employment provisions of the Civil Rights Act of 1964) *with* Schroer v. Billington, 577 F.Supp.2d 293 (D.D.C. 2008) (holding the contrary).

CHAPTER 10. BEYOND IRRATIONALITY AND ANIMUS

1 *See, e.g.*, Adam Winkler, "Fundamentally Wrong about Fundamental Rights," 23 *Const. Comm.* 227 (2006) (noting the variety of doctrinal tests used to evaluate infringements on Bill of Rights guarantees).

2 *See, e.g.*, Roth v. United States, 354 U.S. 476, 496, 503–508 (1957) (Harlan, J., concurring in part and dissenting in part) (arguing that the incorporated version of the First Amendment leaves more latitude for states to regulate speech than the First Amendment itself leaves for Congress).

3 *See ibid.*

4 The one possible exception deals with the Sixth Amendment's requirement for unanimity in criminal law trials, on which different rules exist for the state and federal systems. As Justice Alito recently explained, this anomaly may be due to the unusual lineup of the justices in the relevant cases, rather than a disagreement on the principle that incorporated Bill of Rights provisions mean exactly the same thing as their original versions that bind the federal government. *See* McDonald v. City of Chicago, 130 S.Ct. 3020, 3035 n. 14 (2010).

5 *See* McDonald, 130 S.Ct. at 3101 (Stevens, J., dissenting).

6 To say that the constitutional text is a source of core constitutional meaning is not to say that the text always provides such meaning. For example, some constitutional provisions, from Article I's prohibition on states "pass[ing] any law . . . impairing the Obligation of Contracts" to the First Amendment, are phrased in absolutist terms that courts conclude do not reflect an absolutist meaning. Thus, text *can be* a source of core meaning—but not always and, as reflected by these seemingly absolutist provisions that are not interpreted literally, not even every time it seems to be clear.

7 554 U.S. at 599; *id.* at 628 (describing "the inherent right of self-defense" as "central" to the Second Amendment right); *id.* at 630 (describing use of a weapon for self-defense in the home as the Second Amendment's "core lawful purpose"); *id.* at 627 (approving of an earlier case's limitation on the Second Amendment right to weapons in "common use" at the founding).

8 McDonald v. City of Chicago, 130 S.Ct. 3020, 3036 (2010) (referring to the "central" or "core" meaning of the Second Amendment); *see also id.* at 3036 & 3044 (same, but now speaking only for four justices). *McDonald* also held that the Fourteenth Amendment incorporated the same version of the gun possession right that applied against the federal government via the Second Amendment itself. *See id.* at 3048 (plurality opinion, using the Due Process Clause); *id.*at 3088 (Thomas, J., concurring in the judgment) ("I agree with the Court that the Second Amendment is fully applicable to the States" under the Privileges and Immunities Clause.).

9 For example, lower courts have read *Heller* more broadly, to protect carrying weapons in public. *See, e.g.*, Peruta v. County of San Diego, 742 F.3d 1144 (9th Cir. 2014).

10 *See* Ezell v. City of Chicago, 651 F.3d 684, 704 (7th Cir. 2011) (adopting this reasoning to hold that firing ranges enjoyed at least some protection under the Second Amendment).

11 *See, e.g.*, U.S. v. Masciandaro, 638 F.3d 458, 475 (4th Cir. 2011) (considering a challenge to a federal regulation prohibiting the vehicular transport of a gun in a national park, but resolving the matter on a narrower ground, and noting "the dilemma faced by lower courts in the post-*Heller* world: how far to push *Heller* beyond its undisputed core holding . . . outside the home environment"). For an indication of how difficult it can be to determine what constitutes the "core" of a constitutional right, see *Peruta*, *supra*, at 1153 (noting that *Heller*'s general endorsement of gun bans in "sensitive" public places implies that the Second Amendment gun possession right extends to at least some public places).

12 *See* Katz v. United States, 389 U.S. 347 (1967).

13 486 U.S. 35 (1988).

14 486 U.S. at 40 (footnotes omitted).

15 Despite the California law, the evidence found in his garbage was admitted against him because California had repealed a rule excluding the use of evidence seized in violation of California law, as long as the seizure was legal under the Fourth Amendment.

16 486 U.S. at 55–56 (Brennan, J., dissenting).

17 389 U.S. 347, 364 (1967) (Black, J., dissenting).

18 *See, e.g.*, Smith v. State, 510 P.2d 793 (Alaska 1973) (rejecting claim); *see also* State v. Tanaka, 67 Hawai'i 658 (1985) (reaching opposite result). It should be noted that some of these cases, while resting on state constitutional conclusions, nevertheless held that the state and federal search and seizure provisions are identical. *See, e.g.*, Smith, 510 P.2d at 795 n.4.

19 To be sure, on the facts of the garbage example, the majority's compilation of a majority of state court/state law cases rejecting the asserted privacy claim suggests the lack of a national consensus supporting this claim. But the more general point remains.

20 494 U.S. 872 (1990).

21 *Id.* at 874.

22 *Id.* at 878.

23 *Id.* at 885.

24 *See id.* at 888–889.

25 *Id.* at 890.

26 *Id.* at 890.

27 As the sentence in the text makes clear, the Court did not rely exclusively on this judicial incompetence point when rejecting the balancing approach. Instead, Justice Scalia argued that this rejection flowed also from the Court's precedents, which he may have been shorthanding through his reference to "constitutional tradition." *Id.* at 885.

28 42 U.S.C. § 2000bb(a).

29 521 U.S. at 529 (emphasis added).

30 *See id.* at 513 (noting that the balancing approach rejected by *Smith* "would have produced an anomaly in the law").

31 *See id.* at 530–532 (lack of evidence) & 532–535 (breadth and depth of RFRA's liability rule).

32 Indeed, a leading constitutional law treatise combines its discussion of equal protection–based and due process–based fundamental rights. *See* Chemerinsky, *Constitutional Law*, chap. 10.

33 *See, e.g.*, Joseph Grano, "Prophylactic Rules in Criminal Procedure: A Question of Article III Legitimacy," 80 *Nw. L. Rev.* 100, 101 n. 5 (1985) (suggesting the similarity of methodologies); *see also, e.g.*, Zablocki v. Redhail, 434 U.S. 374, 395 (1978) (Stewart, J., concurring in the judgement) (the fundamental rights strand of equal protection "is no more than substantive due process by another name.").

34 *See, e.g.*, Chemerinsky, *Constitutional Law*, at 793–794

35 427 U.S. 445 (1976).

36 *Compare, e.g.*, Fullilove v. Klutznick, 448 U.S. 448 (1980) (concluding that Congress could use its enforcement power to impose federally mandated race-based set-asides for state construction projects funded with federal funds) *with* Adarand Constructors v. Pena, 515 U.S. 200 (1995) (insisting that federal use of racial set-asides be tested by the same strict scrutiny by which analogous state actions are tested, even when Congress uses its enforcement power).

CONCLUSION

1 It also bears noting that the congruence and proportionality standard itself has no pretense to a historical foundation.

2 Some scholars draw a different lesson from this diversity. For example, Kenji Yoshino has suggested, albeit tentatively, that Americans' "pluralism anxiety" justifies courts refocusing their constitutional attention toward substantive rights under the Due Process Clause, rather than equality rights, which he argues raise concerns about constantly multiplying divisions in American society. Kenji Yoshino, "The New Equal Protection," 124 *Harv. L. Rev.* 747 (2011). This is not the place to engage this argument fully. For current purposes, it suffices to note that at least in some cases enforcement legislation will likely implicate concerns that sound more readily in equality than in protection of fundamental rights, for example, employment discrimination. Moreover, it bears noting that Yoshino's argument focuses, at least partly, on the competence of *courts* to construct a principled equality jurisprudence. Indeed, he concedes that legislatures may be better suited than courts to address equality concerns. That statement, of course, reflects much of this book's thrust.

3 *See* Ackerman, "Beyond *Carolene Products*," 713.

4 *See, e.g.*, Randy Barnett, *Restoring the Lost Constitution* (Princeton University Press, 2013).

BIBLIOGRAPHY

Ackerman, Bruce. "Beyond *Carolene Products*." 98 *Harv. L. Rev.* 713 (1985).

Allen, Francis. "The Judicial Quest for Penal Justice: The Warren Court and the Criminal Cases." 1975 *U. Ill. L.F.* 518.

Amar, Akhil. *The Bill of Rights*. Yale University Press, 2000.

———. "The Supreme Court 1999 Term, Foreword—The Document and the Doctrine." 114 *Harv. L. Rev.* 26 (2000).

Antieau, Chester James. *Modern Constitutional Law*. Lawyers Co-operative Publishing, 1969.

———. *The Original Understanding of the Fourteenth Amendment*. Mid-America Press, 1981.

Baer, Judith. *Equality under the Constitution: Reclaiming the Fourteenth Amendment*. Cornell University Press, 1983.

Benedict, Michael Les. "Preserving Federalism: Reconstruction and the Waite Court." *Reprinted in The Supreme Court in American Society: Equal Justice under Law* 17 (Kermit Hall, ed.). Garland, 2001.

Berger, Eric. "Deference Determinations and Stealth Constitutional Decision Making." 98 *Iowa L. Rev.* 465 (2013).

Berger, Raoul. *Government by Judiciary: The Transformation of the Fourteenth Amendment*. Liberty Fund, 1997.

Bernstein, David. "*Bolling*, Equal Protection, Due Process, and *Lochner*phobia." 93 *Geo. L.J.* 1253 (2005).

Bernstein, David. "*Lochner* Era Revisionism, Revised: *Lochner* and the Origins of Fundamental Rights Constitutionalism." 92 *Geo. L.J.* 1 (2003).

Bernstein, David, and Ilya Somin. "Book Review: Judicial Power and Civil Rights Reconsidered." 114 *Yale L.J.* 591 (2004).

Bickel, Alexander. "The Original Understanding and the Segregation Decisions." 69 *Harv. L. Rev.* 1 (1955).

Brest, Paul. "The Supreme Court 1975 Term—Foreword: In Defense of the Antidiscrimination Principle." 90 *Harv. L. Rev.* 1 (1976).

Burdick, Charles. *The Law of the American Constitution: Its Origin and Development*. Putnam's, 1922.

Chemerinsky, Erwin. *Constitutional Law: Principles and Policies*. 3d ed. Aspen, 2006.

Colker, Ruth. "The Section 5 Quagmire." 47 *UCLA L. Rev.* 653 (2000).

———. "The Supreme Court's Historical Errors in *City of Boerne v. Flores*." 43 *B.C. L. Rev.* 783 (2002).

Collins, Charles. *The Fourteenth Amendment and the States*. Da Capo Press, 1974.

Cooley, Thomas. *A Treatise on the Constitutional Limitations Which Rest upon the Legislative Power of the States of the American Union*. Little, Brown, 1868.

Corwin, Edward. "The Doctrine of Due Process of Law before the Civil War." 24 *Harv. L. Rev.* 366 (1911).

———. *Liberty against Government*. Louisiana State University Press, 1948.

Cox, Archibald. "The Supreme Court 1965 Term—Foreword: Constitutional Adjudication and the Promotion of Human Rights." 80 *Harv. L. Rev.* 90 (1966).

Crenshaw, Kimberle, and Gary Peller. "The Contradictions of Mainstream Constitutional Theory." 45 *UCLA L. Rev.* 1643 (1998).

Crosskey, William. *Politics and the Constitution*. University of Chicago Press, 1953.

Curtis, Michael Kent. *No State Shall Abridge: The Fourteenth Amendment and the Bill of Rights*. Duke University Press, 1986.

Cushman, Barry. *Rethinking the New Deal Court: The Structure of a Constitutional Revolution*. Oxford University Press, 1998.

Egan, Gillian. "Unreasonable Requirements for Reasonable Enforcement: 'Congruence and Proportionality' after *Coleman v. Court of Appeals of Maryland*." 43 *Cumb. L. Rev.* 29 (2012–2013).

Ely, John Hart. "The Constitutionality of Reverse Racial Discrimination." 41 *U. Chicago L. Rev.* 723 (1974).

———. *Democracy and Distrust: A Theory of Judicial Review*. Harvard University Press, 1980.

Eskridge, William. "Channeling: Identity-Based Social Movements and Public Law." 150 *U. Pa. L. Rev.* 419 (2001).

Fairman, Charles. "Does the Fourteenth Amendment Incorporate the Bill of Rights? The Original Understanding." 2 *Stan. L. Rev.* 5 (1949).

———. *The Oliver Wendell Holmes Devise History of the United States Supreme Court*. Vols. 6 and 7, *Reconstruction and Reunion*. Macmillan, 1987.

Fallon, Richard. *Implementing the Constitution*. Harvard University Press, 2001.

Feeley, Malcom, and Edward Rubin. *Judicial Policy Making and the Modern State: How the Courts Reformed America's Prisons*. Cambridge University Press, 1998.

Field, Matthew. *Congress, the Constitution, and Divided Government*. LFB Scholarly Publishing, 2013.

Fisher, Louis. *The Supreme Court and Congress: Rival Interpretations*. CQ Press, 2009.

Fiss, Owen. *The Oliver Wendell Holmes Devise History of the United States Supreme Court*. Vol. 8, *Troubled Beginnings of the Modern State, 1888–1910*. Macmillan, 1993.

Flack, Horace. *The Adoption of the Fourteenth Amendment*. Johns Hopkins Press, 1908.

Foner, Eric. *Free Soil, Free Labor, Free Men: The Ideology of the Republican Party before the Civil War*. Oxford University Press, 1995.

———. *Reconstruction, 1863–1877*. HarperCollins, 1988.

Franklin, Cary. "The Anti-stereotyping Principle in Constitutional Sex Discrimination Law." 85 *N.Y.U. L. Rev.* 83 (2010).

Frantz, Laurent. "Congressional Power to Enforce the Fourteenth Amendment against Private Acts." 73 *Yale L.J.* 1353 (1964).

Friedman, Lawrence. *A History of American Law*. Touchstone, 1973.

Gaffney, Edward. "History and Legal Interpretation: The Early Distortion of the Fourteenth Amendment by the Gilded Age Court." 25 *Cath. U. L. Rev.* 207 (1976).

Gillman, Howard. *The Constitution Besieged: The Rise and Demise of* Lochner *Era Police Powers Jurisprudence*. Duke University Press, 1992.

———. "Preferred Freedoms: The Progressive Expansion of State Power and the Origins of Modern Civil Liberties Jurisprudence." 47 *Pol. Sci. Res. Q.* 623 (1994).

Glidden, William. *Congress and the Fourteenth Amendment: Enforcing Liberty and Equality in the States*. Lexington Books, 2013.

Gold, David. *The Shaping of Nineteenth-Century Law: John Appleton and Responsible Individualism*. Greenwood, 1990.

Goldman, Robert. *Reconstruction and Black Suffrage: Losing the Vote in* Reese *and* Cruikshank. University Press of Kansas, 2001.

Graham, Howard. *Everyman's Constitution: Historical Essays on the Fourteenth Amendment, the "Conspiracy Theory," and American Constitutionalism*. State Historical Society of Wisconsin, 1968.

Hand, Learned. *The Bill of Rights*. Harvard University Press, 1962.

Harrison, John. "Reconstructing the Privileges or Immunities Clause." 101 *Yale L.J.* 1385 (1992).

Hellman, Deborah. *When Is Discrimination Wrong?* Harvard University Press, 2008.

Hurst, James Willard. *The Legitimacy of the Business Corporation in the United States 1780–1970*. University of Virginia Press, 1970.

Hyman, Harold, and William Wiecek. *Equal Justice under Law: Constitutional Development 1835–1875*. Harper and Row, 1982.

Ides, Allan. "Tangled Up in *Brown*." 47 *How. L.J.* 3 (2003).

Kaczorowski, Robert. *The Nationalization of Civil Rights*. Garland, 1987.

Kay, Richard. "The Equal Protection Clause in the Supreme Court, 1873–1903." 29 *Buffalo L. Rev.* 667 (1980).

Klarman, Michael. *From Jim Crow to Civil Rights*. Oxford University Press, 2004.

———. "An Interpretive History of Equal Protection." 90 *Mich. L. Rev.* 213 (1991).

Kluger, Richard. *Simple Justice*. Vintage, 1975.

Kramer, Larry. *The People Themselves*. Oxford University Press, 2004.

Labbe, Ronald, and Jonathan Lurie. *The Slaughterhouse Cases: Regulation, Reconstruction, and the Fourteenth Amendment*. University Press of Kansas, 2005 (abridged edition).

Lofgren, Charles. *The Plessy Case: A Legal-Historical Interpretation*. Oxford University Press, 1987.

Lusky, Louis. "Minority Rights and the Public Interest." 52 *Yale L.J.* 1 (1942).

Macedo, Stephen. *The New Right v. the Constitution*. Cato, 1987.

Magliocca, Gerard. *Andrew Jackson and the Constitution*. University Press of Kansas, 2007.

Maltz, Earl. *Civil Rights, the Constitution, and Congress 1863–1869*. University Press of Kansas, 1990.

Mathews, John. *Legislative and Judicial History of the Fifteenth Amendment*. Da Capo, 1971.

McAward, Jennifer Mason. "Congressional Authority to Interpret the Thirteenth Amendment: A Response to Professor Tsesis." 71 *Maryland L. Rev.* 60 (2011).

McConnell, Michael. "Institutions and Interpretation: A Critique of *City of Boerne v. Flores*." 111 *Harv. L. Rev.* 153 (1997).

McIlwain, C. H. "Due Process of Law in Magna Carta." 14 *Colum. L. Rev.* 27 (1914).

Meyer, Howard. *The Amendment That Refused to Die: Equality and Justice Deferred: The History of the Fourteenth Amendment*. Madison Books, 2000.

Micklethwait, John, and Adrian Wooldridge. *The Company: A Short History of a Revolutionary Idea*. Modern Library, 2003.

Monoghan, Henry. "The Supreme Court 1974 Term Foreword—Constitutional Common Law." 89 *Harv. L. Rev.* 1 (1975).

Nelson, William. *Americanization of the Common Law*. Harvard University Press, 1975.

———. *The Fourteenth Amendment: From Political Principle to Judicial Doctrine*. Harvard University Press, 1988.

Newsom, Courtney. Case Comment, "Free to Discriminate: *Coleman v. Court of Appeals of Maryland* Leaves States with an Incentive to Hire Men over Women." 46 *Loyola L.A. L. Rev.* 755 (2013).

Note. "The Constitutionality of Proposed Federal Anti-lynching Legislation." 34 *Virginia L. Rev.* 944 (1948).

Note. "Legislative Purpose, Rationality, and Equal Protection." 82 *Yale L.J.* 123 (1972).

Note. "Race Segregation Ordinance Invalid." 31 *Harv. L. Rev.* 475 (1918).

Nourse, Victoria. "A Tale of Two *Lochner*s: The Untold Story of Due Process and the Idea of Fundamental Rights." 97 *Cal. L. Rev.* 751 (2009).

Novak, William. *The People's Welfare: Law and Regulation in Nineteenth-Century America*. University of North Carolina Press, 1996.

Powell, H. Jefferson. "Reasoning about the Irrational: The Roberts Court and the Future of Constitutional Law." 86 *U. Wash. L. Rev.* 217 (2011).

Primus, Richard. *The American Language of Rights*. Cambridge University Press, 1999.

Richards, David A. J. "Abolitionist Political and Constitutional Theory and the Reconstruction Amendments." 25 *Loyola L.A. L. Rev.* 1187 (1992).

Roberts, Jessica. "Preempting Discrimination: Lessons from the Genetic Information Nondiscrimination Act." 63 *Vand. L. Rev.* 439 (2010).

Roosevelt, Kermit. "Aspiration and Underenforcement." 119 *Harv. L. Rev. Forum* 193 (2006).

Rossiter, Clinton, ed. *The Federalist Papers*. Penguin, 1961.

Sager, Lawrence Gene. "Fair Measure: The Legal Status of Underenforced Constitutional Norms." 91 *Harv. L. Rev.* 1212 (1978).

Scaturro, Frank. *The Supreme Court's Retreat from Reconstruction: A Distortion of Constitutional Jurisprudence*. Greenwood, 2000.

Scheiber, Harry. "The Road to *Munn:* Eminent Domain and the Concept of Public Purpose in State Courts." 5 *Persp. in American History* 329 (1971).

Sitkoff, Harvard. *A New Deal for Blacks: The Emergence of Civil Rights as a National Issue: The Depression Decade*. Oxford University Press, 2009.

Smith, Steven. "The Jurisprudence of Denigration." *Available at* http://papers.ssrn.com/sol3/papers.cfm?abstract_id=2407244.

Suk, Julie. "'A More Egalitarian Relationship at Home and at Work': Justice Ginsburg's Dissent in *Coleman v. Court of Appeals of Maryland*." 127 *Harv. L. Rev.* 473 (2013).

Sunstein, Cass. "*Lochner*'s Legacy." 87 *Colum. L. Rev.* 873 (1987).

———. "Sexual Orientation and the Constitution: A Note on the Relationship between Due Process and Equal Protection." 55 *U. Chi. L. Rev.* 1161 (1988).

tenBroek, Jacobus. *Equal under Law*. Collier, 1965.

Tussman, Joseph, and Jacobus tenBroek. "The Equal Protection of the Laws." 37 *Cal. L. Rev.* 341 (1949).

Tribe, Laurence. "The Puzzling Persistence of Process-Based Constitutional Theories." 89 *Yale L.J.* 1063 (1980).

Tsesis, Alexander. "Congressional Authority to Interpret the Thirteenth Amendment." 71 *Maryland L. Rev.* 40 (2011).

———, ed. *The Promises of Liberty: The History and Contemporary Relevance of the Thirteenth Amendment*. Columbia University Press, 2010.

———. *The Thirteenth Amendment and American Freedom*. NYU Press, 2004.

Tushnet, Mark. "Thayer's Target: Judicial Review or Democracy?" 88 *Northwestern L. Rev.* 9 (1993).

Waltman, Jerold. *Congress, the Supreme Court, and Religious Liberty: The Case of* City of Boerne v. Flores. Palgrave Macmillan, 2013.

Warsoff, Louis. *Equality and the Law*. Liveright, 1938.

Westen, Peter. "The Empty Idea of Equality." 95 *Harv. L. Rev.* 537 (1982).

Wiecek, William. *The Lost World of Classical Legal Thought: Law and Ideology in America, 1886–1937*. Oxford University Press, 1998.

———. *The Oliver Wendell Holmes Devise History of the United States Supreme Court*. Vol. 12, *The Birth of the Modern Constitution: The United States Supreme Court, 1941–1953*. Cambridge University Press, 2006.

Wilentz, Sean. *Andrew Jackson*. Macmillan, 2007.

Yoshino, Kenji. *Covering*. Random House, 2011.

Zietlow, Rebecca. *Enforcing Equality: Congress, the Constitution and the Protection of Individual Rights*. NYU Press, 2006.

INDEX

ABOUT THE AUTHOR

William D. Araiza is Vice Dean and Professor of Law at Brooklyn Law School. After graduating from Yale Law School, he clerked on the Ninth U.S. Circuit Court of Appeals and for Justice David Souter of the U.S. Supreme Court. He has published widely in administrative and constitutional law.